D1477081

A Gentle Jesuit

A Gentle Jesuit

Philip Caraman, SJ
1911–1998

*'On Saturday evening a dear gentle Jesuit called
Fr. Caraman dines with me.'*

Evelyn Waugh to Diana Cooper (10 September 1962)

June Rockett

GRACEWING

First published in 2004

Gracewing
2 Southern Avenue, Leominster
Herefordshire HR6 0QF

ISBN 0 85244 593 8

Typeset Action Publishing Technology Ltd,
Gloucester GL1 5SR

Printed in England by
MPG Books Ltd, Bodmin, PL31 1EG

Contents

List of Illustrations   vii
Acknowledgements   ix
Preface   xi

Part One   Joining the Jesuits 1911–1945   1

1   The History Boy   3
2   A Lifetime in Training   22

Part Two   The Mayfair Years 1946–1965   47

3   Reveille for *The Month*   49
4   The Golden Circle   70
5   Forty Martyrs – plus One   95
6   Wilderness   128

Part Three   A Nordic Disease 1966–1982   157

7   'An Awful Place'   159
8   Ubique   184
9   Discord in Paradise   214
10   World's End   239

Part Four   A Place of Rest 1982–1998   265

11   The Herb Garden   267
12   A Country Priest   289

Epilogue   322

Fr Caraman's Books   337
CTS pamphlets   338
Note on Primary Sources   339
Select Bibliography   341

Illustrations

1. Philip Caraman – the young Jesuit.
2. The class of 1933 at Manresa House, Roehampton.
3. Scholastic and teacher at Corby Hall, 1939.
4. Students and directing staff at Campion Hall, 1941.
5. The Church of the Immaculate Conception, Farm Street.
6. Fr Caraman, editor of *The Month*, 1953.
   (Photographs – courtesy of the Archives of the British Province of the Society of Jesus.)
7. Graham Greene. (Photograph – courtesy of Hulton Archives-Getty Images.)
8. Evelyn Waugh. (Photograph – courtesy of Mark Gerson.)
9. Sonia Orwell. (Photograph – courtesy of the Orwell Collection, University College of London.)
10. Rosamond Lehmann. (Photograph – courtesy of Roland Philipps.)
11. Dame Edith Sitwell, 1956. (Photograph – courtesy of Hulton Archives-Getty Images.)
12. Fr Martin D'Arcy. (Photograph – courtesy of the Master of Campion Hall, Oxford.)
13. Procession entering St Olav's, Oslo, March 1963. (Photograph – courtesy of Lita Ringnes.)
14. Bishop John Gran. (Photograph – courtesy of Oslo Katolske Bispedomme.)
15. (i) Fr Caraman, Sognesprest, Norway.
       (Photograph – Fr Caraman's private papers.)
    (ii) Mariakirken, Lillehammer. (Photograph – courtesy of Oslo Katolske Bispedomme.)

16. (i) Lita Anker.
    (ii) Fr Caraman with Lita Anker and family.
    (Photographs – courtesy of Lita Ringnes.)
17. (i) Postcard from Iceland to the author.
    (ii) Fr Caraman in tourist mode.
       (Photograph – Fr Caraman's private papers.)
18. Presentation of doves to Pope Paul VI.
19. Fr Caraman with Pope John Paul II.
    (Photographs – Fr Caraman's private papers.)
20. Fr Caraman, painted by unknown artist.
    (Photograph – Fr Caraman's private papers.)
21. Fr John Caraman. (Photograph – courtesy of the Archives
    of the British Province of the Society of Jesus.)
22. Margaret FitzHerbert window.
    (Photograph – Richard Rockett.)
23. (i)   Fr Caraman signing copies of *Western Rising*.
          (Photograph – courtesy of Michael Deering.)
    (ii) Bridge House, Dulverton.
    (iii) Rothwell & Dunworth booksellers, Dulverton.
          (Photographs (ii) and (iii) – the author.)
24. Fr Caraman's grave at Brushford.
    (Photograph – the author.)

Acknowledgements

In writing this biography I have relied heavily on the support of a number of Fr Caraman's closest friends. Foremost among these are Fr Richard Randolph SJ, Fr Olaf Waring, Fru Lita Ringnes, Lady Brigid McEwen, Bridget Grant and Sir Allan and Lady Ramsay. I am profoundly grateful to them all for their constant patience and goodwill.

I am indebted to Archivists Fr Thomas M. McCoog SJ, Fr Geoffrey Holt SJ, and Brother James Hodkinson SJ, for answering my enquiries and guiding my research during numerous visits to the Jesuit Archives in London. The staff of the John J. Burns Library headed by John B. Atteberry, the Senior Reference Librarian, gave me every possible help during my visit to Boston College, and I am grateful to them for their courtesy and patience, particularly in the aftermath of the fateful 9/11. I also wish to thank Clare Austin for her invaluable assistance in tracing letters held in the Manuscripts Department of the British Library.

I am grateful to all those who generously gave their time to grant me interviews, or assisted me with written observations and comments: Fr Philip Endean SJ, Lady Selina Hastings, Fr Robert Miller, Fr Paoli Molinari SJ, Steven Pugsley, Piers Paul Read, Caryl, Richard and Max Rothwell, John Skinner, the late Francis Sitwell, and John Smith.

I would also like to thank Sister Anne Benyon of the Ursulines, Mrs Bond of the Catholic Central Library, Fr Ian Dickie of the Archdiocese of Westminster, Dr Raymond Edwards of the Catholic Truth Society, Robin Gard of the

Diocese of Hexham and Newcastle, Mrs S. Gribbin of St Edmund's Ware, Dr John Harding of the Diocese of Clifton, David Knight of Stonyhurst, the staff of the London Library, Fr Rory Mulligan SM, Dr Joseph O'Shea, publishers Pearson Education, Raleigh St Lawrence, Mrs Tim Todd, Tara Wenger of The University of Texas at Austin, and Fr John Wood of the church of St Teresa of the Child Jesus in Borehamwood. I am indebted also to the Society of Authors for their help and advice.

I am very grateful to all those who have granted me permission to use copyright material: their credits are recorded together with the explanation of my source material in a dedicated passage at the end of this biography.

My deepest gratitude goes to my husband Richard, who has been my research assistant, chauffeur, and technical adviser, and has supported me throughout four years of work with unfailing good-humour and understanding.

Preface

In the last months of his life, Father Philip Caraman made notes for the autobiography which many of his friends considered was long overdue. He jotted down the guidelines he intended to follow: the first of these was 'no gallery of notables'. He had known many distinguished public figures, but reluctance to 'name-drop' and reticence concerning his own achievements were among Fr Caraman's most admirable, and at times frustrating, characteristics. A biographer must dig deep to discover the writers and other prominent people with whom he was associated: without them his story would be only half told, so deeply interwoven was his life with theirs.

Evidence of Philip Caraman's exceptional talent for friendship lies in the index pages of numerous biographies and memoirs, where a surprising number of entries appear under his name. During his lifetime Fr Caraman sought anonymity: he never indicated that he wished the situation to remain so after his death. During the twenty years I knew him, he occasionally dropped hints which might prove helpful to a potential biographer, although he was too modest to suggest that anyone should undertake this work. These clues led me to the papers which form the backbone of this book, and from which I have derived much of my material. It was almost three years after his death, when I discovered that no one else had decided to tell the story of Fr Caraman's life, that I took the first steps along the path leading to this biography.

The part played by Philip Caraman in the lives of those whom he knew was never that of some featureless walk-on extra.

Reactions to this mild-mannered, courteous priest were seldom indifferent: Evelyn and Laura Waugh, and their extended family, regarded him as a valued and much-loved friend: Graham Greene – it is said – hated him: the biographer Garry O'Connor described him as a priest one could imagine in charge of the Inquisition: Alec Guinness addressed him as 'dear, blessed Philip', and offered him a home. Fr Caraman was criticised and disliked by some of his Jesuit brethren, yet won the loyalty and affection of priests of several nationalities both within and outside the Society of Jesus. I was delighted to discover that the loving remembrance of a number of Philip's friends had ensured the preservation of many of his letters: these too have proved a rich source of material for this book.

Few priests can have been represented in such contradictory terms as Fr Caraman. One contributor to a Jesuit obituary notice commented that 'the complications of his character were rather beyond me'. Masked by others, he has never taken centre stage: now it is time for him to stand in the spotlight. In relating the story of Philip Caraman's multi-faceted life, I am conscious that – to some extent at least – I have failed to explore in any great depth either his spirituality or his role as a spiritual director. Sometime in the future perhaps, another writer may embark on this rewarding study.

As a prolific author, for whom books were a passion, Philip Caraman was generous in the encouragement he gave to younger and less well-known writers than himself. I was one whom he urged to 'keep on pushing your pen'. In following his advice, I trust that I have coaxed from the shadows a man who has remained a long time in the wings awaiting his turn to become the principal actor.

June Rockett
Salisbury, 8 September 2004

Part One

Joining the Jesuits
1911–1945

Chapter One

The History Boy

The Jesuit author at the heart of a golden circle of twentieth-century Catholic writers was in speech and manner a typical scholarly Englishman. Only Philip Caraman's features and colouring suggested a more exotic origin. The dark hair and prominent nose betrayed his Armenian ancestry, and he inherited many traits of character from his father's long-suffering, industrious and peripatetic race.

René André Caraman, father of two Jesuit priests, two nuns and five other daughters, was the first member of his family to settle in England, and the first to be granted British citizenship. He was born in 1877 into a family of merchants who had settled in the port of Smyrna,[1] on the coast of Asia Minor, in the late seventeen hundreds. Although they were exiles from their rugged homeland in the mountainous region between the Black and Caspian Seas, the Caramans prospered along with other Armenian families in the town, sharing with them the intelligence and business acumen for which their race was historically renowned.

The earliest surviving document concerning the family, preserved in the church of St Polycarp in Smyrna, records the baptism, on 16 September 1810, of Abraham, son of Artin Caraman of Angora and his 'lawful spouse Catherine'. The godfather was also an Anguriete (from Angora, the ancient name for Ankara), which points to the fact that Artin had only recently settled in Smyrna, having fled there by way of Ankara during one of the recurrent persecutions to which the Christian Armenians were subjected. Three of the signatures on the baptismal register in St Polycarp are in Armenian script.

In the century following Abraham's birth, the Caramans, along with fellow refugees, burgeoned into a coterie of well-to-do families, forming a distinctive and respected Armenian enclave in one of the richest commercial centres in the Eastern Mediterranean. The closeness of the community had its roots not only in ethnic origin, but in a Christian heritage dating back to AD 301. Under a benign Ottoman regime, there was intermarriage and frequent social exchange between members of the Caraman, Issaverdens, Mirzan, Balladur, Muzmuz, de Portu and other families, who were prominent traders, bankers and entrepreneurs. On settling in Smyrna these families generally converted to the Latin rite, and at the same time sought the protection of one of the main Christian European powers, most commonly France or Italy, that over the years had established close trading or political ties with the city. The Armenians set great store on education, at least as far as their sons were concerned, and French Jesuits and Capuchins, Italian Dominicans and Christian Brothers took care of the schooling of their children.

Their Catholic faith was a treasured inheritance, creating a strong bond between the various families. Shortly before his own death, Fr Philip Caraman recalled the gathering that had taken place for the reading of the will after his father's funeral. He remembered in particular the bequest of 'fifty pounds to the Catholic Archbishop for the time being of Smyrna for the adornment of the altars of the Blessed Virgin Mary and of St Anthony in the Basilica of St John the Evangelist, Smyrna. Should no further adornment be necessary the legacy may be retained by the said Archbishop and spent by him at his entire discretion.'[2] He also remembered being told when he was very young that the statue of the Blessed Virgin venerated in the Basilica had been brought all the way from Armenia by a forebear of his paternal grandmother, but added that this could have been just a family legend.

In the prosperous years of the late nineteenth century, many of the Armenians in Smyrna produced large families; although they were officially subjects of the Ottoman Empire, they also enjoyed the political protection of one or other of the European powers represented by a consul in the city. Abraham Caraman's son Artin, who later changed his first name to Pascal, obtained the protection of Italy, and Philip's great-grandfather, Paul Caraman, was appointed a Dragoman of the Kingdom of Naples, a quasi-political role in which it is likely he acted as an intermediary between Turks and Italians. This position passed in turn to his eldest son, André, Philip's grandfather born in 1848, thus giving the family what amounted to dual citizenship, and in time the Armenians of Smyrna gradually assimilated the European culture of the nations by whom they were adopted.

André Caraman, a banker, whom his grandson remembered well, married twice. His first marriage to Anais Issaverdens, a member of the prominent Smyrna family associated with the legend of the Virgin's statue, produced three children of whom René was the second. After the death of Anais, there were two further children from a second marriage to Rosalie Roboly. It was rumoured that at some point André was bankrupted, and it could have been this unfortunate turn of events that prompted his son to move to London in 1897 and set himself up in business in the City. Certainly he was the first member of his extended family to settle in England.

René André Caraman lost no time in seizing the opportunities open to an enterprising young man in the vibrant climate of turn-of-the-century London. He based his trade and future prosperity on his links with the port of his birth. At that time Smyrna was noted for its export trade in tobacco, silk, figs and raisins, and René set himself up as a merchant, importing dried fruit at favourable rates through family connections in Asia Minor. It can be supposed that one of the benefits of his good education was a command of written and spoken English. Although he was a foreigner in London, René did not lack social contacts. His father's position as a Dragoman of the Kingdom of Naples, and the Caraman connections with Italian nobility – one member of the family, the Cavaliere Alessandro Missir de Lusignan, had been in the service of the Royal House of Savoy – ensured that the new arrival was welcomed into the expatriate Italian community.

Long established in the capital, succeeding generations of London Italians had managed to safeguard their unique identity, in no small part through their staunch Roman Catholicism. As an honorary member of this community, the young Armenian would have found the religious situation in his adopted country not unlike that in his native Smyrna. In his autobiographical notes, Fr Philip Caraman wrote that when his forebear Artin fled to Smyrna he 'brought with him a faith tried and tested in the furnace of persecution'. In the early years of the twentieth century the Catholic Church in England was emerging painfully and hesitantly from three hundred years of discrimination, and Roman Catholics, particularly those of foreign origin, were still regarded with suspicion by the general public. As a result, Catholic communities were close-knit and family-based, united in a determination to build schools and churches for the future, reacting much in the same way as René Caraman's forebears had done in their Eastern European enclave. Later accused by some historians of adopting a fortress mentality, early twentieth-century Catholics in London and elsewhere had surrounded themselves with invisible walls primarily for self-protection and the preservation of their newly-won freedom. The Armenians of Smyrna and Roman Catholics in England and Wales were both minority groups dedicated to preserving their religious heritage, and converting others when the opportunity arose.

Once he was in a position to consider marriage it is unlikely that René Caraman would have considered marrying a non-Catholic. The Pasquas, settled in London for sometime, were a very old Latin family with roots in Genoa, and strong connections with Chios, an island off the west coast of Asia Minor. Francesco Pasqua was Dutch consul on the island in 1822 when Greek insurgents attacked Chios against the will of its native citizens, and provoked a massacre of the inhabitants by their Ottoman rulers; his description of the atrocity was the inspiration for Delacroix's painting, *The Massacre*, now in the Louvre. Following the massacre many of the locals fled, and in 1880 Betina Pasqua, a granddaughter of Francesco, was born in Ladbroke Road, London.

René Caraman's future bride was educated at a convent run

by the Sisters of Our Lady of Sion in Chepstow Villas, Bayswater, a short walk from her home. The French order of nuns had built up a good reputation for the education they gave their pupils, and the convent was popular with families of the Catholic gentry, many of whom sent their daughters up from the country as boarders. Despite the strict discipline imposed by the Sisters, the girls were happy and made friendships lasting a life-time. Betina was no exception. Her son recorded that after her marriage most of her friends were from her schooldays and there was nothing foreign about any of them. She always thought of herself as a Londoner, and as English in every way.

Three years younger than her husband, Betina's rejection of her foreign background, and her persistence in speaking no language other than the one she shared with her schoolfriends, were a source of friction at the outset of the marriage in 1903. René was proud of his Armenian roots, and their honeymoon was spent on a visit to his extended family in Smyrna. They travelled by sea, and when her children were growing up Betina confessed that her honeymoon was a hateful memory and she had been thoroughly ill-at-ease with her alien in-laws. In adulthood her second son adopted, whether deliberately or not, his mother's attitude to his Eastern roots. Although well aware that his father was Armenian by birth, Philip Caraman was noticeably reticent on the subject, prompting his friend Evelyn Waugh to remark wryly in 1959, when writing to Lady Mary Lygon, that 'I can offer a very clever Jesuit who says he is French but is really I think a Turk, called Fr Caraman'.[3] The French connection was tenuous at best. Eduard Balladur was claimed as a 'close cousin' by Fr Caraman after the politician stood as a candidate for elec-tion to the Presidency of France, but although Balladur had been born in Smyrna in 1929, the relationship went back to the marriage of Philip Caraman's great-uncle to a member of the Balladur family, and the cousinship was many times removed.[4]

Whatever Philip Caraman felt about his father's lineage in later life, René's entrepreneurial skills and the family ties with Smyrna won them a comfortable lifestyle in a middle-class London suburb. The open spaces of Hampstead had always been popular with those seeking a rural environment within the orbit of London, and the coming of the Tube in 1907 gave nearby Golders Green easy access to the City. Many of the Jews who had prospered in the East End bought the homes being built on developments on the northern outskirts of the capital and René Caraman joined them. Philip was born here on the 11 August 1911, in a house somewhat humorously named Aniteb[5] in Templars Avenue, a pleasant street on the far side of the Finchley Road near Hampstead Heath. He was one of the middle children in a family of nine, of whom only two were boys, an elder son John having been born in September 1905. With his elder brother away for much of the year at school, Philip grew up in a household dominated by women and girls, where the only other male, his father, was a remote figure, either absent on business, engaged in works of charity, or hidden away in whatever seclusion he was able find within his own home. The younger son was marooned in a sea of feminine exuberance, often a butt of teasing by his numerous sisters and their visiting schoolfriends from New Hall.[6]

Family ties with a multitude of Caraman and Pasqua relations were strong, and their grandfather André frequently travelled over from Smyrna to visit them. Various members of their extended family stood either in person or by proxy as godparents to René and Betina's new-born babies. Four of their children were baptised at the church of St Edward the Confessor, the nearest Catholic mission to Aniteb, a short distance from the house on the far side of Finchley Road. Maria and Peter d'Andria, who were cousins of René Caraman through his great-grandmother Monica de Andria of Smyrna, stood for Margarita Mary* born in April 1910 and another d'Andria – Malvina – was godmother to Veronica Mary born in September 1914. Veronica's eldest brother John, then aged nine, was appointed as her godfather. One of Betina Caraman's family, Adelina Pasqua, was godmother to another daughter, Claire Mary, born in 1913, who was the only one of the nine children to survive into the twenty-first century. A requirement for those chosen to act as godparents to a child baptised into the Catholic

* Margarita Maria on her certificate of baptism but in her father's will she appears as Margaret Mary.

Church, then as now, is that they too should be Roman
Catholics. In the days of very large families in the early twentieth century it was customary for the parents' relations to
accept this duty, and in this practice the Caramans were in step
with other members of their Church in England and on the
Continent. An exception seems to have been made in the case
of Philip George Caraman, whose godparents, Alterlius Barry
and Louisa Dudfield, were not members of the Smyrna clan.

Whether or not grandfather André was able to visit England
between 1914 and 1918 is not recorded and Philip Caraman was
too young to remember very much about the First World War.
His only recollection of the conflict was of sheltering under the
staircase when German Zeppelins threatened London. He also
retained a very clear mental picture of his Armenian grandfather, who visited him on more than one occasion when he was
at his preparatory school after the war.

An abiding memory for the siblings in later life was of the
home in Elstree where they moved once the family had outgrown
Aniteb. At the mansion known as The Grange, over the bridge in
Elstree, on the corner of Allum Lane and Deacons Hill Road, the
family kept open house, not only for their relations and Betina's
schoolfriends, but for numerous acquaintances of the seven
sisters. It was a lively and very Catholic household in an area
where the nearest Catholic church was some miles away, at a
time when travel, particularly for a very large family, was not
simply a matter of jumping into a motor car. The family were not
the only Catholics living in Elstree, so in 1925 René Caraman
opened a chapel in The Grange, which quickly attracted a
congregation from the surrounding Hertfordshire countryside.

A Pastoral Letter written by Cardinal Bourne of the
Archdiocese of Westminster, dated Trinity Sunday 1925,
announced that, 'Mass will soon be said in a private chapel in
Elstree until such time as we are able to purchase land and build
a church. The parish will be dedicated to St Teresa of the Child
Jesus to whom we very earnestly and trustfully commit it.' In an
era when the opening of a new church or the inauguration of a
new parish was a cause for celebration, Catholic publications
such as *The Universe* and *The Tablet* gave an account of the first

Mass said in the chapel by a Fr Sims on 14 June of that year. The first collection taken up at this Mass was donated to the Crusade of Rescue, one of several Catholic charities favoured by René Caraman and one to which he later left a legacy in his will.

The parish went from strength to strength. On 20 December the first Benediction was held, and in April of the following year catechism classes were started for local children, for whom this was probably the only Catholic teaching available. The flourishing congregation soon outgrew the chapel in The Grange which held only fifty people, and in 1927 Cardinal Bourne announced, 'Accommodation in the chapel at Elstree is taxed to its utmost and the purchase of land and the building of the church must soon be undertaken'. A site for a church was found in 1932, but Masses continued to be offered at the Grange at 8.30 a.m. on Sundays for some time after the new building was brought into use.[7]

René and Betina Caraman's example of unwavering devotion to their Catholic faith bore fruit in the religious vocations of four of their nine children. Neither boy followed his father into the family business – both were destined to become Jesuit priests, and of the couple's seven daughters two became nuns. Margaret Mary was known as Mother Mary of St John and went to live in a convent in New York, and her younger sister Veronica became a Sister of Charity of Saint Vincent of Paul, but died at the age of only twenty-seven. These four followed in the footsteps of other members of the Caraman's extended family, which had a tradition of giving sons and daughters to the Church. Philip's great-uncle, the brother-in-law of grandfather André, became a monk of the only Armenian monastery in the West on an island in the Venice lagoon. This uncle, Jacques Issaverdens, was a learned man who became an authority on the Armenian liturgy which he translated into English and published in Venice in 1873. His historical writings included a history of his island monastery as well as a major work in English entitled *Armenia and The Armenians,* a book sketching the country's geography and civil and church history.[8] A great-aunt Pauline, one of André Caraman's sisters, became an Ursuline nun; a cousin of Philip's, whom he met at Autun in France in later life, became a Little

Sister of the Poor, with the religious name of Soeur Marie de Saint Polycarp, after the Armenian patron saint.

The love of history, and the books written by Jacques Issaverdens in his island monastery on the Venice lagoon in the nineteenth century, foreshadowed the work which later shaped the life of his great-nephew. Philip George Caraman, without realising it at the time, assumed the scholar's mantle, transforming the studies and research of the Armenian monk into an abiding passion for the history of English Catholicism.

The tranquillity and routine of family life at The Grange were shattered abruptly on the evening of 14 September 1922, when René André Caraman received the news that his birthplace had been destroyed by the Turks. As the best-known representative of Smyrna in the London business community, the report was passed to him by *The Times* in search of a photograph for the story due to appear in the following morning's paper. *The Times* had already covered in detail the events leading up to this horrific climax during the preceding weeks. Following the First World War and the breakup of the Ottoman Empire, Greece had put forward a claim to Smyrna and the surrounding area of Asia Minor, and the mixed-race Greek, Turkish and Armenian population of the port, which had enjoyed a period of calm under the former regime, was thrown into turmoil. Opposing Greek and Turkish forces were soon engaged in hostilities in the hinterland, and terrible atrocities were committed by both sides. Foreseeing the imminent victory of the Turks, many thousands of Greek refugees fled Smyrna which the triumphant army of Mustafa Kemal entered on 9 September 1922. *The Times* reported the 'extreme gravity of the situation' on 11 September, adding, 'it is believed British ships have safely embarked all British subjects in the city'. In the days when the newspaper placed all its photographs on one 'picture page' there was an illustration showing 'a view of the port to the South'.

It seems René Caraman was unable to give the paper the picture they wanted because *The Times* carried no further photographs on Friday 15 September, but told its readers that 'the larger part of the European quarter of Smyrna is burning . . . the fire (as reported by an eyewitness) was started by a Sergeant of

the Turkish regulars who entered a house carrying tins of petro-
leum . . .' The report went on to say that before the outbreak of
the fire about a thousand people had been massacred, but that
the loss of life was feared to be much greater. After the fire,
only the poor Turkish quarter of the port was left standing.
More than three-fifths of the city was destroyed, including all
the banks, business houses and consulates along the quay, seats
of prosperity for the Armenian community over several generations. Fortunately the registers of the Latin church of St
Polycarp survived the fire. The effect on René Caraman and his
family was traumatic. Eleven-year-old Philip, on holiday from
his preparatory school, never forgot his father's horror that the
city believed by the family to be that of St John's Apocalypse,
the birthplace of Homer, the See of St Polycarp, and a centre of
culture since the time of the Roman Empire, had been reduced
to rubble. Before his death Philip Caraman recalled with sadness
that the historic city had been built 'round one of the most beautiful bays in the western world'.

When news of their relations eventually reached England,
René Caraman heard that his stepmother, Rosalie Roboly, had
lost her life during the evacuation, but that other members of his
family, including a much-loved aunt Leontine Issaverdens, had
managed to escape to Italy. This aunt, and a sister-in-law, eventually settled in Naples where René and Betina were later able
to visit them and treat them to a memorable dinner. The destruction of Smyrna also had consequences for Caraman's business,
which suffered, for a while at least, from the loss of exports
from the port. In old age, Philip Caraman revealed that he had
reached 'awareness' at the age of ten. Had he not, the bloody
massacre and destruction of Smyrna and the lasting effects of
these events on his family would surely have jolted a sensitive
child into a perception of the realities of the adult world.

෨

In September 1923, Philip George left childhood behind him
when his parents sent him away to Stonyhurst in Lancashire, the
Jesuit College considered at the time to be one of the leading

Catholic public schools. It is not known whether it was the College's high reputation, or the fact that Jesuits had educated some of the boys in the Armenian community in Smyrna, that influenced the Caramans' decision to send both their sons to distant Lancashire.

Philip was on his own. John Caraman had already left Stonyhurst and Philip remembered the gulf that separated the brothers when they were young, when he wrote:

> We were never together either at preparatory school or at Stonyhurst, and we were seldom at home at the same time. During his Oxford vacations John was mostly abroad ... allegedly working in greater peace than he could have at home where my sisters as often as not had school friends staying; or he was undertaking mammoth walks on the Continent. During one summer he walked to Lourdes, and at [other times] he was in the Ardennes or Vosges.

Many years later Philip recalled how the remote and dashing figure of his elder brother appeared in his life only occasionally, and that he was usually in the company of his Oxford friends, either at Elstree or at Rottingdean, where in the summer the family took a house called The Haven at the top of the steps leading up from the small beach. 'I have a picture of him arriving there one day with steam spurting from the radiator of his small car like an Icelandic geyser. He was off again the next day ...'[9]

As a new boy at Stonyhurst, Philip's life was not made easier by the fact that many of his peers had attended Hodder, the preparatory school on the Stonyhurst estate, and had already formed friendships among themselves before going on to the College. His alien appearance was only one characteristic to set the younger Caraman apart from other boys of his own age. In line with non-Catholic public school practice, where the English cult of games took pride of place, Stonyhurst had recently enhanced the status of sport in the College, substituting Rugby for Association Football in 1921. A contemporary, Geoffrey Holt, recalled that the twelve-year-old Philip was hopeless at games on account of his frail physique, but that he was only too obviously very clever. This combination provoked a good deal of ribbing from other boys and he was teased at school as he had been at home. Holt insisted that the ragging never amounted to bullying and in fact Philip was generally liked by his peers. Perhaps as a result of the teasing he endured in childhood Caraman developed, even at an early age, a wit and sense of humour which would carry him through many trials in later life.

The College was not organised into separate houses with individual housemasters along the lines of many other English public schools, but into Playrooms, grouping boys according to age and occasionally by ability. In 1923 the youngest boys started off in the Fourth Playroom, and gradually moved up the school eventually reaching the First. The Playroom denoted not only a school division but its recreation venue. Artificial houses existed within the various divisions only for competition and games. The author H. J. A. Sire, describing Stonyhurst at the beginning of the twentieth century, says that the Playroom system was designed to prevent sexual corruption or bullying of younger boys by older ones and that discipline was strict and all-seeing.[10] Twenty years later, when Philip Caraman and Geoffrey Holt were pupils, discipline was still strict but generally benign. Holt, who later in his career returned to Stonyhurst as a master, commented:

> there wasn't much chance of a boy having a car round the corner, there were no drugs and boys were not allowed to smoke, except on certain occasions. Alcohol hardly ever came into it. A few daring spirits might go to a public house but if they were caught they got into trouble, and if they were bad enough they might have been asked to leave.

He could not remember a case of a boy being expelled for behaving in this way.[11] But H. J. A. Sire makes the point that insubordination and sexual immorality were both punished mercilessly.

Any boy or girl attending public school in modern times would consider the regime of those days, not only at Stonyhurst but at any other private institution before the Second World War, unbearably harsh. Exeats were unheard of and half-term holidays were never taken, nor were pupils at liberty to go about freely in nearby towns and countryside as they do today. But Catholic schools and convents run by the male and female religious orders, always celebrated the major feast days of the Church with a holiday; for one glorious day lessons were suspended, and treats, both culinary and recreational, were arranged. The greatest feast of the Church, Easter Sunday, was the major event of the school year at Stonyhurst and was celebrated, in Geoffrey Holt's words, as 'a grand weekend after Holy Week', for which the boys, with few exceptions, were obliged to remain at the College. Other schools, even Catholic ones, generally broke up for the Easter holidays a week or so earlier. It was also customary for old boys to return to Stonyhurst for the annual Holy Week retreat.

In every way the paramount ethos of the school was religious. Mass was celebrated every morning, the Angelus bell rang out calling everyone to prayer at the appointed hours, a magnificent procession of the Blessed Sacrament was held on the feast of Corpus Christi, culminating with Benediction in the College grounds, and statues of Our Lady adorned classrooms. The age-old Catholic tradition of devotion to the Blessed Virgin was particularly strong, and in her honour the month of May was marked by 'May Verses', written in either Latin, Greek or English by the boys. A high standard of music enhanced religious rites and liturgy, and there was a fine choir and school orchestra. Philip Caraman featured in neither. He had no musical ability, and revealed in his autobiographical notes that his mother, Betina, had been tone-deaf.

The religious atmosphere permeated the life of a school where the majority of the teaching staff were Jesuits with a vocation dedicated to the welfare and the education, in the widest sense of that word, of their pupils. The boys benefited from the single-minded attention of masters whose duty to them was never deflected by family commitments or outside distractions.

Caraman's first term coincided with the arrival on the teaching staff of a young Jesuit whose career and charisma would later have a major influence on the course of Philip's life. The new boy could not have failed to notice the remarkable figure of the Master of Poetry, Father Martin D'Arcy,[12] who at the age of thirty-five had already impressed his superiors and been marked out for future high office. It is unlikely that the master with the 'beautiful head, wavy hair, delicate features and the eyes of a hawk',[13] often described as Mephistophelean in appearance, would have paid more than superficial attention to the insignificant, bookish twelve-year old among the crowd of junior boys. At that time their future association could not have been foretold.

It was a lay teacher, rather than a Jesuit, who ultimately played a major role in influencing Caraman's interests as he progressed up the school. Maurice Christopher Hollis, known always as Christopher, joined the Stonyhurst staff in 1925 as History Master, at the age of twenty-three. Educated at Eton and Balliol College, he had converted to Roman Catholicism during the year preceding his appointment at the College; after leaving Stonyhurst ten years later he became visiting Professor at Notre Dame University in Indiana, and after World War Two gave up academic work to serve as the Conservative Member of Parliament for Devizes. He was evidently one of those gifted teachers able to instil in his pupils a love of the subject he taught, as Hollis's zeal for Catholic history quickly ignited a spark of interest in the schoolboy which flared into the abiding passion of Philip Caraman's life. And Hollis eventually became another figure in the circle of influential Catholics with whom Caraman was destined to be closely involved.

No boy educated at Stonyhurst could have remained untouched by the school's tradition of English Catholicism, which pervaded the very walls of the Elizabethan house which once had been the home of the Shireburns, a great recusant Lancashire family. The school itself had been founded by the Jesuits at St-Omers in the Spanish Netherlands in 1593 for the education of the sons of English Catholics for whom a Catholic education was prohibited under the penal laws of their own country. In 1794, at the time of the French Revolution, the Jesuits and their pupils were ousted in some disarray from their school on the Continent, and priests and boys travelled by sea to Hull, and thence to Lancashire to the great empty mansion

which had been given to the Jesuits by Thomas Weld of
Lulworth Castle in Dorset, who had inherited Stonyhurst from
the Shireburns when their family line died out.

During penal times, the school at St-Omers had sent a stream
of undercover missionary priests back to England, of whom no
less than fifteen had been martyred for their faith during three
centuries of persecution. Many homes of the great recusant
families had a priest's hiding hole in their walls, and the
Stonyhurst mansion had two secret rooms where Jesuit chaplains
had been concealed. The school also possesses a priceless
archive of manuscripts relating to the recusant past, preserved
in great security behind locked doors, to which ordinary history
pupils would not have been permitted access except under
exceptional circumstances. But Caraman would certainly have
known about this archive, and this knowledge, together with the
school's historical heritage, provided him with the inspiration –
and eventually the research material – for some of his finest
writing.

Surprisingly in the light of his later career, Philip was never
awarded one of the History prizes for which he was eligible to
compete as a sixth-former during his final two years in the
school, nor were his academic achievements particularly
remarkable. He made steady progress in his studies, winning
recognition for General Achievement at the ages of thirteen,
fifteen and sixteen and finally, in his last term, aged eighteen.
He eventually left Stonyhurst with both School Certificate and
Higher School Certificate[14] safely under his belt, showing a
particular aptitude for Religious Doctrine and Classics, both of
which won him prizes during his school years.

It was outside the academic field that Philip came into his
own. The poor physique which had barred him from sporting
activities did not prevent him from joining the popular Officers'
Training Corps, which had an active unit at Stonyhurst during
the years between the two World Wars. Another feature of the
College at that time was the encouragement it gave senior pupils
to speak in public. The school not only had a thriving debating
society, but sent some of its star speakers to share a public
platform with members of the Catholic Evidence Guild. In a

field where wit, clarity and conviction were essential requisites, the eighteen-year-old Philip made his mark. Membership of the prestigious Stonyhurst Union Debating Society was not granted automatically to all those who applied to join; would-be protagonists had to prove their worth by 'speaking for admission'; some boys never impressed their listeners sufficiently to gain membership and gave up after one or two attempts. Sessions followed the format of parliamentary debates in which one side spoke as 'the Government' and the other for 'the Opposition'. Speakers adopted the personae of Members of Parliament, representing a constituency of their choice, usually the town or area of their family home. Philip impressed the Society by his first appearance on the floor of the Chamber on a November Sunday in 1929, and in this inaugural debate, for which the thespian Hon. Prime Minister moved 'that this House approves of Corporal Punishment', Caraman chose to speak as the Member for Nether Wallop. Hilarity greeted his statement that he risked the disapproval of his constituents (the Nether Wallopers) by firmly declaring himself against corporal punishment. He continued that in his opinion 'the whole system was corrupt and far from being a joke, the ferula was an utter abomination. He detested being wallopped'. Following a second debate, speaking as the Member for Elstree, Philip was duly admitted to the Society. In his speech on the motion 'that this House would have liked to have fought in the War', Caraman revealed his growing love of medieval history: he said 'that he much preferred the old days' when combatants donned armour, rather than fighting in unpleasant trench warfare.

The highlight of the Debating Society year was the Prize Debate which took place on 30 March. Of Caraman's speech in opposition to the motion 'the progress of civilisation is and has been the curse of humanity', it was reported that his thought was clear, and, what was best in a debating speech, was brought home even to the slowest wits by the aptness of his illustrations. Caraman's speech was judged the winner, displaying a grasp of essential issues and an enviable power of making these issues clear.[15]

Building on the skills developed in the forum of the

Debating Society, a number of star speakers were encouraged to appear on the very public and demanding platform of the Catholic Evidence Guild. The Guild had been introduced to Stonyhurst in December 1922 with the aim of affording boys an opportunity to play a part in the mission of the Catholic Church in England as it was perceived at that time – namely the conversion of England to the practice of the old Faith. It was intended that boys taking part in this public mission would be given practice in defending Catholic doctrine in the face of a hostile audience. The style of oratory was unashamedly 'soapbox', and the Guild's most prestigious pitch was London's Speakers' Corner, in Hyde Park near Marble Arch. There is no evidence to suggest that Caraman ever appeared on this rumbustious platform, which was the preserve of such famous speakers as Frank Sheed and the Dominican preacher, Father Vincent McNabb. But having been awarded the Guild's diploma for efficient speaking during the previous term, he took part in a rally during the first weekend of the 1930 Easter holidays, performing at pitches in various locations around the capital. Before setting out with a degree of nervousness, protagonists were treated to a hearty meal at The Hut, in the precincts of Westminster Cathedral. The fine spring evening was memorable, apart from anything else, for the fact that the Graf Zeppelin passed overhead just as everyone dispersed to various locations across the capital. Caraman and his party were sent to Walham Green. *The Stonyhurst Magazine* reported that 'After Mr. Ashton[16] had tried, in vain, to thrill some small children with the thought of the Catholic Church, Caraman got up for his maiden speech. The Unity of the Church did not interest Walham Green nearly so much as a man selling magnets, and an ice-cream merchant.'

The following evening at Stamford Hill, 'Caraman wasted his exhaustive knowledge of Unity and Catholicity and his renowned eloquence on a crowd utterly unresponsive to his plea for questions. At the end of half-an-hour's speaking he got down'.[17] Whether or not the Stonyhurst boys and their companions were disappointed by the predictable response to their oratory is not recorded. But the value of this early grounding in public speaking and debate became evident many years later. Although the style of delivery he eventually adopted was far removed from the soapbox oratory of his youth, Philip Caraman was recognised in later life as one of the most notable and sought-after Catholic preachers of his generation.

Not surprisingly Philip passed his last year at Stonyhurst in *Rhetoric* rather than in *Poetry*,[18] and his final term was marked by another success when he won the coveted Harry Keating Memorial Prize for an essay on the Influence of the Church in Public Life. The subject for 1930 was 'The Settlement of the Roman Question'. The adjudicator reported:

> Caraman examined the actual settlement in detail; previous history he introduced only in relation to the theme of the essay. His actual introduction was commendably brief and to the point, and he marshalled clearly the circumstances that led up to the solution of the question. The whole essay was well constructed, though more attention might have been given to details of composition.[19]

The prize itself was for £8. In 1930 a well-produced hardback book cost little more than ten shillings (fifty pence in decimal money) and often less, so Philip returned home to Elstree with a trunkful of books, to the astonishment of his parents and sisters.

His modest silence about his Stonyhurst successes surprised them all. Philip Caraman had to some extent always been on the outer periphery of his large family circle and the distance between the nineteen-year-old and his siblings was extended further by his decision to try his vocation to the priesthood immediately after leaving school. There was one last holiday in the comfortable, upper middle-class world of his numerous relations and their friends, before he joined the novitiate of the Society of Jesus in the autumn of 1930.

Notes

1 The modern Turkish port of Izmir.
2 This is a verbatim extract from the will of René André Caraman, which suggests that Philip Caraman kept a copy of his father's testament until the end of his life.
3 Evelyn Waugh to Lady Mary Lygon, 4 May 1959, *The Letters of Evelyn Waugh*, edited by Mark Amory (Weidenfeld & Nicolson, London, 1980).
4 The Balladur connection is shown in the autobiographical notes made by Fr Caraman shortly before his death.
5 'Aniteb' spelt Betina Caraman's Christian name backwards.
6 Probably the Convent of the Holy Sepulchre at New Hall, Chelmsford, Essex, listed in Catholic Directories of the period as a 'boarding school for young ladies'.
7 *The History of St. Teresa's Parish 1925–2000*. Produced for the parish by Jeff and Caroline Ritchie and other parishioners.
8 Second Edition, St Lazarus, Venice, 1878.
9 Obituary of Fr John Caraman in *Letters and Notices 1982–86*, vols 85–7, Manresa Press, p. 375.
10 H. J. A. Sire, *Father Martin D'Arcy. Philosopher of Christian Love*, Gracewing Publishing, 1997, p. 8.
11 Fr Geoffrey Holt SJ; interview with author.
12 The two upper classes in the College were called *Rhetoric* and *Poetry*. Thus Martin D'Arcy was responsible for one of the senior classes whose pupils included Henry John, son of the artist Augustus John, and Tom Burns, another prominent Catholic who would feature in Caraman's later life.
13 A description of the Rev. M. C. D'Arcy SJ by Louis MacNeice.
14 These examinations were replaced by O Level and A Levels and equated to some extent in standard. But in order to win the School Certificate the candidate had to achieve good marks in a basket of subjects, including Maths and English.
15 Extracted from *The Stonyhurst Magazine* nos. 285, February 1930 and 286, April 1930, pp. 435, 436, 476, 477, 493, 494, 495.
16 Ashton was a senior member of the C.E.G. representing the Westminster Branch.
17 *The Stonyhurst Magazine*, no. 287, June 1930, pp. 544–6.
18 See Note 12.
19 *The Stonyhurst Magazine*, no. 288, July 1930, p. 579.

Chapter Two

A Lifetime in Training

In the decades between the two world wars it was not unusual for several children from the same family to enter the religious life. At a time when large families were fairly common, and religion was still part of the ethos of the majority of Anglican and Catholic middle-class homes, a religious vocation for one or more siblings was considered a natural step. In the first half of the twentieth century English Catholics were still subjected to a degree of discrimination and prejudice by their fellow countrymen and women. Whilst maintaining a low profile as far as possible, Roman Catholics regarded themselves as missionaries in their own country, and prayers for the 'conversion of England' were offered up regularly at Sunday Mass in the Catholic churches which were springing up in all parts of the land.

The Caramans were not unique in 'giving their children to the Church', as religious vocations in a family were described at that time.[1] With a fervently Catholic home life and seven years as a pupil at a Jesuit public school it was natural for Philip George to consider the priestly life as his vocation. And at the age of nineteen he had the example of an admired elder brother before him. After leaving Wadham College, Oxford, the self-confident John Caraman had gone to work in the City, but soon decided that a business career was not for him, and joined the Society of Jesus some two years ahead of his brother. He had already left the novitiate at Manresa House in Roehampton when Philip entered in October 1930, a month after the other novices in the new intake.

It is not known why Philip Caraman arrived late, but Geoffrey Holt, who had entered with him from school, thought that perhaps he had been abroad on a holiday. It is also possible that Philip had been suffering one of the recurrent illnesses that were to plague him throughout his life, or that he had remained at home on account of his mother's ill health. Betina Caraman died the following year at the age of only fifty-one, a blow that overshadowed Philip's first difficult years of Jesuit initiation when the new novices already had much to contend with. Whilst young men taking their first steps in training for the priesthood directly from Stonyhurst were versed to some extent in Jesuit lore, little in their previous education prepared them for the radical differences between school life and the novices' routine. The College was traditionally the source of a steady stream of candidates for the Society, although Geoffrey Holt and Philip Caraman were the only two novices from their school year. In 1929 three Stonyhurst boys had passed on to Manresa, and an earlier year had provided no fewer than nine aspiring Jesuits, including Bernard Basset, who later became a best-selling popular writer on religious themes.[2]

Although the Stonyhurst novices benefited from the presence of a number of old friends in their group, the forming of 'particular friendships' was seen as injurious to community life and soundly discouraged. It is likely that some of Philip Caraman's fellow novices were from a less privileged and well-educated background than the Stonyhurst boys, and learning to accept their less-refined idiosyncrasies provided a salutary lesson in tolerance for the public-school contingent. The biographer H. J. A. Sire records that enduring the crude table manners of some of his fellow novices was a distinct penance for Martin D'Arcy during the time he spent as a novice, as was the rudimentary grasp of Latin – the lingua franca of Manresa House – of the majority of his companions.[3] The house itself was in no way inferior to the grandiose setting of Stonyhurst College, and aspiring Jesuits lived and studied in a beautiful Palladian mansion isolated by large grounds from the village of Roehampton, on the then rural outskirts of south-west London. Built by the Earl of Bessborough in the 1760s, the house and estate of forty-two acres had been bought by the Society of Jesus in 1860, and renamed Manresa. A number of missions in the area, stretching from Kew, Mortlake and Barnes on the banks of the Thames and south as far as Thornton Heath, Worcester Park and Wimbledon, had been administered by the first Jesuits living at Manresa, and in the 1930s they still looked after a number of parishes, including the church in Roehampton village. Today nothing remains of the former glory of the mansion and its grounds, which were taken by the London County Council for housing development after the Second World War; the village lost its rural character and, divided by a main arterial road, was absorbed into the featureless urban sprawl on the outskirts of the capital.

The house and extensive grounds required a great deal of upkeep, and probably for the first time in their lives some of the young gentlemen testing their priestly vocation were obliged to undertake menial tasks. In the class-ridden society of the early twentieth century, religious orders, including the Society of Jesus, still ran a two-tier system in which 'lay' brothers and sisters within an order did the work normally allotted to household servants. But, as part of their training, novices at Manresa were required to do their share of domestic chores, including cleaning, cooking, washing-up dishes and gardening. Geoffrey Holt recalled that the outdoor work was of the roughest kind, consisting principally of digging, weeding and grass-cutting. Apart from being a lesson in humility this domestic training was not wasted, because in later life many of these Jesuits, including Philip Caraman, were well able to cook and care for themselves when they lived on their own in isolated presbyteries. The role played by some of the novices as sacristan in St Joseph's, the Catholic church in the village which in those days had a middle-class, reasonably affluent congregation, was perhaps less arduous.

Recreation had some echo of school days, in the emphasis placed on football as a way for the novices to let off steam. In his biography of the eminent Jesuit Fr Cyril Martindale, Caraman says 'only at football did the novices really become alive. Once Martindale, as an exercise in self-humiliation, tried to play, but on finding himself continuously in the way, he decided it would be more charitable to discontinue'.[4] Philip Caraman wrote with his own lack of athletic ability in mind, and the words probably reflect his personal experience of Manresa games of football. Long walks were also taken in recreation time, and Richmond Park and Wimbledon Common both provided a variety of pleasant and varied routes.

Although domestic chores and periods of recreation were considered integral parts of the daily routine, the basic purpose of the noviceship was the spiritual training of candidates for the priesthood. The years at Manresa were designed as a preparation for a religious life in the Society of Jesus. During these first, and in subsequent years and throughout progressive stages of their training, aspirants had the opportunity to make up their minds whether or not they were prepared to accept a lifetime commitment which excluded marriage, children and a family. Their ability, both to adopt a life in which they might be allotted work they might not want or like, and to accept obediently an assessment of their particular talents by their superiors, was tried and tested in a series of steps of which the novitiate was only the first. The field of work in which members of the Society of Jesus might be called upon to operate was a wide one, and in the early stages of a vocation no one knew what the future might hold in store. Spiritual formation for what lay ahead was the essential factor during the time spent at Manresa.

The basis of Jesuit spirituality has always been the *Spiritual Exercises,* instituted by the Society's founder, St Ignatius Loyola, and aspirants were introduced to this demanding regime of prayer, self-examination and meditation early in the novitiate. Writing nearly sixty years later, Philip Caraman gives a description of the origins and value of the *Exercises.*[5] He tells how at the age of thirty-one Ignatius, almost by chance, found himself in the town of Manresa in the mountains above Barcelona, and how during the ten months he spent there in agonies of soul his heart 'had been raised to an entirely new level of the love of God proportionate to the clarity of his vision ... it was from this period that Inigo [Ignatius] formed the ideas upon which he based his Spiritual Exercises, the little book that was the fruit of his experience, prolonged prayer and illuminations at Manresa'. Caraman gives some detail of the exigencies of the *Exercises,* which begin

> by bringing man face to face with his eternal destiny. After this come the great purifying meditations on the malice of sin and the sufferings of hell. The remaining three sections (Inigo calls them 'weeks' because the full Exercises were arranged to occupy an entire month) are centred round the person of Christ who is presented in compelling attractiveness. This is the new King that Inigo was now serving, ready for his sake . . . to answer his call, endure hardships and undertake any task he might be given. Throughout these meditations the repeated prayer of the 'exercitant' (or person taken through the Exercises) is that he may come to know Christ more intimately and follow him more closely.

Caraman comments that Ignatius's manual instructs the exercitant to seek the will of God not just as an individual but in the unfolding of God's overall plan, and this gives the *Exercises* an enduring modernity. Philip Caraman's spiritual life was moulded by Ignatian teaching from early manhood, but it was only through personal experience and suffering that his spirituality finally reached maturity.

The Novice Master, under whose guidance the young men were introduced to this demanding regime of prayer and penance, bore a heavy responsibility for the welfare of his students, and in Fr William Peers Smith the novices had an experienced mentor. His influence was vital in their spiritual formation and Geoffrey Holt commented that Fr Smith was generally liked and respected by the novices. Although the content of the curriculum gave the students a spiritual maturity in advance of their years and that of their lay contemporaries, it was less successful in educating them in worldly wisdom. Writing many years later, Philip Caraman criticised this lack of direction during his noviceship.[6] And a contemporary and friend of Caraman's, Fr Richard Randolph, who was a late entry to the Society after wartime service in the Army and studying at Cambridge, comments that young men who went to Manresa straight from school, with little experience of life outside an institution, were often charmed from the priestly life by the first woman who decided to set her cap at them. On the other hand it can be said that in social relations with ordinary lay people, Jesuits, on the whole, wear their intense spiritual training lightly, and have the ability to communicate easily without appearing intellectually remote.

At the conclusion of Philip Caraman's initial two years at Manresa, he and his fellow novices made their simple vows, having successfully completed the first of many steps on their journey to final ordination. So many years of further study and spiritual experiment still lay ahead that the Jesuit regime has been described not only as training for a lifetime in the service of God, but as constituting a lifetime spent in training. In 1932 Geoffrey Holt, who had accompanied Philip from school to the novitiate, passed on to the Jesuit college at Heythrop, but Brother Caraman was to remain at Roehampton for a further two years.

The curriculum followed by Caraman in the period between 1932 and 1934 was that drawn up for students in the division known as the Juniorate. Regarded as a foundation for a degree course at university, it was principally scholastic in content with emphasis on classical studies. It is unlikely that Philip had much time or opportunity to follow up his interest in history during the years he spent at Roehampton, although he would certainly have learnt about aspects of Jesuit history and become familiar with the lives of Jesuit saints. One of the most noted Masters of the Juniorate of an earlier generation was Fr Cyril Martindale, whose biographer Caraman would later become.

It is likely that any lapses in concentration on the part of their pupil were treated with understanding by Philip Caraman's tutors in the Juniorate. Having lost his mother early in his noviceship, Philip's father René André Caraman also died very suddenly on 13 March 1933. By his twenty-second year Philip had suffered not only the loss of both parents but also the security of the comfortable home which the couple had made for their large family. René Caraman's funeral on 16 March was a low-key affair for so distinguished a man. The Requiem Mass was said at St Edward's in Golders Green, the church which he had helped to found and where several of his children including Philip had been baptised. After the burial in St Pancras cemetery, René and Betina's children returned to The Grange in Elstree for the reading of his will.

The terms of this testament, drawn up eighteen months before René Caraman's death, were recalled vividly by his younger son over fifty years later. Not only did Philip remember the legacy left by his father to the Catholic Archbishop of Smyrna; he also noted that this 'bequest was *among others*' in the will. Two charities, the Crusade of Rescue and Homes for Destitute Catholic Children, and the Benevolent Society for the Relief of the Aged and Infirm Poor, were also bequeathed fifty and twenty-five pounds respectively, and René explains the lack of further bequests in these words: 'Having during my lifetime tried to do my share in the way of charities and having regard to the smallness of my capital I leave no legacies . . . apart from [these] small amounts . . .'

The lack of capital probably reflected the set-back his import business had suffered after the destruction of Smyrna, and he had certainly done a great deal for Catholic charities. He had also worked tirelessly for the Catholic Church in England since his arrival from Smyrna thirty-six years earlier. Not only had René been associated with the work of the mission in Golders Green and founded the church in Elstree, he had acted as Chairman and Treasurer of the Catholic Huts Council and sat on the Committee of Westminster Catholic Federation. His work for the church was recognised by Pope Benedict XV who, on the recommendation of Cardinal Francis Bourne, created him a Knight of St Gregory in 1920. René Caraman had been equally successful in business, and at the time of his death was senior partner of his firm. He had also acted as Chairman of the London Dried Fruit Trade Association, and was the Founder and first Chairman of the Dried Fruit Importers' Association.

In the penultimate clause of his will, René asked for '. . . the forgiveness of all my friends for any injury I may have done them knowingly or unknowingly. I also ask the forgiveness of all my business friends for all my shortcomings in my dealings with them and for them.' As Edwin May, one of his business partners, was chosen as an executor and trustee, it is unlikely René had acted improperly at any time or was on bad terms with his associates in the City. On the other hand, it probably never occurred to this upright man that unknowingly his relationship with at least one of his own children – his younger son – fell far short of the ideal. At the conclusion of Philip Caraman's notes for his unwritten autobiography the words 'remote father figure' are written, and the irreversible distance between father and son was brought home abruptly to the young Jesuit during the reading of René's will.

Not unnaturally, the elder Caraman's principal concern seems to have been for the welfare of his young, unmarried daughters. One sister, Margaret Mary, had already joined a religious order, and René bequeathed one hundred pounds to the Mother General of the Missionary Sisters of St Joseph's Convent at Patricroft near Manchester, of which community she was a member. The remainder of his estate was to be shared equally among the six remaining sisters. René Caraman made 'no provision for my sons John Andrew and Phillip[sic] George ... as they will shortly be taking or may have taken the vow of poverty as members of a religious Order or Community'. However, it was stipulated that should either of his sons fail to 'persevere in their religious vocation or for any other unforeseen circumstances or causes give up the religious life', then he should apply to the Trustees and to René's daughters for a portion of the estate.

To a certain extent this would have made Philip dependent on the good will of his sisters had he decided to leave the Jesuits either before or after his ordination, but his father was aware that the Society would take good care of his material needs for as long as he was one of its members. In deciding upon this course of action regarding his children, René Caraman stated that he had done so 'after consultation with my son John and in full agreement with him'. The fact that René had never discussed the matter with Philip highlights the second son's status in the eyes of his father. Another small point illustrates their relationship. Throughout the typewritten will drawn up by a firm of solicitors, the younger son is referred to as 'Phi*ll*ip' George. This mis-spelling of the Christian name which appears on both birth and baptismal certificates with a single '*l*' was apparently of so little significance to René Caraman that he either failed to notice it or considered it did not require correction.

Philip Caraman's lifelong fascination with the subject of parent–child and father–son relationships can be explained by his sense of rejection by his own father. In his biography of the eminent Jesuit Fr Martindale, he explores in depth Cyril Martindale's relationship with his father, Arthur Martindale. Caraman relates how, on receiving the news of his father's death in January 1942, Martindale 'at great length went through the changing history of his relationship with his father ... He was to blame for his failure to explain himself to his father in his early days as a Catholic and Jesuit ... It was a relationship that sought understanding on both sides and found it only in small measure ...'[7] Later, wishing to help a friend who wrote on themes connected with the Royal Family, Caraman told her, 'I would have thought something on the relationship between George V and the Duke of Windsor could be placed easily'.[8] Martindale's father lived until the age of eighty-seven. It was unfortunate for Philip Caraman that his own father died in his mid-fifties, long before they were able to attain a degree of mutual respect. In this lack of affection and understanding between René Caraman and his younger son lies an explanation for Philip's quest for the guidance of a surrogate father figure in his later life.

The gradual fragmentation of family life caused by the close deaths of Betina and René Caraman was rendered less painful for Philip when he and John came together as fellow students at Heythrop College. The Philosophy course at Heythrop lasted three years, and when Philip moved there from Manresa in 1934 his elder brother, ahead of him in his Jesuit training, was still studying there. In his contribution to John Caraman's obituary, Philip wrote: 'It was only when our paths crossed at Heythrop for two years that I really came to know him. I don't know the extent to which his decision to become a Jesuit was influenced by his Oxford friends who later became, or tried to become, priests ...'[9] A bond developed between the brothers, which withstood the test of time despite the very different paths they eventually followed in the Jesuit life. John departed for the missions in Southern Rhodesia in 1938, and apart from rare leaves spent the rest of his life in Africa. The brothers visited each other whenever possible and they corresponded frequently; Philip enjoyed receiving John's letters and envied the clarity and conciseness of his writing.[10]

Of all the members of his natural family, the Jesuit John Caraman seems to have been the one to whom Philip was nearest. Although he remained in touch with his many relations, particularly with nephews and nieces, his brother was the only one with whom he appeared to enjoy a lasting understanding. After Philip Caraman's death his only surviving sister Claire remarked that 'once he joined the Jesuits over seventy years ago – that became his life and although we were always in touch, our lives were so very different ... My immediate family ... are scattered all over the world and knew little of Philip ...'[11] Other families whose members have joined the Society of Jesus have made similar comments. A retired Stonyhurst master, married and with a family of his own, described the occasion when he had attempted to organise the funeral of his brother, a Jesuit priest. Although the family's thoughts on the Requiem were listened to politely, the Society made all the arrangements according to their own agenda, leaving the brother to remark that 'the Jesuits take over the lives of those who join them'. From the early 1930s until the time of his death, Philip Caraman regarded the Society of Jesus as his true family.

Although the younger Caraman's relationship with the Society of Jesus was destined to experience many vicissitudes, the period he spent at Heythrop appears to have passed off without incident. The philosophy course was *de rigueur* for Jesuit students climbing the long ladder to ordination and during this stage of their formation they were known as *Scholastics*. The Jesuit College at Heythrop was a relatively new foundation when John and Philip Caraman arrived there, having opened only in 1926 in a grandiose baroque house formerly owned by the Earls of Shrewsbury near Chipping Norton in Oxfordshire. The philosophy and theology scholastics had previously studied at separate institutions, the former at Stonyhurst, whilst the Theologate had been at St Beuno's in Wales. But the Jesuit Superior General, Fr Ledochowski, sent instructions from Rome that Philosophates and Theologates worldwide should be amalgamated into a single *Collegium Maximum* in their own Province, connected to one of the national universities in that particular country. In buying a house some twenty miles outside Oxford, the Provincial of the day, Fr William Bodkin, had thought the College would be affiliated to the University, but his hopes were disappointed. The writer H. J. A. Sire comments that: ' It would have been quite foreign to Oxford's policy to grant any sort of status to a Jesuit seminary even in the High Street, let alone twenty miles outside the city', and Fr Bodkin's aspirations in this respect together with those of his superiors in Rome were rebuffed.[12]

Although the situation was less than satisfactory, both for the younger students of philosophy and their older counterparts among the theologians, Philip Caraman had one advantage over some of his contemporaries. Having learnt Latin from an early age in the classroom, he had fewer problems in understanding the lectures than those without a similar advantage. All teaching at Heythrop was in Latin, so appreciation of the lectures was restricted to the pupils' capacity for understanding the language. A former student relates the story of one of the better professors at the College who emphasised key words and syllables in his discourses so that his pupils were able to grasp their content. But on reading the lecture afterwards nothing made much sense. Eventually the views of former students concerning the College's shortcomings, and particularly the lack of sensitivity accorded to the problems of the younger scholastics, would be taken into consideration by a future Provincial, Fr Martin D'Arcy. Against stiff opposition, Fr D'Arcy attempted to introduce changes in the system of teaching philosophy and theology to scholastics, but he met with little success. In due course, in 1965, the College was turned into a Pontifical Athenaeum with the power to grant degrees, but it was no longer an exclusively Jesuit institution, taking students from some of the smaller religious orders and a number of dioceses. Finally in 1970

Heythrop was closed and the philosophy and theology studies were incorporated in a course at London University with a house in Kensington Square.

For all its vicissitudes, Heythrop in its time could claim at least one notable scholar among those who had passed through the system there. Fr Frederick Copleston is regarded as one of the twentieth century's outstanding teachers of philosophy, and his nine-volume *History of Philosophy,* which evolved during the time he spent teaching at the College, is judged even by agnostics to be admirably unbiased and still remains a much-consulted reference work. It is unlikely that Caraman, a near contemporary of Fr Copleston, looked back on the time he spent at Heythrop with much satisfaction, for his talents – unlike those of some of his fellow Jesuits – were neither primarily nor exclusively academic in nature.

Temporarily released from the hothouse of intensive study, Philip Caraman was sent to teach in a Jesuit school. His obituary in *Letters & Notices* – the official in-house magazine of the British Province of the Society of Jesus – states that he returned to his old school as a teacher in the academic year 1937/8.[13] But there is no mention of him in the listings of the comings and goings of staff in the Stonyhurst records for that or for the previous or subsequent years. Possibly this is one of a number of errors in his official records, or he may have spent only a brief spell as a trainee teacher at the College in preparation for a move to an altogether tougher environment.[14]

What is certain is that at some point Philip Caraman returned to Stonyhurst for a period long enough to allow him to study some of the priceless manuscripts held in the College archives which, when he was a pupil, would have been out of bounds. The Stonyhurst Manuscripts were a principal source of material for a number of his early books, the first of which, *John Gerard. The Autobiography of an Elizabethan,*[15] would be published over ten years later. Caraman was fascinated by the unusual and vivid accounts of persecution left by priests and lay

people who had suffered for their faith during the reign of
Elizabeth I; among the Stonyhurst manuscripts he found the
Collectanea of Christopher Grene, from which he later drew a
number of sketches for *The Other Face. Catholic Life Under
Elizabeth I*,[16] a book whose title was suggested to him by Dame
Edith Sitwell.

Philip Caraman received an enormous boost to his enthusiasm
for English Catholic history when he was posted by his superiors to a school the Jesuits had opened recently in Sunderland.
As part of the long process of Jesuit training and formation, it
was considered advisable to give the Scholastics a period of
practical work at some point during the years before their ordination. In Caraman's case the decision to send him to County
Durham proved beneficial not only in furthering his historical
studies, but also in the formation of his character. Here, in the
industrial north-east of England, he was brought face to face
with poverty and the inequalities of a social system of which,
from the background of a comfortable middle-class home in the
south and with the advantage of a public school education, he
had little previous experience. He gained an insight into the
everyday problems of working-class families, which bore fruit
later in his 'wonderful ability to deal with people on their own
level . . . and his lack of pretence'.[17]

In October 1933 the Jesuits had opened a Retreat House for
men in Sunderland named Corby Hall, after the Jesuit martyr
Ralph Corby. Although the Society of Jesus was strongly represented in other areas of England, at that time it had surprisingly
little presence in the Catholic north-east. This was Benedictine
territory.[18] A previous Jesuit Retreat House had been established
in Gateshead in 1913, but was closed for the duration of the
First World War when the house, Whinney House, was handed
over to the Red Cross Society for a hospital. It had reopened
briefly after the war, but was closed down permanently when
the owner sold Whinney House to Gateshead Corporation. It
seems that the clergy in Sunderland had reservations about the
Jesuits regaining a foothold in the area, and wished to place
certain restrictions on their activities should they return. Despite
this there was an evident need for a retreat house in the diocese,

and in April 1933 a suitable building, Ashbrooke House, came on the market and was acquired by the Jesuits. The name was changed from Ashbrooke House to Corby Hall, and it was blessed and opened as a retreat centre by Bishop Joseph Thorman on 8 October 1933; the first Superior was Fr Paul Whittaker, who was assisted by Frs William Fitzmaurice and Richard Clarke. Later they were joined by Fr Henry Sire. In keeping with the spirit of the times, the centre catered for men only and by 1935 over a thousand had attended retreats there.[19]

By 1937 the Jesuits had also established a secondary day school for Catholic boys in Ashbrooke Road within the catchment area of parishes in the Sunderland area. In many of these close-knit communities the parishioners all lived within call of the church bell, and despite their poverty and the hardships they suffered during the years of the Depression, their devotion to their Faith was unwavering. Philip Caraman met the challenges which faced him at Corby Hall School with energy and compassion, and the period he spent there did more than a little for his own education. He was given an insight into the pride and poverty of the boys he taught when the school fees of £2 a term had to be reduced or waived for families too hard up to find even this small sum. And his own pride received a jolt when he fancied joining his tough pupils in a game of football. In his autobiographical notes he records his 'stupidity', no doubt because he made a fool of himself on the playing field. The school brought the scholastic face to face for the first time with a brand of blatant Irish Catholicism which the English sometimes found hard to swallow and which Caraman himself regarded with scepticism, particularly as he grew older. Until the later part of the twentieth century Catholic parishes had their own distinctive character according to the background of their people. Whilst united in loyalty to Rome and the practice of one Faith, churchgoers in an Irish immigrant mining community such as Sunderland had little in common, other than denomination, with mass-goers in middle-class and predominantly English parishes in places like Elstree or Roehampton. It is likely that Philip Caraman attempted to enliven his classes with flashes of the schoolboy humour which had characterised his performances in the Stonyhurst Debating Society and which he never lost even in old age. But, depending on wordplay and very much public-school in essence, his witticisms were probably lost on his pupils.

All the mainstream subjects were taught at Corby Hall School, including religious knowledge, Latin, French and history. The school also ran a cycling club costing sixpence a term. As an enthusiastic member, Philip made long journeys of discovery into the highways and byways of historic County Durham, and his enjoyment of these excursions more than compensated for any problems in the classroom. He was greatly moved by the celebrated view of Durham Cathedral from the banks of the River Wear, and by a visit to the tomb of the scholar-monk whose writings illuminate the darkness of early Christianity in these islands. In the Galilee Chapel of Durham's Norman cathedral, Caraman spent a long time beside the tomb of St Bede the Venerable, with its top of Frosterley marble and its Latin inscription which he copied faithfully in his notebook.

Inspired perhaps by Bede, Caraman pursued the trail of the county's recusant history, which his own writings later recorded with great success. He had no further to look for one of his subjects than the life and death of the Jesuit Blessed Ralph Corby, in whose honour the school in Sunderland was named, and who had spent most of his early life in County Durham. During the reign of Charles I, Corby had returned to his home county as an ordained priest to work with poor Catholics in Durham and the surrounding villages. Arrested while actually saying Mass, he had been taken to Sunderland for summary trial, and thence by sea to London. Corby was executed at Tyburn on 7 September 1644, a fate shared by several other of Caraman's heroes.

Evidently Philip Caraman made a good enough impression on his superiors to gain permission to spend a long summer vacation in Germany; the money for his journey would have come from Jesuit funds. The decision to grant him leave to travel abroad may have been influenced by the fact that, apart from living in one of the Society's houses, he was now homeless following the death of both his parents and the division of the family estate between his sisters. Thus Caraman was able to follow the lead of many other well-educated young men of his generation,[20] who toured Germany in the years immediately preceding the Second World War and were alarmed at what they saw and heard there. Philip Caraman was no exception. He noted the obvious signs of military activity – the training camps being prepared, the ubiquitous army uniforms, and the Wagnerian drama of the Nuremberg *Parteidag*. Caraman travelled widely on what was surely a limited budget, and his journey not only took him north to Hamburg but east to historic Leipzig, a city which impressed him with the beauty of its medieval buildings and its picturesque streets.

Caraman's grand tour differed from that of his contemporaries because he lodged wherever possible in houses run by the Society of Jesus, and he viewed what he heard and saw from the standpoint of a Jesuit. There was a brief interlude of prayer and recollection during his travels, when he made a retreat at the Jesuit house at Feldkirch in Austria, where the Blessed Rupert Mayer had entered the novitiate in October 1900.

The young Jesuit was given an introduction to Rupert Mayer, who at the time of Caraman's visit was considered one of the most controversial Catholic priests in Germany, having just emerged from serving a prison sentence for his public denouncement of the Nazis. Fr Mayer had served in the First World War as regimental chaplain to the 16th Bavarian Reserve Infantry, known from its original commander, Colonel List, as the List Regiment. One of the soldiers in this regiment was Adolf Hitler. In December 1915 Mayer was awarded the Iron Cross for bravery in the field, and a year later was seriously wounded and lost a leg as a result of his injuries. He had always regarded his mission as that of helping the poor, and after the First World War he returned to his apostolate in Munich where he had been based previously, and worked with the charitable organisation Caritas. Between the wars Mayer was known as the 'Limping Priest' and it was said of him that his own physical suffering helped him to become an understanding, kind and gentle priest. He was also a brilliant and courageous preacher. One of only a few who dared to challenge the Nazis openly,

Mayer was twice arrested and forbidden to preach in public. When Philip Caraman was introduced to him, Mayer was living at the Mariakirke in Starnberg, a village situated on a lake south of Munich where he worked with small discussion groups which were conducted privately. With a limited command of the German language, it is doubtful if Caraman was able to make the most of his visit, but the memory of sitting smoking cigarettes in Mayer's room remained with him until the end of his life. Philip remarked in his autobiographical notes that this was his 'first encounter with a saint'. Mayer was arrested by the Gestapo in November 1939, deported first to a concentration camp and later placed under house arrest in southern Bavaria. He died, much debilitated, shortly after the end of the war whilst preaching at Mass in Munich. He was beatified by Pope John Paul II on 3 May 1987, and some five to six thousand people daily pray at his tomb in St Michael's Church in the city of his apostolate. With the benefit of hindsight, the visit to Rupert Mayer was the highlight of Caraman's journey through a Germany on the verge of war, and he remarks in his autobiographical notes that in old age every detail of this trip was still more clear to him than were details of innumerable other visits he made abroad later in life.

Philip Caraman travelled to Germany by sea, as most people did at that time, and he remarked later that this was the 'first of dozens of crossings of the North Sea'. He lamented that the diary he had kept of this trip was lost, but learnt a salutary lesson because later on he preserved carefully the records he made of his journeys to out-of-the-way places. During the weeks he spent on the Continent at this time Caraman conceived a love of travel, a curiosity for new horizons, which equalled and sometimes eclipsed even his love of history. Fortunately he was able to pursue his twin passions in tandem on many occasions. Less fortunately for Brother Caraman, it was several years before he or anyone else in Europe would be able to make the type of leisurely journey he had enjoyed in the run-up to the Second World War.

The subdued atmosphere of present-day Campion Hall holds few echoes of the position occupied by the house as a centre of Catholic intellectual and social life in the years immediately before the war. The Jesuit hall, set in a quiet lane in the centre of Oxford, is now the home of a number of senior Jesuits, retired after a lifetime of service in parishes, schools and the overseas missions. Originally founded in 1896 with the status of a Private Hall in premises in St Giles, the present building in Brewer Street, designed by Sir Edwin Lutyens, was opened with much ceremony in June 1936 by the Duke of Alba, in the presence of many of the leading Roman Catholics of the day, including Evelyn Waugh and his future mother-in-law, Mary Herbert, who were patrons of the project.

The prestige of the new building and the reputation enjoyed by Campion Hall as a centre of excellence were attributed to the inspiration of its Master and presiding genius, Fr Martin D'Arcy. Recognised as an outstanding writer of philosophic works by his own generation, his books are judged by some latter-day Jesuits to be those of a 'philosophers' philosopher'. Appointed Rector and Master in January 1933, Fr D'Arcy strove to make the Hall 'a shrine of Christian civilisation – something Oxford had been and was no longer'.[21] This influential Jesuit, who guided and befriended a generation of writers, artists and aristocrats, converting a number of them to Roman Catholicism, achieved his aim remarkably quickly. Within a short time the Hall was adorned by a collection of paintings, statues and other pieces, the works of leading artists of the day such as Eric Gill and Augustus John, which are still referred to as the Hall's *objets d'Arcy*. He also built up a collection of magnificent vestments, many of them medieval, bringing a sense of occasion to the celebration of Mass in the Campion Hall chapel.

The high reputation of the Society of Jesus in England during the 1930s was due in no small part to the social cachet enjoyed by Campion Hall under Fr D'Arcy. The Master was renowned for his hospitality, and invitations to his guest nights were readily accepted by prominent men from many walks of life. Graham Greene and Isaiah Berlin, Frank Pakenham and

Maurice Bowra, C. S. Lewis and ex-Chancellor Bruning of Germany were among writers, intellectuals, politicians and foreign visitors who dined at Campion Hall at this time. The dinners were renowned for the brilliance of the conversation, which was orchestrated and directed with unerring skill by Fr D'Arcy. The Rector was at pains to include his undergraduates in these gatherings, for he regarded the young men in his care as his primary responsibility and their welfare and advancement were always close to his heart.

On being appointed Rector and Master of Campion Hall, D'Arcy liberalised the system which until then had discouraged Jesuit undergraduates from taking much part in Oxford life, and which he had found irksome during his own student days some twenty years previously. Under Fr D'Arcy's guidance, the scholastics were encouraged to make friends with their lay contemporaries, their tutors were entertained at the Hall, and Jesuits were permitted to join university societies. Their horizons were widened even further when the new Master invited Jesuits from abroad, some members of other religious orders and a few secular clergy to share their Hall of residence.

The Jesuit intake was small, never numbering more than thirteen to begin with, and the chosen few considered themselves fortunate to have been selected. It is hardly surprising then that Philip Caraman looked forward eagerly to the three years he was to spend at Campion Hall reading History. He was greatly disappointed. His arrival coincided with the declaration of war, and throughout his three years there the University was, in his own words, only 'half functioning'. University life was overshadowed by the departure of the young men, and the death in battle of many of them. Although Oxford was not quite so void of undergraduates as it had been during the First World War, some of the colleges and buildings were requisitioned and only a skeleton staff remained to keep up the traditions and teaching standards of the university. Campion Hall was relatively untouched, but the number of Jesuit students quartered there rose to twenty-one when one of the Society's academic institutions was evacuated from London. At the age of twenty-eight Caraman was among the more mature students; his clerical status placed him in a 'reserved occupation', but it is unlikely that he would have a passed a medical examination had he wished to join one of the armed services. Although in 1941 Philip Caraman was elected President of the Stubbs Society, a university circle of historians named after a renowned nineteenth-century professor of modern history, he confessed that he found his time at Oxford 'frustrating'.

During much of the three years Caraman spent at Campion Hall the Master was away from Oxford and although Fr Basil Gurrin, the Hall's Spiritual Father, was an admirable guide, D'Arcy's absence was unavoidably felt. In August 1939 Fr D'Arcy had set out on what was intended as a brief visit to Washington to take part in a *Pax Romana* congress, but he was stranded by the outbreak of war and had to remain in the United States. He was finally able to return to England by a circuitous route, arriving in September 1940, only two weeks before the start of Caraman's second academic year. The following year D'Arcy went to America in September, this time at the request of the Ministry of Information, returning home in April 1942, a year in which a considerable amount of his time was taken up in lecturing and broadcasting. Fr D'Arcy's contacts in the United States were not without some benefit to his undergraduates, because in the wake of his visits a steady stream of food parcels arrived at Campion Hall from across the Atlantic, enabling the renowned hospitality of the house to continue with a munificence rarely enjoyed elsewhere during those austere times.

Although Martin D'Arcy was heavily involved in life outside Oxford during Caraman's undergraduate years, he was nonetheless able to form an opinion of the scholastic's abilities, and rated his potential highly. Perhaps Philip Caraman made his mark at the dinner nights which D'Arcy hosted from time to time for those luminaries he was still able to gather round his table during the war years. Maybe Caraman's enterprise in travelling round Germany had impressed his superiors, or in private dialogue between the younger man and himself the Rector appreciated Caraman's unobtrusive manner and his willingness to listen rather than try to impress by expounding his own views. It is possible Caraman confided in his superior his disappointment with wartime Oxford, but however it came to pass a bond of friendship was formed between D'Arcy and Philip Caraman which flourished and grew ever stronger with the passage of time.

Whilst he was still Master of Campion Hall, Martin D'Arcy started to introduce his protégé to some of the influential Catholics who were close to him and with whom he felt the young man would be socially at ease. Caraman was given an entrée into the world of old Catholic families and landed gentry, the inheritors of the recusant history that was so dear to him. One of D'Arcy's first introductions did not fit this pattern exactly, because the Herberts of Pixton Park owed their Catholicism to the conversion of their matriarch the Hon. Mrs Aubrey Herbert, daughter of the fourth Lord de Vesci and his staunchly Irish Protestant wife who was a daughter of the tenth Lord Wemyss. Mary Herbert was the long-time widow of gentleman-adventurer Aubrey Herbert, a half-brother to Lord Carnarvon of Tutenkhamen fame, who had died in 1923 aged forty-three. At her great Georgian mansion overlooking the River Exe at Dulverton in Somerset, Mary Herbert dispensed open-handed hospitality; during the war years the large house was home to a strangely-assorted population of retired servants and nannies, evacuees from London, an elderly Austrian countess and her maid, and from time to time family friends like Hilaire Belloc. For some years Fr D'Arcy had been a regular visitor to Pixton, which was also the home of Mary Herbert's son Auberon, and the wartime residence of her three daughters Gabriel, Bridget and Laura. The house was enlivened further by the presence of a number of small grandchildren, including Auberon Waugh who was born at Pixton in November 1939. Gabriel's future husband Alick Dru, Major Eddie Grant who was married to Bridget, and Laura's husband Evelyn Waugh also appeared from time to time, the last on occasion unannounced. Philip Caraman was readily welcomed into this warm, somewhat chaotic, family circle. Bridget Grant, the last survivor of the Herbert sisters, and according to her nephew Auberon the most beautiful,[22] remembered that Philip first came to my family home, Pixton Park – Dulverton, about 60 years ago, having been brought there by Father Martin D'Arcy who was a great friend of my mother's, Mary Herbert. Father Philip was quite young, I don't know if he was already ordained. Philip was very fond both of my mother and my brother Auberon. He was also a great friend of my brother-in-law Evelyn Waugh.

Mrs Grant added that Philip Caraman 'has been a very good friend to several generations of my family'.[23]

Caraman did not meet Laura's husband Evelyn at this time, as Waugh's spells of leave from military service never coincided with Philip's visits. His friendships with the mutually antipathetic Auberon Herbert and Evelyn Waugh began in the period immediately after the war when both men had returned to civilian life. But the young Jesuit was quickly taken under the wing of the formidable Mary Herbert, described by Malcolm Muggeridge as 'a terrific personage, one of those heroic mothers the English upper classes used to produce before they lost their nerve and took to dressing their children in specially faded and patched jeans . . . to show their proletarian sympathies . . .'[24] Mary Herbert's generosity towards Caraman was echoed by her children and grandchildren, whilst he in turn gave them his undying affection and loyalty.

Fr D'Arcy's patronage cannot be explained on the grounds of Philip's academic achievements at Oxford. During Martin D'Arcy's term as Master of Campion Hall, a number of his other Jesuit undergraduates enhanced the prestige of the Hall by winning University prizes and gaining brilliant degrees. In addition to Bernard Basset who won the Stanhope and Lothian essay prizes, other outstanding students included Robert Wingfield-Digby, and Vincent Turner who won a spectacular succession of Firsts. John Coventry gained a First in Classics in 1942, but Philip Caraman who graduated in the same year won no University prizes and went down from Oxford with only a Second to his name. Martin D'Arcy's appreciation of his protégé's abilities was not shared even then by all of Philip's contemporaries, and Fr D'Arcy's favouritism unwittingly caused a ripple of resentment that twenty years later surged into a storm which almost destroyed Caraman in its ferocity.

Meanwhile, in 1942, the new graduate returned to Heythrop to study Theology. The second period of Jesuit training finally came to fruition when on 12 September 1945 Philip Caraman was ordained priest at the Jesuit church of the Immaculate Conception at Farm Street, in Mayfair. His ordination was celebrated within a few weeks of Fr Martin D'Arcy becoming English Provincial of the Society of Jesus, an appointment of great significance in the later career of the younger man.

Notes

1 Among other Catholic families with multiple religious vocations were the Farwells, the Keatinges, the Powers and the D'Arcys. The Farwells of Roehampton had a Jesuit and a Benedictine, Abbot Victor Farwell OSB who became English Provincial. Of two Keatinge brothers one was a distinguished canon of Tunbridge Wells and the other, the Right Reverend William Keatinge, became Senior RC Chaplain of the BEF in the First World War. The Power family gave three sons to the Church, one of whom, John, was a much-loved parish priest in Hertfordshire, and Conyers, the elder brother of the distinguished Jesuit, Fr Martin D'Arcy, was also a Jesuit.
2 Two years older than Philip Caraman, Fr Bernard Basset SJ won the Stanhope and Lothian essay prizes and took first-class honours in Modern History whilst at Campion Hall, Oxford. He taught history at Stonyhurst and another Jesuit school, Beaumont, and was a renowned spiritual director and retreat preacher. His many popular books include *We Neurotics – A Handbook for the Half-mad* (1962) and *The Noonday Devil – Spiritual Support in Middle Age* (1964), which were published along with others of his books by Burns & Oates.
3 H. J. A. Sire, *Father Martin D'Arcy. Philosopher of Christian Love* (Gracewing, 1997), p. 22.
4 Philip Caraman, *C. C. Martindale. A Biography* (Longmans, 1967), p. 69.
5 Philip Caraman, *Ignatius Loyola. A Biography of the Founder of the Jesuits* (Harper & Row, Publishers, San Francisco, 1990), pp. 40 and 41.

6 See Chapter Six, below, 'Wilderness'; final paragraph of chapter and note 52.

7 Philip Caraman, *C.C. Martindale,* pp. 211–13.

8 Philip Caraman, letter to author dated 7 April 1982.

9 *Letters & Notices*, vols 85–7, 1983. Jesuit Archives – English Province.

10 Ibid.

11 Letter to author from Mrs Claire Cradock Henry, dated 23 April 2001.

12 H. J. A. Sire, *Father Martin D'Arcy,* pp. 133–4.

13 *Letters & Notices*, vol. 94, Autumn 1998, no. 414. pp. 831 et seq.

14 In the course of researching this book, the author has noted a number of other omissions and errors in Fr Caraman's official Jesuit CV.

15 Published by Longmans, Green and Co., 1951.

16 Also published by Longmans, in 1960.

17 Fr Caraman's obituary notice: Fr Olaf I. Waring, priest of the Diocese of Oslo, Sept. 1998, and undated letter to author from Fr Waring received 14 August 2001.

18 *The Catholic Directory for 1928* lists only one Jesuit parish, Richmond in the North Riding of Yorkshire, in the dioceses of Middlesborough and of Hexham and Newcastle, whereas the Benedictines ran no fewer than thirteen parishes at that time in these dioceses. Nor are any Jesuit schools listed.

19 *The Northern Catholic Calendar – 1934: 1935: 1936* and *1937.* Courtesy the Archivist, Roman Catholic Diocese of Hexham and Newcastle.

20 Their number included several such as Edward Heath who were later prominent in public life.

21 These words are attributed to the Catholic writer and actor Robert Speaight by H. J. A. Sire in *Father Martin D'Arcy. Philosopher of Christian Love.*

22 Pixton in wartime is vividly described by Auberon Waugh in *Will This Do? The First Fifty Years of Auberon Waugh. An Autobiography* (Century, 1991).

23 Letter to author from Mrs Bridget Grant, Dulverton, Somerset, 22 May 2001.

24 Essay by Malcolm Muggeridge in *Auberon Herbert. A Composite Portrait*, edited by John Joliffe (privately published, 1976).

Part Two
The Mayfair Years
1946–1965

Chapter Three

Reveille for *The Month*

A joke going the rounds of Catholic circles in the 1940s accurately described popular perception of the Jesuit-owned periodical *The Month* at the time. 'I feel very sleepy, there must be a copy of *The Month* in the room', drawled a friend of Tom Burns, so notorious was the once-revered magazine for its soporific effect on readers.[1]

It was Philip Caraman's task to awaken *The Month* from its slumbers, but before the first issue of the periodical under his editorship exploded on the literary world in January 1949, he had to complete a further three years of Jesuit training following his ordination to the priesthood. Initially he returned to Heythrop to continue and complete the fourth year of his Theology course, and possibly in order to retake an exam he had failed earlier which would have qualified him for admission to the inner circle of Jesuits considered eligible for solemn profession. It seems that Fr Caraman did not attain the standards required for this honour at that time, and it was not until much later – on 8 September 1979 – that he was professed.

After his appointment as Provincial, Fr Martin D'Arcy had realised the potential of the near-defunct *Month* as a showcase for Catholic literature and thought. Sensing that Philip Caraman's particular talents could be directed into reviving the Jesuit periodical, D'Arcy chose his protégé for the job. With this assignment in mind, Caraman was given work experience as editor of the Jesuit in-house magazine, *Letters & Notices*. This periodical was, and still is, a very competent publication recording news of interest to members of the English Province of the Society of Jesus. Many of the pieces are obituaries, others, such as those about work in the foreign missions, are of general interest to an almost exclusively Jesuit readership. The short period Philip Caraman spent on *Letters & Notices* in 1947 gave him his first taste of living and working in the great Jesuit complex in Mayfair. The little kingdom of the English Province of the Society of Jesus comprised property in Farm Street adjacent to the splendid Victorian church of the Immaculate Conception, and an imposing red-brick building at 114 Mount Street, overlooking St George's Gardens behind the church. Set in the most fashionable part of London, between Berkeley Square and Grosvenor Square, the Provincial House is opposite the exclusive Connaught Hotel, from where, many years later, the actor and writer Alec Guinness could send a note across to Fr Caraman, saying: 'I am over the road from you. Would you like breakfast tomorrow?'[2]

Before settling in London, Philip Caraman underwent a further year of training in a setting far removed from Mayfair. For the final year of his Tertianship he went to St Beuno's in Wales, a suitably remote environment in which to conduct the third and final stage of a very long haul. The last year of Tertianship was intended as a period in which the spiritual life of the by then almost middle-aged Jesuit was given a final polishing. During this time the Instructor of Tertians inculcated in his pupils the laws of the Society embodied in the Constitution, and the priests in his care once again made the Long Retreat before embarking on the working career allotted to them under their vow of obedience to their Superiors.

In 1948, the Rector and the Instructor of Tertians were both respected Jesuits, with many years of experience in the guidance of younger priests. Fr Ernest Vignaux was a former Master of Campion Hall and had held a senior position at Stonyhurst during the First World War: the Instructor of Tertians, Fr Henry Keane, was a former Provincial whose term of appointment in the early 1930s had been extended beyond the standard six years in that office. Both were considered men of solid achievement, although somewhat rigid outlook, unlike the then Provincial, the more flamboyant Martin D'Arcy.

The regime at St Beuno's under Ernest Vignaux and Fr Henry Keane nonetheless gave Philip Caraman an opportunity for quiet recollection and prayer before being catapulted into the maelstrom of the literary world. The house and grounds, which half a century later are still popular as an Ignatian retreat centre, provided the perfect backdrop for this period of spiritual renewal. Extolled by generations of Jesuits from Gerard Manley Hopkins through to the present day, the magic of St Beuno's setting in the Clwyd Valley was described by Cyril Martindale in his biography of Fr Charles Dominic Plater:

> The scenery is of great beauty. Rhyl and the sea are away to the right; Denbigh to the left looms on its crag; the heavy tower of St. Asaph Cathedral lifts itself from among the trees some four miles distant; and beyond the hills on the far side of the immense valley, yet other hills float upwards till behind them all you see the crest of Snowdon.

The peace and friendly atmosphere of the College won a special place in Fr Caraman's affections, and in later life, when asked for religious direction, he frequently recommended St Beuno's as a suitable place for spiritual renewal.

The months in Wales were intended to prepare the recently-ordained priests for the tasks ahead, and in Fr Caraman's case St Beuno's afforded a vital wellspring of spiritual strength in a time of near despair some years later. Those dark days were as yet far off when he returned to London, in the autumn of 1948, to relaunch *The Month* with enthusiasm, and a head teeming with innovative ideas.

Tom Burns's criticism of the *The Month* at the time Martin D'Arcy became Provincial was fully justified: in both appearance and content the periodical was unattractive and indigestible. Readers were faced with overlong articles presented in pages of close, unbroken print bound in a bland cover. Many of the essays were political commentaries, written by the Jesuit authors who comprised the majority of *The Month*'s contributors. A typical piece of that time by a Belgian Jesuit had the riveting title 'Social Changes in Belgium 1940–1946', and another comatose-rendering essay was entitled

'Pan-Slav and Pan-German – a parallel history of ideas' – worthy subjects, but hardly material likely to attract a wide readership. A complete re-vamp was essential, and from the outset Fr D'Arcy gave his appointee encouragement and support by introducing Caraman to his network of distinguished friends in the world of art and literature.

The younger man used these contacts to good effect. Two of Fr Caraman's main concerns involved the print and layout of the text, and the cover design of the periodical, and in both these areas he was given unprecedented help by leading experts. In the inter-war years, Stanley Morison had been a powerful figure in the Monotype Corporation, and had later designed a new typeface and layout for both *The Times* and the *Times Literary Supplement*, finally taking the editor's chair of the *TLS* in 1945 for a period of three years. A scholarly, committed, albeit quirky Roman Catholic, of whom it was said 'he loved the corridors of power, especially when they led to the dining-room', no one was more knowledgeable on the subject of typography than Morison. His work and advice ensured that articles in *The Month* under Fr Caraman became easy to read and thoroughly modern in appearance.

The new cover had an equally distinguished designer in Reynolds Stone, who suggested alternating colour motifs for successive issues of the monthly. Stone's designs and colours were passed for appraisal to the celebrated art critic and director of the Tate Gallery, John Rothenstein, and to his wife Elizabeth, who soon formed a warm friendship with Philip Caraman. The detailed attention paid to the format, typography, and cover design of the new *Month* achieved one of Fr D'Arcy's main goals. The presentation of the Jesuit publication was judged without hesitation to have overtaken that of *Horizon*, the brainchild of Cyril Connolly and organ of Bloomsbury, which was regarded during the 1940s as the leading literary review.

Horizon had first appeared in January 1940 as a lively and attractive periodical under Connolly's editorship. The first issue ran a series of drawings by Henry Moore, entitled *Reclining Man*, and contributors included H. E. Bates, John Betjeman, W. H. Auden. and J. B. Priestley. In his editorial, Connolly wrote:

A magazine should be the reflection of its time, and one that ceases to reflect this should come to an end. The moment we live in is archaistic, conservative and irresponsible, for the war is separating culture from life and driving it back on itself. The aim of *Horizon* is to give to writers a place to express themselves and to readers the best writing we can obtain ...

Later issues of *Horizon* featured poems by Dylan Thomas, Laurie Lee, and many other leading writers of the time. After the war the number of high-calibre contributors dropped dramatically, many were foreigners, and the tone of the magazine had become distinctly seedy, with the issue of July 1949 giving a 'glimpse of sex-life in prisons'.

Martin D'Arcy envisaged *The Month* as a challenge to *Horizon*, not only as a showcase for the best in Catholic writing, but as a wide-ranging review of literature and the arts. Two prominent writers of the day, Graham Greene and Evelyn Waugh, backed D'Arcy's concept, and Caraman was introduced to both men as plans for the periodical began to take shape. Correspondence between Greene and Fr Caraman dating to October 1948 suggests that theirs was purely a business connection to begin with. On the other hand, the relationship between Waugh and Philip Caraman soon blossomed into a friendship that grew deeper and stronger with the passage of time.

A card sent by Waugh from his home, Piers Court, in September 1948, informed Fr D'Arcy that the writer would 'be in London on Monday and could see the editor of the "Month" then if he is free. Will he come and have a glass of sherry with me at St. James's Club at 12 noon?' It seems extraordinary that Waugh and Fr Caraman had not met previously, given that the Jesuit had become a frequent visitor to the Herberts at Pixton, and had grown close to the family of Waugh's wife, Laura, since his introduction to them by D'Arcy during the war. It was greatly to Caraman's credit that tensions between Waugh and his in-laws never clouded the relationship between priest and unpredictable writer, and from the outset they worked well together.

Evelyn Waugh, to a greater extent even than Graham Greene, had been privy to Fr D'Arcy's plans for *The Month,* and the new editor readily deferred to his literary experience. One of Waugh's suggestions for the reformed magazine probably seemed unexpected at the time, and, to an English Jesuit, somewhat questionable. Waugh had just completed the task of editing, and reducing for a British readership, the autobiography of a then unknown American Trappist monk, Thomas Merton. Originally called *The Seven Storey Mountain*, the version edited by Waugh was published by Burns & Oates and was an immediate best-seller under the Hopkins title of *Elected Silence*. The two men corresponded, and the American wrote in his journal: 'Evelyn Waugh wanted to edit the English edition of *The Seven Storey Mountain* and has apparently already done so. I am glad. I trust him more than anyone else on a job like that . . .'[3] At the time of Fr Caraman's first meeting with Waugh, the author was about to leave for the United States, and planned to visit Merton at the Abbey of Our Lady of Gethsemani in Kentucky during his time there.[4]

Recognising the monk's importance as a Catholic writer, as few other people in Britain in 1948 had done, Waugh urged Philip Caraman to commission work from Merton for *The Month*. Willing to follow his mentor's recommendation, although possibly less impressed by the Trappist's potential than Waugh, the Jesuit handed the job of contacting Merton to his assistant editor, Fr Deryck Hanshell, who at Caraman's request had joined the editorial team from Heythrop. Hanshell and Merton corresponded, and quickly established a personal relationship which transcended business affairs. From his abbey, the monk wrote:

Thanks very much for asking me to contribute to the new Month and to pray for it. I will try to do both, but you cannot expect very much from me either in writing or in prayer, not because I haven't the will but because . . . [sic]. Here is a poem, anyway. As far as prose goes, (you didn't ask me for any but that doesn't matter) I cannot contribute articles but I can let you take your pick from chapters of books, regarding which you might contact T. F. Burns at Hollis & Carter. I will try to send you some galleys of a little book on contemplation that is going to press now. And I would like to see the Month.

Do you know The Society of Jesus has some very promising young poets here especially Daniel Berrigan and Francis Sweeney. The later as far as I know is at Keyser Island, Norwalk, Connecticut. Perhaps you have been in touch with them already.

Please pray for me too. I am just getting close to the subdiaconate. The thought of being a priest terrifies me.

The letter was signed Frate M. Louis Merton CSR.[5] The typescript of the poem enclosed with this letter had been amended in pencil by Merton, and *From the Legend of St Clement* appeared on the title page of Philip Caraman's first number of *The Month*.[6]

&

The new editor limited his own contribution in the relaunched magazine to a brief 'Introductory Note', in which he wrote:

In *The Idea of a Christian Society* Mr. T. S. Eliot deplores a situation in which 'those who should be the intellectuals regard theology as a special study, like numismatics or heraldry, with which they need not concern themselves, and theologians observe the same indifference to literature and art, as special subjects which do not concern them'.

The Month in its new series aims at providing for those interests which go to make a complete culture. It will publish imaginative writing, criticism, and theology which the layman can understand. This number is introduced by an American poet; an English critic discusses in it an important French novelist; and a French theologian gives his views on an English divine. This is a token of our intentions. The list of contributions to appear later will give a better idea of what *The Month* is than a long editorial comment.

The article, 'The Clown and the Philosopher', contributed by Fr Martin D'Arcy to the January issue, is considered by his biographer to be 'one of the finest he ever wrote',[7] and the book reviews kicked off with 'The Redemption of Mr Joyboy', a critical piece by Graham Greene on Evelyn Waugh's *The Loved*

One. Subscribers might well have wondered what other surprises the new editor had in store for them in the months ahead. Accustomed to a diet of erudite stodge, regular readers of *The Month* soon discovered they were in for some shocks. The opening pages of Fr Caraman's second issue in February 1949 featured a short story by Graham Greene, called 'The Hint of an Explanation', in which the author uses the sacred nature of the consecrated Eucharistic host in a surprise denouement. The author was delighted with his editor's treatment of the story, and wrote to Caraman from his villa in Anacapri on 4 March 1949, saying:

> I do want to thank you for the very nice appearance you have given my story in the Month. I hope it won't raise any trouble for you.
>
> I enclose some verses I wrote last year as the result of reading Baron Hugel. Verse is not my métier and therefore I find it impossible to criticise myself properly. If you care to use them, do so; if, as I expect, they are not good enough for publication, put them quietly in the waste paper basket and don't mention them again. I really haven't got any author's pride, in this case.
>
> I expect to be back in England at the beginning of next month, and I look forward to seeing you again. If you have time do drop me a line and let me know how the Month is going and whether Horizon yet hears the note of doom.[8]

Philip Caraman reported that 'The Hint of an Explanation' had indeed cost the magazine a number of subscribers, to which Greene replied, saying that he hoped 'new ones will outnumber the loss'. Far from being consigned to the waste-paper basket, his poem 'Behind the Tight Pupils' appeared later in the year to lead the July issue of the magazine.

Philip Caraman appreciated from the outset that forward planning was essential in producing a successful monthly periodical. During a short apprenticeship working on *The Tablet* at the end of 1948, Fr Caraman came to appreciate the unrelenting hard work that would be required of him in order to maintain the high standard of his first issue. The office of the respected Catholic weekly, at that time under the editorship of Douglas Woodruff, who was a long-standing friend of Fr Martin D'Arcy, was good training ground for Caraman, who relished hard work and never shrank from it.

Pressure was bound to build up as the new series progressed, but Caraman had the foresight to commission work well in advance, writing as early as September 1948 to prospective contributors as far afield as South Africa. His confidence was boosted by some high-calibre, unsolicited, contributions such as Greene's poem, and he soon built up a core of regular features, penned by eminent people of the day. Foremost among these were Edmund Rubbra, the Catholic composer and conductor, who contributed regular notes on gramophone recordings, and the actor Robert Speaight, who was a well-qualified film and theatre critic. Evidence of Fr Caraman's broad-minded approach was a review, written by John Rothenstein, of two books about Aubrey Beardsley which appeared in the second issue of *The Month*'s new series. The publication of a piece about the Victorian artist, who had aroused great controversy by the fantastic and occasionally erotic nature of his illustrations, was not undertaken lightly, and had been the subject of detailed discussion when Caraman visited the Rothensteins at their home the previous November.

The January issue of *The Month* featured extracts from the novel Evelyn Waugh was writing on the life of St Helena, and Caraman knew that he could rely on the author's loyal and continuing support. Under the aegis of Waugh, the magazine published further pieces by Thomas Merton, and the novelist sent Caraman a card in early 1949, saying 'I notice you propose to publish selections from Merton's autobiography, and I have just written my short foreword to the book for Tom Burns. If you care to use it, and Burns does not mind, as I'm sure he won't, I shall be delighted.'[9]

The first of these selections appeared in the March issue, and was followed by another exchange of letters between Merton and Fr Hanshell, to whom the *Month*'s editor had delegated communication with the 'American poet'. Philip Caraman's action over the Merton correspondence may have been simply a matter of office routine, but a more likely explanation lies in

Caraman's lifelong distrust of modern mystics and mysticism, and the scepticism with which he regarded the unconventional in religious thought and practice. Even a member of the Society of Jesus was not immune from his misgivings. Asked if he had known Teilhard de Chardin, Caraman replied that he met him in Paris when 'I was editing my magazine'. Whilst remarking on the Jesuit philosopher's shining goodness and kindness, he commented that Teilhard de Chardin 'was, above all, a poet, who in his writings very often didn't understand what he was saying himself'.[10]

The sub-editor, meanwhile, continued to build on his good relationship with Thomas Merton, who wrote to him in February, 1949, saying:

> This is my first chance to say I got the first issue of the month [sic], and that it looks fine, indeed. I felt very flattered to see St Clement right in the front of such a good-looking and business like magazine. I liked the article on Proust and haven't read the others yet – except the reviews. Evelyn Waugh was here and promised to send us *The Loved One* but didn't . . .
>
> Your remarks about prayer are hard to comment on because I am no authority . . . One has to make room for prayer at every odd interval, banishing noise and keeping one's heart free for God. It means a tremendous amount of courage and detachment, I should think, in a city . . .
>
> I think you asked about paying for the stuff of ours in the Month; pay whatever you pay anyone else – or nothing at all if that is what you pay . . .

Merton followed this up two months later, saying:

> A thought occurred to me about payment for the articles: you could send us books instead of money if that would be conven-ient for you. For instance the book on chant you mentioned. Dom Graham's *Christ of Catholicism* and so on. Also there are some old ones we have been looking for without avail, like Dom Knowles'*English Mystics* . . .[11]

Later the monk reconsidered:

the business about paying by books, that might affect my
agent. I suppose payments from you could come under their
contract and they can't take a royalty by tearing out ten percent
of the pages of a book. So perhaps you had better make the
payments otherwise. In that case they should come through
Curtis Brown Ltd . . .[12]

Evidently the Jesuits decided to send books anyway, because
the monk wrote again in June, saying:

Many thanks for the books, consignments of which have been
coming in. So far we have two packets from Bumpus, including
The Loved One, two books of Dom Graham, the Wellesz and the
one by Mascall which looks interesting alright. I have not had a
chance to get into them, but I devoured some sections of *The
Loved One* before Father Prior had a chance to snatch it out of
my hands. The others can wait as they require leisure . . .

A continuation of this letter to Fr Hanshell reveals Merton's
feelings about his recent ordination:

I am simply floored. One thing that strikes me, and I suppose it
strikes many, is the overpowering sense of how real and how
preponderant has been the influence of Our Lady in all this – the
awareness that this is something that has been brought about by
her, and that she is deeply, personally and triumphantly
concerned, and that she has a great deal more to do too. When
I say this strikes many, I am sure many priests feel the same
thing in their own lives because she makes this one of her greatest concerns of all.
    I have been writing to Father Paul Philippe of the Angelico
who says he has written a book about Our Lady and the priesthood and I hope he is sending us one. Anyway I shamelessly
begged for one.[13]

Fr Caraman shared the monk's deep devotion to Our Lady,
and the American's remarks may have done something to endear
him to the Jesuit. Evelyn Waugh continued to correspond with
Thomas Merton, and passed on news of him from time to time,
on one occasion telling Caraman that he had just received 'a
long letter from Tom Merton – very gay and funny – describ-

ing the centenary celebrations at his monastery, when he was appointed PUBLICITY AGENT for the Trappists . . .'[14]

The eclectic mix of thought-provoking contributions, assembled with flair by the *Month*'s new editor, transformed the magazine. In September 1949 it was praised at length in an article in the *Times Literary Supplement*, which commented that 'it would be hard to point to a livelier monthly review' and lauded *The Month*'s consistently high standards.[15] A number of those providing copy for the periodical were, like Merton, uninterested in payment for their articles, or were happy to be sent books in lieu of money. Shortly after publication of the *TLS* review, Graham Greene requested a copy of Ronald Knox's translation of the Old Testament instead of cash, in the expectation that Caraman could get the book at a discounted price. Greene was delighted that his hopes for the Jesuit monthly had been fulfilled so speedily, and that *Horizon* at last had heard 'the note of doom'.

Evelyn Waugh, more than anyone, rejoiced at Caraman's success and told him: 'Your Month is a great achievement. I am most proud to be in it.' Congratulating the new editor on 'a most varied and vivid production', Waugh could not resist gloating over the demise of the Bloomsbury magazine. '*Horizon* was all opinion and speculation and so failed,' he remarked with relish.[16] Fr Caraman had every reason to feel elated, and found an excuse for celebration when *The Month* notched up its 1000th issue in December 1950. Permitting himself a rare moment of triumphalism, he wrote in his foreword:

> Magazines lie thick in Vallombrosa in these autumnal days, so it is right that the 1000th issue of *The Month* should not pass without a salute. Its survival can no doubt be partly attributed to its connection with a permanent institution. But this by itself is no sure guarantee, and credit must be given to its successive editors, only six in all, in all its eighty-six years, who have adapted the periodical to current needs and tastes . . .

The foreword then gives a brief history of the magazine, and Caraman concludes his editorial by telling readers that:

Throughout its history *The Month* has never been the preserve of The Society of Jesus, or confined to any one type of writing or subject ... In 1865 Newman sent the editor *The Dream of Gerontius* and it was accepted gladly. At the end of the year 1875 or early in 1876, Gerard Hopkins offered his poem *The Wreck of the Deutschland,* but, as he told R.W. Dixon, 'they dared not print it'. The present 1000th number makes its 'amende' by publishing original works from the journals of Hopkins, and associates itself once more with Newman ...

Fr Caraman was no recluse, and the *Month*'s anniversary was an excuse for two celebratory parties. The guest lists were impressive, and included many prominent figures in literature and the arts, who were invited to a cocktail party thrown by Longmans, and to a dinner hosted by the Jesuits.[17] Not all those invited were able to accept but, like the writer C. S. Lewis, sent their apologies and their 'congratulations on your millennium!' They missed a good evening; the parties, like *The Month* itself, were a success. Afterwards Elizabeth Rothenstein wrote to thank Philip Caraman, saying:

> My Dear Philip, This is to wish you a very happy Christmas and all the blessings possible in the New Year ... I'm so glad that Johnny's [her husband John Rothenstein] suggestion that Longmans give you a party worked out so well. They did you very proud, and I hope you will convey to them our thanks once again. Johnny thought it as good a party as he had ever attended. I was glad that Johnny amused Evelyn [Waugh] and kept his bite at bay for the evening ...[18]

With *Horizon* now moribund, and with characteristic boldness, Caraman had earlier approached the review's acting editor for their list of subscribers. By this time, Cyril Connolly had handed over *Horizon*'s remains to the beautiful, recently-married, Sonia Orwell, one in a line of volatile women writers with whom Caraman was associated over the years. Mollified by the Jesuit's charm and humour, Orwell did not resent his request and replied:

> Thank you so much for your very kind letter offering to put me on the Complimentary list of *The Month*. I am so touched and

delighted by this suggestion ... I'm afraid I owe you a great apology for not writing from *Horizon* to thank you for your letter of condolence and to explain our position about the subscribers' list. We feel, somewhat inexplicably, that if we do start again, or if anyone should take the magazine over, that we should not let go of our subscribers' list. I do hope you will forgive us for what must seem appalling meanness of spirit and that you understand that the psychology of the half-dead is always a trifle complicated. If, in a few months time, we decide that *Horizon* has finally expired, we will let you have the lists.[19]

Orwell's courteous letter was remarkable in light of the fact that she had rejected the Catholic church of her upbringing and education, and took a dim view of anything 'jesuitical'. She signed off by sending her good wishes for the future of *The Month,* all jealousy diffused by Fr Caraman's gentle diplomacy.

જી

Philip Caraman's success generated its own momentum, and the magazine attracted attention from some unlikely figures outside the Catholic literary world. Early in the new series, *The Month* featured a review of the film *Joan of Arc*, illustrated with still photographs of a ravishing Ingrid Bergmann playing the lead role. This in itself was an eye-opener for subscribers to the previously tedious tome, and evidently set tongues wagging because, some months later, the editor received a request for a copy of the *Joan of Arc* issue from Vita Sackville-West.[20]

Early in his editorship, Fr Caraman had approached Vita's brother, the Hon. Edward Sackville-West, for a contribution to the magazine. Eddy, as he was generally known, had written a number of pieces and reviews for *Horizon* in 1944 and 1946, including a three-part article on music – a subject on which he was an acknowledged expert – and appraisals of the novelists Ivy Compton-Burnett and Elizabeth Bowen, whom he knew personally. Sackville-West rebuffed Caraman's first approach, saying he would be 'very glad to write something for *The Month* ... but next year', as he was working on a book.[21] But before long, the Honourable Eddy, like many others, was drawn into Fr

Caraman's circle, and wrote a number of outstanding pieces for the *Month*'s editor.

Occasionally Philip Caraman's arts of persuasion proved unsuccessful. In December 1949, an invitation to André Malraux for a contribution was refused by the eminent French writer ostensibly on the grounds of ill health. '... Mon état de santé m'interdit pour plusiers mois encore tout travail supplémentaire, et je ne pourrai malheureusement me joindre à vous cette fois', he wrote. Persisting, Caraman tried again two months later to interest Malraux in his project, but again received a refusal, this time from the Frenchman's secretary.[22]

One of Fr Caraman's most successful projects was conceived early in his time as editor, and involved a number of popular writers. Throughout 1952, *The Month* published a series of essays whose authors were left free to choose as their subject a saint with whom they felt a special empathy. The saints chosen turned out to belong to no one epoch of Christian history, and their lives spanned the centuries from Evelyn Waugh's third century St Helena to psychiatrist E. B. Strauss's St Maria Goretti, who died in 1902 and had only recently been canonised. The final list of twelve contributors did not include Strauss's friend, Graham Greene, who appears to have been irritated by the project. Half way through the series, Greene wrote to Fr Caraman from his address in St. James's Street, London:

> My dear Philip, I am afraid I simply cannot face doing St. Teresa of Lisieux or the Curé d'Ars for different reasons – my dislike of St. Teresa and my ignorance of the Curé. It would really entail an awful lot of work and even reading with absoption [sic] Trochu's life. I am afraid really that you have to count me out of your team. I am sorry, but as you will remember I was very loath to join it in the first place and it was rather agreed on a theoretical basis that I would do my best to provide you with an essay and you could mention my name in the first list of contributors. As a former editor and publisher I think you exaggerate a little when you say you will be 'in a fearful mess' if I drop out. Nobody will remember against you your original list of contributors and in any case nobody expects an editor always to be able to provide the whole of a series of this kind ...[23]

Despite Greene's withdrawal, Philip Caraman did provide his readers with the whole of the promised Saints' series, which proved so successful with readers that he republished the essays the following year in book form.[24] He launched a second series of essays on the saints some years later with a list of new contributors.

Graham Greene's original agreement to write a Saints' essay may have been prompted by a wish to make amends for another article of his, which had only recently appeared in *The Month*, and had unleashed a storm of protest against the magazine's editor. The reprimand received by Fr Caraman came from no lesser authority than the Supreme Pontiff himself. The offending essay, entitled 'Pius XII – The Paradox of the Pope', is still extraordinarily topical some fifty years after its original publication, and could well contribute to the current debate on the subject of this controversial Pope's canonisation.

Greene's essay begins by questioning why Eugenio Pacelli 'already seems fixed on a page of history (rather dull history)' when he was only one in a long line of popes stretching back 'like a column of ants, busy about affairs that often seemed to the world of small importance'. The writer then views the papacy from his own perspective as a Protestant schoolboy in the days before his conversion, and continues by criticising the style and content of Pius XII's Encyclicals, particularly those dating from the war years, saying, 'there are no surprises ... the abstract words, the sense of distance, the lack of fire, make them rather like a leading article in a newspaper: the words have been current too long ...' Greene considers that the 'essential paradox in a Pope so many of us believe will rank among the greatest' was the contrast between Pius XII as high-flying diplomat and his mission as a simple parish priest. The essay compliments the Pope on being a modern man, who had introduced new gadgets into the Vatican 'from the white typewriter and the white telephone and the electric razor, to the short-wave wireless station and the latest television equipment ...' In an emotional conclusion, Greene describes Pius XII 'moving with grace and precision through the motions of the Mass, doing what every priest does every day, the servant of the servants of

God, and not impossibly, one feels, a saint . . .'[25]

It seems extraordinary today that Greene's finely written, carefully considered, essay provoked such a ferocious reaction. Fr Caraman appears to have been taken aback by the strength of the reprimand passed down to him through the Jesuit Father General in Rome; his letter of apology is a model of brevity:

Dear Father General. P. Christi.
Father Provincial has communicated to me the contents of your letter to him of 28 December.
I have written to Father Provincial concerning Mr. Graham Greene's article and the criticisms of *The Month* which have reached your Reverence.
All that I would like to say now is that I was very sorry to hear that Mr. Greene's article caused His Holiness and Your Reverence such distress.
Your Reverence's servant in Christ. Philip Caraman S.J.[26]

This was not the first reprimand to be meted out to Fr Caraman. Three months earlier he had been criticised by a member of the Jesuit administration in Rome over the wording of a paragraph in a book review written by Evelyn Waugh, which was considered 'unsuited to a religious periodical'. Fr Joseph Bolland, a former English Provincial, who later became English Assistant to the General Congregation of the Society, told Caraman that he didn't think *The Tablet,* or the *Church Times*, would have printed it, and remarked that:

Mr Waugh is commenting on the poverty (supposed) of English literary language in forms of expression of the various sorts of irregular sexual relations. Apparently, the expressions currently employed are not physically explicit enough . . . In a religious, and especially a Catholic magazine, it is in the wrong place . . .
It is pretty sure to make some of the readers of *The Month* squirm a little. If modern laymen are invited to contribute to *The Month,* they should write only what can appropriately be printed in a Cath.[sic] magazine . . .[27]

In his review of Greene's *The End of the Affair*, Evelyn Waugh had remarked that:

The story deals extensively with sexual relations and here any writer, however skilful, is gravely handicapped by the lack of suitable words. Our language took form in the centuries when the subject was not plainly handled, with the result that we have no vocabulary for the sexual act which is not quaintly antiquated, scientific, or grossly colloquial. To say that lovers 'sleep together' is an absurdity in describing the hasty incidents of passion occurring in this book. Mr Greene often uses the term 'make love' to describe sexual intercourse. Normally that is an offensive euphemism, but here, where love is often used in its highly spiritual sense, there is an ironical twist in the phrase which frustrates the writer's aim. It is an artistic trap from which, once it closes, there is no escape . . .[28]

Fr Bolland's criticism of Waugh's sober analysis can be explained by the narrow mindset of a small, but powerful, minority holding authority in the Jesuit corridors of power at that time. Bolland's remarks are completely in character for a man who was reputed to have a negative approach to anything outside his own experience, and for one who, in the arena of Jesuit politicking, was known to be hostile to Fr Martin D'Arcy and to those whom he looked on as D'Arcy's disciples.

Whilst *The Month* under Fr Caraman went from strength to strength, in February 1950 Fr D'Arcy had been summarily dismissed from his post as Provincial. Fr Bolland, from the height of his appointment as English Assistant to the General in Rome, was suspected by some to have been the *éminence grise* behind the chain of events leading to the Provincial's downfall, although this was never admitted openly. The letter of dismissal received by D'Arcy cited three main reasons for his Superiors' action, one of which was the granting of too much freedom to young priests under his jurisdiction. D'Arcy was heartbroken. After reading of his disgrace, he called Philip Caraman into his room, and was in tears as he showed him the letter. Fr Caraman told D'Arcy's biographer that his friend and erstwhile Superior had said, 'I'm glad I don't know who my enemies are; it makes it easier for me to pray for them'.[29]

As one of the young priests to whom the former Provincial had granted a great deal of freedom, one wonders if Fr Caraman detected a note of warning in the treatment meted out to D'Arcy by his Jesuit Superiors in Rome. The brilliant and popular former Master of Campion Hall had many friends among politicians, the intelligentsia, and in literary circles on both sides of the Atlantic, and no doubt had aroused the envy and distrust of some of his less worldly and well-connected brethren in the Society of Jesus. And accusations of misjudgement on his part were well-founded. His acquisition of grandiose properties, such as New Wardour Castle and a Victorian mansion at Harlaxton, were allegedly extravagant, and some of the posts he gave to his favourites were controversial.

Philip Caraman took final vows in the Society as a spiritual coadjutor in 1949. He had more than justified his placement as supremo of *The Month,* but his coincidental appointment as Director of *Scriptorum* had caused resentment. Nominally, this post put Fr D'Arcy's protégé in a position of authority over a number of senior priests living and working in a house, known as 'the writers' house', at 31 Farm Street. This house formed a separate community from that in the nearby Provincial headquarters in Mount Street, and was home to a number of eminent and respected Jesuit scholars and authors who had a long string of publications to their credit. Foremost among them was seventy-year-old Fr Cyril Martindale, whose prolific works included a two-volume *Life of R. H. Benson,* the biography of fellow Jesuit, Fr Plater, and a host of popular titles which had brought him fame as a religious broadcaster, and had won him many friends in high places. Another member of the Farm Street community was Fr James Brodrick, author of several acclaimed biographies of Jesuit saints such as St Ignatius Loyola and St Robert Bellarmine. In the early decades of the twentieth century, the English Province of the Society of Jesus had won an enviable reputation for the high calibre of its apologists and authors. Philip Caraman, with only minor academic qualifications and no books to his name, seemed an unlikely candidate for his position as Director of such a distinguished company of writers. The undercurrent of envy, which sprang from D'Arcy's previous acts of favouritism towards him, ran ever more strongly with this appointment. But Fr Caraman's detractors were soon to be proved wrong. Within three years of taking up his post as editor of *The Month,* Philip Caraman justified Martin D'Arcy's faith in him with a best-seller of his own, a book which would outstrip in popularity many of those produced by the elderly men among whom he lived and worked in the writers' house in Mayfair.

Notes

1 Tom Burns, *The Use of Memory* (Sheed & Ward, London, 1993), p. 141. Tom Burns was appointed director of Burns & Oates, the Catholic publishing house, in 1945 and editor of the prestigious Catholic weekly, *The Tablet*, in 1967.

2 Alec Guinness to Philip Caraman, unpublished letter, undated (Philip Caraman Private Papers) (hereafter PCPP).

3 Thomas Merton: *Entering The Silence – Volume 2 of The Journals of Thomas Merton*, edited by Jonathen Montaldo (Harper, San Francisco, 1997), p. 232.

4 After Waugh's visit, Merton commented in his Journal (pp. 245–6) that 'I expected him to be taller and more dashing: but he is very nice and friendly ... He offered to send us books but said that [Graham Greene's] *Heart of the Matter* and *The Loved One* were not suitable [reading] material for our refectory ...'

5 Thomas Merton to Fr Deryck Hanshell SJ, 8 October 1948 from Gethsemani Trappist, Ky. [sic] typewritten letter, signed (Jesuit Archives, 114 Mount Street, London) (hereafter JA).

6 The original typescript of Merton's poem 'From the Legend of St Clement' is in the Jesuit Archives in London.

7 H. J. A. Sire. *Father Martin D'Arcy. Philosopher of Christian Love* (Gracewing, 1997) p. 154.

8 Graham Greene to Philip Caraman, 4 March 1949, unpublished letter, John J. Burns Library, Boston College (hereafter BC) © 2004 Francis Greene.

9 Evelyn Waugh to Philip Caraman, card, 12 January 1949 (BC).

10 Conversation with author, 1 March 1992, Dulverton.

11 Thomas Merton to Fr Deryck Hanshell SJ, 12 February 1949 and 20 April 1949, typewritten letters (JA).

12 Ibid.

13 Ibid. 26 June 1949.
14 Evelyn Waugh to Philip Caraman, undated, from Piers Court (BC).
15 *Times Literary Supplement,* 23 September 1949, no. 2, 486 p. 622.
16 Evelyn Waugh to Philip Caraman, extract from letter dated 1 February 1950 (BC).
17 The publishing house of Longmans, Green and Co. Ltd. printed and produced *The Month* at that time.
18 Elizabeth Rothenstein to Philip Caraman, letter dated 20 December 1950 (JA).
19 Sonia Orwell, 18 Percy Street, W.1. to Philip Caraman, 14 January 1949 (JA).
20 Vita Sackville-West was an acknowledged lesbian. It is a matter of speculation whether or not Philip Caraman was aware of this at the time.
21 Hon. E. Sackville-West, Long Crichel House, Wimborne, Dorset, to Philip Caraman, 9 March 1949 (JA).
22 Letters dated 19 December 1949 and 17 February 1950 (BC).
23 Graham Greene to Philip Caraman, letter dated 20 June 1952 (BC) © Francis Greene 2004.
24 *Saints and Ourselves: Personal Studies by T.S. Gregory, Harman Grisewood, Douglas Hyde, Sheila Kaye-Smith, J.B. Morton, Rosalind Murray, Edward Sackville-West, Henry Slessor, Robert Speaight, E.B. Strauss, Evelyn Waugh and Antonia White,* edited by Philip Caraman SJ (Hollis & Carter, 1953).
25 Graham Greene, 'Pius XII – The Paradox of the Pope' (*The Month,* December 1951, vol. 6. no. 6, pp. 327–39).
26 Philip Caraman to Father General, The Society of Jesus, letter 13 January 1952 (JA).
27 Fr Joseph Bolland SJ to Fr Philip Caraman, letter 12 September 1951 (JA).
28 Evelyn Waugh in *The Month,* September 1951, vol. 6, no. 3, p. 175.
29 Based on H. J. A. Sire, *Father Martin D'Arcy. Philosopher of Divine Love* (Gracewing, 1997).

Chapter Four

The Golden Circle

Fifty years after it was first published Fr Caraman's *John Gerard: The Autobiography of an Elizabethan* is still a good read.[1] The story of the gentleman–priest who moved about in disguise in high society, whilst working quietly to bring those whom he regarded as heretics and schismatics back to the Catholic faith, seems to belong more to the realms of fiction than to minutely-researched history.

The origins of the book lay in the text of an eighteenth-century Latin manuscript in the Stonyhurst archives, which was a copy of a document written during the reign of James I by Gerard himself. Under orders from his superiors, the priest had recorded all that had happened to him in the eighteen years he worked in the English mission during penal times at the end of the sixteenth century, and during the years leading up to the Gunpowder Plot. The original version of Fr Gerard's autobiography was lost when the Archives in Sant'Andrea, the novitiate of the Roman Jesuits, were scattered at the time of the suppression of the Society of Jesus in 1773. A number of copies of the original text, some fragmentary, had been made, but the Stonyhurst manuscript was considered to be the oldest complete version of John Gerard's story.

An English translation of the Stonyhurst manuscript had been made in 1870, but Fr Martin D'Arcy, in his role of Provincial, considered that the language of the Victorian version was dated, and suggested that Philip Caraman should retranslate and re-edit Gerard's story in modern idiom. It was work close to Caraman's heart. His love and knowledge of recusant history are evident in every page of the book, and in the numerous footnotes and appendices with which he embellishes the narrative. The book works well on several levels; it is at once an adventure story, an account of the spiritual progress of a hunted, missionary priest, and a vivid historical record of the era it depicts. The most dramatic episode in Gerard's chronicle is his escape by means of a rope down the walls and across the moat of the Tower of London, despite being weak from brutal torture.[2] Throughout his narrative Gerard acknowledges the inner strength he received from God in times of suffering, particularly during his trials in the torture chamber, and the age of religious uncertainty and persecution which engendered his tribulations is brought alive in the many details of Caraman's research.

The book was an immediate success. *John Gerard* quickly went into reprint and, within three years, into translation; a second edition came out in 1965. In retrospect, Fr Caraman considered that in addition to the fact that the Jesuit's autobiography was intrinsically a page-turner, the timing of the book's publication was fortuitous. Appearing soon after the revelation of the horror of the holocaust camps, and of the atrocities perpetrated by the Japanese on their prisoners-of-war, the realisation that a similar type of barbarism had been directed against fellow-countrymen in England a mere four hundred years earlier acted as a talking point.

Prospects for Philip Caraman's first book were greatly enhanced by an imaginative Introduction by Graham Greene. The author, who was then in the heyday of his popularity, wrote a glowing and enthusiastic foreword, in which he spoke of the book's 'excitement and immediacy' and of Caraman's 'excellent translation' from the original Latin manuscript. The sympathy and insight lavished by Greene on his Introduction to *John Gerard* hints at the way in which his association with Philip Caraman had progressed in the short time since the Jesuit had taken over the editorship of *The Month*. Evidence suggests that initial contacts between novelist and priest were of a purely business nature, but Fr Caraman's lively wit and his talent for friendship soon transformed their relationship into a deeply personal one. Greene's early letters are addressed to 'dear

Father Caraman' and signed 'yours ever', but within a year of Caraman taking over *The Month* this had moved on to 'dear Philip' and 'love Graham', and eventually became 'my dear Philip' and 'affectionately Graham'.

The success of the relaunched *Month,* and a generous budget from the trust fund which financed the magazine, enabled Caraman to woo and retain his writers with gifts. It was perhaps in response to this generosity that eminent authors were prepared to contribute to *The Month* for little or no payment. One of his first gifts was a bottle of green chartreuse which he sent to Greene, and was deemed by the recipient to be 'a magnificent present such as no editor has ever made me before'. Thanking Fr Caraman, the author invited the priest to join him in sampling the bottle, and thus began a series of social calls to Greene's London flat, first at 5 St James's Street and later at C.6. Albany. Both flats were within easy walking distance of the Jesuit house in Mayfair, and during these visits the two men tasted, among other drinks, 'an ordinary George IV whisky, and one bottled in America' produced by Caraman, which Greene considered might be 'an interesting variant'.[3]

Over the whisky tasting, conversation flowed easily on a range of topics. During their discussions on literature, a subject of deep interest to both of them, Greene aired his forthright opinions on the style and content of the work of his contemporaries, some of whose books they exchanged. These literary conversations occasionally spilled over into letters. Before leaving on a trip to Malaya, Greene wrote:

> Could you let me have that Diary I lent you back before I go away. I like to have all my manuscripts etc. in order on leaving.
>
> Did I by any chance lend you a proof copy of *Brideshead Revisited* sometime ago? This is a very special copy on hand-made paper inscribed by Evelyn [Waugh] and I lent it to somebody whom I trusted and have suddenly realised that it has never been returned. I don't know who I do trust with books apart from you! ...[4]

Previously Caraman had lent Greene a book written by a leading Jesuit author, Fr James Brodrick, which Greene found

'too sticky to finish. His [Brodrick's] style is curiously difficult to read easily. I don't believe he ever reads aloud to
himself!'[5]

In the course of these meetings talk turned to the craft of
writing and to English usage. It is interesting to note that an
identical phrase referring to a particular form of medieval
torture is employed by both authors in books they were working
on simultaneously. One chapter in Philip Caraman's *John
Gerard,* describing the betrayal and imprisonment of Catholic
laymen and women, is entitled *'Peine Forte et Dure'.* This
phrase also appears near the beginning of Greene's *The End of
the Affair,* where Bendrix expresses the feeling that 'the enormous pressure of the outside world weighs on us like a *peine
forte et dure'.*[6]

There was further bookish discussion in November 1953 in
connection with the German translation of *John Gerard,* two
years after the book's first publication. The German publishers
wanted permission to omit certain references in Fr Caraman's
notes which they felt would not be of interest to the ordinary
German reader. Caraman readily gave this permission, but when
the same problem arose with a passage in Graham Greene's
Introduction to the book in which he referred to the archetypal
Victorian characters, Archdeacon Grantly and Mr Micawber,
Greene was not prepared to give the German publishers, Messrs
Raber & Cie, *carte blanche* to alter his text. He argued:

> I should have thought that Longman's [the English publishers]
> were underrating the Germans a great deal when they think that
> they haven't heard of Micawber. I should think Dickens is as
> well known in Germany as he is in England. I agree however
> that Archdeacon Grantly is a bit wide of the mark for them. I
> think [it] best to let them submit a text showing the omissions
> and alterations, only they'd better do it in English.

Greene was better pleased with an article which Fr Caraman had
just published in *The Month* written by W. Peters. In a critical
essay entitled 'The Concern of Graham Greene', the author
analysed the spiritual content and nuances of Graham Greene's
novels, concluding that '. . . we might say that Mr. Greene's

novels have their triangular plots too: Satan and God fighting for the affection and loyalty of man . . .' While complaining about German ignorance, Greene wrote: 'I very much enjoyed the article by W. Peters. It was rather a change after the unpleasant ones I've been receiving lately! From my point of view it seemed extremely good, intelligent and perceptive'.[7]

Heartened by a favourable review, and – in the manner of all authors known and unknown – protective of his own work, Greene was always ready to defend his corner. When Philip Caraman showed him a critical piece, Greene commented that he rather wished it had not been brought to his attention because 'one would much rather not attack one's critics, but human nature is weak'. And another review in *The Month,* mentioning one of his novels, provoked a complaint from Greene to the editor, asking Caraman 'to tell whoever the reviewer is that if he read *Brighton Rock* with a little more care he would find that the whole point of the book is that Pinkie was redeemable. In fact the author thinks exactly the opposite of what the reviewer says'.[8]

It is probable that in the early years of their relationship Philip Caraman was to some extent overawed by Greene's reputation and authority in literary matters. The junior in age by seven years, Caraman was undoubtedly callow in many respects compared to the worldly-wise and experienced Greene. The long years of Jesuit training had conferred on the priest a certain authority in matters philosophical, theological, and spiritual, but Caraman still had much to learn concerning practical human morality from the older man. Intrigued as he himself was by sexual *mores,* Greene spared his celibate friend nothing, and his letters to Caraman are smattered with titillating references. Perhaps Graham Greene felt a need to educate the inexperienced Jesuit in the ways of the world, whilst leaning on Fr Caraman for guidance amidst his own moral turmoil. Since the time of his conversion to Roman Catholicism, and throughout his life as a Catholic, Greene sought the company of a succession of priests with whom he could mull over his religious reservations, and with each of whom, in turn, he formed a close relationship. Among Greene's former clerics-in-waiting were two

Dominicans, Frs Bede Jarrett and Gervase Mathew, and the Jesuit Cyril Martindale. By the time Greene came to know Philip Caraman well Fr Martindale had retired to the country in poor health, and with his departure the younger Jesuit provided a listening ear for Greene's tortured Catholicism. Whether Fr Caraman was also Greene's confessor, as Fr Martindale had been, is uncertain.

In an extension to his work as a novelist, Graham Greene was also involved in the theatre at the time Philip Caraman was editing *The Month*. Not only was Greene writing plays and overseeing the adaptation of his published stories for stage and screen, he was deeply involved in details of their production. Early in 1956, rehearsals for a stage version of *The Power and the Glory* were causing concern to the adapter, Denis Cannon, and the play's producer Peter Brook. Paul Scofield, due to take the leading role of the Whisky Priest, was playing Hamlet to great acclaim whilst at the same time Brook was rehearsing him for the Greene play. Scofield seemed to be experiencing problems in getting into the skin of his next character, and Greene, who frequently attended rehearsals, called on Fr Caraman's help, writing:

> Can you tell me how I could get the formula for the conditional Absolution? In THE POWER AND THE GLROY [sic] the priest gives conditional Absolution to the dead murderer. Schofield [sic] for some reason is anxious to get these words as early as possible ... I would much like to arrange eventually a conference of Peter Brook, yourself and Gervase (Mathew) so that all opinions can be taken, both Jesuit and Dominican!

Philip Caraman stepped into the breach, and a greatly-relieved Greene expressed his praise in a further letter:

> I can't tell you how grateful I am for your cooperation ... You flung yourself into the situation magnificently. No other priest that I know would have been so completely helpful to Scofield ... You won everybody's heart by the clarity and the ease of your exposition.[9]

Despite this, Scofield's apparent inability to get into the role of the Whisky Priest continued to cause alarm, but John Gielgud recalled Peter Brook telling him that the play suddenly came to life at the last dress rehearsal, when everyone was in complete despair and thought the play was going to flop. A sideline to this is that long before, as a child, whilst staying with his maternal grandparents during his summer holidays, Paul Scofield had attended a Catholic church and practised as a Catholic for a brief period.[10]

Greene's noted generosity to his friends, and the Jesuit's evident enjoyment in being involved in *The Power and the Glory*, prompted Greene to invite Caraman to rehearsals and performances of some of his other plays. But Fr Caraman's attendance at the theatre was strictly limited by adherence to his priestly vow of obedience. A rule in place during the eighteenth century, and reinforced by Cardinal Manning in the nineteenth, banned priests living in the Archdiocese of Westminster from attending theatrical performances in certain places. In inviting Caraman to a dress rehearsal of *The Potting Shed* at the Globe Theatre, Greene mentions that this would avoid difficulties imposed under the ban. Alternatively, if Fr Caraman 'felt able to go to a theatre outside the Westminster diocese', he wondered if he would like to see the play in Brighton. On another occasion, Caraman had to refuse an invitation to a play because of this stricture.[11]

Philip Caraman's love of theatre was deeply implanted, and was destined to lead to some unusual encounters later in his life when he was no longer living in London. Meanwhile his spiritual wavelength embraced Alexander Korda, with whom Greene had been closely associated for many years both in work for the screen and in a social capacity. Graham Greene's official biographer, Professor Norman Sherry, credits Korda with saving Greene from committing suicide during one of the writer's bouts of depression. The two men had also set up a small limited company, Graham Greene Productions, which handled business affairs.[12] In January, 1956 Korda died suddenly after a massive heart attack, and Greene wrote immediately to Fr Caraman asking him to say some Masses for his old friend, adding 'he had for a long time been on the very verge of the Catholic Church'. According to Greene, Korda had been put off the Church at the last moment by a meeting of Rank executives and the Catholic Society at which Korda witnessed a large number of Dominicans sitting down to a feast with the film magnates.[13] Philip Caraman's reply to Greene's request for Masses was surprising. The Jesuit wrote: 'Actually I said Mass for Korda at Brighton as soon as I read of his death in *The Times*. I have often heard you and Catherine speak of him. From all you both said I seemed to know him . . .'[14]

It is apparent that Fr Caraman spent a considerable amount of time in the company of both the long-married Greene, and his mistress Catherine Walston. During the early years of the priest's association with the writer, Greene was deeply and passionately involved with the woman who is credited with being the inspiration for his novel *The End of the Affair*, and the model for the book's heroine, Sarah. Greene's biographers, particularly Professor Sherry, have devoted extensive research and space to the writer's adultery with the beautiful, wealthy and intriguing woman, whose husband, Henry Walston, seemingly turned a blind eye to her unfaithfulness. As the liaison with Catherine progressed, Fr Caraman was called upon by Greene to give religious instruction to Dorothy Glover, the ex-mistress whom he had discarded in favour of Mrs Walston.

The Catholic actor and writer Robert Speaight, who had preached Becket's sermon in *Murder in the Cathedral*, and acted as theatre critic for *The Month*, was said to be responsible for Greene's first meeting with Catherine Walston. Speaight, who had a reputation for theatrical gossip, may also have had a hand in introducing Fr Caraman to Catherine, who – like Greene – was a convert to Catholicism. Philip Caraman stayed at the Walston home, and knew Henry and the couple's children. The priest was also well aware of the situation between Greene and his mistress. Fifty years later, it is still rumoured that Philip Caraman not only condoned the illicit relationship, but may even have blessed it in an unofficial ceremony.

Evidence suggests that the opposite is true, and that far from sanctioning the affair between Greene and Catherine, Fr

Caraman tried to persuade them that their liaison was wrong in the eyes both of God and of the Catholic Church. The biographer W. J. West mentions that the affair between the two was causing problems 'in their families, and with their religious advisers', and in a letter to Catherine, quoted by Professor Norman Sherry, Greene wrote '... don't let Philip [Caraman] or anyone make you think you are *bad* for my writing. You've produced perhaps the best book.' This was a reference to *The End of the Affair*.[15] It is clear that Fr Caraman disapproved of Greene's behaviour, and that over the years he gently attempted to separate them. In 1951, in a handwritten postscript to a typed business letter to Caraman about publication of one of his pieces in *The Month,* Greene added: 'Thank you for your other messages. I *don't* believe that my relationship with C. is wrong, and I don't believe that we shall be cut off forever. G.' The lovers frequently sent postcards to Philip Caraman when they were living together at Greene's house in Anacapri, where the writer liked to have Catherine beside him when he was working on a book. Brief messages from Graham, such as 'Catherine sends her love, and so do I', seemed designed to tell the Jesuit that his efforts to end the relationship were in vain.[16]

The affair did come to an end eventually, much to the chagrin of Greene, as Professor Sherry has described, and by 1956 Graham and Catherine had parted. Fr Caraman's reaction to this news is not recorded, but a clue to his feelings is contained in a letter found among his private papers after his death. It was many years since he had been in touch with Catherine Walston when, in 1975, he sent her a copy of his latest book *The Lost Paradise*. In her letter of thanks, Catherine wrote:

> What a lovely surprise arriving home after being in Venice for five weeks and finding a book of yours by YOU ... You have had quite a life after leaving *The Month.* So many things that you used to want have come about since those days. I am contented and happy being a wife, a mother and a grandmother but I do very little and will be on crutches for the rest of my life ... Come down again sometime, or let's meet for lunch in London ...Well, dear Philip... Love Catherine.[17]

In the last years of her life Graham Greene's beautiful ex-mistress was a cripple, and she died in 1978 at the age of sixty-two. It is possible that Greene believed that Philip Caraman was responsible for the break-up of his liaison with Catherine; there was a gradual cooling in the relationship between the writer and the Jesuit, particularly after Greene made his home in France. Ostensibly they remained on good terms, and still corresponded and collaborated on literary matters, but their meetings became infrequent, and the friendship, which once had been close, gradually faded away.

~

A sizeable body of literature has been inspired by attempts to explain the complexities of Graham Greene's work and character and the writer's complicated attitude to the Catholic Church. Apart from the official biographer, Professor Norman Sherry, numerous other writers have produced memoirs and essays on Greene, all of them fascinated by his multi-faceted life, soul-searching, and seemingly elusive nature. Not only later commentators, but those close to Greene during his years in London, were puzzled by him. Even Philip Caraman admitted to another friend of Greene's, Edward Sackville-West, that 'I don't claim to understand Graham well (who does)?' Fr Caraman's remark was prompted by a review written by Sackville-West for *The Month* about one of the early studies in the Greene industry entitled *The Art of Graham Greene*. The reviewer named his piece 'The Electric Hare', and likened Greene to 'the electric hare whom the racing dogs are not *meant* to catch'. He added that the authors of the study, Kenneth Allott and Miriam Farvis, were 'as greyhounds, efficient enough ...' Complimenting Eddy Sackville-West on his piece, Fr Caraman told him that he was 'delighted with your article on Graham. It is the best thing I have ever seen on him, and the comparison between him and an electric hare is brilliant ...'[18]

Although Edward Sackville-West never enjoyed the popularity of Evelyn Waugh and Graham Greene, in his day he earned the respect of his contemporaries in the literary world, and was taken seriously by them. He was homosexual, and a member of a circle of men of the same proclivity, including Raymond Mortimer, Denton Welch and Desmond Shawe-Taylor, with whom he shared Long Crichel House in Dorset. He was received into the Roman Catholic Church in 1947. Following his conversion he was taken up by Evelyn Waugh, with whom his relationship had not previously been a particularly friendly one. He stayed with Evelyn and Laura Waugh at their home, Piers Court, and in 1951 Graham Greene spent a weekend with him at Long Crichel house. It was after this visit that the Hon. Eddy wrote his article for Fr Caraman, whose influence as editor of an acclaimed and influential arts magazine was by then generally recognised. Amongst the coterie of prestigious Catholic writers, Philip Caraman was regarded with respect both for his achievements at *The Month* and for his willingness to act as priest and spiritual adviser. Sackville-West expressed a wish to a friend that he could 'find a really efficient spiritual director, with whom I could keep up a constant relationship ...'[19] He turned to Fr Caraman. In the course of their association, Philip Caraman was invited by Eddy to give an opinion in a dispute between himself and Raymond Mortimer involving money. Fr Caraman discussed the matter at length in a long letter based on Jesuit principles, looking at the dilemma from both sides, and concluding that 'on the moral issue both you and Raymond Mortimer are entitled to your conflicting views. This sounds terribly Jesuitical ...'[20]

The friendship between Sackville-West and the Jesuit was warmer and less demanding for Caraman than his relationship with Graham Greene. In January 1953, when Fr Caraman was seriously ill, Greene wrote to the priest asking him to say a Mass for an acquaintance, a woman who was not a Catholic, who had just committed suicide in a gas oven, adding that Caraman was 'the only priest I know to whom I can make this kind of appeal'. Greene apologised for being too busy to visit Caraman in hospital, and as an afterthought added: 'I wish you'd tell me how you are and what's the matter. Are you in need of books?'[21] But it was to the Hon. Eddy that Fr Caraman wrote when he escaped from London to recuperate in Ireland two months later. Appreciating material comforts and the peace of the countryside after the trauma of his illness, he told Sackville-West:

> I am staying with Fr. O'Sullivan, who has certainly trained his novices to attend to his friends. As soon as I arrived yesterday afternoon my car was driven round to the garage and filled with petrol and thoroughly looked over. Hot water bottles were bought in, my pyjamas warmed ...
>
> I am beginning to think I have missed my true vocation, I feel so attracted to work in the remote bog- and sea-bound parishes of the west: but I have madmen, suicidal depressives and hysterical women lined up to see me instead when I return to London.[22]

The nature of Fr Caraman's illness is not known. His personal file in the Jesuit Archive in London gives no clue, and Society records referring to this period of his life have apparently been destroyed. As Graham Greene's note implies, Caraman himself was reticent concerning his ill-health, and remained so in respect of other bouts which he suffered from time to time throughout his life. But from later remarks it can be inferred that the illness in 1953 involved surgery, and was probably, to some extent at least, caused by stress and overwork. His industriousness, and his dedication to the spiritual welfare of those who turned to him for guidance, imposed weighty burdens on his frail physique and sensitivity. Philip Caraman's popularity, and his reputation as a patient listener attracted a growing retinue of anguished souls and attention-seekers.

The work of maintaining the high standards Philip Caraman had set in his early issues of *The Month* demanded his unflagging attention, and the success of his first book prompted calls for a sequel. When he was taken ill in early 1953, Fr Caraman was working on the translation from the Latin of a second Elizabethan autobiographical manuscript, and the complicated and time-consuming historical research that accompanied it. Buried in the copious notes he appended to the autobiography of William Weston, lies a hint of the stress Fr Caraman was experiencing at the time. In a footnote to a chapter recounting what

he terms the 'somewhat nauseous subject' of the exorcisms prac-
tised by Weston and other priests in Elizabethan England,
Caraman notes that 'it is probable that in a number of cases
William Weston was over-credulous and the victim of deception
at the hands of malicious or *hysterical women*' (my italic.JR).
The new book also entailed going abroad. Although Philip
Caraman always welcomed any excuse for foreign travel, other
commitments piled up whilst he was away in Spain, France and
Italy.

Perhaps the greatest strain placed upon Fr Caraman involved
human unpredictability rather than routine office work. His
distaste for life in Mayfair, expressed partly in jest in his letter
to Sackville-West, reveals his longing for the opportunity to
nurture his own spiritual life, and to work on his own books and
research without interruption. It would be a long time before
that happened: meanwhile he returned from Ireland to the suici-
dal depressives and hysterical women who would continue to
occupy his attention for a further ten years.

The names of the majority of those who sought Fr Caraman's
ministry will never be known. The Jesuit house in Mayfair has
always had an open-door policy, under which visitors seeking
religious advice may ring the doorbell and be directed to a
priest. The legacy of their long training, and the ethos of the
Society, bestow on Jesuit priests a well-earned reputation as
perceptive father-confessors. By the time Philip Caraman was
living in Mayfair only a few Jesuits were still working as private
chaplains; nevertheless, local residents still sought him out on a
personal basis. Some of the writers with whom Caraman was
associated through their contributions for *The Month* were also
troubled by religious doubts and moral problems which he was
called upon to resolve. Antonia White, a Catholic by birth, had
only recently returned to the Church after a lapse lasting many
years, when she was asked by Fr Caraman if she had any ideas
for a possible article for his magazine. The writer, then in her
early fifties, with a tempestuous love-life behind her, and –
according to her daughter – a history of nervous breakdowns,
became one of Philip Caraman's regular contributors. The piece
she sent him in response to his original approach was one she

had offered to Cyril Connolly eight years earlier which he had been turned down for publication in *Horizon*. Abridged from an exchange of letters between White and a man named 'Peter', the article about her return to the Church describes her conflicting thoughts and feelings about Catholicism. Fr Caraman brought out the article in August 1950 under the title 'Smoking Flax', and some years later this essay was the starting-point for the publication by John Guest of Longmans for *The Hound and the Falcon,* one of White's most successful books.[23]

Antonia White had some standing as an intellectual, and at one point was involved with the community of French Dominicans who published *La Vie Spirituelle*, a revue relating religion to the arts. Through this connection, White was invited to lecture in French on Graham Greene's novel *The Power and the Glory*. The 1952 'Saints' series in *The Month,* slighted by Greene, received a notable contribution from Antonia White on the subject of St Thomas Aquinas, whose teaching and personality she had grown to love, even though her mind was 'incapable of carrying off more than a few stray crumbs' of Aquinas's profound and subtle thought.

The second series of 'Saints' featured an essay on St Monica by another woman writer, who at that time was almost unknown to the reading public in comparison with Antonia White. Her name was Muriel Spark. In the early 1950s Spark's success as a novelist lay in the future, and, with a failed marriage behind her, she was struggling to eke out a meagre living from writing. At one point when she was extremely ill she was helped financially by Graham Greene, who sent her monthly cheques often accompanied by a few bottles of red wine. In her own words, the wine was intended to 'take the edge off cold charity'. In 1951, Spark won a short-story competition run by the *Observer* which attracted 6,700 other entries, and this launched her into the public eye.

In the autobiography Spark published in 1992 she describes what happened to her on one particular day, which in its entirety stood out vividly in her memory. On 24 July 1953 she had been invited to a 'lovely' champagne lunch at the Ritz at which she sat next to the poet Edmund Blunden. Her account continues:

On the way home from that lunch I bumped into Father Philip
Caraman, a 'Farm Street' Jesuit, editor of *The Month*. Philip
Caraman was a much-loved friend of a great many writers,
known and unknown, Catholic and otherwise. Philip said if I
would walk back with him to the office he would give me a book
to review. On the way there, I felt in the mood to entertain him
with some amusing stories. He gave me the book to review and
a cheque for fifteen pounds for having made him laugh.[24]

During the year of this meeting with Fr Caraman, Muriel
Spark was already thinking of becoming a Catholic. Following
a careful study of the theological writings of John Henry
Newman, she was received into the Church at Ealing Priory by
Dom Ambrose Agius on 1 May 1954, and was then gently and
surely guided through her Confession by Fr Caraman. He also
helped her with the work of editing a selection of Newman's
letters, lending her a bundle of the Cardinal's original letters to
various Jesuits which she had with her all the time she was
working on the book. Muriel Spark never forgot Fr Caraman's
kindness: as time passed, their relationship deepened, and she
remained loyal to him when her talents eventually received
recognition – a much-cherished friend until the end.

In contrast, Philip Caraman's association with the best-selling
romantic novelist, Rosamond Lehmann, was short-lived and
unsatisfactory. Of the many women who turned to him for spiritual guidance, she was probably the most emotional. Volatile,
egotistical and promiscuous in her dealings with men, Lehmann
was devastated by the sudden death of her daughter Sally, whom
she adored. She sought comfort in the spiritual world. Seizing,
as he hoped, the opportunity to effect her conversion to
Catholicism, Eddy Sackville-West, a friend of Lehmann's,
introduced her to Fr Caraman and invited them both to stay at
Cooleville, the house he had bought in the village of Clogheen
in Tipperary. The Hon. Eddy's attempt at proselytising was a
failure. In a letter to Michael De-la-Noy, Sackville-West's biographer, Lehmann recalled the visit with distaste, describing
Eddy's efforts as well-meaning but extremely painful. She was
upset because she believed no one had paid proper attention to
her during the visit, and was disappointed because the other

guests were clumsy Irish priests, rather than the refined social gathering she had expected. Fr Caraman's memories of the visit, his second to Cooleville, were somewhat different. He recalled Eddy being very kind to Rosamond Lehmann, and told De-la-Noy that although she was 'thinking of becoming a Catholic at the time, she didn't in fact ... because she persisted in a desire to explore spiritualism even if received into the Church, and it was this that proved the sticking point'.[25]

Philip Caraman's previous visit to Eddy at Cooleville had been a happier occasion, which he recalled with relish, remembering in particular the excellence of the food.[26] The interior of the early nineteenth-century mansion had been decorated by Sackville-West with maroon flock wallpaper, highlighted with enormous white roses in the drawing-room, in keeping with the house's Victorian origins. Although the cook was a simple Irish girl, Eddy had trained her up to his own high standard of cuisine. The maids were dressed in red uniforms, and the host took to donning a red dinner jacket, affecting his typical eccentricity. During the years Philip Caraman was editing *The Month,* he had grown accustomed to being entertained lavishly by his literary friends in their grand homes, and learned to accept their eccentric behaviour with ease and humour. Thus, in Fr Martin D'Arcy's eyes, Fr Caraman seemed the ideal priest to give religious instruction to Dame Edith Sitwell, one of the most notably flamboyant and aristocratic writers of the twentieth century, whom Caraman described after her death as 'an eccentric woman and an eccentric Catholic'.

ॐ

With her baroque appearance, adorned with silver paint, oriental turban and enormous bracelets, her tapering fingers weighed down by rings glittering with turquoise and topaz, Edith Sitwell failed to see the irony of her remark to Fr Caraman that Rosamond Lehmann was the most advanced exhibitionist she knew. By turns carping and compassionate, egotistical and thoughtful, devoted to her brothers Osbert and Sacheverell but critical of her many friends, in due time the *grande dame* of

English poetry displayed the full range of her emotions for
Philip Caraman's benefit. Sitwell's attitude to Rosamond
Lehmann was typical of her relationship with many of the
writers whom she entertained and corresponded with. In June
1949 she swore undying loyalty to Lehmann, saying '. . . never
– never – never think I have "gone away", as people do, sometimes . . . If I am devoted to anyone, I am devoted to them
forever, and never change, unless *they* throw *me* out. Even then,
I don't change . . .' Three months later she wrote to Osbert,
telling him, '. . . if I have to refuse to be defended in order to
please *all* the men Rosamond has dossed down with, my life
would be a little difficult . . .'[27] Similarly, when she heard on the
literary grapevine that Lehmann was looking for spiritual consolation following her daughter's death, Sitwell told Fr Caraman
she was very glad that '. . . poor Rosamond is going to enter the
Church. Her daughter's death was a great grief to her, and I
think she feels her life is over. She will now find comfort . . .'
On learning that Eddy Sackville-West's attempt to convert
Lehmann had failed despite Fr Caraman's counselling, Dame
Edith told the Jesuit that she had been convinced from the start
that Rosamond had only turned to him wanting to chew over her
experiences, having worn everyone else out with her problems.

Edith Sitwell's doubts concerning Lehmann's motives
occurred some four years after her own reception into the
Church in 1955. Sitwell's journey to Rome had been a gradual
one, paced slowly over a period of years, under the influence of
the Catholic poet Roy Campbell, who had grown close to her
after he defended her work in an article in the *Poetry Review* in
August 1949. Her reading of mystic writers, combined with a
natural intellectual and religious curiosity, and the serenity she
said she saw in the faces of the peasant women praying in
churches in Italy, all contributed to her interest in Catholicism.
In April 1955 Sitwell wrote to Fr Martin D'Arcy, whom she had
first met in Oxford in the 1930s and had come to know well
during his years in London as Provincial, telling him she wished
to enter the Catholic Church. Her letter found D'Arcy in the
United States, where he had accepted an appointment at Notre
Dame, Indiana. He replied to her letter, expressing his pleasure

and telling her, 'I had felt God's love moving in your last volumes of poetry'.[28] The ex-Provincial immediately referred Dame Edith to Philip Caraman, convinced that his protégé would lead her discreetly and wisely along the final steps of her way.

When Fr Caraman received Sitwell's first, respectful letter saying she hoped she was not trespassing too greatly on his kindness, but would be '... most deeply grateful if you could ... spare your valuable time to see and advise me before I go to Italy ...' the Jesuit called on her within a few days. He didn't have far to travel. Dame Edith's London base was the Sesame and Imperial Pioneer Ladies' Club in Grosvenor Street, where she held regal sway over the staff and other members of the Club. She generally spent the summer at Renishaw Hall, her brother Osbert's seat near Sheffield, and in winter the family migrated to the Castello di Montegufoni, near Florence, another of their stately homes, where they also stayed from time to time at other seasons of the year. Immediately after Philip Caraman's first visit, Sitwell wrote to him expressing her profound gratitude:

> I can only say that after our meeting I had a sense of happiness, safety and peace such as I have not had for years and in an infinitely greater degree than these have ever come to me. What a fool I was not to have taken this step years ago. I can never thank you for what you have done for me. I am sending for the books and shall study them each day, then I will, as you with great goodness suggested, write to you.[29]

And write to him she did, incessantly and at length, for the rest of her life.

Dame Edith's earliest letters to Fr Caraman reflect the seriousness with which she approached her preparation for the big step that lay ahead, and the humility with which she accepted the spiritual direction of her mentor. Sitwell, who could subdue distinguished guests round her dinner table into agreeing with her most outrageous diktats, meekly complied with Caraman's programme of reading and study. After arriving in Italy, she told him she was reading St Thomas Aquinas, and would read the Missal daily as he had suggested; these books, together with Fr D'Arcy's *The Nature of Belief*, 'make one see doubt ... as a complete failure of intellect. Then again I see that purely intellectual belief is not enough ... There has to be a sixth sense in faith.' Sitwell confided in her director that prayer had always been a difficulty for her, that when she tried to pray she felt very far away from God, 'as if I were speaking into the darkness'. In reply, Fr Caraman told her that prayer is a two-way movement, a converse not a soliloquy, and that 'we must leave God to act'. Edith confided deeply personal problems to her spiritual director. She told him that she was 'under daily temptation to great anger' because of the situation that had developed between her beloved – homosexual – brother, Osbert, and his long-time companion David Horner. Horner had deserted her crippled brother, but had returned to live in their home, in Edith's opinion treating Osbert most cruelly. Philip Caraman tried to help her understand David, and emphasised the positive side of the relationship with Osbert, namely Horner's kindness and loyalty in the past. In the short term, the priest's counselling diffused her anger and she told Caraman that she was 'profoundly grateful for the prayers you offer up for Osbert and for me. I am *certain* that these are helping me and I feel centred and more at peace than ever before.' Painstakingly the Jesuit listened to all Edith's concerns, gently laying them to rest and bringing her, momentarily at least, the tranquillity she had seen reflected in the faces of the peasant women, and which she had seldom experienced in her own emotionally-charged life. She wrote to Caraman from Montegufoni: 'I believe, and trust with all my heart, that I am on the threshold of a new life. But I shall have to be born again. And I have a whole world to see, as it were for the first time, and to understand as far as my capacities will let me'.[30]

On her return to England, Sitwell was delighted when Fr Caraman agreed to travel up to Renishaw Hall in early July for the final stages of her religious instruction. The ceremony of her reception was arranged for 4 August, and took place at the Jesuit Church of the Immaculate Conception in Farm Street. Edith had wanted Roy and Mary Campbell to stand as her godparents, but they were living in Portugal and the poet was in ill health. In their place, Evelyn Waugh acted as her godfather. He was afraid that the occasion might be marred by the intrusion of the press, and curious sightseers, as his own reception had been many years earlier. On 19 July, Waugh wrote to Fr Caraman:

> I am an old friend of Edith's and love her. She is liable to make herself a little conspicuous at times. She says she will be received in London. Am I being over-fastidious in thinking Mount St. Mary's much more suitable. What I fear is that the popular papers may take her up as a kind of Garbo–Queen Christina ... There are so many malicious people about to make a booby of a Sitwell. It would be tragic if this great occasion in her life were in any way sullied.[31]

Waugh's fears were well founded. Edith Sitwell was sixty-seven at the time of her conversion, and had been created a Dame of the British Empire the previous year. Her position as a serious author and poet was long established, but her celebrity status in the eyes of the general public rested more on her reputation for eccentricity than on her writing. Her penchant for self-advertisement was renowned.

Waugh need not have worried. Dame Edith decided that this important day in her life should remain private and, as far as possible, low key. Sitwell's supporters in the church numbered only six, and no pressmen or photographers got wind of the occasion. Edith chose her guests carefully. Two weeks before the ceremony, she wrote to Caraman to tell him about

> my old friend Alec Guinness (we are very fond of each other but he thinks I have a heart of stone, insensible to the sufferings of others). He tells me he is being instructed and is going to become a Catholic. He does not know that this is also true of me. He has had a very sad childhood, but he is now happily married ...[32]

Guinness, who had known Edith for some years at the time of her conversion to Catholicism, and had fallen out of favour with her in the past, was one of the guests. The actor gives a witty description of the Farm Street ceremony in his autobiography, mentioning that Fr Philip Caraman SJ, who received Edith into the Church, was in time 'to become a loving friend of mine'.[33] The occasion marked Guinness's first meeting with Evelyn Waugh, who also described the proceedings vividly in his diary. The Guinness account refers to Sitwell's 'reconciliation' with the Roman Catholic Church, and Waugh describes how, prior to the reforms of Vatican II, it was necessary for Edith to renounce in public 'all manner of heresies'. Having recanted her supposed errors, Sitwell, swathed from head to toe in black, received conditional baptism and was then led into the confessional by Fr Caraman. Meanwhile the other guests, who included Fr Martin D'Arcy, a Portuguese poet, an old and rather dotty friend of Edith's named Evelyn Wiel, and Quentin Stevenson, a Catholic poet with whom Edith later fell out, gathered in the sacristy. The church ceremony was followed by a splendid lunch at the Sesame Club, presided over by Edith, at which the wine flowed freely late into the afternoon.

In his letter thanking Edith for the lunch, Evelyn Waugh wondered whether, as her godfather, he should warn her of the fallibility of the 'human aspect of Catholicism', and told her that the world had its fair share of 'Catholic bores and prigs and crooks and cads'. He felt that, 'not all priests are as clever and kind as Fr D'Arcy and Fr Caraman.'[34] Philip Caraman also felt responsible for Edith Sitwell's happiness, and was anxious that she should feel at home in the Church. A few days before she was received, he wrote to Eddy Sackville-West to give him the news of Edith's conversion, and told him: 'As she knows so few Catholics, I feel that she would very much welcome a message from you. It would make her feel she is among friends in the Church'.[35]

Although the other Jesuits in the Mayfair community must have been fully aware that Edith Sitwell's reception was taking place in their Farm Street church, it seems none, apart from Martin D'Arcy and Philip Caraman, was present on 4 August. Certainly no other priest was invited to the banquet at the Sesame Club that followed. But the Jesuits were involved in the very public ceremony of Dame Edith's confirmation that took place at Farm Street two months later. The cream of Catholic London made up the large invited congregation, and the proceedings were conducted by Archbishop Roberts, a former Jesuit Archbishop of Bombay, who was living in the Mayfair house at the time. Afterwards, the congregation went over to the Connaught Hotel to a cocktail party hosted and paid for by the Jesuits. It was reported that after Dame Edith had left the party, Fr Caraman announced: 'Before we separate I just want to say that any of you who would like to ask Dame Edith to a meal, is free to do so'.[36] Caraman probably had Edith's welfare at heart, and in expressing her 'endless gratitude for a great and moving experience', she thanked him profusely for 'a happy and wonderful occasion – ending with an unforgettably delightful party'.[37] But in the eyes of some of his guests the priest seemed to overreach himself. Sitwell's respect for her spiritual director was not shared by all her fellow Catholics in London society.[38]

When the recently-ordained Philip Caraman was appointed editor of *The Month*, his task was to transform a tired magazine into a readable and influential publication: nothing more. He could not have foreseen that his success would suck him into a social merry-go-round, and mark him out as a 'popular priest'. The twentieth century witnessed a surge in English Catholic writing, from beginnings in the Chester–Belloc era to a high point at a time when *The Month* was enjoying its greatest prestige for the quality of its articles and reviews. Networking, to use a term unheard of in the 1950s, played an important part in the success of *The Month* and of its contributors, the celebrated writers who featured regularly in its pages. Philip Caraman was on everyone's guest list, and he played a prominent part in the private lives of many of the authors who wrote for him. The galaxy of Catholic writers was in the ascendant, but few of its stars realised the burden their friendship placed on the taut energy and boundless patience of the Jesuit at the heart of their golden circle.

Notes

1 Published by Longmans, Green and Co., 1951.
2 In an ITV documentary, *The Tower*, (2002) it was wrongly stated that *two* Jesuit priests had escaped in this way. In fact Philip Caraman identifies Fr Gerard's companion as John Arden, a Northamptonshire Catholic layman.
3 Based on letters from Graham Greene to Fr Philip Caraman SJ, undated, and 20 June 1952, John J. Burns Library, Boston College (hereafter BC) © 2004 Francis Greene.
4 Ibid. 17 November 1950.
5 Ibid. 20 October 1949. Fr James Brodrick had written a number of books on the lives of Jesuit saints, including a long biography of the Dutch Jesuit, St Peter Canisius (1521–97). Originally published in 1935, this vast tome was reissued by The Carroll Press of Baltimore in 1950, and is written, staccato style, in short, clipped sentences. It is not an easy read. The book referred to by Greene was Fr Brodrick's *Procession of Saints*, which was published in 1949 and was reviewed in *The Month*.
6 Edition published by The Folio Society, London 1997, p. 32.
7 Letter, Graham Greene to Philip Caraman, 16 November 1953 (BC) © 2004 Francis Greene; and W. Peters, 'The Concern of Graham Greene', *The Month* vol. 10. no. 5. November 1953, pp. 281–90.
8 Letter, Graham Greene to Philip Caraman, 19 June 1959 (BC) © 2004 Francis Greene.
9 Ibid. 25 January 1956 and 9 March 56.
10 Based on Garry O'Connor, *Paul Scofield – The Biography* (Sidgwick & Jackson, 2002), pp. 15, 97, 132, 133 and 134.
11 Based on letters from Graham Greene to Philip Caraman, 24 January 1958 and 19 June 1959 (BC) © 2004 Francis Greene; and letter to author from Fr Ian Dickie, Diocesan Archivist, Westminster Diocesan Archives.
12 Based on Norman Sherry, *The Life of Graham Greene* vol. 2. 1939–1955 (Jonathan Cape, London, 1994) p. 507; and W. J. West, *The Quest for Graham Greene* (Weidenfeld & Nicolson, London, 1997) p. 142.
13 Based on letter from Graham Greene to Philip Caraman, 24 January 1956 (BC): Cited by W. J. West (note 12 above).
14 Letter, Philip Caraman to Graham Greene, 26 January 1956 (BC). Ibid.
15 W. J. West: p. 142, and Norman Sherry: pp. 502–3.

16 Based on Graham Greene's letters and cards to Philip Caraman, (BC) © 2004 Francis Greene.
17 Letter from Catherine Walston to Fr Philip Caraman, 23 October 1975, Philip Caraman Private Papers (hereafter PCPP).
18 Letter from Fr Philip Caraman to Edward Sackville-West, 12 June 1951, British Library (hereafter BL). 'The Electric Hare' was published in *The Month* vol. 6. no. 3. September 1951, p. 141.
19 Based on Michael De-la-Noy, *Eddy – The Life of Edward Sackville-West* (Arcadia Books Ltd, 1999), first published by The Bodley Head, 1988.
20 Letter from Philip Caraman to the Hon. Edward Sackville-West, 2 March 1956 (BL).
21 Letter from Graham Greene to Philip Caraman, 20 January 1953 (BC) © 2004 Francis Greene.
22 Letter from Philip Caraman to Hon. Edward Sackville-West, 29 April 1953 (BL).
23 Antonia White, *The Hound and the Falcon. The story of a recon-version to the Catholic Faith* (Longmans, Green and Co., 1965).
24 Muriel Spark, *Curriculum Vitae* (Constable & Co, Ltd. 1992), p. 202.
25 Based on Michael-de-la-Noy, *Eddy: The Life of Edward Sackville-West*, and letter, Philip Caraman to Michael De-la-Noy, 29 May 1987 (BL).
26 Ibid.
27 Letters quoted in Richard Greene's *Selected Letters of Edith Sitwell* (Virago Press, 1997).
28 Based on H.J.A. Sire, *Father Martin D'Arcy* (Gracewing, 1997), p. 164.
29 Edith Sitwell to Fr Philip Caraman, 29 April 1955 (BC) © Francis Sitwell 2004.
30 Letters from Edith Sitwell to Philip Caraman, 7 May 1955, 20 May 1955, and 3 June 1955 (BC) © Francis Sitwell 2004.
31 Evelyn Waugh to Philip Caraman, 19 July 1955 (BC), quoted by Victoria Glendinning, *A Unicorn Among Lions* (Weidenfeld & Nicholson, 1981). Fr Caraman gave Glendinning access to his papers before these were placed in the John J. Burns Library in Boston College.
32 Edith Sitwell to Philip Caraman, 19 July 1955 (BC) © Francis Sitwell 2004.
33 Alec Guinness, *Blessings in Disguise* (Hamish Hamilton Ltd, 1985).
34 Victoria Glendinning, *A Unicorn Among Lions*, p. 319.

35 Philip Caraman to Edward Sackville-West, 29 July 1955 (BL).
36 Victoria Glendinning, p. 319.
37 Edith Sitwell to Philip Caraman, 30 September 1955 (BC) ©
   Francis Sitwell 2004.
38 Based on author's conversation with Lord Longford, 13
   November 1997; Lady Longford (then Lady Pakenham) attended
   Dame Edith Sitwell's confirmation.

Chapter Five

Forty Martyrs – plus One

'What has happened to *Weston*?' Evelyn Waugh enquired when publication of the book was overdue. Pushed to one side by its author's other commitments, Philip Caraman's second Elizabethan autobiography eventually came out in 1955 after Edith Sitwell's reception into the Catholic Church. Waugh's interest was fraternal. Following the precedent set by Graham Greene with *John Gerard,* he had written a Foreword to the book, in which he tells readers that 'Father Caraman who has already served John Gerard so well, now gives us a very different character in William Weston'. Waugh points out that the work of editing was of even greater importance than in the previous book, as the 'gentle, self-effacing little narrative that forms the core of the book, tells us little of the hero'.

Although William Weston was a contemporary of John Gerard, and both Jesuit priests faced the perils of working in England during penal times, their stories are complimentary rather than repetitive. Caraman's second Elizabethan narrative was, like his first, based on a manuscript in the Stonyhurst archive, but the original document was in such poor condition that Fr Caraman's translation was made from an early seventeenth-century transcript preserved in Rome. Weston was fourteen years' John Gerard's senior, a man of frail health and contemplative nature. Both were imprisoned in the Tower of London. Whereas Gerard made a dramatic escape, Weston says that he 'spent five years in the Tower, and seventeen years altogether in prison'. Of his years in the Tower, four were spent in solitary confinement, and he was released on the death of Queen

Elizabeth broken in body, his eyesight impaired, and with his memory of his experiences blurred by his ordeal. Like *John Gerard*, the autobiography of *William Weston* is enhanced by Caraman with fascinating historical background and details gleaned from exhaustive research. Although the second Elizabethan narrative was appreciated by historians and published in New York as *An Autobiography from the Jesuit Underground*, it was a more sombre tale and did not attract the same popular success as Fr Caraman's first book. As the Foreword points out, Gerard was an 'unambiguous man of action', whereas Weston was 'the mystic beset with the mystic's devils, drawn to the desperate'. In general, readers preferred the ripping good yarn to the tale of psychological predicaments. Waugh, with some insight, concludes, 'If any is tempted to suppose that the discipline of Ignatius produces a uniform type, he will find assurance in the careers of these two holy and heroic men'.[1]

In acknowledging the work of those who had helped him with *William Weston*, Philip Caraman thanked Evelyn Waugh 'for his Foreword and for much valuable advice'. Over the years the literary debt was a mutual one. Initially Evelyn Waugh gave Caraman support and guidance when the Jesuit, who was eight years his junior, was finding his feet as editor of *The Month*. Not only did Waugh help Fr D'Arcy's protégé with introductions to eminent contributors in the world of literature and the arts; he even administered an occasional schoolmasterly reprimand over Caraman's writing style and grammar. Once the younger man was established and running the magazine with aplomb, Philip reciprocated by helping Evelyn Waugh with a number of his literary projects. The first of these was *St Helena*, a book Waugh was writing about the third- to fourth-century empress and saint, mother of Constantine the Great, who is credited with the discovery of the true cross in Jerusalem. Caraman acted as Waugh's consultant on Jewish and religious history, and gave the book's author much vital background material on the saint herself. The first three chapters of *Helena* were published in *The Tablet* in 1945, but an essay summarising the essence of Waugh's work and feelings about the saint appeared in the first 'Saints' series in *The Month* in 1952, and was reprinted in the anthology the following year.

The Month came to the rescue when a long article of Evelyn Waugh's was – rarely for him – rejected by a number of other publications. He had been to Goa to witness the final exposition of the relics of the Jesuit missionary to India, St Francis Xavier, and on his return had been offended when *The Sunday Times*, the *New Yorker,* and even lesser periodicals such as *History Today* and the Catholic *Universe* and *Tablet* had turned it down.[2] Fr Caraman ran it in the December 1953 issue of his magazine, but it was among many other Waugh pieces for which the author waived payment. Early in the same month, the writer had added a postscript to a letter to Caraman, requesting back-up in a literary vendetta he had embarked on against the historian Hugh Trevor-Roper, who had just published an essay entitled 'Sir Thomas More and the English Lay Recusants'. Waugh believed that Trevor-Roper was anti-Catholic, and enquired of Caraman:

> Have you read Roper in this week's *New Statesman*? I spotted four errors in the first three lines & have written about them. I seemed to find a dozen others. I am sure that someone better educated than I am could find a hundred. Would it not be a good thing to employ one of your learned friends to go through the articles with a fine comb and expose them all in a long article. It is time Roper was called to order and this article seems a happy opportunity. E.[3]

Any previous favours requested by Waugh were insignificant compared to his plea for help in connection with work on the biography and papers of the eminent convert Monsignor Ronald Knox, who had appointed Waugh as his literary executor. Writing the life and sorting and editing the documents of the prolific author and orator presented Waugh with an overwhelming task. As the biography neared completion, Waugh reminded Caraman that 'you were so very kind as to offer your help to me in dealing with Ronald's spiritual life, a subject [on] which I am far out of depth. Is it too much to ask you to have the great good to read [the enclosed] pages and return them with your comments?'[4] By early 1959 letters about Knox's papers were flowing thick and fast in Caraman's direction. Waugh asked for advice. He said that his role as executor, as agreed with Knox, was merely to grant permissions for publication. Could someone be found to edit the mountain of papers he had inherited? The priest, who seemed incapable of refusing any job, however onerous, that required urgent attention, said that he would take on the work of collecting and editing Knox's sermons himself. Waugh breathed a sigh of relief and wrote, 'I did not dare hope you would take on the job yourself. It is very noble of you . . .'[5] In return, Waugh promised to pass the sum of £150 allotted for the work on Knox's orations over to Fr Caraman, who needed financial backing to trace some of the sermons. One of these was Knox's panegyric for G. K. Chesterton, and Caraman confirmed the correct date of this sermon through Chesterton's erstwhile secretary, Dorothy Collins.[6] Waugh's executorship caused him a certain wry amusement. ' I wonder how many people are buying Ronald's *A Priestly Life* under the impression that it is a biography of J. B. Priestley?' he queried.[7]

Waugh expressed his gratitude for Caraman's labours on the Knox legacy, when he told the priest that he was 'the last of the Jesuits of popular imagination'.[8] The bond of affection and respect that had developed between author and priest during the ten years of their association was further deepened by Caraman's support. But the long slog on Knox's biography, and the responsibilities of executorship for his literary estate, caused ill-feeling between Waugh and other members of the Catholic establishment. Although he had received help with his work on Knox from the editor of *The Tablet,* Douglas Woodruff, and from Tom Burns, supremo of the Catholic publishing house Burns, Oates and Washbourne, Waugh quarrelled with both men. He took exception to Woodruff's criticism's of his attitude towards the hierarchy, and he tried to wrest the publication of Knox's sermons from Burns, with whom he had shared a volatile relationship going back over some thirty years. In his autobiography, Tom Burns outlines his chequered association with Waugh. It is not a favourable portrait. Despite paying tribute to Waugh's loyalty to the Church and mentioning his many private acts of 'compassion and courtesy', he also dwells on what he terms the 'coarse, snobbish, [and] alcoholic' aspects of Waugh's character.[9] Fr Caraman was brought into the dispute between Burns and Waugh over publication of the Knox sermons, assuming the role of peacemaker, and he was eventually able to persuade Waugh that he was in the wrong and should give way.

Whilst in private they indulged in the ego clashes and intellectual disagreements common in the creative world, the Catholic literary circle of writers, publishers, reviewers and journalists formed a remarkably self-supportive and homogeneous group, a Catholic anti-Bloomsbury set. The strength of this literary establishment contributed in no small measure to the air of optimism pervading English Roman Catholicism during this period of the mid-twentieth century when the long shadows of penal persecution and discrimination were receding, and a strong minority spirit was in the ascendancy. The prestige of its authors, and international acclaim for their work, boosted the self-confidence of the increasingly middle-class, educated, minority community in a country where Catholics had for so long, in Newman's words, been a *gens lucifuga*.

On social occasions, the writers' circle tended to be religiously exclusive. Despite their differences, and some years before the Knox contretemps, Waugh asked Tom Burns and his Spanish wife Mabél, to host a lavish party in their London home for Clare Boothe-Luce, the celebrity wife of the proprietor of the American publications *Time* and *Life*, who was an ardent convert. The Catholic intelligentsia gathered in the house in Victoria, and Philip Caraman, who was still building his reputation as editor of *The Month*, was among them. The Jesuit followed up his introduction to Booth-Luce with an invitation to her to contribute to his magazine, but he was turned down as he had been by Malraux. The international standing of his *Month* had not then been fully recognised. In Caraman's case social exchanges were viewed as work opportunities. Shortly before the Burns party, he had tried to arrange a potentially memorable event at the scene of his own former triumph, the Stonyhurst Debating Society. Evelyn Waugh backed him up, saying that 'if Graham Greene can come we might have a debate with the boys.

We disagree on all essential subjects.' But the debate had to be postponed for some time because Greene turned down Philip's invitation, saying: 'I should love to join Evelyn and you at Stonyhurst ... the only thing is that I expect to be abroad [at that time]. Do ring me up again, my cupboard is well stocked after my absence ...'[10]

Whatever Waugh may have confided in private to Caraman concerning Graham Greene, any disagreements he had with his fellow Catholic author were not reflected in published criticism. At the time of the novel's publication, Waugh was one of very few people who knew that *The End of the Affair* was inspired by Greene's affair with Catherine Walston. Faithful in his own marriage to Laura, Waugh nevertheless took a lenient view of Greene's extramarital liaison with Catherine, who seems to have charmed Evelyn with her generosity and warm personality, as she charmed so many men. His review of Greene's autobiographical novel, which Fr Caraman published in *The Month* and which resulted in the reprimand he received from Fr Bolland, was a glowing one. In private, Philip Caraman told Waugh that: 'No contribution I have ever received has given me such pleasure ... I thought [the book] beautifully written and a great technical achievement, but I read it with sadness.'[11]

By the time Fr Caraman came to know him well, Greene was irrevocably separated from his wife Vivien. In contrast, the stability of Waugh's marriage and family background was the true foundation for the friendship between writer and priest, overriding any ties formed by their literary association. The Jesuit had been a regular guest at Pixton Park since his first introduction to Mary Herbert during the war. Although relations between Waugh and his Herbert in-laws were often prickly, Caraman was also made welcome by Evelyn, and by Laura with whom he had a warm friendship. As the Waughs' children reached adulthood, Philip grew fond of them too and took an increasing interest in their development. Visits to the Waugh home, first at Piers Court and later to Combe Florey, were generally social calls although on occasion Caraman was called upon to stand in for a parish priest away on holiday. With sensitivity, Waugh told the priest: 'Please do not suppose that we only turn to you in difficulty. You are always most welcome here when ever you can come.'[12] His attitude to Caraman's visits was markedly different from his reception of Laura's unmarried brother Auberon Herbert, whom he disliked intensely. A family friend described how meetings between Laura and Auberon were fraught with difficulties. Auberon would enter Combe Florey by the back door and meet his sister in the kitchen, where on occasion they would be surprised by Evelyn. Malcolm Muggeridge, who knew both men, said that the hostility between Herbert and Waugh was mutual and left this description of their relationship:

> Whenever the subject of Waugh cropped up ... Auberon never failed to acknowledge Waugh's qualities, and the weird, outrageous sanctity which underlay his outward acerbity and boorishness. When Waugh's scandalous intimate journal was posthumously published, Auberon was deeply distressed, on Waugh's own account and for the sake of his sister, and showed no particular chagrin at the rough handling he received himself. In Waugh's case, the hostility was doubtless due to the fact that Auberon possessed all the credentials, social and genealogical, for being numbered among the Brideshead elect, and yet continued to be, in his own vein, an outsider. Waugh the brilliant success, the much-sought after wit and celebrity, looked askance at an aristocratic, affluent brother-in-law.[13]

The brothers-in-law had one thing in common – their friendship with Fr Caraman. Auberon Mark Henry Yvo Molyneux Herbert, who lived with his mother at Pixton, was eleven years' Caraman's junior and was the only English officer to have served in the Polish Army during World War Two, having been turned down for the Irish Guards because of his flat feet. He was an upper-class eccentric, in the mould of Eddy Sackville-West and Edith Sitwell, whose foibles and flairs were humoured and appreciated by Philip Caraman. Herbert's abilities were considerable. He was a brilliant linguist, speaking five or six European languages fluently, and was a renowned wit with a rich and imaginative vocabulary in his own tongue. One day, in a fashionable London eating-house, he asked for a vodka and

tomato juice. 'You want a Bloody Mary?' queried the barman.
'No, that's precisely what I don't want' Herbert replied. 'The
odious roadhouse jauntiness of that name turns a magnificent
drink into wormwood and simultaneously traduces the memory
of a noble and deeply wronged Queen.' A godson of Hilaire
Belloc, Herbert's devotion to the pre-Vatican II Catholic Church
was boundless. In Fr Caraman's eyes, his Christianity was
edifying, although on occasion alarmingly unrealistic, as he
espoused one noble, distant and half-forgotten cause after
another, from Canada to Cracow and Taiwan. Although
Herbert's idealism was often quixotic, as a leading patron of the
large Polish exile community in England after the war he gave
much sound and lasting practical help. This was particularly
altruistic in view of the fact that he had been defrauded of
£60,000 from his current bank account by a Pole whom he had
trusted. After the family chapel on the Pixton estate was closed,
Mary Herbert founded the present small Catholic church in
Dulverton, which was dedicated to St Stanislaus of Cracow in
recognition of Aubrey's association with the exiled Poles.

The church of St Stanislaus was established in 1955. Fr
Caraman took an interest in the church building and its congregation from the beginning, and the parish was destined to play an
important role in his later life. The year before the church was
opened it was to Philip Caraman that Laura Waugh turned in a
time of crisis. The story of what has been termed 'the Pinfold
episode' in Evelyn Waugh's life, as related by Caraman, has
been written up by the author's two principal biographers, and is
well known. In February 1954 Waugh, disturbed and unwell,
had travelled by sea to Ceylon. On the island his health deteriorated further, and the delusions from which he had been suffering
for some time reached a climax. He was experiencing hallucinations, hearing voices, and was generally disorientated. An
anxious Laura was preparing to go out to Ceylon when her
husband managed to get back to London by plane, and she was
waiting for him at the Hyde Park Hotel when he arrived. Laura
called Philip Caraman, who rushed over to the hotel the same
evening. During dinner Evelyn's behaviour was manic; he told
his friend that he believed he was possessed by the Devil, and

wondered if the priest should perform an exorcism. With his distrust of the paranormal, Caraman sought a more prosaic explanation, and immediately telephoned the Catholic physician and psychiatrist Dr E. B. Strauss, who was a friend of Graham Greene's and a contributor to Caraman's magazine. Strauss's diagnosis was decisive and reassuring. Waugh's problems were caused by bromide poisoning and the cure was straightforward. The author's hallucinations later inspired one of his stranger novels, *The Ordeal of Gilbert Pinfold*. Although the cause of Waugh's illness would no doubt have been discovered eventually, Philip Caraman's willingness to drop everything when Laura called him proved crucial and immensely reassuring.

ॐ

Fr Caraman's many friends and acquaintances knew that they could always rely on his support. However inopportune their pleas for help might be from the point of view of his own work, his sympathy and quiet advice was at their disposal. His detractors may have considered him a sycophant, kowtowing to the whims of his celebrity friends, and there may have been an element of truth in this accusation in his Mayfair days. But then, and later, he was equally prepared to go to great lengths for other, unknown, people who turned to him for help. By temperament, the more gifted creative writers in Caraman's circle were also the most demanding. On the night of his mother's death in September 1959, Graham Greene wrote immediately to Philip Caraman from Paris, asking the priest 'to say a few masses [for her]'. On another occasion, the writer enclosed a cheque for two guineas with a request for masses to be said for 'a young Swede called Stig Dagermann, who has committed suicide. His wife is a friend of mine, and although not a Catholic would like this to be done.' A telegram from Greene in Paris was more peremptory, demanding that Philip 'look up Trevor Wilson. Seems in bad state. Melancholy and friendless in London. Address Overseas Club.' Another call on the Jesuit's time was a request from Greene for contributions to his Chestertonia collection, should Caraman happen to come across any suitable papers in the course of his literary work.[14]

While Greene seemed to be oblivious of any inconvenience he might cause, his thoughtlessness was overshadowed by the urgency of Edith Sitwell's constant demands. Her bombardment by letter of Fr Caraman, as of so many others in her circle, was gruelling, particularly as the Jesuit was meticulous in replying to his correspondents.[15] Once the euphoria of her reception into the Church had evaporated, the tone of polite courtesy adopted by Sitwell in her early letters to her confessor gave way to the emotional torrents she poured down on her other intimate friends. Dame Edith's principal biographer remarks that:

> the Church with its confessional relationships, took her and her anxieties on its shoulders more acceptingly and more reassuringly than could have the mother, lover – or analyst – that she had never had ... She never reneged or lost her faith, and she retained her close and confidential relationship with her confessor.[16]

Father Caraman shouldered Sitwell's burdens with good humour, but her appreciation of his patience did not prevent her from increasing the load whenever she felt the urge to do so. She wrote to him from Renishaw Hall:

> I am so grateful to you for all your goodness to me. And I shall come to confession immediately on my return [to London]. And now, I have once more to place a burden on you – one which may save someone from utter despair, so I know you will not refuse it.
>
> I have a friend – one whom I have never known very well, but she came to me yesterday in her appalling grief (I have never seen anything more dreadful) – who I have told must receive instruction to become a Catholic because that alone can help her, and she says she will. I have told her also that she must tell you of her grief and consult you as to what she must do, because you are greatly wise ...[17]

Thus the break-up of the long-standing marriage of the Secretary of the Society of Authors who, according to Sitwell, had run a string of mistresses and finally deserted his wife of thirty years for a girl of twenty-three, brought yet another distraught woman to Philip Caraman for comfort and advice.

Edith Sitwell was at her amusing best when she regaled her confessor with snippets of literary gossip, occasionally launching into a tirade when one or other of her writer friends offended her sensibilities. She told him she was exceedingly displeased with Quentin Stevenson, the young poet who had attended her reception at Farm Street, because 'he met *everyone* who could be of use to him through me', but had ceased to visit her when, in her opinion, he had got what he wanted. She was also upset by Graham Greene's praise for Vladimir Nabokov's controversial novel *Lolita*. She told Caraman that:

> I tremble to think what Mr John Morgan, the anti-Lolitist, will say when he finds where Graham has got himself to. As you know I am a staunch adviser of Graham and am *very* fond of him as a person but I must say I draw the line at Lolita and so does Osbert. The two things that shock me most after blasphemy are cruelty and the corruption of children, and some of the book is quite [?] unreadable. The first few pages are sad and idyllic though. It was sent me by the American publishers ...[18]

Sitwell's views on literary matters were generally sound and well considered, and one of her most memorable poems was among a number of contributions she made to *The Month*. The verses 'His Blood Colours my Cheek' were published in 1958 and dedicated to Fr Martin D'Arcy. Dame Edith also took a genuine interest in Philip Caraman's writing, and gave him sensible advice and encouragement. His third book came out in 1957. *Henry Morse: Priest of the Plague* was dedicated to Dame Edith Sitwell, who wrote to him ahead of publication from her eyrie in the Sesame Club, saying: 'Only four days more and that wonderful book will be available to everyone. I wish it, with all my heart, the great success it deserves. I am deeply proud of, and grateful for, the dedication, which I treasure'. She added that news of Roy Campbell's death 'was a great shock and grief to me'.[19]

Henry Morse was the first of Caraman's books of which he was the original author. Unlike the autobiographies of his

Elizabethan Jesuit predecessors, John Gerard and William Weston, which he had translated, the story of the priest who worked among victims of the plague in penal times was Caraman's own. To a modern reader, the writing style seems curiously stilted compared to the flowing translations from the Latin of his previous books. Caraman inscribed the copy of *Henry Morse* which he gave to Martin D'Arcy, 'with deep gratitude for all you have done for me', expressing his continuing affection and respect for his former Superior.

Edith Sitwell also had a hand in another of Fr Caraman's books three years later. *The Other Face: Catholic Life under Elizabeth I* is an anthology of stories and snippets covering many aspects of religious life and the persecution of Catholics in Elizabethan England.[20] The extracts had been gathered by Caraman over some eight years from manuscripts and rare books he had studied during the course of his research work. The origins of the book lay in a personal and haphazard collection he had made as he went along of little known stories, sharply defined character studies, and unusual details. Various chapters deal with features such as 'The Gallows', 'Pursuivants', 'Anabaptists and Others', and 'Practice and Belief'. In an extract from the section entitled 'The Queen', he quotes a letter from Elizabeth I to the King of Scotland, in which she thanks 'God that you beware so soon of Jesuits, that have been the source of all these treacheries in this Realm, and will soon spread like an evil weed, if at the first they be not weeded out . . .' The book is an important contribution to historical studies of the first Elizabethan age, and, enlivened with snatches of humour, it is never dull reading. Writing at the time of Philip Caraman's death, another Jesuit, Fr Richard Randolph, described *The Other Face* as being 'of great importance as an antidote to the establishment view of the Elizabethan era as a Golden Age. Modern Englishmen generally have little idea of what persecutions were inflicted on our Catholic forebears over some three hundred years, and some are surprised to find that Catholics have ever felt persecuted.'[21] The title of the anthology, which illuminated little known aspects of sixteenth-century England so vividly, was suggested to Caraman by Dame Edith

Sitwell, and the book greatly enhanced her confessor's standing as an Elizabethan scholar.

Sitwell's inspiration was some recompense for Philip Caraman's solicitude in guiding her through her complex personal relationships. A couple of years before the publication of the priest's anthology, Edith wrote to Caraman revealing the tensions between herself and her brothers Osbert, and Sacheverell (Sachie) and his wife Georgia. She described Sachie as

> A most deeply loving character, his heart is warmth itself but he has no tact, he suffers from a great sense of grievance. My father injured him greatly, but it is not my father that he is angry with. He adored Osbert. Really the whole thing is too dreadful . . . O. is sweet, lovely and loving character . . . He worries so much about everybody but . . . he has had an *awful* lot to put up with from G. When his father died in very mysterious circumstances – I am practically certain he was murdered in Switzerland during the war – it was discovered he had made many wills. The first that came to light left *everything* to Reresby over Osbert's head. Nobody likes to be disinherited without reason.[22]

The letter reveals the friction between herself and Osbert on the one hand, and Sachie and Georgia, who lived at Weston Hall in Northamptonshire, on the other. Dame Edith's biographer cites money troubles as the cause of the division between them. But Edith and her younger brother and his wife were united in their anxieties concerning Osbert's situation vis-à-vis his unfaithful companion David Horner, who accompanied the family on a voyage to America shortly after Edith had written this letter to Caraman. The Jesuit was drawn even deeper into the family's councils when Sachie sent him a report on the state of play from on board ship.

Echoing Fr Caraman's mutual friendship with the incompatible Evelyn Waugh and Aubrey Herbert, the priest's closeness to Dame Edith did not prevent him from establishing a warm relationship with Sacheverell and Georgia Sitwell, who were not Roman Catholics. Caraman was a welcome guest at Weston Hall, and following a somewhat ambiguous review he had published in his magazine of Sacheverell's book *Journey to the Ends of Time: Volume 1: Lost in the Darkwood,* he wrote to the author, fearful that he might have been offended by the reviewer's comments. Anthony Levi's review of Sitwell's 'kaleidoscopic series of meditations on death and the possibility of survival', concluded that 'the sheer cultivation of the writing makes this a fascinating book, and the author's clarity and sensibility go a long way to redeeming the speculative weaknesses. The main weakness in Mr. Sitwell's viewpoint is an insufficiently developed humanism.'[23] Fr Caraman need not have worried. Georgia told him that 'we both think it is a most gratifying review especially considering the divergence of your views and experience and it shows your Catholicity in the widest and I think the best sense of the word'. Sacheverell followed this by writing:

I could not possibly be offended by the *most* intelligent review in The Month. I am so much touched by your attitude ... by your kindness and affection. A very great, and I think vital, difference has been made to Edith's life, and I never have it out of my mind that everyone I admired in the past had this belief and revelation that is so far denied to me, but I hope not forever ... With my thanks and love to you.[24]

Georgia and Sacheverell Sitwell did not follow Dame Edith's path into the Church, but their letters illustrate why Fr Caraman's Catholic friends were anxious to introduce him to anyone whom they considered ripe for conversion. Unwittingly he had assumed the role of missionary to the intelligentsia. Not all who called upon him were as insensitive as Eddy Sackville-West had been in the case of Rosamond Lehmann. Evelyn Waugh was a little more subtle in trying to steer his friends down his own path to Rome. One whom he considered might benefit from Fr Caraman's ministry was Lady Mary Lygon. Waugh wrote to her in 1959 suggesting a choice of priests she might like to meet. He could introduce her, he said, to either a Spanish priest 'called Alfonso de Zuleueta', or to 'a very clever Jesuit who says he is French but is really I think a Turk, called Fr Caraman of 114 Mount Street', or to just 'a simple English gentleman'. The following year Waugh wrote to Philip Caraman about Mary Lygon:

[She] is an old and dear friend of mine whom I always try to see when I come to London. She is in distressed circumstances . . . She knows no Catholic priest and her Anglican–Orthodox faith is dim. I think it is very important that people like her should at least know the name of a priest to turn to if they feel desperate (as she may well do). I don't suggest you should do anything about her. Simply that if the moment comes she should turn to you.[25]

Following his introduction to Lady Mary, Fr Caraman promised Waugh that he would try to help her. Another of the writer's friends whom he wanted Philip to meet was Lady Diana Cooper. Trying to arrange a weekend meeting with her at his favourite London haunt, he told her that he would be at the 'Hyde Park Hotel . . . all Saturday and Sunday. On Saturday evening a dear gentle Jesuit called Fr. Caraman dines with me. I'd like you to meet him . . .'[26] After Waugh's 'gentle Jesuit' and the famous socialite beauty were finally introduced on another occasion a month later, Caraman told him that he too 'liked Lady Diana very much', and that he would love to meet her again but wondered how this could be arranged.[27] Three years later, when Philip was living in Norway, Waugh suggested that Lady Diana might call on Fr Caraman in Oslo during a trip she was making to Scandinavia, but the meeting never took place because Diana Cooper changed her itinerary.

A more unexpected encounter did take place, and this too was probably through an introduction from Evelyn Waugh. The ballerina Moira Shearer, a Catholic, and her husband Ludovic Kennedy were friends of the Waughs during the 1950s. Some thirty years later, when Kennedy had declared himself an atheist and had become a strong advocate of euthanasia, Fr Caraman revealed that on one occasion he had been invited to talk to him. 'But it wasn't any good', he added with a shake of his head and a wry smile.[28] With other candidates Caraman was more successful, and when a journalist named John Mortimer was received into the Church the Jesuit rejoiced that as far as the left-wing press was concerned the Catholic rot had set in. At a time when prayers for the conversion of England were still said on Sundays in every Catholic church in the country, Fr Caraman manned a very fashionable mission post in the heart of Mayfair.

ⓦ

The centenary of the Restoration of their hierarchy in 1950 was marked with jubilation by Catholics in England and Wales, and culminated in a triumphant gathering of 85,000 people in Wembley Stadium on 1 October. The Westminster Eucharistic Congress of 1908 had been condemned in such bitter terms by correspondents to *The Times* newspaper, and had run into so much anti-Roman prejudice, that the main event was cancelled at the last moment: in contrast the centenary celebrations in 1950 aroused little comment or opposition. After the war correspondents to *The Times* were more concerned with the price of butter and the unreliability of the electricity supply than with religion. The Vatican and the hierarchy sensed that the time was ripe to honour publicly the martyrs whose courage and fortitude had laid the foundations for the survival of the Church and enabled its glorious revival. Catholicism in England and Wales during penal times was Philip Caraman's scholastic speciality, and he was the obvious choice for the appointment of Vice-Postulator or Promoter when the Cause for the canonisation of Forty Blessed Martyrs, executed in defence of the Faith during religious persecution under Henry VIII and Elizabeth I, was resumed in 1961 at the request of the Catholic hierarchy of England and Wales.

The history of the Cause is part of the story of the beatification of a whole phalanx of men and women who shed their blood in England in the defence of the Catholic religion from the time of the schism of Henry VIII right up to the end of the seventeenth century. It is beyond doubt, and historically proved, that those who died under Henry VIII and Queen Elizabeth I in defence of the primacy of the Pope were regarded by their contemporaries as the equals of those martyred in the early persecutions of the Church, and that like the latter they were considered worthy of veneration and cult. From the time of Pope Urban VIII[29] the promotion of their Cause of Beatification was considered, and the first necessary steps were taken, although the Catholic authorities in England were not in a position to do this themselves directly at that time. Towards the end of 1642, the Procurator General of the English Benedictine Congregation presented a formal request to the Holy See that the Archbishop of Cambrai and the Bishops of St-Omers and Ypres be delegated to draw up the canonical processes. As the process got under way, the Papal Brief and the Archbishop's decree were seized by the English authorities and brought to the attention of Parliament, and proceedings to beatify the Martyrs were suspended. The Cause then lapsed until after the Catholic hierarchy was re-established in 1850.

In 1859, Cardinal Nicholas Wiseman, the first Archbishop of Westminster, petitioned Rome for a special Feast, Mass and Office in honour of all the English martyrs of ancient and of more recent times. The Vatican's Congregation of Rites replied negatively. The petition was turned down on the grounds that Feasts are granted only in favour of those whose cult has been legitimately approved by the Holy See. The Cause fell victim to bureaucratic procedural differences between the Vatican and the hierarchy, and stalled again. Eventually the Sacred Congregation accepted the opinion of the English bishops that work on the Cause should not be delayed any further, and on 16 April 1873 decided that the ordinary processes should be drawn up. Thereafter the complicated procedures necessary for recognition of the martyrs went forward slowly over a period of many decades. A group of English and Welsh martyrs was successfully honoured in 1935, and others were beatified during the first half of the twentieth century.

After the success of the 1950 Centenary celebrations, the Catholic hierarchy was encouraged to promote the Canonisation, not of the entire company of martyrs, but of a limited group of them. The Sacred Congregation of Rites gave their approval, and the decision to go ahead was passed to Fr Paul Molinari, a Jesuit residing in Rome, who was appointed as Postulator of the Cause. He arranged to present it to the Sacred Congregation in

a *Supplex libellus* dated 1 December 1960. Although the formal
decree under which the Cause was reassumed was not promul-
gated until 24 May 1961, the groundwork was started in the
winter of 1959. Fr Caraman wrote to Evelyn Waugh in
February 1960, apologising for the fact that he had not been in
touch with him for some while. Revealing the extent of the task
that lay ahead of him, he told Waugh that:

> Since we last met I have been appointed Vice-Postulator of the
> Cause of the English martyrs. From the middle of Dec. to the
> middle of January, I was in Rome getting the Cause in motion.
> On my return I have been occupied seeing the Bishops to get
> their agreement on a select list and procedure. I still have *The
> Month* and, in my appointment as Vice-Postulator, I was already
> engaged in plans for a quarterly ascetical review (to start in
> January 1961) for priests and religious ...[30]

Following Fr Caraman's discussions with the Bishops, a
group of forty martyrs was selected for canonisation, eleven of
whom were chosen from among nearly two hundred already
declared as Blessed on three successive occasions between 1886
and 1929. Their beatification had been won on the grounds of
the 'confirmation of cult' rather than on documentary historical
evidence. Although there was a sure knowledge of facts relating
to their imprisonment, trial, and execution, the process of
canonisation required that each of the eleven should comply with
the rigorous demands of the Historical Section of the Vatican
before they were considered worthy of sainthood. The work
involved was staggering. In the case of each of the eleven,
archives were scrutinised for any document that might throw
light on the facts relating to their martyrdom; cures and favours
granted through their cult were thoroughly investigated and
documented, and papers and pamphlets were written and
published. The fast-tracking to sainthood introduced in recent
times under the papacy of John Paul II was not then in place,
and apart from the detailed work involved, the process cost a
great deal of money. The expenses, not only of the Promoters
of the Cause, but of the Devil's Advocate chosen to scrutinise
it, had to be met by the hierarchy. Philip Caraman's team in

England included another Jesuit, Fr James Walsh, and a layman, Paddy Barry, all of whom reported regularly to Fr Molinari in Rome.[31]

When he was appointed Vice-Postulator of the martyr's Cause, Philip Caraman had been editing *The Month* for eleven years. During this time he had transformed the Jesuit magazine into an internationally acclaimed publication: literary flair, imagination, and unremitting routine work had maintained the high standard he had set in 1949. The magazine had brought him influential contacts, and had made him many friends, but the social side of his work, and the high-profile conversions to Catholicism won by his patience and dedication, were not included in his job description as editor. In the eyes of his Jesuit confrères these were sidelines. After Fr D'Arcy's departure the burdens imposed by Caraman's extra-curricular activities were not fully appreciated by his superiors. His books and his writing were regarded to some extent as a sideline: he was after all Director of *Scriptorum*, nominally in a position to regulate his own work. Fr Caraman had driven himself too hard and for too long, and his appointment as promoter of the martyrs' Cause brought the realisation that the work involved was more than even he could cope with. His new task was in many ways a compliment to his past achievements, employing his talents in a wider – national – context than previously. But Philip's frail physique could no longer cope with the demands which his nervous energy placed upon it. Whilst outwardly he appeared to be riding the crest of the wave of prestige and success, his health was steadily declining, and he was often in pain.

It is unlikely that Fr Caraman complained to his Provincial. As in the case of his major illness and hospitalisation in 1953, his personal file in the Jesuit Archive records no health problems at this time. Lacking close family members to whom he could turn, Caraman shared his problems with some of his friends, who in turn reciprocated the sympathy and understanding he had shown them over the years. During his stay in Rome to set the Cause in motion over the Christmas of 1949, Fr Caraman wrote to Edith Sitwell to tell her he had been taken ill during his visit. In the new year she expressed her concern, saying 'you must still be feeling *very* weak and utterly unfitted for such overwork as is being put on you'. Two weeks later she wrote again in alarm from Castello Montegufoni telling him that she 'was horrified when I received your letter ... from Rome, and wrote to you immediately in London ... I said how dreadfully distressed I was to know in what shocking pain you had been.' In her second letter she could not resist relating her own woes to her confessor, telling him that 'I have had two very bad accidents – the second being the result of travelling long before I was fit to do so'.[32] After Fr Caraman's return to London, it was Alec Guinness's turn to express concern. He sent a note over to Farm Street from the Connaught Hotel telling Philip that he hoped he was feeling better. 'You *appeared* fit and strong at Mass this morning, but I was anxious for you last night.'[33] In addition to his other work, Fr Caraman was included in the rota of Jesuits who took the services in the church of the Immaculate Conception, regularly celebrating Mass and preaching there. His ministry in the hushed beauty of the dignified Victorian church alongside the house in which he lived and worked was a duty dear to Fr Caraman: a treasured commitment, however tired he felt.

Fr Caraman's health continued to cause him problems throughout the following months, although he was able to make a retreat which renewed his spiritual resources, and he took a break from his office in the summer, returning to Farm Street in September. He received a note from Evelyn Waugh welcoming him home, and adding: ' I hope you have recuperated your strength. Margaret was much worried at your tendency to overwork. She is used to her father's idle habits and is aghast at your industry ...'[34] By this time Margaret, Waugh's second daughter, known as Meg to her family, was one of a group of girls recruited by the Jesuits to work in the office which they had set up for the Cause in the 'writers' house' at 31 Farm Street.

As the constraints of office routine, and the volume of work in connection with the Cause, threatened to overwhelm him, Fr Caraman permitted himself the occasional escape. His prestige as a writer versed in Catholic medieval history had won him an enviable commission. The Provincial of the English Province of the Ursulines of the Roman Union asked him to write a biography of the foundress of their Order, St Angela Merici. No life of this saint, whose importance in the Counter-Reformation is considered by some historians to place her alongside her contemporary, St Ignatius, had previously been written in England. At the time Fr Caraman was commissioned to write the book, reliable sources were still few and far between, and although several previous biographies of St Angela had been written, Caraman considered that only by visiting the places associated with the saint would it be possible to reach new conclusions. With funding from the English Province of the Ursulines, the Jesuit enjoyed *carte blanche* to travel in St Angela's footsteps from her birthplace on the southern shores of Lake Garda, to Jerusalem, Bethlehem and other sites of Christian pilgrimage in the Holy Land. He also had an excuse to visit towns in northern Italy such as Cremona and Venice, where Angela had stayed for a time, and her principal base in Brescia. Fr Caraman's travel-research was at once exhaustive and responsible, but there is little doubt that he made the most of it.

He found other legitimate excuses to escape from the increasing constraints imposed on him by the demands of the Cause. Apart from the biography of St Angela, he was also working on a book about Fr Henry Garnet, the Jesuit Superior in England at the time of the Gunpowder Plot, who was executed on 3 May 1606. Fr Garnet was a leading character in the stories of both John Gerard and William Weston, and Fr Caraman had unearthed many interesting details about his ministry in penal England whilst researching the autobiographies of his two previous Jesuit heroes. A packet of Garnet's correspondence had recently been discovered in archives in Rome, and the Jesuits considered a book about their martyr, his exploits during times of persecution, and his connection with the Gunpowder Plot, would provide a good showcase for this new material.[35]

On a visit to the Jesuit novitiate at Harlaxton, Fr Caraman had been introduced to John Skinner, the head novice: the young man and the celebrated editor of *The Month* immediately established a rapport. Later, when Skinner was a Jesuit scholastic teaching at Mount St Mary's, the two met up again and set out together in a Morris Minor, borrowed from Skinner's mother, to do some research. More than twenty years Caraman's junior, Skinner recalls that in those days the priest seemed to him to be 'terribly dashing', and had been great fun as a travelling companion. Certainly on this expedition he regained some of his customary sparkle and charisma. John Skinner drove Fr Caraman around for three amusing days, during which they went to Rushton Hall, the home of Sir Thomas Tresham, a leading Catholic layman at the time of the Plot, and afterwards to Baddesley Clinton; as a result of this field trip Caraman was able to confirm that this house had been Fr Garnet's country headquarters when he was in hiding.[36] He describes the house as a 'beautiful and perfectly preserved mansion ... secluded and difficult to find'. The fifteenth-century moated manor house near Solihull is now in the hands of the National Trust, but was still in private hands at the time of the Jesuits' visit. John Skinner recalls that Fr Caraman had not planned ahead. He simply knocked on the door of the house and said 'I'm Fr Philip Caraman and I'm writing a book about Henry Garnet, and I'm wondering if I could just see the house'. The astonished owner allowed them in, and Garnet's author was delighted to find the priest's hiding-places and a house little changed since the time the martyr had stayed there nearly four hundred years earlier. Finally the pair called in at Stonor, the ancestral home of Lord Camoys in the Oxfordshire Chilterns, where, in Skinner's words, they just 'rolled in for lunch'. Here the family were old friends of Caraman's – he had dedicated *The Other Face* to the Stonors – and they received a great welcome. They were treated to a grand lunch of salmon brought down from Scotland the previous day, eaten with two 'very beautiful Georgian silver forks', rather than fish cutlery, which was served in a pretty dining-room. At the end of the trip John Skinner returned the Morris Minor to his mother at Leatherhead and, in gratitude for the loan of the car, his passenger presented her with a beautiful lavishly-produced missal, which Skinner believes Caraman had edited himself. Little did any of them realise that within a short time the missal would be rendered obsolete following the introduction of the vernacular mass by the Second Vatican Council.[37]

Lighter moments, such as the excursion with John Skinner, grew fewer and further apart as work for the Cause grew more hectic. In order to carry out the detailed work involved, Fr Molinari and Fr Caraman decided to co-opt a number of reliable historians to collaborate with them by carrying out necessary research in the archives and libraries of the different dioceses and religious orders in which the martyrs had mostly lived or to which they had belonged. Once these historians had agreed to help, the Postulators held regular meetings with them to monitor their findings, and to collate the mass of documentation they produced. The hierarchy had to be regularly up-dated on the progress of the Cause, and regular meetings were held with the diocesan representatives appointed by the Bishops' Conference, and also with Bishop Petit of Menevia who acted as a link between the Jesuits and the hierarchy. The three Jesuits heading the operation, Frs Molinari, Caraman and Walsh, were involved in frequent meetings, either in Rome, London or in one of the dioceses involved in the martyrs' Cause. An efficiently-run office was needed to administer the paperwork. Whilst *The Month*'s offices remained at 114 Mount Street, as they had been throughout Fr Caraman's years as editor, rooms were set aside in the 'writers' house' at 31 Farm Street for work on the Cause, and he engaged secretaries and other clerical staff.

In the small kingdom he had established at 31 Farm Street, it seems that Fr Caraman felt free to distribute largesse and hire staff according to whim. he eventually acquired a team of eight women of varying abilities, covering a wide age-range. Among the younger members of staff were two of Evelyn Waugh's daughters, first Margaret, and then later, when she was old enough, Hattie. Of the two, Margaret was at that time the better qualified to work as a secretary. An attractive, clever girl of eighteen, who had failed to win a place at Oxford, Meg was charming and compassionate, although prone to fits of depression. Her cousin Ann Fleming, wife of James Bond's creator Ian, said she had 'tremendous poise', and Martin Stannard, one of Waugh's biographers, speaks of her 'articulate shyness, a disturbing combination of modesty and wit,' which men found intriguing.[38] Of Waugh's six children Meg had always been his favourite. When she complained of being unhappy at her convent school, he had allowed her to leave, and as she grew older he seemed to welcome her company in a way he never did that of his sons or other daughters. Much to Waugh's displeasure, Meg wanted to live in London, but had neither a job nor enough money to support a lifestyle which included frequent parties, smoking and drinking: her father strongly disapproved. Knowing Waugh's feelings, Fr Caraman found a place for Meg in his office, and was pleased to find that she was a 'quick and most intelligent worker'. Soon he was able to write to her father to tell him that Margaret was 'proving invaluable'.[39] The following day, a delighted Waugh thanked the Jesuit for his letter, saying:

> I am delighted to learn that Margaret is giving satisfaction. I knew from her that she was exhilarated by the work for you. She is a delightful girl, but capricious and intermittently lazy. I am enormously grateful to you for finding her a task worth doing, instead of selling dubious antiques or acting as a receptionist to a businessman, as most failed University girls do, particularly one which will keep her tight bound to her Faith.[40]

Writing later in May to Nancy Mitford, Waugh again expressed his pleasure over Meg's job, saying 'Margaret now works in London canonising 40 martyrs at £10 a week. No London season for her. Can't afford it ... She is very happy canonising.'[41]

In taking Margaret Waugh under his wing, Fr Caraman felt to some extent responsible for her. He sent Evelyn and Laura regular bulletins about her welfare. He was worried by her frequent late nights, her smoking and her drinking, fearing that her health would suffer, and expressed his concerns to her father. Despite her partying, Meg's work was surprisingly competent, and within a year she was promoted from routine office duties to writing pamphlets on the martyrs' lives. Fr Caraman was delighted with the result. He was able to tell Waugh that:

Fr D'Arcy thinks that Margaret's pamphlet on Nicholas Owen is a gem. I have read it three times and I think it is very good ... I should like to see her tackle a full-length biography of Philip Howard. This will require more self-discipline than she has at present ... I do hope you are happy about [her] development. Although on the surface she has many childish qualities, in other ways ... she is mature beyond her years. She has an independence and sound sense that owes much to her deep devotion to you.[42]

Waugh responded immediately to the Jesuit's letter. He thought Margaret would 'do a good pamphlet on Philip Howard', but doubted if she had the 'diligence to manage a full-length book'.

She is very happy making herself useful (I hope) in your office, and gossiping on the coffee table. I don't believe she has the stamina for prolonged solitary work. It was very kind of you to suggest her working at home for a week. There would be many distractions for her during her sister's and brothers' holidays. After they return to school it would be a good plan if you can impress on her that she will have to work office hours here. She seems to think that you are offering her a holiday without pay.[43]

Between them, her father and her employer continued to monitor Meg's life, and it is hardly surprising that she wanted, without wounding the feelings of either priest or parent, to become independent of both.

Late in the summer of 1961, Fr Caraman suggested to Waugh that Meg might stay with her elder sister, Teresa, in Rome and help him with some research he had to do in archives in that city. He told Waugh that he needed to be in Rome 'in the second half of October while Cardinal Godfrey is there. Together we plan to push the Cause forward with the Congregation of Rites in the *hope* of arranging for the canonisation when all the Bishops are present in Rome for the Council'.[44] The promoters of the Cause were wildly over-optimistic. Vatican bureaucracy grinds extremely slowly and the Second Vatican Council was due to open within a year of Cardinal Godfrey's and Philip Caraman's visit to Rome. Too much work remained to be done, and it would be several more years before the Forty were canonised.

Pressure to speed up the tortuous procedures for the Cause was only one of many problems bearing down on Fr Caraman. Every time he returned to Farm Street, the atmosphere there grew heavier and less congenial. The situation in the twin Jesuit communities in Mayfair has been described as 'interesting' by one of the priests living there at the time. Certainly it seems to have been far from tranquil. It appears that traditionally there was a loose arrangement under which the writers at 31 Farm Street came under the aegis of the community at the Jesuit house in Wimbledon, South London. This meant that they enjoyed a good deal of independence from Mount Street, the seat of their immediate superior and of the Provincial. In the late 1950s the then Provincial, Fr Desmond Boyle, had considered moving his headquarters out to Wimbledon, but abandoned the idea when the inconvenience of such a move became apparent. His successor as Provincial, Fr John Coventry, a contemporary of Philip Caraman's at Campion Hall, decided that it was time to end the anomaly, and that Farm Street and Mount Street should become one community. Fr Caraman opposed the idea, and received the support of Fr Martin D'Arcy who, by this time, paid only fleeting visits to London. From the spring of 1959 onwards, the former Provincial began a decade of lecture tours across the United States, and spent more time in universities on the other side of the Atlantic than he did in England: during this period of his life his longest stay in Farm Street was only eighteen months. By the end of 1962, Fr D'Arcy's influence over the direction of the English Province was almost negligible, and his role in policy-making was marginalised. Over-tired, and lacking the time and space in which to consider the situation calmly, Fr Caraman's reactions in trying to defend his territory seemed, in the opinion of some of his fellow-Jesuits, egotistical and abrasive. Another problem was Fr James Walsh's tacit support for the Provincial, an attitude in Caraman's co-worker on the Cause which made it increasingly difficult for the two men to work together harmoniously.[45]

Errors were beginning to creep into work emanating from the Farm Street office. In the summer of 1962, the *Westminster Cathedral Chronicle* had published an article written by

Margaret Waugh about one of the Forty Martyrs, Blessed John Plessington. After publication, the bishop's secretary of the Shrewsbury diocese wrote to Fr Caraman questioning the accuracy of the article, pointing out that documents in their archives showed that the manner of Plessington's martyrdom had been incorrectly described by the writer, and questioned her research. Caraman replied that, 'Margaret is away at present but as soon as she returns I will show her your letter and see what she has to say'.[46] Waugh's daughter did not react well to criticism of her work. She told her father that she thought it was time she changed jobs: he did his best to dissuade her. Neither Waugh nor Fr Caraman realised she was in a state of emotional turmoil, and had more on her mind than the disembowelling of a seventeenth-century martyr. Meg was on the point of announcing her engagement to Giles FitzHerbert, and her state of hypertension affected her relationship with some of the other girls working in Farm Street. The situation was exacerbated further when Fr Caraman gave her unpaid leave before her wedding in response to a plea from Laura: her mother considered that Meg was unfit for work and suffering a bad bout of depression. The atmosphere in the office grew increasingly fraught.

Had Fr Caraman been weighed down with fewer commitments he might have had time to calm the frayed nerves of his staff; had he been less tired he might have appreciated some of the reasons behind the growing hostility of his brother Jesuits. Apparently it never occurred to him that his success and popularity, and his celebrity friendships, were a source of unspoken envy among his more retiring brethren. In some measure he had only himself to blame. Despite extreme weariness, often rising at five o'clock to recite the Divine Office and get through the day's work, he continued to accept invitations to lavish social engagements that were outside the normal orbit of other priests in the Mount Street community.

Within a few days of a visit to Manchester to direct a formal enquiry into an alleged miracle attributed to one of the forty martyrs, which he described as 'a long and expensive process',[47] Fr Caraman attended a gala evening celebrating Dame Edith Sitwell's seventy-fifth birthday. Organised by her nephew

Francis Sitwell, a public audience of 3,000 gathered in the Festival Hall for a performance of *Façade* conducted by Sir William Walton. Philip Caraman related that 'Edith sat in her invalid chair [in the Royal Box] like a queen on a throne. At the end of the concert the whole family received a great ovation.'[48] After the concert, Philip was one of sixty guests invited to a private party at which he was seated between Cyril Connolly and Reresby Sitwell. Many other prominent figures in the arts world were at this dinner, including Sir Kenneth and Lady Clark, Stephen Spender, the novelist L. P. Hartley, John Lehmann and Sir Charles and Lady Snow. It was a long evening. Shortly afterwards, Fr Caraman attended another, much smaller, select dinner given by Ann Fleming before Margaret Waugh's wedding, and two days later he conducted her marriage service. His sermon on this occasion was memorable. Evelyn Waugh expressed gratitude for his copy of the address, adding:

> I shall treasure it not only as a souvenir of the day, but also as a beautiful literary composition. I have heard countless expressions of admiration for it and the whole conduct of the ceremony, from Christians and heathen alike.
>
> You have been a wonderful friend to Meg during her time in London, all the time unobtrusively standing between her and malign influences ... I don't expect to be in London much this winter. If you feel the need of a quiet retreat from your office, Laura and I would so love it if you came here. Diana [Cooper] liked you awfully – she should be in the Church.[49]

Fr Caraman's impressive address eventually reached a far wider audience than the congregation at Margaret Waugh's wedding. Nearly forty years after it was first written, Fr Olaf Waring, a Norwegian friend, said Philip had given him a copy of the sermon, which 'is so good that I have translated it into Norwegian and used it many times in both English and Norwegian. I only changed 'plighting of troth' to 'exchange of vows' for Americans.'[50]

Dame Edith's Gala, and the Waugh family gathering, momentarily raised Fr Caraman's spirits, but within a few days of the wedding the shadows closing in on him over the past two years returned, and now they were darker than ever before. At the end of the summer he had stayed with Laura and Evelyn, and in thanking them for their hospitality had told Waugh that,

> I was very happy to discover, that, among other things in common, we both desire to enter a better life. It is a desire that has been in Fr Martindale for thirty years: and, while he has done his utmost to achieve it, he still shows no signs of dissolution. So, be prepared for a ripe old age.[51]

World-weariness was only slightly mitigated by a shaft of humour.

After Meg's marriage, the thought of working in an office no longer enlivened by her sense of fun was hard to contemplate. 'I can't thank you enough for bringing her into my drab routine life', Fr Caraman told her father. Although she was planning to return to work after her honeymoon, he felt she would leave 'when she starts her family'. He added sorrowfully, with a lame attempt at light-heartedness, that he hoped Meg would pray for him 'when I am dead'.[52]

The Waughs' offer of 'a quiet retreat' from Farm Street was taken up with alacrity. Fr Caraman no longer had close ties with his own large, but now scattered, family; two of his seven sisters had died, another was a nun, and his brother John was in distant Rhodesia. There was no parental home where he could relax and take refuge. The bond of mutual affection between the priest and the Waughs at Combe Florey, and the Herberts at Pixton, had deepened over the years to the point where they had, within certain limitations, assumed the role of surrogate family. As the winter of 1962 closed in, he accepted the Waughs' invitation, saying he was supplying for Fr MacDonald, the priest at Pixton, over the weekend of 25 November, and wondered if he might move over to Evelyn and Laura on the following Monday or Tuesday. He explained that:

> I need a rest for three or four days, for I am making disastrous mistakes and losing my faculty for judging persons and situations. It would be a perfect relaxation if I could come then (or

later), work in the morning, rest and do manual labour in the afternoon, bath and read (or talk) in the evening . . . If nothing is said outside the house, I have no scruple in saying Mass at Combe Florey. (I could bring with me all that is needed). Jesuits have this privilege, but the Bishops can make difficulties over it . . . I have had a fascinating letter from Fr. [Bernard] Basset in Rome describing scenes at the Council. The accidental results of the meeting will be far greater than the intended ones. [53]

It was inevitable that talk between Waugh and Caraman would turn to the Second Vatican Council which had opened on 11 October. Events in Rome had taken an unexpected turn; the Church, which had provided Waugh with a bedrock of unshakeable faith for over thirty years, and through which Fr Caraman had dedicated his priestly ministry to God, was in turmoil. The Roman Curia had hoped that the Council would be over by Christmas, that the bishops could return home quietly, and that everything would go on as it had done for generations. It soon emerged that Pope John XXIII's Council was not going to comply with the wishes of the Vatican's civil servants. Great changes were in the wind in respect of the liturgy, the introduction of Mass in the vernacular, the role of the laity in the Church, and attitudes to ecumenism. Waugh was greatly affected, and a few days before Fr Caraman's visit had published a landmark article in the *Spectator* entitled 'The Same Again, Please'[54] in which he put forward cogent arguments in favour of maintaining the status quo. Fr Caraman cherished tradition, and was largely in agreement with him.

The turmoil engendered by events at the Council was yet another disturbing influence on life in the Jesuit communities in Mayfair, to which Fr Caraman reluctantly returned from the peaceful Somerset countryside. His stay at Combe Florey had lasted only a few days. Writing from Farm Street to thank Waugh for his hospitality, he revealed that it was only the needs of someone who had called upon him for spiritual direction that had brought him back to London. He had spent many hours on the following Sunday talking to the man, and was 'very hopeful that he would become a Catholic'. Fr Caraman added that 'Combe Florey is incomparably more peaceful than Farm Street

... I am most deeply grateful to you and Laura for giving me such a wonderful and happy change.'[55] It was a short respite. Fr Caraman had dredged the depths of his spiritual and physical resources, and on the brink of a complete nervous breakdown was ill-prepared for the bitter trials ahead.

Notes

1 *William Weston. The Autobiography of an Elizabethan*, translated from the Latin by Philip Caraman (Longmans, Green and Co.), 1955.
2 Based on Selina Hastings, *Evelyn Waugh. A Biography* (Sinclair Stevenson, 1994), p. 554.
3 From Mark Amory, *The Letters of Evelyn Waugh* (Weidenfeld & Nicolson, 1980), p. 642.
4 Evelyn Waugh to Philip Caraman, 21 June 1958, John J. Burns Library, Boston College (hereafter BC).
5 Ibid. 11 January 1959.
6 Philip Caraman to Miss D. Collins, 11 May 1959, British Library (hereafter BL).
7 Evelyn Waugh to Philip Caraman, 13 April 1959 (BC).
8 Ibid. 1 May 1959.
9 Tom Burns, *The Use of Memory* (Sheed & Ward, London, 1993), pp. 61–6.
10 Graham Greene to Philip Caraman, undated (BC). In 2003, Raleigh St. Lawrence, who taught History at Stonyhurst in the 1950s, recalled seeing the slight figure of Fr Caraman escorting a 'melancholy-looking' Greene and 'a grumpy-visaged' Waugh to the station after the debate, which eventually took place after Greene's return from his travels.
11 Philip Caraman to Evelyn Waugh, 27 May 1951 (BL).
12 Evelyn Waugh to Philip Caraman, from Piers Court, 10 August 1952 (BC).
13 Malcolm Muggeridge, *Auberon Herbert – a Composite Portrait*, edited by John Joliffe (privately published by Compton Russell, Tisbury, Wilts, 1976).
14 Based on Letters, Graham Greene to Philip Caraman, various dates (BC).

15 The Dame Edith Sitwell Collection in the Harry Ransom Humanities Research Center at the University of Texas at Austin contains 40 autograph letters, and one incomplete autograph letter, from Fr Philip Caraman to Dame Edith. Included with these is a typed manuscript with translations from Latin on an extract concerning Queen Elizabeth I's religious observations on the defeat of the Armada.

16 Victoria Glendinning, *A Unicorn Among Lions*, pp. 317 and 320.

17 Letter, Edith Sitwell to Philip Caraman, 13 June 1959 (BC) © Francis Sitwell 2004.

18 Ibid. 19 February 1959 © Francis Sitwell 2004.

19 Ibid. 2 May 1957 © Francis Sitwell 2004.

20 *The Other Face: Catholic Life Under Elizabeth I* (Longmans, Green and Co., 1960).

21 *The Month*, June 1998, pp. 250-1.

22 Letter, Edith Sitwell to Philip Caraman, 14 February 1957 (BC) © Francis Sitwell 2004.

23 Anthony Levi, *The Month*.

24 Letters, Georgia Sitwell and Sacheverell Sitwell to Philip Caraman, 5 December 1959 and 12 December 1959 (BC) © Francis Sitwell and Reresby Sitwell 2004.

25 Mark Amory (editor), *The Letters of Evelyn Waugh* (Weidenfeld & Nicolson, 1980) p. 539.

26 Artemis Cooper (editor), *Mr Wu and Mrs Stitch. The letters of Evelyn Waugh and Diana Cooper.* (Hodder & Stoughton, 1991), pp. 295 and 318-9.

27 Letter, Philip Caraman to Evelyn Waugh, 26 October 1962 (BL).

28 Conversation with author.

29 Pope 1623-44.

30 Philip Caraman to Evelyn Waugh, 9 February 1960 (BL).

31 Based on Document 148 produced by Sacra Rituum Congregation Section Historica, *Westmonasterien. Positio Super Martyrio et Cultu ex Officio Concinnata*, 1968 Jesuit Archives (hereafter JA); and letter to author from Fr Paolo Molinari SJ, 3 June 2002.

32 Edith Sitwell to Philip Caraman, letters, 10 January and 25 January 1960 (BC) © Francis Sitwell 2004.

33 Alec Guinness to Philip Caraman, 16 January 1961, Philip Caraman Private Papers.

34 Evelyn Waugh to Philip Caraman, 17 September 1960 (BC).

35 Conversation with Fr Thomas M. McCoog SJ, Jesuit Archivist, 20 August 2002.

36 Philip Caraman, *John Gerard*, p. 264.

37 Based on author's interview with John Skinner, 28 February 2002.
38 Martin Stannard, *Evelyn Waugh. No Abiding City. 1939–1966.* (J.M. Dent & Sons, 1992), p. 424.
39 Card, Philip Caraman to Evelyn Waugh, 1 May 1960 (BL).
40 Letter, Evelyn Waugh to Philip Caraman, 2 May 1960 (BC).
41 Evelyn Waugh to Nancy Mitford, 18 May 1960 (Mark Amory, *Letters*).
42 Letter, Philip Caraman to Evelyn Waugh, 21 April 1961 (BL).
43 Letter, Evelyn Waugh to Philip Caraman, 22 April 1961 (BC).
44 Letter, Philip Caraman to Evelyn Waugh, 13 September 1961 (BL).
45 Based on *Letters & Notices*, vol. 94. Autumn 1998. no. 414. pp. 833/4 (JA).
46 Letters (JA).
47 Letter, Philip Caraman to Evelyn Waugh, 10 October 1962 (BL).
48 Ibid.
49 Letter, Evelyn Waugh to Philip Caraman. 23 October 1962 (BC).
50 Letter to author, 21 July 2002.
51 Letter, Philip Caraman to Evelyn Waugh, 16 September 1962 (BL).
52 Ibid. 26 October 1962 (BL).
53 Ibid. 8 November 1962 (BL).
54 23 November 1962, pp. 785–8.
55 Letter, Philip Caraman to Evelyn Waugh, 2 December 1962 (BL).

Chapter Six
Wilderness

The month of January 1963 was one of the coldest and bleakest of the twentieth century. As staff struggled to work through ice and snow, tempers were frayed and the goodwill and tolerance of the Christmas season had evaporated. The sequence of events leading to a final showdown between Fr Caraman and his Provincial, Fr John Coventry, began with an office squabble and rapidly escalated into a crisis which affected the last thirty-five years of Philip Caraman's life as a Jesuit.

Ostensibly it started with a prank that got out of hand and provoked an extreme reaction from some of the secretaries working in Farm Street for Fr James Walsh. After a honeymoon in Italy, Giles and Margaret FitzHerbert had set up home in Westbourne Grove, and decided to decorate their flat with unusual stuffed animals, scouring local markets on a Saturday for additions to their collection. Evelyn Waugh thought this highly amusing: he advertised in the national press on Meg's behalf for big game, and gave Fr Caraman a stuffed monkey to add to the newlyweds' menagerie. At a time when the threat to wildlife was not yet fully appreciated, and hunting was still considered acceptable, offers of wild animals poured in; the press arrived in force at Farm Street, one newspaper asking if they might photograph Fr Caraman presenting his assistant with a rhino. This was too much for one or two of the older women in the office, who for many months had been upset by Meg's *joie de vivre*. The fact that the priest had found a job for her eighteen-year old sister Hattie, who had no qualifications and whom he employed as a general dogsbody, was also resented.

The action had been prompted by generosity, but was a serious misjudgement on Philip's part: it was frowned upon by his superiors in Mount Street, and went down badly with some of the women in Farm Street. One embittered woman in particular, whom Meg described as 'malicious and untruthful',[1] resented the favouritism shown by Philip Caraman to both Waugh's daughters, particularly to Margaret. The woman lodged a formal complaint initially with her own boss, Fr Walsh, and then with the Jesuit Provincial, Fr Coventry, accusing Fr Caraman of being infatuated with Meg, and saying that he was hated by other members of his staff. The woman's allegations received a sympathetic hearing. The turmoil in the adjacent house provided the Mount Street hierarchy with a perfect opportunity to dismiss Fr Caraman, and rid themselves of his unsettling presence and worldly ways. The noise and laughter, and the constant stream of visitors to the office in Farm Street, had become an increasing nuisance and distraction to the other clergy, particularly the more sober and austere members of the community, and the furore caused by the menagerie joke was the last straw.

At first, Fr Caraman appeared to accept the situation calmly. Having long expected just such a confrontation with his superiors, it came as little surprise when the storm finally broke, although he was distressed by the Provincial's decision to exile him to Campion House, an establishment run by the Jesuits in the outer London suburb of Osterley. This establishment was a diocesan house of studies for men with late vocations requiring tuition in subjects such as Latin, where the Superior was Fr Clement Tigar, who had been working alongside Philip Caraman and James Walsh on the martyrs' Cause. Fr Caraman sought to make a more dignified withdrawal from Mayfair: he requested permission to remain in Farm Street until June to put his affairs in order and mitigate the disgrace of immediate demotion to a minor appointment in a satellite house. He said he would then like to go over to Ireland and work in peace writing up the Cause of the Blessed Oliver Plunkett. Meanwhile he paid a flying visit to Somerset to explain to Evelyn Waugh what had happened, and to seek reassurance in the comforting atmosphere of Combe Florey.

On his return to London, the situation deteriorated cruelly. Meg, out of misconceived loyalty, and in a state of hypertension – on top of everything else Giles was in hospital – led an office mutiny in support of Fr Caraman. On 15 January, she and Hattie, together with Mary Keen and Audrey von Lintzgy, both of whom remained loyal to the Vice-Postulator, considered their views had been misrepresented by the troublemaker in their midst and sent letters of resignation to Fr Walsh. In a fit of paranoia, Meg saw enemies everywhere, and decided that Fr Walsh's recent visits to Rome on business in connection with the martyrs' Cause had really been motivated by a plot to remove Fr Caraman. She refused to change her mind when Fr Walsh, in great agitation, begged her to withdraw her resignation; he admitted that Meg's relationship with Fr Caraman, and accusations concerning his infatuation with her, were merely a means of 'getting through to him' that he must leave.[2]

When Fr Coventry heard of the girls' action he was infuriated: this was the last straw. By now the priests involved were drowning in a maelstrom of female histrionics, and even the Provincial was out of his depth. On the day following the resignations, Fr Caraman wrote to Waugh, explaining:

> Yesterday I was too upset to be able to write and thank you and Laura for your wonderful kindness to me ... You will never know what a comfort and support you have been ... I should tell you that last night, in the presence of a witness, I was severely reprimanded by Fr Coventry for reading to Meg the paragraph in his letter [of dismissal] to me that covered our relationship and its supposed effect on the staff. I was also reprimanded for staying with you without his permission. At the same time he laid on my shoulders *all* the blame for this unhappy situation. I accepted the reprimands without attempting a defence.

Fr Caraman explained that his reasons for informing Meg of the allegations concerning their relationship were motivated by his anxiety lest 'gossip' should reach Giles or Waugh 'in an underground way: and so destroy or endanger friendships that I value'. He added that in his opinion the 'gossip' only existed on 'the tongues of some one or two malicious people in intrigue against me'. Fr Caraman told Waugh that other, more damaging, accusations had been made, but that some of the charges against him had been toned down. He also remarked that, with the exception of the one troublemaker in their midst, the other girls were 'all distraught at the departure of Meg, who was loved by everyone', and that after their departure he sadly missed the girls who had resigned.

Towards the end of this heart-rending letter, Philip Caraman requested Waugh to write to Fr Martin D'Arcy, who was then at Boston College, to enlist his support. He concluded on a note of optimism. Imploring Waugh to 'pray for me, that all will be well with me spiritually', he added that:

> Many blessings will come through this unhappy and shabby intrigue in which my friendship with Meg is only one of many sticks used by the Provincial to beat me with. I bear him no resentment. He is a clever man, but unintelligent.[3]

From the perspective of almost half a century, none of the priests involved in the affair emerges with much credit. Fr Walsh was the weak link between Provincial and Vice-Postulator and failed to establish an understanding between them. Hovering in the background was the distinguished figure of another Jesuit, Fr Tom Corbishley, the Superior of Mount Street, who was – nominally at least – responsible for the administration of the community. Somewhat older than Philip Caraman, and from a non-public school background, he had enjoyed a distinguished career in the Society: he followed Fr Martin D'Arcy as Master of Campion Hall after the war, and had served as Vice-Provincial. The author H. J. A. Sire relates that during his six-year tenure of office in Mayfair as Superior, starting in 1960, Fr Corbishley 'exercised his office in a particularly distinguished way, introducing the social practices of Oxford to the extent of holding dinners for eminent figures such as Archbishop Ramsey and Harold Macmillan'.[4] But it was also said of him that he 'had the difficult, nay impossible, task of making his writ run all over the property', and when difficulties 'became too difficult Father Tom retired to bed like a Russian president retiring to his dacha or an American president going to Martha's Vineyard.'[5] Certainly Fr Corbishley seems to have abrogated his responsibilities on this occasion, leaving the Provincial to deal with the thorny matter of Fr Caraman's recalcitrance on his own.

Both the Superior and Fr Coventry were in a difficult position vis-à-vis Philip Caraman: all three priests were disciples and friends of Fr Martin D'Arcy, and shared a deep respect for their former mentor. Fr Coventry said of the former Provincial's fall from office that 'It was the blackest day of my life when I heard he had been taken off',[6] a sentiment shared by Fr Caraman. Possibly on account of their mutual friendship with Fr D'Arcy, the relationship between the two priests was a difficult one. Three years younger than Philip Caraman, and his contemporary under D'Arcy at Campion Hall, Fr Coventry had overshadowed *The Month*'s editor academically, winning a First Class Honours degree in Greats, later going on to become a successful Rector of Beaumont, the Jesuit public school, before reaching the Province's highest office. Despite his many achievements, Fr Coventry seems never to have won Fr D'Arcy's confidence to the same extent as Philip Caraman, and their association was darkened by a cloud of sibling rivalry dating back over twenty years. Certainly there is evidence of a clash of temperaments in Fr Caraman's peevish remark to Evelyn Waugh, that Fr Coventry, in his opinion, was 'a clever man but unintelligent'. This uncomfortable personal relationship may explain Fr Coventry's reluctance to discuss calmly and authoritatively his differences with Fr Caraman over the integration of the Mayfair communities before reconciliation of their opposing views was impossible. The impasse facing brother Jesuits during the bitter winter of 1963 could perhaps have been avoided had the Provincial been someone other than John Coventry, who was the wrong man in the appointment to give Fr Caraman quiet and reasoned advice when he most needed it. Whilst Philip paid due respect to Fr Coventry's academic prowess and rapid promotion, the Provincial had reason to envy his confrére's talent for friendship, and the host of celebrities with whom he had surrounded himself. When the two men came face to face, it was Fr Coventry who held the reins of power, but whose man-management skills were sadly lacking: he seemed unaware of Fr Caraman's poor state of health, and he made no allowance for the heavy workload responsible for an obvious case of nervous breakdown. Ultimately, the Provincial bore the responsibility for Philip Caraman's embitterment, but he revealed the depths of his own dilemma when many years later he warned Fr Jock Earle, on his appointment as Provincial, that 'you'll lose all your friends'.[7]

In retrospect Fr Caraman believed himself to have been a victim of fraternal jealousy: there was justification for this belief, but his own conduct in the affair was far from blameless. Knowing that his relationship with Margaret Waugh was both innocent and platonic, he nonetheless allowed his affection for her to become all too obvious. In taking her under his wing, he may have regarded her as a much-loved younger sister, but his attitude towards her inevitably left observers with a false impression. In the office, he treated her to lunches during the working week, overlooked her shortcomings, indulged her absences, and valued her work on the Cause beyond that of his other employees. Describing his ' dear gentle Jesuit' to Diana Cooper, Evelyn Waugh added that the priest was 'in love with Meg'.[8] He did his friend few favours with this flippant remark, although he frequently joked with his daughter that Caraman had a 'crush' on her. It seems extraordinary that a priest who was so wise in counselling others, could have been so naive in his conduct towards Meg, and so insensitive to the nuances of his personal relationships with other members of his own community. His distraught letter to Waugh reveals a man at odds with himself. Caught in a web of worldly affairs as a successful editor and confidant of the rich and famous, the spiritual calm for which he yearned seemed to elude him. He enjoyed his friendships and the social life they brought him, spent money flamboyantly on his projects, and was reluctant to concede ground to his critics, whilst still striving to pursue his priestly ministry and fulfil his obligations to the Society of Jesus.

From the vantage point of an outsider, Evelyn Waugh viewed Fr Caraman's situation dispassionately and sensitively, and was able to pour balm on his friend's wounded pride. Replying to the priest's agonised letter and the news of the Provincial's severe reprimand, Waugh wrote:

> It was, as always, a delight to us all to have you here, I wish that the circumstances had been happier. I have had no letter from the Father Provincial. If he writes I shall reply with suitable respect and severity. I will certainly write to Father D'Arcy as you suggest. You speak of 'the blessings which may result from the intrigue'. I can name one already. I have from time to time in the last thirty years been aware of various quarrels among clergy, and have noticed that they often seem to be so rancorous, envious and dishonest as the laity. Your behaviour in this whole business has been a shining example of humility and obedience with every mark of supernatural grace. It has done more to fortify my belief in the divine institution of the priesthood in general, and in the divine institution of the Society of Jesus in particular, than any event in my life as a Catholic.[9]

From Boston, Fr D'Arcy reacted immediately, promising Waugh he would forward to Rome a letter Waugh had written in support of Fr Caraman and saying that he was 'so distressed by what has been happening'. He feared that a 'strong letter' of protest he had written to the Provincial had done no good, and added that although he would love to see friends like Waugh again in England he was alienated 'by what has happened and is happening at home'.[10]

From Somerset, Waugh did everything he could to rally support for his beleaguered friend. He wrote to Graham Greene, telling him that Fr Caraman was 'suffering one of those disasters which happen to Jesuits and which we outside the Society can't hope to understand'. He suggested that it would be an act of friendship if he looked up the priest as though unaware of his difficulties, although he realised that Greene had 'rather lost sympathy with him lately'. Waugh added that the reverse was not the case: Caraman's affection for Greene had not declined.[11] Somewhat reluctantly, the writer agreed to look up the Jesuit, admitting that it was several years since he had sought Fr Caraman's company. It is probable that the part Greene believed the priest had played in ending his affair with Catherine Walston continued to rankle, and may have been one reason why he and Caraman had not met for some time. But underlying this was possibly another, subtler, reason for the cooling of Greene's friendship. Towards the end of his novel *A Burnt-Out Case,* which was written at the time when *The Month's* editor was at the height of his popularity, and was published exactly two years before his disgrace, the book's principal character, Querry, tells Dr Colin that 'it needs a very strong vocation to withstand success. The popular priest and popular architect – their talents can be killed easily by disgust [of praise].' It is a matter of speculation whether Greene had Fr Caraman in mind when he penned these words. If he did so, the Jesuit seemed unaware of the allusion. Writing to thank the author for the signed advance copy of the novel, he told Greene:

> It is a superb book and even greater than *The Power & the Glory*, which for me, up to this week, has been your finest. I feel sure it will be recognised, almost universally, as one of the best novels of the 20th century. I know from Eddy [Sackville-West] who is reviewing it for *The Month,* that Raymond Mortimer has written a 'raving review' in the *Sunday Times.*[12]

Greene's sense of perception regarding the clash of interest between popularity and priestly vocation was not acknowledged.

When Greene and Caraman finally met for lunch, the occasion was a friendly one, which the writer said he had much enjoyed, although his final comment on Caraman's predicament proffered little comfort. 'I hope that the comedy of the situation will more than outweigh the shock!' he told the priest, adding, as an afterthought, 'you know that all your friends are behind you'.[13]

In the weeks and months following his public disgrace, Fr Caraman found little comedy in his situation: he put a brave face on events, fulfilling his commitments with as much dignity as he could muster, whilst facing an uncertain and unwelcoming future with trepidation.

An announcement in the Catholic Press in December 2000 informed readers that after one hundred and thirty-six years of continuous publication *The Month* would close the following April; observers realised that the magazine had been in slow decline for decades. Apart from brief periods of revival, notably under the editorships of Fr Peter Hebblethwaite, who later left the Society of Jesus, and then the layman Hugh Kay in the 1980s, the new *Month* never again attained the international reputation and acclaim it had enjoyed when Fr Caraman was in the chair. Long after his dismissal, he continued to think of *The Month* as 'his' magazine, and the loss of the editorial appointment was a bitter blow, not only to Philip Caraman's pride but also to his solicitude for the future of the publication.

Throughout his fifteen years as editor, Fr Caraman's commitment to *The Month* had been unstinting and wholehearted. Whilst Fr D'Arcy had provided the inspiration for the magazine's triumphant revival, it was Caraman's unremitting labour and flair that had guaranteed its success. He had witnessed the demise of *Horizon,* and learnt a lesson from its closure: *The Month's* success in replacing 'fluff' with 'Catholic thinking'[14] was not the only reason why its rival had shut down. The Bloomsbury publication had closed after a period of editorial negligence: the directors, Peter Watson and Cyril Connolly, had lost interest in the daily running of the magazine, seldom visited its office, and left the routine work to Sonia Brownell. *Horizon* was finally buried when she left shortly after her marriage to the dying George Orwell. Although Fr Caraman knew his Jesuit successor was unlikely to behave irresponsibly, he nevertheless feared for his magazine's future, reporting to Evelyn Waugh that 'at Easter [1963] I hand over *The Month* to Fr Moffat, a man a few years older than me: pleasant, fairly capable, but unimaginative ...'[15] The blow to Fr Caraman's pride was a personal defeat which tested his Jesuit vocation to the limit. Another renowned Catholic editor, Tom Burns, who ran *The Tablet* for a similar period of fifteen years, said that 'editing is a drug, a stimulant that few men relinquish willingly'.[16] Willing or not to relinquish his appointment Philip Caraman had no choice in the matter: he was bound by his vow of obedience to observe the decision of his Provincial.

To what extent the Jesuit hierarchy in Rome guided Fr Coventry's hand, or backed the Provincial's notice of dismissal, is not clear. Certainly articles published by Fr Caraman in *The Month* had upset his superiors in Rome on more than one occasion: the pieces written by Waugh and Greene[17] were not the only ones for which he had been reprimanded. Fr Bolland, who had been official censor of *The Month* for many years, continued to hand out criticism with gusto. On one occasion a letter written on behalf of the Father General accused *The Month* of 'a lack of candour' in connection with an article Philip Caraman had published on relations between Israel and the Catholic Church in the Holy Land; apparently the Jews and the friends of Israel had been outraged by 'false, distorted and exaggerated statements and comments' in the article, and were demanding that these be 'publicly repudiated' without delay. Fr Caraman was criticised for his unwillingness to apologise for the article, and failing to retract the allegations made in it with sufficient speed. Another black mark against Caraman was a tongue-in-cheek piece he published about a nun and mystic, Mary Bunn. The Jesuit Fr Roy Steuart had written about her in his memoirs, which were aired in *The Month,* the editor little realising not only that Bunn was still living in the Cistercian convent in Ghent, but that the lady was highly regarded by Pius XII. The wrath of the Carthusians (who had been appointed her mentors) descended on Farm Street in the form of three monks in voluminous robes, whom Caraman received in his small room, inviting them to be seated, saying 'that is if you can find somewhere to sit'.[18] The Carthusians' threat to report the matter to Rome was yet another incident contributing to Fr Caraman's reputation as a loose cannon. Small wonder that his superiors both in London and in Rome welcomed a pretext to silence him for ever.

Handing over the editor's appointment was a dismal task, not least because it entailed the loss of an excuse to circulate in the world of literature and the arts where he had been such a popular figure. As he wound up his affairs, Fr Caraman wrote to Evelyn Waugh, suggesting a visit to Combe Florey 'to thank you for all your kindness to me during my fifteen years as Editor', adding, 'since you have never accepted any remuneration for all you have done for *The Month*, I am arranging for a feast of caviar when I come down to see you . . .'[19] The extravagant gift was no doubt paid for out of the magazine's generous budget, representing one last fling before the key to its coffers were handed over to his successor. Fr Caraman always sought ways in which to reciprocate the generosity of his friends: for a priest under a vow of poverty this was never an easy matter. Whilst obedience to an unsympathetic superior was painful, the curtailment of the financial independence he had enjoyed as editor of *The Month* was equally hard to bear. In disgrace, Fr Caraman was still welcome at Combe Florey, but his visit in the depths of that bleak winter was discouraged by Waugh, who reported that 'the effect of the frost is far from over here. Only half the water system is in action . . . We are therefore ill-placed for hospitality . . .' Nevertheless he suggested that the priest might accept these discomforts as part of his 'Lenten privations'.[20]

Another penance suffered by Fr Caraman during that most galling of Lents was the knowledge that he was shortly to be evicted from his quarters in Farm Street. His room, aesthetically furnished and decorated, had become part of his *persona*, and uncertainty about where he would live disturbed him. Half-way through Lent the matter was settled. He was told that in Easter week, following a retreat at Stonyhurst, he was to remove himself to Claver House, a Jesuit hostel for foreign, mostly African, students in Pimlico, where the superior was Fr Paul Crane, a sympathetic man with a radical social apostolate, who did what he could to ease the plight of his brother Jesuit. Sending Laura Waugh this news, Fr Caraman told her:

> I have been allotted a minute bedroom in Pimlico (65 Belgrave Road) where there is not space for a bookshelf or a writing table. But I am glad to have it for it will keep me centrally housed or bedded in London . . . I shall probably do all my work in the reading room of the London Library . . . I look forward very much to seeing James [Waugh] at Stonyhurst in Holy Week.

He also told Laura that he had dined with Hattie, and that he was trying to arrange a job for her with his publisher, Longmans: he was concerned because she was still unemployed following her resignation two months earlier from the Farm Street office. He took this opportunity to express his gratitude to Laura Waugh, on whom the domestic burden of his frequent visits had fallen. He told his hostess:

My visits to Combe Florey have kept me sane and have taken me out of myself at times when I have become afraid of doing something desperate or despairing. I am intensely grateful to you and Evelyn. I can think of nowhere where I could have been more happy . . .[21]

The Provincial's decision to allow him to remain 'centrally housed' within easy reach of Mayfair, was probably governed more by expediency than by leniency. Although *The Month* had been taken away from Fr Caraman, it was impossible to find anyone else to take on the the Forty Martyrs: the hierarchy were still pressing for the necessary procedures for their canonisation to be completed as speedily as possible, and the Vice-Postulator had established a friendly and irreplaceable rapport with the diocesan bishops who were involved. His letters to the clergy involved in the Cause were no less warm in tone than those to his many personal friends, and his correspondents included the Abbot of Ampleforth, the Rector of the seminary at St Edmund's, Ware, and several bishops and their secretaries. In the three years since its inception the Cause had gained national momentum: diocesan activities included rallies, pilgrimages, and other high-profile events down to parish level, with the object of galvanising the support of the laity and promoting general awareness. The Society of Jesus had accepted responsibility for promoting the Cause, and could hardly remove the Vice-Postulator because of an internal dispute without losing face and publicising their private grievances.

Fr Caraman dealt with problems that arose in connection with the martyrs in a sensitive and discreet manner, and a newcomer would have found it difficult to acquire his intimate knowledge of the details involved. When the Abbot of Ampleforth made an

error omitting a key phrase in a submission concerning Alban
Roe, one of the Benedictine martyrs, Caraman politely blamed
himself, saying he should have noticed the error, and that he had
been able to rectify the matter without troubling the Abbot
further. Other problems were constantly arising. Shortly after Fr
Caraman was banished to Claver House, the Bishop of Clifton,
Joseph Rudderham, wrote to him saying:

> I tell you in confidence that the bishops gave their careful atten-
> tion to [your report] regarding possible opposition to the
> furtherance of the Cause, and they studied the memorandum on
> this matter which has been prepared by Fr Molinari. They agreed
> that His Grace, the Archbishop of Birmingham, when in Rome,
> should at his discretion express to Cardinal Bea the strong view
> of the Hierarchy that work for the Canonisation should proceed
> inasmuch as the bishops did not consider that it would interfere
> with the Ecumenical Movement.[22]

Fr Caraman's forecast of the way in which the upsurge in
ecumenism would affect the process of canonisation was perceptive, and further evidence of the reason why the Jesuit
Provincial found it impossible to replace him as Vice-Postulator
of the Cause.

The move to Pimlico made Fr Caraman's working conditions
considerably more difficult: indispensable but marginalised, his
presence in the Farm Street office was barely tolerated. In the
months following his confrontation with the Provincial, Philip
Caraman was subject to abrupt mood-swings, at times elated and
full of optimism for the future, at others in the grip of despair.
Following Fr Cyril Martindale's death at Petworth, he told
Laura Waugh that 'everything is working out well for me ... it
may be possible for me to escape to Australia (where he
[Martindale] had many friends and much influence) next winter,
to write his life there, and in the boat'.[23] His appointment as
Martindale's official biographer had been at the express wish of
the distinguished Jesuit, who had entrusted his personal papers
to Fr Caraman. This was another appointment which Fr
Coventry could not repudiate, although he vetoed Philip
Caraman's escape to Australia. It was in another country, and

only after a delay of nearly three years, that the book was eventually started.

Another bright spot resulted from an enjoyable luncheon at Brown's with the publisher John Guest, who told Caraman – in great confidence – that Edith Sitwell and Evelyn Waugh had been made Companions of Literature. After the meal, Fr Caraman immediately wrote to Waugh with the news, saying: 'It made me very happy. I had been asked for my recommendations, and without hesitating for half-a-second I had given the names of you, Edith and Graham: it was really a wonderful reassurance of my judgement to find that you and Edith were 'tops': and without any near rivals'.[24] In his excitement, Philip's hand-writing degenerated from its customary clarity into the untidy scrawl that characterised several of his letters about this time. In his state of euphoria he seemed unaware that Waugh already knew of the Companionship, having been offered it by the President of the Royal Society of Literature a couple of weeks earlier, and that the writer was decidedly underwhelmed by the prospective honour. Although Fr Caraman was a member of the Royal Society, it is likely that his was only one among many recommendations that had been sought, and that his jubilation at the success of his nominees was a natural reaction to bolster his own badly dented self-confidence. The award ceremony at the Skinners' Hall on 25 June provided a happy interlude in that otherwise black year. Dame Edith and Sir Osbert were too ill to attend, although Sacheverell Sitwell stood in for his sister, and during the banquet Caraman, along with Laura Waugh, Ann Fleming and Meg, was treated to a witty speech of acceptance from Evelyn.

Following this family gathering, Caraman paid a brief visit to Combe Florey, and he was still in good spirits when he went about the martyrs' business to stay at Archbishop's House in Cardiff, where the foibles of his fellow-guests caused him some amusement. But following another confrontation with Fr Coventry in August he was again despondent. After a summer spent either in London or travelling on work for the Cause, Fr Caraman felt in need of a holiday: when the Provincial refused to let him go, he broke down. Worn out both mentally and physically, he called on the FitzHerberts in Westbourne Terrace to find Meg, who was pregnant, in a highly emotional state, which was aggravated further by her visitor's neurosis. He had been seeing Meg regularly since she left Farm Street, but on this occasion, in trying to soothe her and crying out for sympathy himself, he only made matters worse for both of them. In a 'state', as she called it, Meg told her father that she felt she could no longer cope with Fr Caraman's visits. She wrote:

> The thing is he's gone all soft and sloppy again ... I wouldn't mind if he was going away but now he'll be in London the whole summer and I can't avoid seeing him because I'm supposed to work on this book with him ... The trouble is it's just when he's like this it would be wicked to do anything unkind – I feel I'm his only wall to lean against and if I turned on him he'd collapse.
>
> The other trouble is he still doesn't realise he had a crush on me and his whole life at the moment is his belief in his innocence and the malice of his enemies and I don't know what would happen if he stopped believing it.

A distraught Meg considered Fr Caraman's behaviour 'unedifying' and wondered if it would be a good idea if Fr D'Arcy, who had returned from America, had a word with him 'as a priest to a priest'.[25]

Later Meg regretted her outburst about Fr Caraman's erratic behaviour, and told Waugh that she felt 'rather mean about the whole thing'. She admitted that she had got herself into a 'state' because she was 'generally low', and that when she had seen the priest again a couple of weeks later 'he was much better'. In an upbeat letter dealing mostly with family affairs, she remarked that she spent a lot of time house-hunting, and that 'there are a surprising number of pretty houses in Notting Hill, Islington and Kentish Town and Camden Town under £8,000'.[26]

Throughout this difficult period, Fr Caraman had been trying to complete his biography of Henry Garnet. Amidst the turmoil of his disgrace and the exigencies of the Cause, and with impossible working conditions, he was on the verge of abandoning the project on more than one occasion. Meg, who had worked as his research assistant, knew that Fr Caraman prized this book above all his other commitments, and continually urged him not to give up. He admitted it was only her 'constant but kindly taunts' that kept him going because 'there were always excuses at hand to do other things, even to write other books'.[27] With Meg's encouragement and the co-operation of friends, he managed to overcome these difficulties, and made a sustained effort to finish the book, and pass his manuscript and a revised typescript over to Longmans.

As autumn approached, Henry Garnet's biography was still a year away from publication, but Fr Caraman was encouraged by the appearance of his biography of St Angela towards the end of September. Longmans brought out a well-produced and designed book, with a selection of excellent illustrations and photographs collected and shot by Fr Anthony Powell. *The Life of Angela Merici Foundress of the Ursulines (1474–1540)*[28] is a lucidly written account of the saint's life which relies heavily on secondary sources. In the years since this book was written, researchers have discovered new documentation; conscious of the fact that primary material had not been fully investigated, Fr Caraman admits that although his book 'leaves out no known fact about Angela herself' he could not claim to have written the definitive biography. Supported by the author's travels, the freshness of the book lies principally in its topographical character. Caraman clearly admired his subject, and is at pains to emphasise her role as 'the greatest of all the peacemakers of her time', who was 'never known to have failed when she attempted to reconcile warring individuals'. He also valued Angela's 'power of sympathy', which the author considered 'lay in her very simplicity. She attributed nothing to herself.'[29] The author took the opportunity to air his personal views on mystics, remarking that although Angela had many authentic mystical experiences, she kept them to herself and to her director. She was said to have considered 'false mystics in greater danger of perdition than even infidels'.[30] From a reader's point of view, the book's lack of anecdotal detail concerning the saint's charitable works is regrettable: but lack of primary material would account for this omission.

A leitmotif throughout Fr Caraman's text is the parallel he

draws between the career of the foundress of the Ursulines and that of St Ignatius and the Society of Jesus. Writing of Angela's stay in Venice, he notes:

> Once again, her career ran parallel with that of Ignatius Loyola, who would have been known to many of her more important callers in Venice, and whose mission at this period sent him to the same cities as Angela, set on the same intention of finding the exact purpose which God had for him and his companions.[31]

Caraman concluded that the similarity between the two saints was very close and that 'their spirit is the same'. Devoting the latter part of the book to a detailed examination of the *Rule* set out by Angela for her Company, he draws attention to sections that 'reproduce exactly what is known of the practice of St Ignatius at Rome during the years when these Constitutions of Angela's Company were still being written'. In his emphasis on parallels in the lives of these two great saints, Fr Caraman wrote a testimony to his own unflagging devotion to the Society to which he had pledged his life. Despite the difficulties he was experiencing at the time the book was written, his loyalty to the Jesuits was never in question.

When Evelyn Waugh acknowledged his courtesy copy of *St Angela*, he told Fr Caraman that 'you are very fortunate in having a task which took you to so many places. Martindale, I fear, will lead you to fewer aesthetic treats.'[32] Treats were rare in his dreary bed-sit in Pimlico, but Philip glimpsed an avenue of escape, low in aesthetic merit perhaps, but offering the possibility of freedom and adventure. As his *annus horribilis* drew to a close, the future was beginning to look more encouraging, and prospects for writing his biography of Fr Martindale in more auspicious circumstances were distinctly brighter.

❧

On a visit to Caldey Island in May 1957, Fr Caraman had been present at the ordination of John Willem Nicolaysen Gran, the first Norwegian to become a Cistercian. The ceremony in the monastery of Our Lady and St Samson off the Welsh coast marked an important milestone in the life of Norwegian Catholicism: shortly after Philip's dismissal from Farm Street, John Gran was appointed Assistant Bishop of Oslo, the first Norwegian to be consecrated bishop since the Reformation. Writing with this news, the forty-three year old bishop invited Fr Caraman to his consecration ceremony in Oslo in March 1963.

In the years between John Gran's ordination and his appointment as bishop, Fr Caraman's interest in Norwegian Catholicism had been awakened. Above all he was intrigued by the position of the Society of Jesus in this Lutheran country, from which – until the year before John Gran's ordination – all Jesuits had been banned. Under Article One of the 1814 Norwegian Constitution, Jesuits, monks and Jews were excluded from the kingdom, whose royal allegiance was a subject of dispute between Sweden and Denmark at the time. Gradually a more liberal view of non-Lutherans prevailed: firstly, in 1851, Jews were admitted, then in 1897 the monastic orders, and finally in 1956 the Jesuits were allowed to return. The editor of *The Month* perceived parallels with the persecution of Jesuits and the position of the Catholic minority in England following the Reformation. In the summer of 1958 Fr Caraman toured Scandinavia, meeting a number of prominent Norwegian intellectuals and artists, both Catholic and non-Catholic, and in 1959 he devoted an issue of his magazine to the Church in Norway. The articles were written by leading Norwegian scholars, and included a piece by Hallvard Rieber-Mohn, a Dominican attached to the Priory in Oslo since 1953, who made a plea that the 'Nordic mind, this lost jewel' should be led back to unity with the Church of which it was a part: another Dominican, Finn D. Thorn contributed a piece entitled 'Does Hell Exist', which dealt with a doctrinal controversy in the Church in Norway. John Gran sent in an article on the 'English Influence on Norwegian Monasticism', and an essay on 'The Reformation in Norway' by Oskar Garstein, a leading historian, was also included. No review of the Church in Norway would be complete without a piece about the internationally acclaimed author, Sigrid Undset, who converted to Catholicism in 1924 in the middle period of her literary career, and this was written by A. H. Winsnes.[33]

Recognition on this scale in an internationally important publication was generally welcomed by Norwegian Catholics, and won Philip Caraman a number of friends in the small Catholic circle in Oslo. Following his visit to the country in 1958, Philip also struck up a warm friendship with two married sisters, both artists, Wenche Koren and Lita Anker, who hovered on the periphery of this circle, and visited him in London. Later, in 1964, news came of John Gran's promotion and appointment as Bishop of Oslo. As head of the church in Norway he had no hesitation in inviting Fr Caraman to work in his diocese, and as Fr John Coventry's term of office drew to a close there was every prospect that the invitation would be favourably received by the Jesuits. The new Provincial, Fr Terence Corrigan, who took up his appointment in October 1964, was sympathetic; Fr Caraman would establish a Jesuit presence in a missionary field which had been closed to the Society since the Reformation. Meanwhile, Philip had exchanged his shoe-box in Pimlico for a room in Great Peter Street, and wanted to leave as soon as possible for Oslo after a short holiday in the Mediterranean to armour himself, as Evelyn Waugh phrased it, 'against the regions of the Arctic'.[34]

Fr Caraman's wish for an early end to his wanderings in the wilderness beyond Mayfair was not fulfilled as speedily as he hoped. The process for the Cause for the Forty Martyrs dragged on, and the biography of Henry Garnet was not finally published until the end of the year. The book represented a landmark piece of historical writing, and Caraman's perseverance was completely justified. It was a pioneering biography of the priest who was Superior of the Jesuits in England during the reign of Queen Elizabeth I and the early years of the reign of King James I. Fr Caraman had spent more than fourteen years researching it; in the process he transcribed and translated from the Latin more than a hundred and fifty letters or fragments of letters written by his subject, in addition to the letters sent to him. Some of Garnet's letters were between five and ten thousand words in length; a number of these had been used in previous historical studies, but the most revealing had been discovered by Philip in archives in Rome in 1952, when he had been working on other books connected to the Jesuit mission in penal England. Fr Caraman's translation and editing of *John Gerard, The Autobiography of an Elizabethan*, and his second book on the Jesuit, William Weston, contained numerous references to Henry Garnet, who was their heroes' contemporary. John Gerard and Garnet had been good friends, and companions in several hair-raising episodes of near-capture by spies and pursuivants.

Garnet's story, however, differs from those of Gerard and Weston in several important respects. As Superior, albeit in hiding from the authorities, his was the responsibility not only for the welfare of other Jesuits working in England at the time, but for important matters of policy concerning the Catholics in their care, and their loyalty to the monarch and the civil authorities in a hostile environment. During the twenty years he worked in England, there were one or two interludes of relative calm, and Caraman notes that within Garnet's 'own lifetime there was formed the nucleus of a Jesuit province which, in the esteem of the Church, was to have a record matching even the Provinces of the Indies and Paraguay'.[35] The success of the Society's mission incurred the wrath of powerful enemies, who were resolved to rid themselves and the country of the Jesuits for ever. The historical importance of Fr Caraman's book lies in its analysis of the way in which the government under Sir Robert Cecil was determined to involve Garnet personally, as Jesuit Superior, in a plot against the Crown. 'If anything is determined against me individually it will come entirely from the fury and hatred that the heretics have against the Church ...', Garnet predicted with uncanny premonition.[36]

Enter the Gunpowder Plot. This lurid episode in English history originated in Catholic hopes that the accession to the throne of James I, son of the Catholic Mary Queen of Scots, might usher in a period of increased tolerance for Catholics after the intense persecution they had suffered under Elizabeth I. In Scotland James had seemed relatively well disposed to

Catholics, and after his arrival in London the new king tried to steer a middle course between mild persecution and limited freedom. In alarm Cecil, who feared a Catholic revival, protested that priests were openly saying Mass again: before long his influence on the King prevailed, the hopes of the monarch's Catholic subjects were dashed, and many of their leading laymen were prepared to revolt.

The origins of the Plot lay in the disillusionment of a coterie of well-born Catholics who had expected better treatment from the new king; Henry Garnet was involved in their stratagems, but not in the role in which he has been cast by Protestant history. Fearing that the more hot-headed aristocrats might attempt some act of violence which would reflect badly on the majority of peace-loving Catholics who were loyal to the Crown, Garnet wrote in alarm to Claudio Aquaviva in Rome. He sent repeated requests to the Jesuit General imploring him to obtain severe papal censures, even excommunication, of all Catholics who entered into any conspiracy or rising against the State. With the knowledge that he had the backing of Rome in his condemnation of violence, Garnet sought out Robert Catesby, whom he considered one of the most bellicose of putative Catholic plotters, and 'cautioned him most severely against rushing headlong into mischief. Catesby denied that he intended any plot.' Although he managed to extract a promise from Catesby that no action would be taken for the present, Garnet was still suspicious, and the Jesuit's worst fears were confirmed when another priest, Fr Tesimond, revealed to him in the secrecy of the confessional that Catesby did indeed have a plot in hand.[37]

In the sacred seal of sacramental confession, lay Garnet's dilemma over the Gunpowder Plot. Fr Caraman goes to great lengths to emphasise this point in his study of the Jesuit's alleged involvement: wishing to avert certain catastrophe for English Catholics, Garnet could not reveal anything he had heard in confession or forewarn the authorities of what he knew. Thereby was he implicated in the eyes of his accusers. Following Guy Fawkes's bungled attempt to blow up King and Parliament on 5 November 1605, Garnet became the most wanted man in England: he sought refuge at Hinlip, a large house near Worcester, and despite a prolonged and thorough search managed to escape detection for some weeks. Eventually, on 27 January 1606, after spending eight days in unbearable conditions in a cramped hiding-hole in Hinlip, Garnet and his companion, Fr Oldcorne, were captured. Garnet's trial and guilt centred on his knowledge of the Plot, which it was alleged had been planned at his instigation. He put up a spirited defence. When one of his accusers, Nottingham, making a theoretical case, asked the Jesuit if a man should tell him in confession that he intended to stab the King, was the priest not bound to reveal this knowledge, Garnet replied, 'My Lord, unless I could know it by some other means, I might not'.[38] Inevitably Garnet was found guilty of treason for not revealing the Powder Plot and sentenced to be hanged, drawn and quartered. His bloody execution was carried out in St Paul's Churchyard on 3 May, and he was generally considered to have suffered a martyr's death by many people in the crowd of witnesses. The Cause for Garnet's canonisation was begun very quickly by his friends in Rome, for he was considered 'an example to the world of a priest's fidelity to the secrets confided in the sacrament [of Confession] that was the true cause of his execution'.[39]

Whilst the public continues to follow the ancient dictum to 'Remember, remember the Fifth of November', singeing fingers and disturbing neighbours with pyrotechnics in the process, few people now realise the origins of the tradition, and even fewer have any knowledge of the intricate history of the Powder Plot. Writing in 'circumstances that demanded much patience and endurance',[40] Fr Caraman made an important contribution to a controversial event, and his biography provided later historians with new material. The book received a glowing notice in the *Times Literary Supplement*, whose reviewer remarked that:

If the sufferings of Catholics in the England of Elizabeth I are not fully appreciated today the fault can hardly be laid at Fr Caraman's door. For many years he has carried on concentrated researches which by nature of the evidence, combined with his skill in presentation, he has made known in some highly success-ful books. In this, the latest of them, he is again busy with the

Elizabethan religious underworld he knows so well: a cloak-and-dagger world, where dedicated Jesuits carried on their work of ministering to the spiritual needs of the faithful in English country houses, hiding behind sliding panels in secret chambers while spies ... hunted them down in the service of a government scared by this stealthy invasion from Rome ... Through these scenes of insecurity, tragedy and death the figure of Fr Caraman's hero moves quietly towards what he must have known would ultimately be for him a martyr's death ... No one before Fr Caraman has thought of giving him the full-scale biography he deserved ... [This book is] an important contribution for the student of religious controversy, while for the layman the exciting incidents Fr Caraman marshals with such skill and his easy flowing narrative give his book the quality of a first rate adventure story.[41]

Henry Garnet was dedicated to Margaret FitzHerbert; Paddy Barry, with whom Philip was working on the Cause for the Forty Martyrs, also assisted him, delving into the records of London libraries on his behalf. The author acknowledged the help and hospitality of a number of friends in whose houses he was able to work 'while I was both their elusive chaplain and eremitical guest', and made particular mention of 'Mr and Mrs Evelyn Waugh who, for days on end, many times suffered my moods and depressions as I strove to continue the book when it was in danger of dying ...'[42]

Meanwhile another old friend of Evelyn and Philip was approaching her end. In the spring of 1963, whilst away on a cruise with her nurse, Sister Farquhar, and her secretary Elizabeth Salter, Dame Edith Sitwell had suffered a severe haemorrhage, and was flown home from a hospital in Bermuda. On her return Fr Caraman, who was experiencing his own personal crisis, immediately visited her and gave her the Sacrament of the Anointing of the Sick, normally administered to Catholics in danger of death from sickness or old age. Dame Edith had been in poor health for some time, frequently writing to her confessor with reports of accidents which had befallen her: her biographer attributes these recurrent disasters to the fact that she was drinking heavily, although she never showed it in any obvious way.[43] Philip surely knew about her weakness; nevertheless he continued to feel responsible for her spiritual welfare and called on her whenever he could.

Dame Edith survived, and in the spring of 1964 moved to a cottage in Keats Grove in Hampstead, which she named Bryher House. Here Fr Caraman called regularly, taking Holy Communion to her about once a month. Over the years, Edith had become one of Philip's most sympathetic friends, and in his time of suffering she listened attentively, her cats beside her, as he related his woes. Her nephew, Francis Sitwell, tells the story of one visit when, carried away by the tale of his own misfortunes, Philip absent-mindedly consumed a plateful of cats' biscuits, which he thought were meant to accompany the drinks they were having. Mr Sitwell wondered if Philip was hungry.[44] Maybe he was – being dependent on the frugal fare of Claver House at the time. When he could forget his own problems, Fr Caraman shared Edith's mischievous sense of humour, and would no doubt have been amused to hear of the reply his spiritual daughter had sent to one of the many letters she received from the public. One 'very nice new lunatic' wrote to Sitwell from Dublin, telling her that:

All R.C. priests have lots of illegitimate children – usually by their 15-year-old nieces. I am replying that I know they have. My own dear confessor often brings round his happy little brood of ten to have tea with me. Four are by his own niece, but he is sadly forgetful about who are the mothers of the rest. There were eleven, but unfortunately he ate one in a fit of absent-mindedness, one Friday . . .[45]

Fr Caraman was abroad when Dame Edith died on 9 December 1964: her funeral Mass was at the Jesuit church in Farm Street. Although she had not attended Mass regularly for several years, and rumours concerning her commitment to Catholicism had surfaced from time to time since her conversion, her confessor was always at pains to deny that she had any regrets or had turned her back on the Church. He told Evelyn Waugh that he was 'absolutely certain that rumours of this kind are utterly and wholly without the slightest foundation'.[46]

Among the papers Fr Caraman passed to the library of Boston College he left a signed portrait of Dame Edith by Cecil Beaton, and a handwritten note, dated 16 August 1985, confirming that the report that Sitwell had given up her Catholic faith, which had found its way into some books about her had 'no basis whatever'. He recorded that he had taken Holy Communion to her regularly when she lay bedridden in her Hampstead flat, and that she had received the last Sacraments from Fr Martin D'Arcy. On hearing the news of her death, he wrote to Sitwell's brother, Sir Osbert, who replied from Castello di Montegufoni:

> Your most kind and sympathetic letter reached me here two days ago and has greatly comforted me. I must say I find her loss appalling, and I doubt whether I shall ever get used to it. Although I am not a Catholic I know how much your visits must have meant to Edith. I thought her cottage was very pretty though she seemed rather far away up there: her bedroom seemed to exist in space only. The last time I saw her she seemed fairly well and cheerful. As you know I too was abroad at the time of her death – perhaps this was just as well, as I am sure that I could not have stood the strain had I been in England... I am very grateful for what you have done for her.[47]

Sir Osbert lived on, bound to his wheelchair, until 1969, and Fr Caraman remained in contact with him and other members of the Sitwell family for several more years. With Dame Edith's death and his exile from Mayfair, a high-profile phase in Philip Caraman's life was drawing to a close, but behind the scenes he retained the friendship and respect of Cardinal Heenan, with whom he had been associated through his work on the martyrs' Cause. The procedures for the canonisation of the Blessed Forty were nearing completion, and the remaining work had been passed over to Fr Clement Tigar, a Jesuit who had stood for the Archdiocese of Westminster on the panel of representatives, and whose efforts to authenticate medical cures had been thorough and painstaking. Philip Caraman's move to Norway received the moral support of his father-in-Christ, Martin D'Arcy, who wrote from the Center for Advanced Studies at the Wesleyan University in Connecticut where he was lecturing during the spring semester of 1965. Wishing Fr Philip 'a happy Easter', and mindful that finance for his transfer to Norway could pose a problem, Fr D'Arcy said:

> Tell [the Provincial] if you like that I have received some personal money gifts which normally I would hand in, but ... the donors ... would gladly have the money used for your purposes. I do hope Cardinal Heenan is not over-confident in his hopes for the Martyrs.
>
> I confess I contemplate my Indian Summer of a life with melancholy ... So much in the world is going just contrary to what I hoped. The England I have known is no more and the English Province is in the doldrums. Oxford and Campion Hall again are disappointing ... In my last letter ... I said that I had hoped you might keep an eye on my things when I die. There are a number of treasures, there are lots of books with dedications in them – some letters, diaries, parts of MSS. I have lost a good lot when [another priest] was given my room [at Farm Street] ... Anything might happen again, especially with Superiors who are antipathetic and quite indifferent. The old learn that all can be lost except the love of God.[48]

Evelyn Waugh was also becoming increasingly despondent, and Fr Caraman, preparing to move abroad, seems to have grown uncharacteristically neglectful of his friend. Waugh was puzzled when the Jesuit failed to acknowledge a copy of his new book *Basil Seal Rides Again or The Rake's Regress* which he had sent in the autumn of 1964, and in the summer of 1965 he complained to Meg that he had written to Philip suggesting a farewell meeting and had not received a reply. He told his daughter that her sister, Hattie, was collecting subscriptions for a joint present with Auberon, and that 'your mother will subscribe to this. I should prefer to give him something on my own.' He asked if Meg could suggest anything suitable within his means, because '[Fr Caraman] has been so very munificent to me'.[49] At the end of July he contacted Philip again, saying that Harriet had told him that the priest's date of departure was 'settled and soon', adding:

It would be a great pleasure to see you before you go, I'm sure you have much to do. Can you get away for a night here, or will it be more convenient if Laura and I come up to London for the day? We shall quite understand if you're too busy to see us, but it would be sad if after all these years and all you have done for us we should part without further meeting.

Waugh commented in a postscript that he was 'astounded at the closure of Beaumont', and was very glad that he had not sent his son Septimus there, as he had considered doing.[50]

A momentous chapter in Fr Caraman's life was drawing to a close, but the painful events surrounding his dismissal from Farm Street continued to haunt his spirit, and cast a shadow over his reputation for many years to come. Over thirty years later Lord Longford remarked, at mention of Philip's name, that 'there was some trouble, wasn't there?', and Francis Sitwell similarly remembered his dismissal, although neither could recall the circumstances.[51] With the wisdom of hindsight, Caraman felt that his training in the Jesuit novitiate had left him unprepared to cope with the situation. Three years after the débâcle he wrote, 'no-one directed the novices to meet the real difficulties they would encounter – jealousies, the possibility of idleness, disillusionment'.[52] Idleness played no part in his life at that time, but he dreaded the *longueurs* of unemployment, as would any man accustomed to challenging work might fear the empty hours and uncertainty of redundancy. Fr Caraman had suffered bitter disillusionment, and experienced the effects of jealousy, but he set out for Norway with the good wishes and prayers of many loyal friends and with every intention of starting a new life in surroundings far removed from Mayfair.

Notes

1 Letter, Margaret FitzHerbert to Evelyn Waugh, 9 January 1963, British Library (hereafter BL).
2 Ibid. 16 January 1963 (misdated 16 April).

3 Letter, Philip Caraman to Evelyn Waugh, 16 January 1963 (BL).
4 H. J. A. Sire, *Father Martin D'Arcy. Philosopher of Divine Love*, p. 180.
5 *Letters & Notices*, vol. 94. Autumn 1998, no. 414, pp. 833 and 834. Jesuit Archives (hereafter JA).
6 H. J. A. Sire. p. 156.
7 *Letters & Notices*, vol. 94. Autumn 1998, no. 414, p. 822 (JA).
8 Artemis Cooper, *The Letters of Evelyn Waugh and Diana Cooper*, p. 295.
9 Letter, Evelyn Waugh to Philip Caraman, 17 January 1963, Philip Caraman Private Papers (hereafter PCPP).
10 Letter, Fr Martin D'Arcy to Evelyn Waugh, 21 January 1963 (BL).
11 Based on Martin Stannard, *Evelyn Waugh: No Abiding City 1939-1966,* p. 469.
12 Letter, Philip Caraman to Graham Greene, 13 January 1961, Boston College (hereafter BC).
13 Letter, Graham Greene to Philip Caraman, 15 March 1963 (BC).
14 'I want to produce ... an *Horizon* with Catholic thinking in place of the fluff.' Letter, Philip Caraman to Evelyn Waugh, 12 October 1948 (BL).
15 Letter, Philip Caraman to Evelyn Waugh, 22 February 1963 (BL).
16 Tom Burns, *The Use of Memory*, pp. 150, 151.
17 See Chapter Three above, 'Reveille For *The Month*'.
18 Based on interview with John Skinner, author of *Sounding the Silence* (Gracewing 2004).
19 Letter, Philip Caraman to Evelyn Waugh, 22 February 1963 (BL).
20 Letter, Evelyn Waugh to Philip Caraman, 23 February 1963 (BL).
21 Letter, Philip Caraman to Laura Waugh, 18 March 1963 (BL).
22 Letter, Bishop Joseph Rudderham to Fr Philip Caraman SJ, May 1963 (JA).
23 Letter, Philip Caraman to Laura Waugh, 18 March 1963 (BL).
24 Letter, Philip Caraman to Evelyn Waugh, 2 April 1963 (BL).
25 Letter, Margaret Waugh to Evelyn Waugh, 16 August 1963 (BL).
26 Ibid. 9 September 1963.
27 Philip Caraman, *Henry Garnet 1555-1606 and the Gunpowder Plot* (Longmans, Green and Co., 1964). Preface xiv.
28 Published 1963.
29 Philip Caraman, *St Angela Merici*, p. 85.
30 Ibid. p. 141.
31 Ibid. p. 65.
32 Letter, Evelyn Waugh to Philip Caraman, 25 September 1963 (BC).

33 *The Month*, February 1959, vol. 21. no.2.
34 Letter, Evelyn Waugh to Philip Caraman, 14 November 1964 (BC).
35 Philip Caraman. *Henry Garnet 1555–1606 and the Gunpowder Plot* (Longmans, 1964), p. 136.
35 Ibid. p. 312.
37 Ibid. p. 322.
38 Ibid. p.415.
39 Ibid. p. 440.
40 Ibid. Preface xv.
41 *Times Literary Supplement*, 24 December 1964, issue 3,278, p. 1167.
42 *Henry Garnet*, Preface xiv.
43 Victoria Glendinning, *Edith Sitwell – A Unicorn Among Lions*, p. 324.
44 Francis Sitwell in conversation with author. This anecdote is also related by Victoria Glendinning, p. 354.
45 Undated letter, Edith Sitwell to Maurice Bowra, *Edith Sitwell – Selected Letters*, edited by John Lehmann and Derek Parker, (Macmillan, 1970), no. 205.
46 Letter, Philip Caraman to Evelyn Waugh, 9 January 1956 (BL).
47 Letter, Osbert Sitwell to Philip Caraman, 19 January 1965 (BC). © Frank Magro 2004.
48 Letter, Fr Martin D'Arcy to Philip Caraman, 26 April 1965 (BC).
49 *The Letters of Evelyn Waugh*, edited by Mark Amory, (Weidenfeld and Nicolson, 1980).
50 Letter, Evelyn Waugh to Philip Caraman, 29 July 1965 (BC).
51 Conversations with author.
52 Philip Caraman, *C.C. Martindale. A Biography* (Longmans, 1967), p. 73.

Part Three
A Nordic Disease
1966–1982

Chapter Seven

'An Awful Place'

The ferry crossing from Newcastle to Kristiansand and Oslo was a journey Fr Caraman would make many times, but the North Sea passage was in essence more than just a short excursion from one European state to another. The sea-voyage, more often than not rough even in summer, was a journey into a little-known country very different in atmosphere and culture from others on the same continent. Whereas the economic and trau-matic effects of the Second World War had largely receded in other Western European nations by the mid-1960s, Norwegians could not forget the brutal treatment they had suffered under Nazi occupation, and, with its vast oil reserves not yet exploited, the country was still relatively poor and unmaterial-istic compared to others with which Philip Caraman was familiar. In Norway the majority of families did not own a car, restaurant dining and wining was a luxury, and plain fare was the staple diet of most people. Even in the capital city life was austere in comparison to that in London, and entertainment was far simpler than much of the hospitality Fr Caraman had enjoyed during his heyday as editor of *The Month*.

As Philip crossed the North Sea in one of Fred Olsen's ferries, a sense of anticipation and adventure motivated him to keep a diary which he intended to write up daily, but as events and engagements crowded in on him after his arrival the entries became increasingly intermittent.[1] From the outset he was intrigued by Norway's history, culture and language, and the idiosyncratic social conventions of its people: all were unlike anything he had encountered on his previous travels. In the spirit of a responsible missionary, Fr Caraman's observations were inspired by his intention to participate as fully and as speedily as possible in local life. He got off to a good start: fellow priests in the diocesan house which was to become his home welcomed him with a party on the evening of his arrival on 6 September, and from his base in Akersveien, conveniently located near the Catholic Cathedral and within easy walking distance of the centre of Oslo, he sallied forth to accept a flood of invitations even before his crates were unpacked.

The only other English-speaking Catholic priest in Oslo at that time was a New Yorker of Norwegian extraction: twenty-one years younger than Philip and Jesuit-educated, Fr Olaf Waring had arrived in Oslo some two years earlier, full of missionary zeal. Despite the difference in their ages, the two priests quickly established a strong rapport, which over the years developed into a close friendship. Having recently completed his own Norwegian studies at Oslo University, Fr Waring was the ideal interpreter for Philip, who was at once fascinated by the nuances and vagaries of the Norwegian language. At dinner with Bishop John Gran two evenings after his arrival, Fr Caraman was absorbed by a conversation – in Norwegian – about different elements in the language and a controversial movement to preserve its purity. A week later he was intrigued to learn that in a remote mountain valley 'three words are used for "2" people: according whether [sic] they are 2 men, 2 women, man and woman.' Within ten days of his arrival, Caraman was devoting most of his afternoons and evenings to studying Norwegian and comparing it to other Scandinavian languages: he noted that Swedish was a more controlled language with a larger vocabulary and capable of more nuances than Norwegian. He considered this was possibly 'because of the nature of the country, only forests (not mountain ranges) divide the people'. He noted, with some foresight, that 'while quarrels take place in Norway on language, English is entering by [the] back door'. Fr Caraman's mastery of the language had not progressed sufficiently to rescue him from an embarrassing situation when he was left to hold the fort at Akersveien two months after his arrival: he records that he was faced with taking a service of Rosary and Benediction when all the other priests in the house had gone away to attend a funeral. 'All went well', he says, 'until I started the *Salve Regina* in Norwegian at the end: I hadn't looked at even the first words thinking the congregation would join in: no response and had to go through unprepared in dim light: near disaster: got into deeper waters.' In due time Caraman became reasonably fluent in the language, although he was never completely at home with the pronunciation. Fr Waring recounts that this led to many hilarious incidents, adding that he thought Philip 'just could not dismiss the notion that the sounds were somehow vulgar'.[2] It is more likely that the Jesuit's faulty pronunciation was a consequence of his lack of a musical ear.

Fr Caraman's Norwegian studies embraced a wide spectrum: the finer points of the country's history, and of its religious and social culture, were all matters of intense speculation, and frequently the source of humorous comment. The peculiarities of local gastronomy were of more than objective interest. During his Mayfair years Philip Caraman had enjoyed the hospitality of some of England's most discriminating bon viveurs, and although not all matched the standards of haute cuisine set by Eddy Sackville-West at Cooleville, the priest had acquired a taste for good food and fine wine. Philip's gastronomic expectations were sadly disappointed in Norway, although dining out with new friends and acquaintances provided some relief from the dull fare served up in the Akersveien house. Food was always a subject for comment: following an out of town excursion to a restaurant in Frognerseteren with Fr Waring, he remarked that they had lunched on reindeer: a dinner at the home of the ecclesiastical historian Oskar Garstein was notable for the 'best (home made) bread in Norway'. A conversation with one of Norway's numerous, dedicated, fishermen inspired a long diary entry on the sacred ritual of cod consumption:

the fish is to be eaten with akvavit chased by beer or with *red* [sic] wine: cod in Oslo is 'alive' 24 hours after it is dead: in seaports (also in Oslo) cod-eating groups or societies have President (entitled to 3 glasses of akvavit along with head of cod) ... cod always boiled: and with boiled potatoes and butter sauce:

to be brought to point of boil three times: but not left to boil at any stage. Entrails served on dish: cut up tongue, roe etc.

The protocol of dining-out intrigued Fr Caraman. In a country with probably the severest drink-driving laws in the world, he noted that taxis were all occupied between seven and eight in the evening and from eleven-thirty onwards in taking people to and from parties. It is considered 'something of an insult to the host to drive up in a private car', he wrote, because this suggested that the 'guest is not prepared for [a] good evening'. At one very formal dinner attended by Philip the guest of honour was General Sir Robert Bray, the Commander-in-Chief of the NATO headquarters at Kolsas on the outskirts of Oslo. The priest commented firstly on the long, formal speech of 'welcome to the table' made by their Norwegian host before the meal, and the General's equally long 'takk for maten' oration at the end. Philip noted that an explanation for the expression 'one over the eight' probably lies in the Norwegian custom of raising a glass and toasting each guest round the table if more than six are present. 'Eight individual drinks – too much', he declared.

The articles on Catholicism in Norway published in *The Month* in February 1959 were later reissued as a symposium in booklet form: through contacts provided by contributors to his magazine, Fr Caraman quickly established good connections with members of the History Faculty of the University of Oslo. However intrigued he may have been by the idiosyncrasies of everyday Norwegian life, Philip's abiding passion for history overrode all other outside interests. He jotted down every snippet of unusual information and every anecdote he heard relating to the country's Christian heritage, the position of Catholics in the country, and the ethos of the Lutheran State Church.

Early in September he was invited to Sunday lunch with the Dominicans where he was 'very kindly received indeed' by the acting Superior, Hallvard Rieber-Mohn, a leading contributor to *The Month*, and other members of the small community. On this and similar outings in the company of historians he learnt, among other things, of the folk-lore relating to Norway's patron saint, St Olav, who claimed the throne of Norway on the strength of his belief in his descent from the Norse god, Odin.

He picked up an old Norwegian proverb relating that 'in his old age the devil becomes a monk: meaning he thinks of the Church after a gay life'. Caraman noted with thinly-disguised contempt that 'if Lutheran Ministers "consecrate" too many altar breads, they put them back in the cupboard and reconsecrate them the next time they hold a service. Sometimes wine left in base of chalice [is placed] on or behind the altar: flies settle in it.' He also wrote with compassion about a Catholic priest in a sparsely populated parish who was 'on his own for weekday Mass: no server for Sunday: therefore tied bell to his ankle and had harmonium keys let into altar: ventriloquist stunt in answering himself'. Little did Fr Caraman realise when making this entry in his diary that he himself would one day be in a similar situation to that isolated Catholic priest.

One story related to Fr Caraman both surprised and moved him: he learnt that there had been one Jesuit in Norway at a time when the exclusion order under the country's 1814 Constitution was still in force. On his first day in Oslo, Philip was told that a young Jesuit, Xavier Rénom de la Baume, who had been conscripted into the French Army in 1939, had been killed when the Chasseurs Alpines had fought a rearguard action near Namsos during the German invasion. Fr Caraman offered up his first Mass in Norway for his French brother, mindful that the main purpose of his coming to Norway was to establish a Jesuit presence in this unlikely missionary land. A letter of welcome from his English Provincial, Fr Corrigan, served as another reminder of this point, although to some of his Norwegian friends, Fr Caraman's presence was a matter of speculation. Lita Anker, at that time a non-Catholic, said, 'You never told me when we met first, when I asked you about the Jesuits, that the Jesuits were started to do down the Lutherans. I read that since.' And another enquired, 'Are you going to pinch Lutherans? Is that why you have come?' Overtly at least, it was not John Gran's intention to employ Fr Caraman as a propagandist against the State religion, but his original plans for the Jesuit's pastoral role in Norway were never realised. The Bishop's intention was for Philip to become the official chaplain to the English-speaking community in Oslo, which was a sizeable one at the time. In addition to foreign diplomats and businessmen and their families, a considerable number of Americans, Canadians, Dutch, German and British personnel attached to the large NATO establishment were Roman Catholics, providing a steady source of income for their pastor. Geographically, the NATO headquarters at Kolsas was situated in the parish of Stabekk administered by Dutch Marist priests from their presbytery alongside a modern church. Fr Waring recalls that when the Marists heard of the Bishop's decision 'they raised a storm of protest – saying that no "Jesuit" (even worse an *English* Jesuit) was going to function within *their* area. So Philip took the English Mass in St Olav's in central Oslo . . . The English-speaking community was thus deprived of an excellent priest.'³

Once again, it seems, Fr Caraman was the object of jealousy, this time from outside the circle of fellow-Jesuits, whose company he sorely missed despite his recent difficulties within the family of the Society. When he went to Norway in 1965, apart from time away travelling or on holiday, Caraman had spent forty-two years studying, living and working in Jesuit houses and institutions. He was both adaptable and eager for new experiences, but when – just after his arrival in Norway – he heard that Bishop John Gran had written to a mutual friend saying 'God bless Philip for his pluck', he believed he had been 'foolhardy, not brave'. He also admitted that 'never for three and half years, since [Cardinal] Godfrey died, have I felt so depressed: almost black gloom without a break visible'. He considered his depression was caused by fatigue, the dreary weather, and 'most of all by distance I felt I was from friends'. A couple of days later he received a solicitous letter from Fr Martin D'Arcy who clearly understood the younger priest's feelings. Hoping that Fr Philip was 'off to a good start', he wrote: 'I am sure it will be a lonely life at first. Here there is rain and cold weather. I had a letter from Evelyn [Waugh], alas! incredibly depressed and saying that he did not expect to meet me again in this life so sorry was his condition'. Fr D'Arcy continued his letter by asking if he had lent Caraman a framed drawing inscribed to him by Eric Gill, which he could not trace, remarking that 'it's strange how things disappear'. He concluded his letter by relating that Cardinal [Heenan] had suggested that Farm Street might become a parish 'if we like. We did like – apparently, and I am again saddened.'[4]

The news that the weather was as gloomy in England as in Norway may have brought Fr Philip some consolation. His Mediterranean blood rebelled against the rain that had greeted his arrival and continued to fall incessantly throughout his first week in Oslo; he was badly affected by the darkening days of autumn which presaged the mid-winter gloom of this northern land, unalleviated as yet by the sparkling snow. The rains that autumn were in fact unprecedented, breaking a previous record set up in 1887: the River Aker burst its banks, and the morning papers carried front-page pictures of cars driving down city streets axle-deep in water, the river flowing into the windows of houses, and old men being carried piggyback across roads.

Philip Caraman's depression lifted when he went out to dine with Lita Anker, who had prepared a special meal for him. Her company, and the friendship of her family, were the brightest spots in his life during the early weeks of his time in Oslo. Lita's sister, Wenche Koren, was the first person he had called upon on the day of his arrival, and the family's welcome, and their obvious affection for Philip, compensated for his sombre living conditions and the austere ethos of his adopted country. Cultured, cosmopolitan and vivacious, the sisters brought a much-needed glow into his life, much as Margaret FitzHerbert had done during the dark days at Farm Street. Lita Anker was seriously considering becoming a Catholic at this time, and Fr Caraman was impressed when he saw that she had included *The Imitation of Christ* among the books she had collected to study in Spain, where she – like so many other affluent Scandinavians – spent the winter. He was astonished to hear that Lita had 'worked all through *Henry Garnet* in Spain. She had no English–Norwegian dictionary, but only English–Spanish, and Spanish–Norwegian, and by this method she got through it'. The sisters and their extended family owned several properties, including a country home on the island of Malmoya, on the eastern side of the Oslo fiord, and two houses and a studio in the remote mountain valley of Flatdal, where, so Philip was told, the electric heaters were left on throughout the winter, so cheap was electricity. Later he stayed in all these houses, but the history of the family intrigued and delighted him as much as their generosity. Insofar as Norway could be said to have an aristocracy at all, the family of Lita's husband, John Anker, fitted this description. The Ankers were a prosperous clan of whom it was recorded at the beginning of the nineteenth century that they 'sent their linen to be washed in England', and whose grand house in Oslo was eventually demolished to make way for the railway station on the eastern side of the capital. In 1814, more than a hundred of the country's leading citizens gathered at the manor house owned by Karsten Anker at Eidsvoll some eighty kilometres outside Oslo: here, on 17 May, they signed the Norwegian declaration of independence. The momentous event is celebrated by a painting hung in the Storting, the Norwegian parliament, and the Anker house in Eidsvoll is now a national monument open to the public.

New friends, however distinguished and welcoming, could not fill the void felt by Fr Caraman at his separation from those he had left behind in England, and about whom he was becoming increasingly concerned. The news of Evelyn Waugh's depression was relayed to him not only by Fr D'Arcy but also by Meg FitzHerbert who was alarmed by her father's health and mental state. Nor did Philip Caraman leave the past behind him when he crossed the North Sea. His personal and professional involvement with so many celebrated English literary figures was well known in Oslo, and it was suggested that he might lecture on Evelyn Waugh's work the following year. On one occasion he fell into what he describes as a 'violent argument' with one of his new acquaintances over Edith Sitwell, and he considered carefully an idea put forward for a series of lectures on other writers and on a number of prominent Catholics with whom he had been involved, including Cardinal Heenan, Graham Greene, Stephen Spender, Angus Wilson and Muriel Spark. Meanwhile, in an attempt to cheer up Evelyn Waugh and to reassure him of his continued friendship, Philip sent a box of Norwegian chocolates to Combe Florey for Waugh's birthday. From Somerset came an acknowledgement hinting at some of the causes of Waugh's disillusionment with life: on All Souls Day, he wrote:

> How kind and dear of you to remember my birthday! Thanks most awfully for the royal box of chocolates. I fear that winter must be setting in dark and drear, but anyway you will be free from many of the embarrassments of the Church in England which increase daily. I enclose a photograph to remind you of us all. We are not, I fear, a photogenic family. The English Jesuits arc not behaving well — you are, but away.[5]

Philip Caraman's first Christmas in Norway was far from cheerless. Bishop Gran returned from a long visit to Rome in time for the holiday, bringing news of the Second Vatican Council with him. In his appointment as editor of *The Month,* Fr Caraman had been close to the heart of current affairs and privy to first-hand reports on the momentous events taking place in the Vatican. Out on a limb in Oslo, he enjoyed hearing up-to-date news of the Council from John Gran, and was amused when the Bishop told him that 'a Swedish observer at the Council told him [the Bishop] that Norway in Lutheran Church is what Spain is in R. C. Church – extreme, unbending, fierce'. A Norwegian Christmas, and the traditional dishes served at this time of year, were unlike anything Philip had experienced before. A week before the Feast he went to a traditional *Julebord* in one of the local restaurants, and was amazed at the buffet table groaning under great dishes of lobster, oysters, eels and herrings, many varieties of cold meat, and assorted desserts topped with lavish helpings of whipped cream. After the principal meal on Christmas Eve, he walked through deserted streets: the first, unsullied, snow of winter had just fallen and the hushed city looked lovely in the dark, with lights sparkling on graves in the cemetery. For once, the drunks who usually lay about the streets at night were absent: the previous evening there had been so many he felt it was unsafe to walk through the east end of the town to visit the Franciscans. Mass was celebrated at midnight in the usual way and, writing to Evelyn Waugh three days later, Fr Philip told him:

Before Christmas there seemed so many English-speaking people in Oslo in need of my services that I had no time for letters. I have preached here every Sunday since my arrival to the same little congregation, so that they know me well ... I hope and pray you are keeping well and warm. Here the temperatures are appallingly low: but the houses are warm. When the church was already crammed for midnight Mass, another 150 people were let in ...[6]

With New Year's day came the deep snows of winter, causing Caraman and a group of fellow priests to be late for a party given by the bishop when their car was stuck in a drift. A few days later the citizens of Oslo, Fr Philip among them, took to the ski slopes surrounding the city, to revel in the vigorous exercise they had looked forward to during most of the previous year. Although physically unsuited to participate in the national sport of cross-country skiing, Philip was nonetheless determined to join in as far as possible, and gamely accompanied a group of Norwegian friends out into the hills. On his third outing he was told he was wearing the distinctive bonnet of a smart Oslo Ski-club. This, he decided, 'explained much. I did not ski as a world-champion.' He made a few more attempts at the sport, travelling on crowded public trams with the young, the fit, and entire families making their way to the slopes, but he soon abandoned his efforts to emulate their prowess. Later in the winter, he was awoken in his room at the top of the tall house by 'heavy snowfall from roof against my windows during night: one great crash from gable: then number of small ones like [a] person trying to break in: TROLL!' With amusement, Philip noted the 'perils of walking Oslo streets during the thaw: choice of death: run over by car or brained by block of ice from roof'. Fortunately he succumbed to neither peril.

Fr Caraman's sense of humour and his enjoyment of the ridiculous, which seemed to have deserted him during his time of trial two years earlier, were restored. Despite the loneliness he professed to feel, and the bouts of depression from which he suffered occasionally, Norway acted as a catharsis, and he was beginning to enjoy life again. Although he complained of feeling tired from time to time, more often than not this was caused by a run of late nights out, although he was reluctant to admit this was the reason: he could not claim, as he had done in London, that his fatigue was caused by overwork and extortionate demands on his time. Although the congregation at his Sunday Mass had steadily grown in size, and he had built up a core of admirers in the English-speaking community who sought his spiritual advice and his company, in no way was he over-stretched as he had been in the past. His days followed a steady routine of mornings spent in writing, afternoons in studying, and evening visiting.

Caraman still received a great number of letters from friends and acquaintances in England and on the continent, among whom Fr D'Arcy was one of the most faithful. Philip had suggested that his father-Jesuit might visit him in Norway some-time during 1966, but D'Arcy – politely – implied that he was not keen on the idea, saying he felt his health was not up to the journey. When Philip persisted with his invitation, the older man said he had looked into possible flight schedules, but had decided that the projected visit was 'turning into a nightmare. Could I not put it off indefinitely?' pleaded the seventy-eight-year old. Caraman failed to appreciate how age and frailty had affected D'Arcy's ability to travel abroad as frequently as he had in the past. Although he never visited Fr Philip in Norway, Martin D'Arcy wrote regularly with news of the English Province of the Society, and the comings and goings of the Mount Street community. He reported that Fr Coventry, who had filled another post in Mount Street following his term as Provincial, had moved on, and later he told Philip that Fr Walsh too had left. It is notable that despite both Fr D'Arcy's and Fr Caraman's recent problems within the Society of Jesus these letters were never derogatory nor malicious.[7]

Part of Philip Caraman's day was devoted to correspondence, but he had more time for his own writing during his first six months in Norway than at any time for many years. He was juggling no fewer than three books at the time, so space to concentrate on them was invaluable. Early in the new year of 1966, he received the second proofs of *The Years of Siege* from his publishers. The sequel to *The Other Face,* the well-received

anthology describing Catholic life during the reign of Queen
Elizabeth I, follows the same pattern as its predecessor in the
series, illustrating aspects of Catholic life in the period from the
accession of James I to the death of Cromwell in an anthology
of quotations and vignettes. The second book differs in mood
and incident from *The Other Face*, to reflect the changing
historical background. During the reign of James I, as Fr
Caraman had shown in *Henry Garnet,* Catholics, particularly
Jesuit priests, were subjected to almost unremitting persecution,
particularly following the discovery of the Gunpowder Plot: for
a period of eleven years under King Charles I's personal rule,
they enjoyed greater toleration than for some time. During the
Civil War, and under the Commonwealth, Catholics were again
abominated, the Puritans' 'apprehension of Popery having
carried them so far to the other extreme that they [had] now lost
all moderation and decorum'.[8] Although no less readable and
informative than the preceding book, *The Years of Siege* is
slimmer in content and coverage. It is padded out with two
lengthy extracts which are not altogether relevant to the subject
matter: one relates in detail the 'Defence of Wardour Castle' in
1643 by Lady Arundell against the Roundhead Army, and
another describes the missionary foundation of Maryland in
1634. Both are readable stories, but fall outside the parameters
originally set by the book's editor. Caraman collated the material during his exile from Mayfair shortly before he moved to
Norway, and at a time when he was overcome with other
commitments and beset with difficulties. He admits in his
Introduction that 'the raw matter for this second volume has
been difficult to gather ... It is a period largely uncharted by
Catholic historians. Whether as a result of the Civil War or
other upheavals, the records of Catholic families are deficient
during these years ... I have failed to find much material I
sought ...'[9] A third book in the series, which Caraman had
envisaged would cover Catholic life in England during an
unspecified period following the death of Cromwell, was never
written. Either through boredom with the subject, or more probably owing to the difficulty of gathering relevant material, Fr
Caraman's creative ideas had changed direction by the time he

reached Oslo. Once he had unpacked the crates containing his papers and had settled into his new home, two books were in the forefront of his mind. The first he started working on immediately, more through a sense of duty than with much enthusiasm: the second engrossed his thoughts long before he started writing it.

The biography of Fr Cyril Martindale, which Philip had been tasked to write immediately following the death of the distinguished Jesuit in March 1963, had barely been started two and a half years later. On his retirement from Farm Street, Fr Martindale had given the younger man many of his personal papers, but the turmoil in Caraman's life at the time Martindale died had shunted the biography on to the back burner. Once he had sorted out his papers, Fr Philip started writing methodically, noting early on that he was 'averaging 2 pages a day: hope to have ms. ready for revision by June or July [1966]'. In fact, with considerable leisure for writing, the book went much more quickly than anticipated, and shortly after Christmas 1965 he was able to write to Graham Greene to say he was nearing the end. Contact with Greene was an essential ingredient of the biography: Martindale had played an important role in the writer's personal and spiritual life, and almost certainly had been the confessor of both Greene and of his lover, Catherine Walston.[10] Following a visit to Fr Martindale at his retirement home in Petworth in 1959, Fr Philip had written to Greene, telling him:

> I am just back from a visit to Fr. Martindale. He is in bed and very weak and for the first time in his life losing interest in the work he is doing. He asked after you, but after nobody else. He may get better – so often he has appeared to be dying and has recovered ... I will keep you informed.[11]

When Fr Caraman wrote to Greene from Oslo, asking if he had any letters from Fr Martindale 'of exceptional interest', which might help with the biography, the writer replied that he had 'a mass of letters of Fr Martindale's, but most ... are too personal to send, or quote from'.[12] Ultimately the biography made no mention of Martindale's involvement with Greene, except for a brief reference to the Jesuit's opinion of *The Power and the Glory*.

Throughout the months Fr Caraman was working dutifully on *C.C. Martindale*, his mind was buzzing with ideas for his next book, a concept which had engaged his enthusiasm since the moment he arrived in Oslo. This was to be a book quite unlike any other he had worked on previously: a book about Norway, its Christian roots and history, the lives of its people in the twentieth century, and their Viking heritage. It was with this travel book-with-a-difference constantly in mind, that Fr Caraman noted in his diary everything he felt would be of interest when he started writing. As the Jesuit biography neared completion, he was planning a leisurely journey across Norway to add zest and first-hand background to the next book. As the snows started to melt, and the days lengthened into spring, he looked forward eagerly to travelling through the Norwegian mountains and fiords to the kingdom's northernmost borders in search of material. Instead, the despatch of the completed manuscript of the Martindale biography, and the start of Fr Philip's long journey, were delayed by a protracted visit to England and an unforeseen turn of events during his stay there.

Disturbing accounts concerning the deterioration in Evelyn Waugh's health had continued to reach Fr Caraman in Norway. Martin D'Arcy was not alone in describing the writer's state of utter depression in letters to Oslo: Margaret FitzHerbert also wrote regularly to Philip Caraman, her anxious letters alerting him to her father's condition. Waugh, it seemed, had lost all interest in living, he ate very little, slept badly, was unable to write, and, according to some accounts, appeared at times to be hallucinating. Fr Caraman was deeply concerned, and from so great a distance felt unable to help and advise as he had done in the 'Pinfold' crisis twelve years earlier. Having re-established contact with Graham Greene over the Martindale biography, Philip told him the alarming news about Waugh. Greene wrote back: 'I'm shocked to hear about Evelyn. Is there no priest other than yourself whom he knows and likes and whom you could ask to go and see him. Alas that [Eric] Strauss is dead. I don't myself believe in 'almost incurable melancholy'. I have seen wonders done with electric shock treatment.'[13]

One of the principal causes of Waugh's depression was his disillusionment with the manner in which decisions made at the Second Vatican Council were affecting Catholic life: in particular he detested the new vernacular Mass and pined for the Latin liturgy. 'I now cling to the Faith doggedly without joy. Church going is a pure duty parade,' he told one correspondent.[14] Fr Caraman understood and sympathised with Waugh's predicament. Although he was short of funds, being financially dependent on little more than pocket-money for travel and expenses at that time, with the help of friends Philip returned to England in time for Easter. According to a note in his diary, it is possible he first spent a few days at Stonor Park before he moved on to stay with Mary and Auberon Herbert at Pixton, where he had been a frequent guest for nearly a quarter of a century. Waugh, longing to attend Easter Sunday Mass in the Latin rite, had invited an old friend from Downside, Dom Hubert van Zeller, to celebrate privately for the family at Combe Florey: the Abbot refused the monk leave of absence from his community, thus adding to Evelyn's state of paranoia. But Fr Caraman needed no permission to celebrate a Latin Mass, as he had explained to Waugh on his visit to the family in the autumn of 1962, and arranged to take the service on the morning of Easter Sunday in the Catholic chapel in Wiveliscombe, a village on the edge of Exmoor between Combe Florey and Dulverton. In the congregation that Easter day were Laura and Evelyn Waugh and most of their family, and Mary Herbert, her son Auberon, and her daughter Bridget Grant. It was a joyous occasion. Waugh's depression had lifted: he radiated bonhomie, even towards his brother-in-law Auberon with whom he was normally barely on speaking terms.

After Mass, the Herberts returned to Pixton, while Caraman went back to Combe Florey with the Waughs for Sunday lunch. The story of what followed was related later by Fr Caraman himself to Evelyn Waugh's biographers, and has been retold in

various versions by a number of authors. Four of Laura and
Evelyn's six children were staying in the house at the time,
Hattie, James, Septimus and Meg with her husband Giles
FitzHerbert and their children. Whilst lunch was being prepared
following their return from church, the family dispersed to their
various pursuits about the large house: Laura was supervising
the preparation of the meal, while Philip and Harriet sat quietly
in the bow window of the drawing room playing a board game.
It was presumed that Waugh had retired to his library, but when
lunch was ready he could not be found. Searching the house,
Laura discovered him in the downstairs lavatory: he had died
there, apparently of a sudden and massive heart attack. The
family was stunned. Fr Caraman immediately administered
Conditional Absolution, and then telephoned Fr Formosa, the
local parish priest, asking him to come with his oils to anoint
the dead man: a doctor was also called as a matter of routine,
and later an undertaker.

So much has long been known about Waugh's dramatic death.
But one detail concerning Fr Caraman has been omitted in biographies of the writer. Among the papers the Jesuit deposited in
the John J. Burns library in Boston College is an envelope
containing a cheque for ten guineas made out to him, and dated
and signed by Waugh on that Easter Sunday, 10 April. On the
envelope Philip wrote: 'Cheque given to me by Evelyn Waugh
at Combe Florey on the morning of his death. This is almost
certainly the last thing he ever wrote.' The priest may have been
short of funds, but he never cashed the cheque, preferring to
keep it as a last memento of Waugh's thoughtfulness and affection.[15]

As the household at Combe Florey tried to come to terms with
what had happened, and absent members of the family were
contacted with the shocking news, Bridget Grant drove over
take Philip Caraman back to Pixton. He remained in Somerset,
and conducted Waugh's funeral service five days later at the
church of St Teresa of Lisieux in Taunton, followed by a simple
burial service on the hillside just outside the boundaries of the
Anglican churchyard at Combe Florey. The Requiem Mass in
Westminster Cathedral the following week was a grand occasion

attended by many celebrities of the day, including leading politicians and figures from the arts world, Catholic and non-Catholic alike. Permission was granted for the Mass to be celebrated in Latin by Mgr George Tomlinson, in the presence of Cardinal Heenan, who was a long-standing friend of Evelyn Waugh: the Apostolic Delegate, Archbishop Cardinale, was also present. Fr Caraman preached a deeply moving panegyric to the packed congregation. In paying tribute to the writer's talents, he pointed out that Waugh 'sought perfection in his craft and came nearer to achieving it than perhaps any man of his time. But the way he cultivated his gifts was only one manifestation of his fidelity – the virtue marked the whole man.' Waugh's faithfulness – to his craft, to his friends, and above all to the Church of his adoption – was the principal theme of the sermon. Caraman did not shirk mention of the 'crisis caused by the Vatican Council' in Waugh's religious life, and said that although it was a struggle for the deceased man to accept the new liturgy, 'he did accept it, and with enviable fidelity ... To those who were with him on his final day – his family and a priest (he surely prayed for this) – nothing was more manifest than the way God had arranged his end as a mark of gratitude to a faithful servant.' Approaching the end of his tribute, Fr Caraman begged 'all here to pray for him now', and concluded by saying that Waugh's family 'can be certain that God above all others cannot fail in faithfulness to those who have been loyal to him. *Requiescat in pace*.'[16]

With these heartfelt words Philip Caraman paid his official farewell to the man who, over the years of a deepening relationship, had stood beside him when he was desperate, and to whom he, in return, had given support in times of crisis. Theirs was a friendship based on mutual respect, courtesy and affection. There is little doubt that when they first met Caraman stood in awe of Waugh's formidable reputation: he never lost his deference for the writer's literary talents and achievements, but for the man behind the writing he developed a filial and lasting devotion. Initially Waugh regarded the younger man merely as one of Fr D'Arcy's disciples whom he was prepared to help in a new and demanding literary appointment: as the years passed, and Philip became almost part of his extended family, Waugh began to appreciate the wit and humour, the capacity for hard work, and the quiet spiritual advice of his 'gentle Jesuit'. The abrasiveness which soured many of the writer's other relationships was notably absent from his friendship with Philip. Waugh's 'dislike of this life', which Michael Holroyd believes was directed towards others, was notably absent from his relationship with Fr Caraman.[17] Replying to a letter of condolence, Margaret FitzHerbert told Lady Diana Cooper that her father's death 'was a kind of wonderful miracle':[18] he had died on Easter Sunday, following a Latin Mass, and in joyous mood.

The part played by Fr Caraman in the peaceful end to Waugh's life can only be guessed at. There is no doubt about the sentiments of the writer's family: on her return home after the grand Requiem, Laura wrote to Philip:

> I did love your panegyric. It said all I wanted said and it was lovely being done by you who loved Evelyn. Thank you from the bottom of my heart. I am asking Teresa Waugh [wife of Auberon Waugh] to make copies of it so that all the children can have one – I am so happy that you were here on Easter Sunday; both for the Mass and for your presence in the house.
>
> Evelyn had been so unhappy for the last three years that I know I should accept his death with thanksgiving for God's kindness to him that perhaps in time I will manage it and knowing it is a comfort ... I would have liked to have seen you again before you left. I meant to ask you back to lunch with us after the requiem but I suppose I was dazed and didn't – Oh! I did love the panegyric – it was beautiful.[19]

Fr Caraman returned to Oslo drained emotionally, but his sense of loss was assuaged by the gratitude of Waugh's family. In early May he received a letter from Mary Herbert, who had been ill following the private funeral at Combe Florey, and was unable to get up to London for the Requiem Mass. Writing from her villa in Portofino, where she was recuperating, she told Philip how sad she was not to have seen him again after they parted in Somerset. She continued her letter:

I heard from those who were [in Westminster Cathedral] that your sermon was of very great beauty. I know it meant a great deal to Laura ... but it wasn't only the family who said how deeply moving they had found it, but from people who were quite remote. I was so glad you stayed those last days with us. We all felt very close to each other in the [?wake] of the huge disaster that had come, and your presence from the Easter Sunday Mass with Evelyn to his last resting place on the hillside made the whole difference. His last meetings outside Wiveliscombe church I hold too for the extraordinary atmosphere of kindliness and peace it conveyed.

Laura's mother added a postscript to her letter: 'Ever so grateful for all the long friendship you have given me and so many of my family'.[20]

Graham Greene was living in Paris at the time Waugh died, and wrote to Fr Caraman saying that he thought 'Evelyn's death seemed to be an extraordinarily nice and suitable one. It was good too that you were in the house at the time.'[21] Father Martin D'Arcy was another of Waugh's close friends to have missed the Requiem, although Philip Caraman had spoken of him in his panegyric, and had written to him in Boston after the ceremony telling him how tired he felt. D'Arcy's somewhat irascible reply followed Philip to Oslo:

You presuppose that I know all that happened at the death of Evelyn and after. In fact I know very little, and your letter told me quite a lot of what he was doing when he was dying ... But did he die suddenly? Was he found dead? Were you in the house and able to give him Absolution if not the Last Sacraments? How broken was Laura? – and the children? You mention a 'cathedral sermon'. Was this at Westminster? I thought probably there would be a Requiem at Farm Street after about a month. I miss him very much.[22]

Fr D'Arcy sympathised with Philip's tiredness, but said he must be 'very satisfied that the book is through the censors'. This was the Martindale biography which had been cleared for publication by the Jesuits whilst Fr Caraman was in England. Once the book had passed the Society's vetting procedures, the

author drew a sigh of relief and sent off his manuscript shortly
after his return to Akersveien. He had been away longer than
intended. The long days of the Nordic summer were not to be
wasted in a gloomy building in Oslo, and he was impatient to
start his journey. Reminding himself that Trollope had begun
work on a new book the moment the previous one was finished,
Philip noted that he set out on the first lap of his journey to
Hamar on 10 May, the day after sending *C.C. Martindale* to
Longmans, and exactly one month after Evelyn Waugh's death.

The weather was kind: although snow still lay on the high
ground and in the valleys, the sun was warm and he 'jogged
along' in his little car at between fifty and sixty kilometres an
hour. On that first day Fr Caraman's thoughts turned to Evelyn
Waugh; arriving in Hamar in the afternoon he had the 'comfort
of saying [my] Breviary at end of [the] journey', and he also
said a 'Mass for E.W.', noting that he intended to continue this
practice every tenth day of the month for the next year, and that
the last sentence in his homily would always mention Waugh.
This was in line with a promise he had made to Laura before
they parted. As he drove on Fr Caraman was often reminded of
his dead friend. In a country which still carried the scars of the
Nazi invasion and of their scorched-earth retreat in 1944, and
where in remote country areas foreigners were still eyed with
suspicion, he recalled 'E.W.'s last comment on Italians cheating
Germans'. Later Caraman received a letter from Osbert Sitwell
that had been forwarded from Oslo. Writing from Castello di
Montegufoni, the aesthete said:

> I feel I must write to you about the death of Evelyn, as I know
> how close you were to him. He is a great loss to us all. It is sad
> to think that we will not see him again in this world, and there
> will certainly be no one to take his place. I was so sorry for
> Laura.[23]

In the midst of a long, and at times gruelling, journey Fr
Caraman still kept in touch with his friends, and complained that
he was having to write about five letters a day: correspondence
reached him at various prearranged postes restantes along his
route. Only a few days into his journey, he complained to Fr

D'Arcy that he was feeling ill and tired; he hadn't appreciated how tortuous the roads were across the mountains, nor how badly rutted in many places after heavy snowfall. Notorious among his friends for his bad driving, he complained of commercial traffic and lorries tail-gating him on the narrow highways and mused that the 'pace of the Lord's business' was slower. Entertained by Philip's comments, yet wearied by another moan about how tired he felt, Fr D'Arcy made fun of his protégé, telling him that 'those who drive badly always get tired. I of course never get tired. I have always thought that one of your few failings was that you are not athletic. I keep slim but muscular even in Bostonian weather . . .'[24]

Philip Caraman had temporarily abandoned the road when he received D'Arcy's letter, having travelled through the western fiords on one of the ferries that are a lifeline for the people along that rugged coast. With some trepidation, Philip braved the roads again for the most demanding part of the journey over the inhospitable terrain confronting the Arctic close to the border with Russia. He described this venture in his book:

> I was driving north to Kirkenes before there was any certain information on the state of the road. And I was driving back – something that had rarely been done before, since any man in his right senses would return along the good roads through Finland or Sweden. And I knew nothing about the working of a car beyond the fact that it needed occasional refuelling. What would I do in case of a breakdown? Simply open the bonnet, for this is what I had seen others do in these circumstances.[25]

At the height of the Cold War, he describes how 'the road to the nearest border check ended abruptly at a small farm sloping down to a narrow strip of water'. For fifteen minutes he stood near the barriers of barbed wire, ditches, fences and poles, but saw neither man nor animal during his silent vigil.[26] He later admitted to Lita Anker that the border 'looked very sinister. The road was fearful in places – in fact only the new foundations existed. Although I had escaped punctures all the way, I had three in one day driving from Alta to Kirkenes.' As Caraman crossed the bleak and treeless landscape of grey waters, and drove along byways closed for much of the year, he may have recalled something Evelyn Waugh had told him before his visit to Scandinavia eight years earlier. Based on his own experience of a pre-war trip to the country with his friend Hugh Lygon, when a venture to climb a glacier near Spitzbergen had gone disastrously wrong, Waugh had warned Philip that 'Norway is an awful place'.[27]

In the course of his summer-long journey there may have been one or two occasions when Fr Caraman agreed with what Waugh had said to him, but for most of the time he was too absorbed in the customs and culture of the remote areas he visited, and the history of the towns and villages where he wandered, to feel dispirited. The drive was demanding, but even in the far north of Norway the weather was sunny and very warm, and he thoroughly enjoyed most of his stopovers. In places where there was a Catholic church he lodged in the presbytery, occasionally he stayed with people to whom he had an introduction, more often in hotels of varying standard or in simple boarding houses.

Wherever he stopped, he commented on the food. At a simple hotel by the lake of Majavatn, used mainly by fishermen, the menu 'was unappealing with the fishballs, meat cakes and sausages to which the Norwegians remain so perversely addicted'. On another occasion Philip was offered 'the most delicious smoked salmon I had tasted in any country . . . caught on Friday, smoked over the week-end, eaten on Wednesday, that was how it should be treated'. It was of course wild, not farmed, salmon. When stopping with friends or near a Catholic church, he said Mass: at Hamar he had taken the opportunity to go to confession, believing it would be his last chance to do so in English for some months. He was disappointed not to have been able to say Mass on Whit Sunday in the chapel of the military cemetery at Narvik where the French Jesuit, De La Baume, was buried: the chapel, like the hotel bar and almost everything else, was closed because it was a holiday. On another occasion the 'sun reached down to the valley in the middle of my Mass which I began at 6.15 a.m.': it was a promising start to a new day. On a weekday, at Hammerfest, he had a multinational

Philip Caraman – the young Jesuit.

The class of 1933 at Manresa House, Roehampton, when Philip Caraman was a Junior. (He stands at the right-hand end of the middle row.)

Scholastic and teacher at Corby Hall, the Jesuit school in Sunderland, in 1939. (Philip Caraman is seen, standing, centre.)

Students and directing staff at Campion Hall, Oxford, in 1941. The Master, Fr Martin D'Arcy, is seated centre. (Philip Caraman stands near the middle of the third row.)

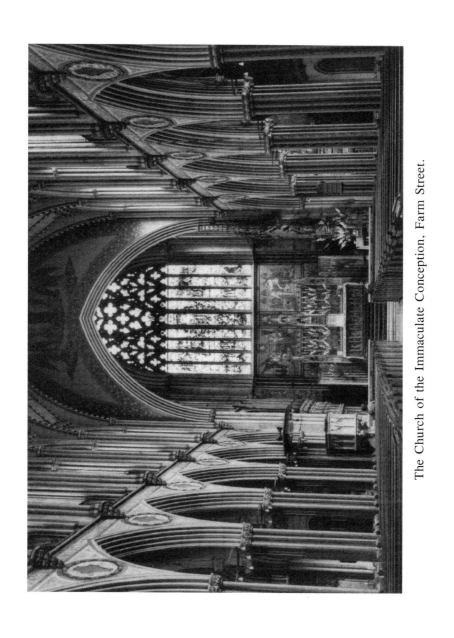

The Church of the Immaculate Conception, Farm Street.

Fr Caraman in 1953 when he was editor of *The Month*. His talents and personality won him many friends in the world of literature and the arts.

Graham Greene dispensing hospitality. Philip Caraman was a regular visitor to the writer's London flat in the early 1950s.

Evelyn Waugh at Combe Florey, where Philip Caraman often stayed with the writer and his wife, Laura.

Sonia Orwell on her last day at *Horizon*.

Novelist Rosamund Lehmann's belief in spiritualism defied Fr
Caraman's efforts to bring her into the Catholic Church.

Dame Edith Sitwell in 1956, the year after her reception into the
Catholic Church by Fr Caraman.

A portrait of Fr Caraman's mentor and friend, Fr Martin D'Arcy, painted in 1939 by Augustus John.

Fr Caraman (last – wearing a black biretta) in the procession entering St Olav's on the occasion of the consecration of John Willem Gran as Bishop of Oslo in March 1963.

John Willem Nicolaysen Gran, first Norwegian-born Roman Catholic Bishop of Oslo since the Reformation.

Sogneprest in Norway. Fr Caraman regarded his pastoral
work in the country as 'missionary'.

The imposing Mariakirken in Lillehammer, where Fr Caraman spent two
isolated winters. In 1982, he said that he did not have 'even a cat in the
congregation' on Ash Wednesday.

The artist Lita Anker. She illustrated Fr Caraman's
Norway and became a close friend.

Fr Caraman spent many enjoyable hours with Lita Anker and her family in
Spain and in Norway.

A card sent by Philip to the author following his visit to Iceland. On it
he wrote, 'this picture shows the Pope playing hide and seek.'

Philip Caraman in tourist mode. His passion for travel matched his love
of history.

The presentation of doves to Pope Paul VI by Fr Caraman was part of the elaborate ceremonies celebrating the Canonisation of the Forty Martyrs in St Peter's on 25 October 1970.

Fr Caraman was a great admirer of Pope John Paul II.

Portrait of Fr Philip Caraman SJ by an unknown artist.

Philip's elder brother, Fr John Caraman SJ, went to Rhodesia (Zimbabwe) in 1938, and devoted his life to the African missions.

Window commissioned by Fr Caraman for St Stanislaus Church, Dulverton, in commemoration of Margaret Fitzherbert and her work for the Cause for the Forty Martyrs of England and Wales.

Signing copies of *The Western Rising* in 1994, watched by publisher Steven Pugsley and bookseller Caryl Rothwell.

Bridge House, Dulverton, was Fr Caraman's home from 1986 until shortly before his death in 1998.

Philip Caraman enjoyed popping across Dulverton High Street to the bookshop opposite Bridge House.

Pray For The Repose
Of The Soul Of
Fr PHILIP GEORGE
CARAMAN SJ

Died 6th May 1998, Aged 86

R.I.P.

Qui Mariam Absolvisti,
Et Latronem Exaudisti
Mihi Quoque Spem Dedisti

A country priest, buried in a country churchyard. Fr Caraman's grave at Brushford, with the verse he chose from the *Dies Irae*.

congregation of 'Norwegians, Germans, Finns and Dutch in the little church . . . mostly off the ships going to the North Cape'. In another remote area of the far north, he said Sunday Mass in the house of the local dentist, whose wife was a Catholic from Glasgow: finding a congregation of five gathered in the living room, Fr Caraman commented that 'this was a true church of the diaspora. The first missionary journeys of St Paul must have had many points of resemblance to the present-day excursions of a Catholic priest in Norway.'[28]

One of the last places on Caraman's itinerary on the way back to Oslo was Flatdal where the Anker family had a summer retreat. He lingered here contentedly in the company of John and Lita, their extended family and children, and their friends in the artists' colony in the beautiful Telemark valley, which he describes as a valley 'of legends, song . . . turf-roofed houses, mountain trolls, writers, silversmiths and painters'.[29] During these days in Flatdal, was Philip reminded of childhood summers when his own large family had gathered on a Sussex beach, long ago before he entered the Society of Jesus, before his parents died and his siblings were scattered?

With August and the first hint of Nordic autumn in the air, Fr Caraman returned to base in Oslo, well pleased with the summer he had spent exploring and gathering material for his book. The journey was one of which he was proud and he enjoyed talking about it for several years afterwards. But the book itself progressed more slowly than he hoped at first it would: the writing took two more years, and publication another after that. Philip Caraman was distracted, as he was on numerous other occasions in the middle years of his life, by other commitments and by his own innate restlessness.

Notes

1 Except where noted separately, this chapter is based on entries from the diary which was found among Philip Caraman's personal papers, and on extracts from a collection of letters written by him

to Lita Anker, together with the author's personal experience of living in Norway at about this time.

2 Fr Olaf Waring, submission dated September 1998 for Fr Caraman's obituary notice in *Letters & Notices* and copied to author.

3 Fr Olaf Waring, letter to author, undated, circa 11 August 2001.

4 Letter, Fr Martin D'Arcy to Philip Caraman, 11 September 1965, John J. Burns Library, Boston College (hereafter BC).

5 Letter, Evelyn Waugh to Philip Caraman, 2 November 1965 (BC). The 'royal' chocolates were either the variety labelled 'Kong Haakon' or that called 'Kong Olav'. Both were extremely expensive.

6 Letter, Philip Caraman to Evelyn Waugh, 28 December 1965, British Library.

7 Based on letters from Fr Martin D'Arcy to Philip Caraman, 16 September 1965 et. seq. (BC).

8 Philip Caraman, editor and compiler, *The Years of Siege* (Longmans, Green and Co., 1966). Quotation p. 152.

9 Ibid. pp. 2 and 3.

10 Based on Norman Sherry, *The Life of Graham Greene*, vol. 2, pp. 284 and 298.

11 Letter, Philip Caraman to Graham Greene, 1 October 1959 (BC).

12 Letter, Graham Greene to Philip Caraman, 3 January 1966 (BC).

13 Letter, Graham Greene to Philip Caraman, 31 January 1966 (BC).

14 To Lady Mosley, 30 March 1966, in Mark Amory, *The Letters of Evelyn Waugh*, p. 639.

15 Envelope and note signed by Philip Caraman on 25 July 1981 (BC).

16 *The Tablet*, 30 April 1966, p. 518. The full text of the panegyric appears at the end of this book. © The Tablet Trust. http://www.thetablet.co.uk

17 Michael Holroyd, essay on Evelyn Waugh, *Works On Paper* (Little Brown and Company, UK, 2002), p. 165.

18 Letter, Margaret FitzHerbert to Lady Diana Cooper, 14 April 1966, British Library.

19 Letter, Laura Waugh to Philip Caraman from Combe Florey House, undated (BC).

20 Letter, Mary Herbert to Philip Caraman, 30 April 1966 (BC).

21 Letter, Graham Greene to Philip Caraman, 25 April 1966 (BC).

22 Letter, Fr Martin D'Arcy at Boston College to Philip Caraman, 25 April 1966 (BC).

23 Letter, Sir Osbert Sitwell to Philip Caraman, 20 May 1966 (BC) © Frank Magro 2004.

24 Letter, Fr Martin D'Arcy to Philip Caraman, 1 June 1966 (BC).
25 Philip Caraman, *Norway* (Longmans, Green and Co., 1969), p. 88.
26 Ibid. p. 147.
27 Postcard, Evelyn Waugh to Philip Caraman, 29 June 1958 (BC).
28 *Norway* p.119.
29 Ibid. p. 181.

Chapter Eight
Ubique

In the twenty years following his dismissal from *The Month* Fr Caraman never settled in any one place for more than a few months at a time. The pattern of his travels crossed countries and continents, at times defying the efforts of even his closest friends (and occasionally those of his biographer) to locate him. The dominant thread in this pattern was always Norway. Once he had established a base either there or in England he was up and away on a bewildering number of visits and holidays with friends, or on journeys of research and exploration. On several occasions he claimed to be comfortably ensconced in one place or another, but in reality was never content to remain anywhere for long; engaged in work on one book, he had the next in mind to provide an excuse to do what he enjoyed most – travel. The clues to Philip Caraman's whereabouts at any particular time during these nomadic years lie in his diaries and in letters he wrote to friends, but at times even these sources are contradictory and haphazard.[1]

Once Fr Caraman had been relieved of the appointment of Vice-Postulator of the Cause of the Forty Martyrs, and with only a vague and undefined role to play in Norway, he was free of specific obligations. The passing of friends who formerly had relied on his spiritual advice also lightened the burden of his perceived responsibilities, and allowed him freedom to follow a path of his own choosing. In Oslo, Bishop Gran proved to be the most lenient of superiors; in London, a succession of Jesuit Provincials seemed happy to permit him to do more or less as he pleased within certain parameters. His books were as good an excuse as any to roam at will, just so long as his writing and royalties provided financial backing. The English Province of the Society of Jesus may have taken a lenient view of his wanderings as recompense for his disappointment at their refusal to agree to Fr Caraman's wish to set up a Jesuit mission in Norway. He went to Oslo believing the country to be a potential missionary field, a view strongly reinforced by his summer journey. But the Province did not have priests to spare, and his request to allow other members of the Society to join him was refused. Caraman believed an opportunity had been lost, and relayed his disappointment to Meg FitzHerbert, with whom he had kept up a regular correspondence since he left England. Her sympathy was expressed with characteristic bravura: 'your superiors are foul to you. You are amazingly good the way you take it – I would like to mow them all down with a machine gun', she told him.[2]

Shortly after he returned to Oslo in August 1966, Fr Caraman told Lita Anker that he had begun his book on Norway, and added, 'I think I may have great fun writing it'. But two months later he was complaining that he had so much to do that he had been unable to get on with it. 'I got stuck . . . in the middle of the second chapter . . . At present the next chapter or two is boiling up inside me which is perhaps a good thing.' He claimed to have been 'occupied incessantly' catching up on his correspondence, preparing a lecture for the Katolsk Forum on Graham Greene's latest novel, *The Comedians,* and writing his Sunday sermons. He was also planning to leave Oslo for some weeks, because he hated the 'mist, rain, low clouds, semi-darkness' that descended on the city in midwinter. Abandoning his book, he left for Paris in early December. His excuse was that he had to go to England to do some 'odd jobs' and to see his publisher. The journey to London took in Malmo in Sweden, where he visited an Englishman and an Irishman in prison for smuggling, Copenhagen, where he attended the preview of an exhibition of Wenche Koren's tapestries, and Paris, where he had a cousin and many friends. He found that the 'whole of Paris' seemed to be 'given over to a Picasso exhibition – Petit Palais, Grand Palais, Bibl. Nationale. After 1907 he seems to have played about like a madman with his talents. But his ceramics were a revelation.' Fr Philip claimed that it was cheaper to travel by this route, than to fly directly from Oslo to London and back. He spent Christmas 'on a small private island in the middle of Lake Erne' in Ireland, and then moved on to spend a few days with the Herberts at Pixton Park: before catching the boat back to Norway he stayed with the McEwen family at Marchmont in Berwickshire. He returned in time for the 'real winter', claiming he enjoyed 'the snow, the cold, the ice and the crisp air.' Only a relatively short time of the seven or so weeks Philip was away from Oslo had been spent in London dealing with business affairs.

Discussions between Fr Caraman and John Guest of Longmans provided a genuine reason for his absence, and were probably long overdue. *The Years of Siege* had been published in the previous October, with a dedication to Mary Herbert, but the biography of Fr Martindale had raised one or two difficulties, and was again the cause of a delay in Philip Caraman's plans for his book on Norway. Having returned to Farm Street from America, Fr Martin D'Arcy had acted as an intermediary between Longmans and Fr Caraman over editorial changes to the manuscript of *C. C. Martindale:* most of the corrections suggested by John Guest appear to have been matters of spelling and punctuation. The book went straight into page-proof, and immediately on his return from his summer excursion Fr Philip wrote to Graham Greene with this news, and asked him to read the book:

> Can I ask Longmans to send you bound proofs in the hope that you will genuinely like the book and be able to write a few sentences in commendation, which they can use for publicity? ... This would greatly help to put the book over to a more general public ... I think I have been honest in the biography and not shirked the problems of drink and affections for men, particularly the latter. At least those who knew him will (I think) recognise this.[3]

Greene readily agreed to Fr Caraman's request, and two months later wrote to say he had read the biography of

Martindale with 'a lot of pleasure and admiration for the way you balance the tightrope'. He duly sent John Guest a quote to use as publicity. Following their meeting with Caraman, Longmans went straight ahead with the book, which came out in March 1967. A month after publication the author claimed that the book had caused 'quite a stir in England and I get about 20 letters a week from people I know and don't know about it'. This was not surprising as Fr Martindale was a controversial, complex and charismatic character. Privately, Graham Greene told Caraman that he had 'two little criticisms' of the biography, one of which related to Fr Martindale's enforced stay in Denmark, where he had been trapped for the duration of the Second World War, having arrived in Copenhagen on a lecture tour on the eve of the German invasion. Throughout the 'five empty years' during which he could 'see nothing, hear nothing, say, imagine, believe nothing' – and feel nothing save the cold, the Jesuit had kept a diary on which Fr Caraman based an important chapter of the book.[4] Greene remarked that he was 'glad that he knew [Martindale] well only after his Denmark years. I doubt whether I would have loved him as much at an earlier period.' He also criticised Fr Caraman for avoiding the 'modernist issue' in Martindale's life.[5] The book's author conceded that he should have been more explicit in connection with the accusations of modernism levelled against Martindale:

> It was a time when any priest of intelligence was 'suspect'. I remember Fr Devas telling me that he himself was accused of modernism, indeed had his ordination postponed simply because he spoke in praise of Tyrrell who had been his teacher at St Mary's Hall. Devas added that he never understood what modernism meant.
>
> My trouble is that in writing I often assume facts are known by readers when I have no reason for thinking that they should know them.[6]

The modernist controversy had rocked the intellectual element of the Catholic Church in England at the beginning of the twentieth century, and as a result Fr George Tyrrell had been excommunicated, and had left the Society of Jesus in February 1906.

Even in the early 1960s it must have been a difficult book to write. Certain episodes in Martindale's apostolate, such as his ministry to the Holy Child Settlement in the slums of Poplar in London's East End, might be misinterpreted today: helpers in the centre considered the priest showed 'favouritism to certain youths', when he took them up to a secluded rooftop to hear their confessions in private. Whilst trying to make the biography, as he said, 'an honest and interesting study of a priest's life', not only was Fr Caraman looking over his shoulder at the Jesuit censors, but he was also conscious of the trust that had been placed in him by the dead priest. On the whole he manages to draw a sympathetic portrait of his fellow Jesuit, and to some extent Caraman's understanding is based on empathy with his subject. Temperamentally they had much in common. Both men were highly strung, suffering frequent bouts of illness, and many of the traits in Martindale's personality, which are highlighted by Philip Caraman, are reflected in his own: unwittingly this book is the closest the author ever came to self-revelation in a published work. Intellectually and academically the two Jesuits were poles apart. Martindale had been notably successful at Oxford, winning a number of prizes; at the end of his second year he had been offered fellowships at three Colleges, and 'in the history of the University few undergraduates could have made such an impression on their teachers'.[7] But, like Caraman himself, faced with a choice between a 'life of scholarship and that of a people's priest', Martindale greatly preferred the latter.[8] Both Jesuits loved to give presents whenever they had the means to do so: Caraman quotes a letter in which Cyril tells a friend that he is giving him a book 'because there is no pleasure in life like giving things to people one is fond of'. The words mirror exactly the biographer's own sentiments and actions.[9]

The review of *C. C. Martindale* in the *Times Literary Supplement* is not as complimentary as that of Fr Caraman's biography of Henry Garnet, but it is a fair and perceptive assessment of the book, which is only a little over two hundred pages in length:

Philip Caraman is a distinguished historian of recusant life in Elizabethan England, so, predictably, his biography of Fr Martindale begins with genealogies ... A disproportionate attention to this not very interesting ancestry does at least establish the essential Englishness of a priest whose influence was to transcend the inherited categories of class and race ... The 'important' affairs are faithfully chronicled by Fr Caraman: the Duke of Marlborough's marriage, the royal visitors in the parlour at Farm Street, the set-piece sermons and speeches. But what [Fr Martindale] really achieved can only be guessed at, though his diary and immense correspondence provide his biographer with some important evidence.

... Fr Caraman admits in his preface that he has been selective in the use of the material he had at his disposal. ... It could hardly have been otherwise, for it would be impossible in a biography of this length to give any adequate account of a life of such prodigious activity. [The author's] purpose was to present the priest rather than the many enterprises in which he was involved. A biographer must be allowed his right to choose, and Fr Caraman has provided a carefully organised account of Cyril Martindale's evolution as a Jesuit and a priest. If there is some hesitancy in interpreting crucial episodes – the circumstances of his decision to join the Society of Jesus and the difficulties he experienced with his superiors are hardly analysed – this marks a reticence of which Fr Martindale would have approved.[10]

Fr Caraman's hesitancy in analysing the 'difficulties' Fr Martindale had experienced with *his* superiors may be explained by his memory of recent events at Farm Street, and the anguish he still felt over his dismissal from *The Month* by Fr Coventry. The book was dedicated to 'Evelyn Waugh – Master and Friend – and to his wife Laura', and in his preface Fr Caraman expresses his debt to 'John Willem Gran, Bishop of Oslo, who ungrudgingly allowed me to write this book in time that belonged to him'. He acknowledges a long list of people who had helped him with letters and recollections of Martindale. This gave rise to a wry comment from Philip to Lita Anker to whom he had promised a copy of the biography as a late Christmas present. 'Don't think this is a cheap present', he told her, 'the publisher gives me six copies of which I have to give three to the Jesuits. I have a list of 35 people – friends and others who have helped me in one way or another – and these 35 copies I have to *buy*.' On this occasion his generosity to friends was somewhat stretched.

Even before he received the correspondence engendered by *C. C. Martindale,* and despite John Gran's relaxed attitude to how he spent his days, Fr Caraman complained that 'the number of jobs I get given grows every day. There is always a pile of unanswered letters on my desk, and I average about thirty a week.' Whilst grumbling that his writing was being endlessly interrupted by callers, lectures, and other demands on his time, he admitted that some, at least, of the interruptions were enjoyable. A Norwegian Pastor friend gave a lecture on the Jesuits to some eighty students from the Theological Faculty of the University, and afterwards Caraman spent an hour and half answering questions, which were put to him in Norwegian, and to which he replied in English. 'I enjoyed the evening very much', he said, no doubt delighted that his Norwegian was up to the situation. Three weeks later he was invited to present a paper on 'Morals and Modern Man' at a big conference in Oslo attended by academics from several Scandinavian, French and English universities. This was not quite so enjoyable, and he claimed that preparing the paper required 'a lot of effort' on his part.

Fr Caraman worked every morning, and three evenings a week, in the *Oslo Katolske Bibliotek,* which was housed in the diocesan building in Akersveien where he lived. Visitors knew where to find him, and a friend of Lita Anker's, identified only as Nini in letters, regularly went in every Friday to help with the books and organise library shelves. Philip's writing and other work was put aside while she was there, but he looked forward to her visits at the end of the week. 'We have coffee together and a great many laughs', he told Lita, 'I have come to know her quite well and I really do like her very much'. It amused him that Nini was always promising to ask him to dinner, but never got around to actually inviting him: her visits were a welcome distraction from his more serious commitments.

Meanwhile the Norway book was making little progress.

Caraman's expectation that the manuscript might be ready for the typist by Easter proved over-optimistic, and in order to write in peace he decided to go up into the mountains and 'live like a hermit for a fortnight'. In the depths of the Norwegian winter, the snow still deep in the valleys, he travelled up Gudbrandsal to the small town of Lom. From here he wrote to Lita Anker, who was wintering on the Costa del Sol, to tell her that he was

> living in a small house on a hill about one mile out of Lom, all alone, in order to get on with my book on Norway. I make my own meals and my table looks very colourful with *vinmonopolet* red wine, oranges, bread, butter and cheese. Usually there is hot soup: occasionally a hot main course: but I can eat, work, sleep, exercise myself as I like.
>
> ... I have trained the man at the Kolonial [supermarket] in Lom to leave my packet of provisions in the snow at the end of the lane leading up to the house: I also told the post office that I had put out a letter-box there, but so far nothing has been found in it. Perhaps tomorrow. There is a fire burning now in the *stua* and I shall go to bed when it dies out. Altogether a very happy life. And my writing goes well.

During his hectic days in Mayfair, Fr Caraman had confided in Eddy Sackville-West that he yearned to retire to an isolated bog: his desire for seclusion was fulfilled now on a snow-bound hilltop in Norway, but it is unlikely he would have continued to be happy there for more than a few weeks. His mood alternated between a longing for isolation and a need for stimulating company, constantly tearing him between sociability and solitude. Even there, in the tranquillity of his temporary hermitage, he was considering expeditions into unknown territory later in the year: a long trip to Africa during the darkest days of the Nordic winter, and an excursion to the desolate island of Spitzbergen in midsummer. He had not managed to make the difficult journey to this outpost of northern Norway the previous year, and during his stay in Lom he wondered if his book 'should have a chapter on Spitzbergen. It will be an excuse for going there.' Warming to the idea, Philip asked Lita if her husband, John, might like to accompany him, and added 'he can paint polar bears for a change'.

The last chapter of Fr Caraman's book describes his voyage on a small coaster through the polar ice to Spitzbergen, which at that time had no airfield and was far removed from the tourist trail. In June 'the weather was like midwinter on the Norwegian mainland'. He talked to the people of this most remote of all mining communities: visited a mine, where, clad in 'woollen underclothes and woollen shirt, two sweaters, jersey and overalls', he was still cold: discussed the finer points of wild-dog and bear-hunting: experienced the 'contrasts of the place ... the noise of gales and the abrupt stillness'.[11] John Anker did not accompany Caraman on this journey, but Lita's sketches of churches, sacred statues, ruins, isolated harbours and the polar bears of Spitzbergen eventually illustrated Philip's book on Norway.

ॐ

In the early months of their friendship, Lita Anker had given Fr Caraman a sketch she had made of the route to her house in Spain, showing electric cables, a river bed and other houses. He was delighted with it, and when he heard from her sister that she had started drawing again, he asked her to illustrate his Norwegian book with diagrams of the route he had taken on his journey the previous year. 'There could also be other little drawings at the foot of the chapters', he added.

Lita agreed, and her illustrations contributed atmosphere and originality to his text when the book was eventually published. Their collaboration was harmonious, reflecting the deepening relationship between Fr Caraman, and the artist and her family. From the time of his arrival in Oslo, Philip looked forward increasingly to spending his free time with the Ankers, and with Lita's sister, Wenche: in time the affection he felt for them, and which they returned in good measure, made him almost an honorary member of the family. Fr Caraman greatly missed Lita's company during the long months she spent away from Norway, but they kept up a regular and lengthy correspondence, and his letters paint a vivid picture of the warmth of their friendship. Lita celebrated her thirtieth birthday at the time Philip was in Lom, and her children, Iver and Elinor, were then of early school age. During her absences in Spain, Fr Caraman – in late middle age – assumed the role of a concerned uncle, or that of a much older brother perhaps, showering her with advice on Iver's schooling, and fussing over her health much as he had done over Meg Waugh when she worked for him in Farm Street. Philip was delighted when Lita told him that concerns about Iver's education in Spain had been resolved. 'Everything seems to be working out much better than you anticipated', he wrote, 'I can't tell you how relieved I am to know that everything has been settled in such a satisfactory way'. Philip's delight was heartfelt: 'I always feared that Iver, wherever he went, would have a very difficult first term or two; but I seem to be completely wrong, thank God. If he really likes going to school, it does not matter how long he spends there. Before long you will have a lot of his school-mates running round your property.' When Lita wrote to say that Iver had been ill, Philip remembered his own childhood: 'I come from a large family, and whenever any of my young sisters got measles, mumps, or chicken pox or anything else, my mother would put the rest of us in a big bed together to make sure that we all got it and so her life would be made easier: a very sensible thing to do with a large family.'

John Anker suffered with a bad back; Philip was full of sympathy, telling him that he didn't think 'doctors anywhere know how to treat a back that gives pain: at least, it is my experience that every doctor has his own theory. Backs get out of order suddenly, and the only thing to do is to wait until they get themselves right again, just as suddenly.' When Lita told him that she had angina, he advised her 'you ought to find out whether it was what they call in England "false angina", which has all the same pains as real angina but is not so serious'. Some years later, he was even more concerned when he heard from Wenche that Lita had cracked her skull and might need an operation.

That sounds very serious indeed. It is one thing to be brave (we *all* know you are brave) but it is quite another thing to be foolish. Thank God you have John to stop you doing anything silly. You say that it takes at least a fracture to get you Norwegians down: that is just what you have. So obey John. That is not being sissy.

The affectionate relationship had lighter touches. Philip delighted in teasing Lita: the managerie of animals she had collected in Spain was a particular butt of his humour. 'I think you will have so many animals soon that you will never be able to visit Oslo again, unless you take the pig, the three hens, the owl, the cat, the dog, the pigeons and the squirrels in a trailer behind your car. I should like to make a film of it,' he told her.

Fr Caraman was also very fond of Lita's sister, but the relationship was more remote. Wenche Koren was an artist of international standing, who held exhibitions outside Norway, and received major commissions for her tapestries. When Sir John Gielgud visited Oslo to give readings at the Opera House, she was appointed to act as his hostess for the occasion, and for the reception at the British Embassy which followed. 'She made the evening tolerable for Gielgud', Caraman reported, adding regretfully that he didn't see very much of her because she was working furiously. 'Her life is all stitching and cutting out,' he added.

Eventually his library assistant, Nini, also won a place in his affections. 'She has become a great friend,' he wrote, when at long last he had dined with Nini and her husband. 'I find her instinctive simplicity and generosity immensely attractive, and she is far more intelligent than she herself realises.' Nini confided her problems to him, and during her visits to the Catholic library they had 'long talks together'.

Fr Caraman's affection for the sisters, and to a lesser extent for their friend, is undoubted. Beyond the reach of censorious eyes, and far removed from the Farm Street goldfish bowl, the bond between the Jesuit and the young Norwegian women did not attract the attention nor suffer the misrepresentation which had affected his friendship with Meg FitzHerbert. In the meantime, perhaps, he had learnt that a degree of discretion was advisable. He remained in close touch with Waugh's daughter until the time of her death in 1986, but she, Wenche Koren, Lita Anker and Nini were among a line of other creative, attractive and vivacious women with whom he shared close and loving friendships. Women trusted him, probably because they knew instinctively that the relationship had no sexual undertones: he readily gave affection, and welcomed it in return, particularly within the setting of a happy family where he sensed husband and wife were living in harmony. Maybe, subconsciously, he sought compensation for the loss of his natural family, and for the warmth of the laughing girls among whom he had grown up, and from whom hc had bccn scparatcd so young. Of his seven sisters, only the youngest, Claire, remained close to him until the end of his life, and she had her own family and personal concerns.

Describing Fr Cyril Martindale's work at Campion Hall during the First World War, and his contacts with the young men whom he encountered there, Fr Caraman wrote in the priest's biography:

> Wartime Oxford [gave Martindale] greater freedom in displaying the immense affection that inspired his work and accounted for the immeasurable good he did as a priest. His personal affection for others, as he was already well aware, constituted the greatest problem of his life as a priest. . . . when there was no risk of misunderstanding or misinterpretation . . . he gave his affection full rein.

Caraman relates that many years after the war, Martindale had advised a young Jesuit as follows:

> Go easy about 'feelings'. They are human and no human thing is negligible, because God-made. They have not to guide us: but you do not want a shrivelled heart. We need *fully* to love people, if we want to do them any good. A technical apostolate is perfectly barren.[12]

Was Philip Caraman the young priest to whom the distinguished Jesuit had given this advice? The biography emphasises that Martindale 'gathered many devoted friends', among whom, in later life, Graham Greene was one, although the book does not mention this. Like the priest about whom he wrote, Fr Caraman also had many friends for whom he had a profound affection, but – unlike Martindale – many were women with whom Philip seemed able to develop a special rapport.

There was a further dimension to Fr Caraman's relationship with Lita Anker. Unlike some of the other women with whom he was associated who were 'cradle Catholics' like himself, he also acted as her spiritual adviser and mentor as she hovered on the brink of conversion. His letters on the subject of her religious hesitancy are no less affectionate than those in which he discusses family matters, but are more serious in tone, and demonstrate the depths of his patience and understanding for anyone who was thinking about becoming a Catholic.

Lita Anker had been attracted to the Church while living in Spain, and had gone to a Spanish priest for instruction in the Faith. Like Dame Edith Sitwell twelve years earlier, she discussed with Fr Caraman what books she should read to help her make up her mind. His advice is down-to-earth, but surprising:

> St. John of the Cross is about the toughest spiritual reading you could find. I don't think there is anyone who is more difficult to understand: the reason is that it is quite impossible to communicate in human language the kind of spiritual experience he had. There are odd sentences and passages that I can follow, no more. Are you reading him in Spanish? The poems are a different matter, really moving. He was a great poet.

He always recommended St Thomas Aquinas to those he directed, but of other writers he was more dismissive. When Lita enquired about Bronowski's books, he told her he would arrange for copies to be sent to her from his bookseller in London, but that she should 'take only the proven statements of Bronowski seriously, the rest is theological bull-shit'. As Lita came closer to the Church, Fr Caraman urged her to read 'that little book called *What Law and Letter Kills*. You can pick it up, open it anywhere, and read it for five or ten minutes. I feel sure it will help you far better than any help I can or could give you.'

Although he was at pains not to upset Lita's relationship with her Spanish priest, Fr Caraman sympathised with the anguish she was experiencing over the important step she was about to take. He told her that he

> understood [her] fears and feelings completely: but I think also that you are braver than you know. Somehow, in church on Saturday night before Easter, I felt you were in distress: it was the day you saw the Padre: I hope he was helpful to you.
>
> There is much I should like to tell you, but one thing you must remember is that all who become Catholics, whatever their age or circumstances, have to pay a price, but though it seems a big price at the time, it is very little indeed for the deep happiness and manifold blessings you have in return.

John Anker did not like the idea of his wife becoming a Catholic, and Caraman tried to allay Lita's fears on that score, saying John would 'eventually be happy about it', and that she should rely on 'the Padre and on your prayers: you will come through your loneliness all right: I am sure of that'.

When Fr Caraman heard a few weeks later that Lita had been received into the Catholic Church in Spain, he told her that he was 'immensely happy', but if her Padre agreed he thought that, as she was Norwegian, she ought to keep her Confirmation until she returned later in the summer. The ceremony is given great prominence in Norwegian churches, and Philip told her that 'we can arrange for it to be done privately in the chapel here [in Akersveien] by John Gran'.

The patience with which Fr Caraman directed and helped Lita Anker through her own particular religious maze is an example of the gentle guidance he lavished on all who chose him as their spiritual mentor. Reading his advice to her, it is understandable that people like Evelyn Waugh, Edith Sitwell and Eddy Sackville-West, who had found their home in the Catholic Church, should commend others to him. Talking to her biographer, Lady Selina Hastings, Rosamond Lehmann recalled her meetings with Fr Caraman. 'He used to come and see me', she said, 'and have a little drink and smoke a little cigarette, and say "Don't worry, you've been given a great grace"'. Lehmann eventually chose spiritualism rather than the Church, but Philip concentrated on giving her reassurance, and never sought to intimidate her.[13] Although Catholicism had (and still has) a reputation for inflexibility, Fr Caraman never emphasised rules and regulations. Quite the contrary: he told Lita to remember that 'you are only bound to go to Mass when you can reasonably get there. If you can't leave your children or your house, then that is that. A Catholic is bound to go only when he *can* go. There are many Catholics in Norway, living up the valleys, who can only go to Mass in summer.

Those who turned to Fr Caraman for spiritual comfort and guidance probably had no inkling of the burden they laid on him. In contrast to an expensive therapist, it was he, the counsellor, who paid the price for their outpourings. In one of his letters to Lita he revealed how much it cost him to listen patiently and to give advice to others:

> The months between the end of summer and *Julebord* time were so depressing. Cod liver oil did not help much. So many people in distress came to see me and I felt I could do so little for them. I had to conceal my own low spirits. But all this is another way of saying that I am selfish. Go on praying for [me] for yours are Norwegian prayers and perhaps the only Norwegian prayers I get.

These remarks reach the heart of Fr Caraman's personal understanding of his vocation as a priest, and illustrate the pastoral role which he believed he was called upon to fulfil. Fr Olaf Waring relates that on one occasion he and Philip

> were going to meet some people whom I, frankly, did not quite approve of. I had some misgivings, and while Philip was not without misgivings either, he nevertheless did not hesitate to remind me that some of our rather important priestly forebears were fishermen whom the Lord quite specifically turned into 'fishers of men'. So Philip, with that wonderful little muffled grunt of his – 'humph' – remarked, 'We must always be fishing.'

Recalling this story thirty years later, Fr Waring incidentally captures a mannerism of Philip's speech, which would grow more pronounced with age.[14]

Despite the depression he often felt, Fr Caraman gave the best of himself to his ministry: in Oslo this entailed working quietly among the English-speaking community, saying Mass in English, preaching sermons, and guiding a small, scattered and unofficial flock. His homilies in the dimly-lit chapel on Sunday mornings were prepared with great care, but spoken seamlessly, without notes, in so relaxed and convincing a manner that they seemed to come without forethought straight from the heart. Fr Caraman did not base his sermons exclusively on the text of the Sunday's readings. In one memorable homily he spoke of the beauty of the Psalms, and told the congregation that the verses of Psalm 138 (139) found a deep echo in his own spiritual life: at least one of his listeners was inspired to look up the words when she returned home.

> Lord, thou hast proved me and known me:
> thou hast known my sitting down, and my rising up.
> Thou hast understood my thoughts afar off:
> my path and my line thou hast searched out.

There were more unexpected facets to Fr Caraman's ministry in Oslo. Fr Olaf Waring describes one unusual incident when the Jesuit was given permission to say the prayers of exorcism for a couple who had been experiencing 'weird' happenings in their flat in central Oslo. Fr Waring says that Philip 'was quite aware of the fact of satanic influence', and after he had performed the exorcism of the flat everything returned to normal there.[15]

This was a rare departure from the orthodox. The mainstay of Fr Caraman's life was the Mass. It was for the Mass that the English martyrs, to whom he had devoted so much of his work, had died: it was the loss of this Holy Sacrifice from the churches of Norway that he mourned: the daily celebration of Mass was the focal point of his days. After Philip Caraman's death, Fr Waring bemoaned the fact that for some priests the Mass has become almost exclusively 'a social reality' instead of 'that personal devotional, essential, element of the priest's life in the spirit, as illustrated in Pope Paul VI's encyclical *Mysterium Fidei*.' He praised the example given by Fr Caraman in this 'crucial area' of a priest's life when they were both living in the presbytery in Oslo:

> Younger priests no longer viewed their day and their Mass as integral parts of a whole, and unless they were absolutely required to say Mass they preferred not to do so. There might be no congregation for them that day, a not surprising phenomenon in a country where the Catholics were less than half of one per cent of the population. It was a grace for me and example, to live in a presbytery where the 'Jesuit Father' never missed a day's Mass whether there was a congregation or not.[16]

By the summer of 1967, Fr Caraman was sufficiently confident of his understanding and performance in the Norwegian language to offer his pastoral services to Bishop Gran as an acting parish priest during the long holiday period, when regular incumbents went away. John Gran was only too pleased to accept; six months earlier he had invited Caraman to stay on in Norway, and the Jesuit, somewhat hesitantly, had agreed to do so. The decision had been made only after a great deal of heart searching. In explaining his dilemma to Lita, Fr Caraman made a rare allusion to his roots:

> All my life as a child, youth and a priest, I have lived in London. Give me Paris, Rome or Vienna, and I should be in my own climate. Oslo is different ... I will stay; although there are so many people in Oslo I like very much, it was a hard decision to make. Certainly your prayers ... must have helped me a great deal. So you are to be thanked (or blamed) according to what happens. But go on praying almost every night.

After his expedition to the Arctic region of Spitzbergen in June, followed by a flying visit to England, Philip spent three weeks running a parish in the port of Stavanger, and later spent a weekend acting as *sogneprest* in Hamar. But devotion to pastoral duty did not give him the courage to spend another dank, dark autumn in Oslo. As summer ended, with his book on Norway still unfinished and with no permanent appointment on offer, Fr Caraman left Norway for the warmth of Africa, and a visit to Rhodesia where his brother, John, had been working as a missionary for the last thirty years.

ꙮ

At the time of Fr Caraman's visit, Rhodesia (now Zimbabwe) was in crisis. The government under Ian Smith had made a Unilateral Declaration of Independence from Great Britain, sanctions had been imposed, and for a time the prospect of war between the mother country and its former colony was openly discussed. Caraman told John Anker that he had completely lost trust in Mr Harold Wilson (then British Prime Minister), but thought that 'he is so clever that he is certain to be in power for the next eight years. He is no statesman, but he is perhaps the most cunning politician in Europe.' During his travels around Rhodesia, Philip carefully noted the effects of the political situation on life in the country. The journal he wrote during the weeks he spent in East Africa is in other respects somewhat confusing: the pages covering Rhodesia are neatly written in sequence, but a description of a visit to Ethiopia and Eritrea is undated, written hurriedly and possibly retrospectively, and the pages covering these countries are almost illegible and contain numerous erasures.

From a study of the diaries it seems that he travelled to Kenya, Ethiopia and Eritrea before touring Rhodesia. The only hint of his stay in Kenya is contained in an entry in which Fr Caraman relates that he met two men from Claver House, the Jesuit house for African students in Pimlico to which he had been banished by Fr Coventry, who were begging on Kenyatta Avenue in Nairobi.

Philip Caraman was plainly fascinated by Ethiopia, and his breathless description of his visit to the country contains some surprising comments. At a time when the British generally believed that they had won a victory by ridding the country of Mussolini's occupying army, Fr Caraman – possibly recalling his own Italian roots – reveals that several educated Ethiopians to whom he talked 'admitted that if the Italians had stayed on another twenty years, they would all be better off today. In the six years of occupation Musso [*sic*] did reveal the Roman genius for colonisation.' The Italians had given them roads and buildings, and lavished thirty per cent of their national revenue on the country. Caraman added that 'experts reckon that if the agricultural resources of Ethiopia were developed, the country could feed the entire African continent'. But the principal interest of the Jesuit's visit lay in the country's religious heritage: of the Coptic churches he wrote: 'The paintings that cover [the church] are proof that all the Christian dogmas are there: but all in a very Jewish framework. There are ritual cleansings, impure foods, emphasis on the letter of the law. Behind the altar is the Holy of Holies, which only the priests and deacons enter.'

Fr Caraman travelled as widely as circumstances permitted in Ethiopia: 'by chance' he made a flight in a small local plane from Addis Ababa along with a 'handful of passengers', that circled low over the Blue Nile falls and overflew the 'square Coptic monastic churches surrounded by mud huts on the islands on Lake Tana'. The plane also ventured to Gondar, and then to Aksum, 'the ancient Holy City', which 'at first appeared like any Ethiopian township – rows of mud huts, streets filled with donkeys and fly-plagued children, dung everywhere'. But a tour of the town revealed fascinating relics of a past age, and 'an old castle where the rains wash up ancient coins among the excavations'. The excursion had risky interludes: at one point the plane 'landed with a splash beside our baggage piled forgotten in the middle of the field. The pilot walked 200 yards in a straight line to see whether the ground was dry enough for a take-off.' At the end of the trip Philip concluded that 'it was a relief to be airborne and flying to Asmara'.

Amidst the whirl of his intensive travels round East Africa, Fr Caraman could not foresee the significance of the Ethiopian leg of his journey. He was enjoying an extended holiday, his Norway book was still unfinished, and at the time he didn't have the slightest intention of writing about the country. It was another eighteen years, and several books later, before his experiences in this unusual Christian land came to fruition in his tale of *The Story of the Jesuits in Ethiopia*.

For the first three weeks of his visit to Rhodesia, Philip Caraman was in the competent hands of his elder brother, for whom his admiration was undiminished by years of separation. The two Jesuits had kept up a frequent correspondence, and the younger Caraman always enjoyed John's letters, saying, 'he wrote with a clarity and concise niceness that I envied'[17] – a valuable compliment from a successful writer to a man of action. John was quite unlike Philip in character. After thirty years in Africa, he was – according to his brother – tired out by 'the exertions of his pioneering years, caring for the Africans from Nyasaland or working on the mines or farms throughout the country'. Staying with John in the Umvukwes Mission, Philip found him an excellent host, despite the frugality of his living conditions.

> His [John's] parishioners supported him more in kind than in cash, for he reckoned that his food expenses for the year, [at 1967 prices] amounted to £30. Going round the countryside with him we would return with old window frames, bags of cement, unwanted furniture, unused bricks and much else, all gifts to cut down the expense of another out-school or a convent for the African Sisters.[18]

John Caraman's success as a missionary was achieved by a forceful character, which echoed his father, René's, personality. Fr Richard Randolph, who knew him well during the years when he also was working in Rhodesia, reveals that the elder Fr Caraman was affectionately known as 'Hitler', and was renowned for always being 'given' what he most needed.

Nonetheless, John Caraman's parishioners obviously regarded him with respect and some affection: local Catholic farmers at Umvukwes had a whip-round the day before he set out on his holiday with Philip, and presented him with £23 to help with expenses. It is likely that Philip managed to finance his stay in Africa, at least in part, with revenue from articles he had written for Catholic weeklies in England, and from some of the royalty payments on his books which had been allowed him by the Jesuits: under Caraman's vow of poverty these were generally made over to the Society. With the elder brother as guide, the pair set off in Fr John's car on a comprehensive tour of Rhodesia, which took them south into Matabeleland, west to the Victoria Falls, and east into Mozambique, before returning to Umvukwes.

Whenever possible the Caramans stayed at Catholic mission stations, where, more often than not, John was well known by the priests in charge. Other legs of the journey were purely for sight-seeing and were touristic in nature. Philip's journal covers a wide variety of subjects: the nature of missionary work in the country: the people and their culture: tourist excursions and mishaps: the effect of sanctions and UDI on Rhodesia, and his own experiences resulting from the political situation there. At their first stop at the mission station of Kutama, his interest was focused on a workshop in a satellite farm where the priest in charge, Fr Hannan, was working on a 'new edition of his Standard Shona Dictionary for the Government, and a translation [into the Shona language] of books of the Old Testament not in the Anglican canon'. Philip Caraman was intrigued by the nuances of the Shona language, just as he had been by Norwegian when he arrived in Oslo. 'It was clear that Shona has few generic words but is very rich in specific words.' He was surprised to learn that the language was 'rich in conceptual words, but lacked words that were equivalent to notions derived from Greek and Roman civilisation'. His curiosity was aroused by African art. Towards the end of their journey the brothers spent a night at Serima, and Caraman recalled that this mission had been described by Evelyn Waugh in *Tourist in Africa*. Here he discovered 'the only Catholic attempt to develop native Christian art . . . no other attempt anywhere to use African arts (except music) for church.' In the workshops attached to the mission he watched boys aged between twelve and eighteen busy carving wood, and remarked that the enterprise was 'totally uncommercialised'. He was struck by 'two very remarkable native paintings in the church', one depicted the miracle of the multiplication of the loaves and fishes, and the second was of the Last Supper.

The younger Caraman was content to listen, watch and learn during his stays at the various posts they visited. On one occasion he sat quietly through a debate on missionary methods between John and another priest, feeling himself unqualified to contribute to the discussion. But a stay at the 'large village' of Umtali, which was the local headquarters of the Irish Carmelite mission, elicited a forthright comment:

[The] Irish in bulk (i.e. religious congregation) in British territory would seem not to make good missionaries. Why among all the priests in Scandinavian countries is there not even one Irishman or even half an Irishman? There are twenty theologates or houses of study for different Orders and Congregations in Dublin alone each holding down ten to fifteen priests (presumably among the best men) and yet reluctance to join up.

Within two years this criticism concerning the lack of Irish missionaries in Scandinavia would become obsolete, when a remarkable young Irishman, the Marist Fr Rory Mulligan, joined the Stabekk community near Oslo, and devoted his life's ministry to the Catholic Church in Norway.

Along the tourist trail, the Caramans lodged in camps and occasionally in hotels. They stayed in a chalet on the Wankie Game Reserve, and were rewarded by generous sightings of elephants, giraffe, buck, crocodiles, baboons and buffaloes. Philip recorded that the temperature was over 105°F when they checked in to Robins Camp, where, in the early evening, they had a frightening experience. On the road running through the Reserve, they watched

a pride of eight lions frolicking about twenty-five yards off the track. Interesting to see how happy a passing truckload of Africans was to see *us* happy – rather an endearing characteristic of Africans. An hour later the lions were still there ... [when] another car-driver called out and pointed to flat left tyre on side facing the lions. Fierce injunctions at camp against stepping out of car, but [we had] no alternative. I kept watch on lions who were darting out and playing like puppies and watching John get pump out of car ... tough German from neighbouring car pumped furiously.

They breathed a sigh of relief as John got back into the car, and they headed back to the camp where they spent a very hot night: on another occasion Philip recorded a temperature of 110°F–120°F, remarking that they were touring Rhodesia during the 'hottest time of the year in the hottest place' in the country.

Fr Philip was duly impressed by the grandeur of the Victoria Falls, where the priests said Mass in the Victoria Falls Hotel, attended by a congregation of seven Europeans. They were given a 'free lavish breakfast' in the '*very* grand' hotel, which was crowded out by an American tourist party. This taste of luxury was in sharp contrast to a night they spent at a Jesuit holiday house in the mountains near the Mozambique border: the place turned out to be no more than a primitive hut, without water or electricity, although the setting amidst 'lovely hills and panoramas' was beautiful. Philip wrote: 'John is too old for "camping". I could stay here for days and write.' He remarked that the climate was 'cold like a Norwegian summer day'. Any reminder of the cosy hermitage at Lom where he had stayed earlier in the year stopped there; although they had planned to stay another night in the hut, they found it was 'too sordid and cold', and they left the following morning.

It was when the Caramans tried to get over the border into the Portuguese colony of Mozambique that they experienced the impact of the political crisis in Rhodesia at first hand. Early in his visit to the country, Fr Philip had applied for a visa in Salisbury (now Harare): the paper had not arrived either there nor in Bulawayo when they passed through. At the border the immigration officer pretended to look aghast when he saw Philip's British passport, although John, with a Rhodesian passport, had no problems. At the mission station Philip was told that it was a question of luck whether he got through, depending on the mood of the official who dealt with him. After remarking on the radical differences in atmosphere and architecture between the Portuguese and British colonies, Fr Caraman described the 'queue of Rhodesian cars passing through to the Portuguese post where there was petrol on sale at special prices for "tourists", who turned back immediately after filling up'.

Throughout their tour of Rhodesia, they were regaled with stories of the brutality of the armed gangs which were – even then – disrupting the formerly peaceful country. In the run-up to what eventually developed into a full-scale civil war, Fr Philip learnt that 'terrorists' were responsible for a decline in candidates for the novitiate in some missionary areas where they were particularly active, and everywhere the Frs Caraman lodged the talk inevitably turned to 'terrorist' activity. In a racially unbiased and detailed summary of the political situation engendered by Ian Smith's UDI, Philip predicted that 'relations with England will never be good again'.

Throughout the weeks Fr Philip spent in Rhodesia, his thoughts frequently turned to Norway. At one of their stops, the brothers met two priests who knew the country well, and the talk at lunch that day was 'entirely about Norway', which, Philip thought, seemed 'odd in the middle of the African veldt'. As John Caraman sat down, exhausted, on the grave of Cecil Rhodes, his sibling admired the vista, remarking that the view was 'impressive but unusual. Norway has spoilt me forever for scenery.' And during the final week of his Rhodesian visit, which was spent in Salisbury, Fr Philip was asked to lecture on what was now regarded as his special area of interest: he gave a well-attended talk to an audience of Anglicans and Catholics on 'Religion in Scandinavia', and spoke to the Presidium of the Legion of Mary on Norway. From a discussion with Father Dove, whom he considered was destined for high ecclesiastical office, Caraman concluded that it was 'more clear than ever that there is need for "youth" work in Rhodesia as much as in Norway'.

Preoccupation with his adopted country did not hasten Philip's return there. His obsessive passion for travel goaded him into trying to cram into his tour as many East African countries as he possibly could. He was 'bored' with Salisbury within two days of arriving there, although he had to spend almost three weeks in the city to honour pre-arranged appointments before leaving for Zambia. One meeting was with the local representative of his publishers, Longmans. A discussion on possible subjects for books may have seemed unimportant at the time: one suggestion was for a biography of the Elizabethan Jesuit, Fr Persons, who had played a major role in the lives of Henry

Garnet, John Gerard and William Weston. A second possibility was noted in Fr Caraman's journal simply as 'Paraguay', with the comment that 'obvious tension lies in racial questions'.

The tours of Zambia, Uganda and the Sudan with which Philip hoped to crown his East African safari did not turn out as he hoped. The Zambian visit in particular irritated him. Arriving at Lusaka airport, he was held up by an immigration official who decided to declare him a prohibited immigrant: after protracted wrangling, in which Caraman was supported by his Jesuit host, he was permitted to stay in the country for only three days on condition he remained in the capital.

He fared better in Uganda. Throughout his travels his path was smoothed by a network of Jesuit contacts, and at Entebbe airport he was met by an African priest, Fr Barnabas, 'who had the chief immigration officer in tow'. The official was 'a tall, handsome, African, who gave me VIP treatment'. Fr Caraman said he had the 'sensation of entering a Catholic country', although Uganda was only about one-third Catholic. The highlight of his stay was an invitation to attend the funeral Mass of Prince Alfred, the younger son of the Kabaka of Buganda: this turned out to be a colourful and noisy occasion, at which Philip and an English girl with a dog were the only Europeans present among a vast crowd of several thousand Africans. Much of his time in Uganda was spent in a vain attempt to obtain a visa for the Sudan, but after several unsuccessful visits to the Sudanese Embassy, he finally ended up with an unsatisfactory transit visa, for what was the seventh and final country on his prolonged African tour.

Fr Caraman's journals are enlivened by delightful and humorous vignettes of encounters he had along his way. He describes a morning in Umvukwes when, before he started saying his Mass, a four-year old African boy went up to him, and the Jesuit's server 'helped me to find out what he wanted. It was simply that he wanted to "pray".' Another experience, in Uganda, was disturbing:

A mad African with a panama hat and red band followed me . . .
I seem to attract mad Africans: he divided world into seven

classes of people which he recited for my instruction. I remember only the last (coming after Sadducees and Pharisees), namely the hypocrites. I thought he was going to enlarge on my fittingness for this class, but he included only in his seventh class Arabs and Americans (strange bedfellows). He stepped into sun and across the street, starting his litany anew.

Philip reiterated that he seemed to have 'a peculiar attraction for crazy Africans'.

On returning to Oslo, with his experiences in Africa still fresh in his mind, Fr Caraman preached once again to the English-speaking congregation in the sombre chapel in Akersveien. One of his first sermons was a moving homily on the subject of Catholic missionary work, and its importance to the country he firmly believed to be his own particular territory – Norway.

❧

Fr Caraman's fervent preaching was born, in part, from a sense of frustration. His plea for the establishment of a bona fide Jesuit mission in Norway continued to fall on deaf ears in London, and with no permanent parish or fixed appointment there was little to keep him in the country. Although Bishop Gran was happy for him to remain, and Philip was still undecided about whether or not he wished to do so, the time had come for other options for his future to be explored. Caraman's reputation as an historian and writer had been firmly established with his successful books, and through his work on the Cause for the Canonisation of the Forty Martyrs, and he had more than one option to consider. He was about to take up the offer of the post of Catholic chaplain to Bristol University when Cardinal Heenan invited him to become Professor of Church History at St Edmund's College, Ware, in Hertfordshire: at that time the College embraced both a boys' school and the Westminster diocesan seminary of Allen Hall.

In 1968, the appointment suited Fr Caraman's mood well, promising him congenial work in an environment conducive to writing. He sought Fr Martin D'Arcy's approval, and the old

priest, writing from California, confirmed that he considered the
post 'quite a good idea, and you will like it – though of course
it is a little hard on the students. But you will have time to mug
up something no doubt, and at the worst you can always call on
Fr O'Higgins.'[19] The reference to the priest who was an exact
contemporary of Fr Caraman's in the Society of Jesus and as an
undergraduate at Campion Hall, exemplified D'Arcy's gentle
teasing concerning his protégé's lacklustre academic qualifications. Philip was not particularly amused by this leg-pull:
attached to the letters addressed to him by Fr D'Arcy, which
were deposited in Boston College, he left a note saying this
remark referred to his student days at Oxford, when D'Arcy had
said Fr O'Higgins 'was the greatest historian of the English
Province, and that I [Caraman] was jealous of his reputation. It
was a *joke* [sic] that he made from time to time.' Whether or
not Philip liked it, the joke had a basis of solid fact. Fr
O'Higgins had a background of enviable academic qualifications: he gained a doctorate in 1966, and held the appointment
of Oxford don and tutor at Campion Hall into old age, devoting
his life to the study of history. There is no doubt that in
academic terms Fr O'Higgins outshone the gregarious Caraman.

Fr D'Arcy's letter also sent the latest news of the Mayfair
community, where he was still based. ' I will try for the present
to put up with Farm Street. I hope and pray for a change of
bosses there,' he told Caraman, who certainly sympathised with
him. Philip still shuddered at mention of the place, and dreaded
the thought that he might one day have to return there.
Supportive as ever, Martin D'Arcy added a postscript to his
letter: he had heard from the Jesuit, Fr Sweeney (poet friend
of Thomas Merton), with whom Caraman corresponded regularly, that Philip was 'short of cash, so I wrote to Fr Vavasour
[in London] suggesting that if he had any stipends to send some
to you'.[20] Fr Caraman was getting into the habit of pleading
poverty; no doubt on this occasion his protracted tour of Africa
had proved more expensive than he had originally intended.

He needed royalties, and the Norway book was not yet
finished: in the spring of 1968 he made one last effort after
many distractions, and completed the writing and the preface

before he left Oslo. The book was so unlike all his previous
work that he was unsure of how it would be received. When he
started writing it, he had promised to 'try it out' on Norwegian
friends like Bishop Gran, Rieber-Mohn, the Ankers, and
Wenche Koren, before giving it to Longmans. 'I shall probably
be expelled from Norway when it appears', he quipped, and
added, 'it will be very much *my own* book'. He thought 'the best
parts of it are about North Norway'. When John Guest of
Longmans went through Lita Anker's drawings, 'he was
delighted' with them: Philip praised her work and, when the
publisher suggested paying her £100, he told her that 'this
seemed to me inadequate. I will find ways of making it more
after talking with my agent.' For a long time he agonised over
a title for the book, toying with no less than eight different
names: these ranged through various 'Viking' options from
Vikings Today to *In Quest of the Viking,* and on to the pompous
Inside Norway – A Personal Guide for Native and Tourist.
Finally all were discarded in favour of a simple *Norway.*

Before taking up his appointment at Ware, Fr Caraman spent
part of the summer in London – but not in Mayfair. He had
some constructive meetings with his publisher, but otherwise did
not much enjoy the weeks he spent in the capital. Having said
farewell to Norway, he immediately pined to be back there.
Mulling over Lita Anker's illustrations for his book, he said
'they made me want to come back soon for a visit ... [the
drawing of] Flatdal made me rather sad. What a peaceful place
– two days in London have left me exhausted.' He hated
London, and could not remain there 'after the wide open spaces
of Norway'. The idea of living at St Edmund's College appealed
to him more. 'It is well out of London, half way to Cambridge
and in the country ... I have two rather big rooms there and a
garage for my old car. Somehow I already miss Norway. I was
settled there and I am not yet settled here,' – well, only insofar
as his peregrinations allowed him to settle anywhere for more
than a few months at a time.

Before 'settling' in Ware Fr Caraman enjoyed a stimulating
few weeks. He visited the Herberts at Pixton, went up to
Berwickshire to see the McEwens, and rounded off the summer

with a week in Rome, where he stayed with Giles and Meg FitzHerbert, in order to 'advise about a film'. The film has not been identified, but the greater part of his journey to Italy was made on the private yacht *Clonsilla*, on which he sailed from Dublin, firstly to Gibraltar, thence to Venice and along the coast of Yugoslavia to Dubrovnik, from where he flew to Rome. The summer cruise on the luxurious mini-liner was made at the invitation of Honor Svejdar, a wealthy friend and a member of the Guinness brewing family on whose estate in Ireland Philip stayed on several occasions over the years: he had received her into the Church following an introduction from the actor Sir Alec Guinness, whom Honor regarded as a 'cousin'. Philip went ashore in Venice to lunch at the Cipriani hotel with Osbert Sitwell; 'an English playwright who lives in Venice', also unnamed in Fr Caraman's description of the cruise, acted as the party's guide to the Dalmatian coast.

During the idle days of his September voyage, the Jesuit realised that for the first time in many years he had no book in prospect. Writing from *Clonsilla's* anchorage in the Venice lagoon, he told Lita Anker:

> I have *suddenly* got a great impetus to work. For a long time I have been turning over a number of ideas for a new book and have been dissatisfied with them all: those that appealed to me most were impossible without much travel abroad – and I shall be tied down to Ware until next Easter. But last night at dinner, in the middle of a lot of party conversation on other things, I decided to begin an anthology of the writings of Thomas More. Such a book does not exist. It is something I can do while I am preparing my daily lecture ... Thomas More wrote much in Latin and these parts I should have to translate.

The dinner-party chatter may well have touched on the recent success of Robert Bolt's screenplay about More's heroic martyrdom, *A Man for All Seasons*, but Philip's anthology never materialised. The academic discipline of preparing and delivering lectures to the students of St Edmund's College quickly proved too dull and constricting, and the impetus to travel directed Fr Caraman's thoughts towards something far more challenging and exciting. It would be another seven years before his next book was published, and it was destined to bring him pleasure, pride and pain in equal measure.

Notes

1 Unless annotated separately, the text of this chapter is based principally on three 'African' Journals found among Philip Caraman's private papers, and on letters he wrote to Lita Anker.
2 Letter, Margaret FitzHerbert to Philip Caraman, 23 August 1966, private papers (hereafter PCPP).
3 Letter, Philip Caraman to Graham Greene, 6 August 1966, Boston College (hereafter BC).
4 Philip Caraman, *C. C. Martindale. A Biography* (Longmans, 1967), ch.11.
5 Graham Greene to Philip Caraman, 17 October 1966 (BC) © Francis Greene 2004.
6 Letter, Philip Caraman to Graham Greene, 20 October 1966 (BC).
7 *C. C. Martindale,* p. 90.
8 Ibid. p. 136.
9 Ibid. p. 112.
10 *Times Literary Supplement*, 23 March 1967, no. 3,395. p. 247.
11 Philip Caraman, *Norway*, pp. 198–207.
12 *C. C. Martindale*, pp. 126–8.
13 Selina Hastings, *Rosamond Lehmann*, pp. 356–7 (Chatto & Windus, 2002).
14 Fr Olaf Waring, submission for Fr Caraman's obituary notice, September 1998.
15 Fr Olaf Waring, letter to author, 21 July 2002.
16 Fr Olaf Waring, September 1998.
17 Fr John Caraman's Obituary notice, *Letters & Notices*, vols 85–87, 1983, Jesuit Archives.
18 Ibid.
19 Letter, Fr Martin D'Arcy to Philip Caraman, 3 April 1968 (BC).
20 Ibid.

Chapter Nine

Discord in Paradise

As he looked out from the window of his room in Allen Hall,
Fr Caraman's thoughts followed the road lying beyond the
college gates: it runs to Colchester and the port of Harwich,
from where ferries make their regular crossing of the North Sea
to Scandinavia. His mind flew further yet, across the Atlantic to
the countries of South America, which to him were still
unknown territory. Reminders of his last book, and plans for the
next, captivated his imagination to the exclusion of almost
everything else. Fr D'Arcy's jest concerning his students of
Church History was a valid one. Caraman decided that 'the
young men' were 'not a bad lot on the whole', but he left only
the faintest of footprints in his appointment as their Professor of
Church History. The college archives contain no trace of the
lectures he delivered, nor of his participation in any extra-
curricular activities during the time he spent there.

The idea for a study of the seventeenth and eighteenth century
Jesuit Reductions[1] in Paraguay came to him towards the end of
1968, and harked back to the conversation he had when he was
in Rhodesia the previous year. His decision to go ahead may
have been strengthened by a visit to the Jesuit archives in Rome
during his stay in the city following his cruise on board
Clonsilla. The subject was not one that covered a ground-break-
ing area of research, but the excuse it would afford for extensive
travel surely played a part in his choice. The Reductions were
regarded by many historians and sociologists as an idyllic model
of benign and harmonious colonisation: as Caraman pointed out
in his introduction to the book, there had been a continuous flow

of books about the Jesuit Republic since the end of the seventeenth century. In the twentieth century the Society's unique
experiment had inspired two major works, Cunninghame
Graham's *A Vanished Arcadia,* and Hochwalder's play, *The
Strong are Lonely (Sur la Terre comme au Ciel)*, which had been
staged both in London and in Paris as recently as the 1950s.[2]
The London production had starred Donald Wolfit in the role of
the Jesuit Provincial, and *The Month,* under Fr Caraman, had
run a review of the play. He considered that the principal interest of his own chronicle did not lie in the originality of the
subject, but in its importance as a study of the 'treatment of a
primitive people and its preparation to take its place in a more
developed society'.[3]

Research into this fruitful field for writers and historians
was continually throwing up new material, and it was
Caraman's intention to make the best possible use of the most
recent studies, and of work which had been done mainly by
Spaniards and South Americans since the publication of *A
Vanished Arcadia* in 1901. Most of the information and mate-
rial Fr Caraman required was lodged in the Jesuit Archives in
Rome, in other European institutions in Madrid and
Stockholm, and in libraries and archives in Buenos Aires.
Within a few days of arriving at Ware, Philip's intention to
remain there until the following Easter was abandoned, and he
was arranging to return to Italy during the Christmas vacation.
This foray into the Jesuit archives was treated as a working
holiday, and he availed himself of an invitation to stay with
Osbert Sitwell in his mountain castle outside Florence for a
few days in the New Year. Thereafter he took every opportunity to escape from his 'settled' and comfortable existence
at St Edmund's, spending the intervals between academic
terms away doing preliminary research which was frequently
combined with visits to friends.

Once work on the book was under way, Caraman announced
his new project to Graham Greene, then living in Paris, who
immediately expressed his interest. 'How amusing that you have
been working on the Paraguay Reductions while I have been
visiting Paraguay', he replied. Greene had taken photographs of

some of the Jesuit ruins in remote areas of the country: he wondered if Philip might like to use his pictures. Fr Caraman told him it would be a long time before he started to arrange illustrations for his book, but welcomed the offer to look at Greene's photographs.[4]

This time Caraman had no difficulty in finding a title for the book: it was taken from a line in G. K. Chesterton's poem 'To the Jesuits', which Philip had published in 'his magazine' when he was editor:

> You bade the Red Man rise like the Red Clay
> Of God's great Adam in his human right,
> Till trailed the snake of trade, our own time's blight,
> And man lost Paradise in Paraguay.[5]

Graham Greene, another Chesterton fan, took a spasmodic interest in *The Lost Paradise* throughout the years Fr Caraman was working on it, but when the priest sent him a preview copy of *Norway*, Greene merely complimented the author on his ability 'to make so readable an account of such a dreary country!'[6] Philip probably chuckled at this reaction which was in line with Evelyn Waugh's opinion of a country which neither of his friends knew well, and for which he himself at that time felt such affection.

With the publication of his long-awaited book on the country imminent, Fr Caraman could not resist the lure of spending the best weeks of the long holiday in Norway, where the short – often glorious – summers are one of Europe's best-kept secrets. Bishop Gran was delighted that Philip could take over one of his parishes during the incumbent's absence just as he had done two years earlier. The Jesuit's spell of duty in the pretty south coast town of Arendal gave rise to a revealing incident. A family from Fr Caraman's erstwhile English-speaking flock in Oslo was astonished to find him saying Sunday Mass in the local church, and invited him to dine at the beach-side hotel where they were holidaying. Among other guests in the hotel, whom the family had got to know during their stay, were the author Roald Dahl, his movie-star wife Patricia Neal, and their children, Tessa, Theo, Lucy and Olivia. Wondering if Dahl had come across

Philip Caraman on the literary circuit, the hostess mentioned to him that the priest was expected to dinner; his reaction was negative. When the popular author and his family were pointed out to Philip, he too was puzzled, 'never heard of him,' said the Jesuit of Dahl. Neither writer knew anything about the other, so far apart were their creative circles.

Norway was the last of his books to be published by Longmans. English reviews of the book highlighted the affection with which Fr Caraman presented his portrait of the country, and Lita Anker's drawings were praised. In September, Philip wrote to tell her that 'my agent has just fixed up an American edition of *Norway*': he had money again, and offered to send Lita £50 'for your horse'. In jubilant mood, he could not resist the chance to tease her about her ever-growing managerie.[7]

Towards the end of his life, when he looked back over the full range of his work, Caraman regarded this book with particular affection. It was published at a time when there was a dearth of good English travel writing on Norway, and is written from an unusual standpoint. The writer points out that 'it would be ridiculous ... to assume that [the book] gives a Jesuit or even a Catholic view of the country – the first is a chimera, the latter an absurdity',[8] but he highlights the historical Christian associations of the places he had visited during his extensive travels, and his idiosyncratic portrait of the Norwegian people is vivid and amusing. It was this presentation of their culture that he feared might offend some of his readers in Oslo and elsewhere in the country. Based on observations he had made in his journal, he remarks in one passage that:

It is characteristic that the principal morning paper [*Aftenposten*] should be called 'Evening Post': it surprises no one in a country where the political 'Left' is the Right Wing party, 'free teaching' given for a substantial fee, *middag* (midday meal) taken in the evening ... the guest arriving for dinner is greeted with 'good day', and the tourist in search of entertainment finds the 'autumn show' running in early summer.[9]

Philip need not have feared that his humour would antagonise his Norwegian friends. He was assured of a warm welcome whenever he returned there, which he did on many occasions for a dozen or so more years.

Before returning to Ware for the autumn term, Fr Caraman spent a month at the Jesuit *Istituto Storico* in Rome, where he became a familiar figure over the following years. On this occasion he informed Lita Anker that he was 'very happily settled' there and was taking regular Spanish lessons, because 'sometime in 1971, I shall have to visit Madrid to look up some documents for the book I am writing'.

He was also in the early stages of planning a lengthy journey to South America, and wrote to Graham Greene updating him on the progress of his book. Greene repeated his offer of 'some excellent coloured photographs ... of the Jesuit ruins in Paraguay which you might find useful', and gave Philip some advice:

Paraguay is a charming country in everything except its politics. The priests however are having a rather harried time there and I see that one Jesuit was expelled the other day to Argentina. The Archbishop has excommunicated the Minister of the Interior and the Chief of Police. You will be very much under observation if you go as a priest probably now. If you are going to a hotel don't go to the horrid new one in the town but go to the ex-house of Lopez's mistress – the Gran del Paraguay which is charming and excellent and abundant food and not expensive.[10]

Before Fr Caraman could explore this intriguing possibility, he had to complete the remainder of his appointed time at St Edmund's College. Working in England, in a job for which he had been recommended by the Archbishop of Westminster, he was once again involved in the fall-out from his former post as Vice-Postulator of the Martyrs' Cause; reminders of his dismissal from Farm Street were also uncomfortably close. Most galling was a rejection he received from the priest who had taken over his former job as editor of *The Month*. Embittered, Caraman complained to Fr D'Arcy, who was now living in Mount Street. The aged Jesuit did his best to calm his protégé, saying that he was 'sorry about the rejection of the review, but I don't think it is out of malice or spite. I can see that the flow of superlatives might have put Fr Moffat off. If accompanying the praise there had been a faint sound of criticism, all would have been well, so I guess. I am sorry.'[11]

The delay in achieving the desired goal of Fr Caraman's years of toil on the Cause for the Canonisation of the Forty Martyrs, was a frustration which he had been able to keep at arm's length when he was based in Norway. While he was abroad, Fr D'Arcy had sent him newsletters from time to time. Most were depressing. He reported that the Cause seemed 'to be drooping. Why doesn't Cardinal Heenan do something?' And: 'It is a shame that Fr Tigar should go on struggling so manfully for the Martyrs while the Postulators [the Catholic hierarchy] do so little. But hasn't the Cardinal rather backed away too? Too much hobnobbing with the Archbishop of Canterbury!'[12]

Towards the end of November 1969, it appeared that the desired canonisation would not be delayed much longer. D'Arcy, heartened by the prospect, complimented Fr Caraman: 'You have played your part in what will come about, even though there are those who don't want to admit it . . .' he told him.[13] Once more both were disappointed. Three weeks later, Fr D'Arcy contacted Philip again: it was his turn to express indignation. He reported that:

> There is a mess over the Canonisation of the English Martyrs. *The Tablet* asked the Archbishop of Canterbury about it and printed his answer in *The Tablet*. It said that such a step would 'interfere with ecumenism'. Righteously indignant, Fr Tigar prepared a letter to *The Tablet* – but owing to the influence partly of Fr Walsh – the Provincial has forbidden those in the Province from writing about the matter – in defence of our martyrs – it makes my blood boil![14]

D'Arcy's vehement reaction to the *Tablet* article may have been generated, at least in part, by his dislike of the magazine's editorial management under Tom Burns. The previous editor, Douglas Woodruff, was one of Fr D'Arcy's most fervent disciples, but after his retirement in 1967 Burns welcomed most of the changes instituted by Vatican II, turning *The Tablet* in a direction very different from that favoured by Woodruff. The traditionalist D'Arcy deplored the policy adopted by Burns, who in turn considered that the Jesuit 'in his last years [had] a closed mind'.[15] Fr Caraman followed in his mentor's footsteps. He also enjoyed Woodruff's friendship: at one point there was a suggestion he might act as private chaplain to Douglas and his wife, Mia, but the idea came to nothing. Philip adopted D'Arcy's stance vis-à-vis Burns. The stand-off appears to have been mutual. Although Burns mentions several priests, including Martin D'Arcy, in his autobiography, he ignores Fr Caraman, who for his part plainly disliked the *Tablet*'s new editor. A degree of professional rivalry may have been involved, and any personal animosity was probably aggravated by Philip's fall from grace in 1963.

Publicity concerning ecumenical opposition to the canonisation of the Martyrs brought out into the open a problem which Philip Caraman had foreseen more than six years earlier. Diplomacy finally overcame this last obstacle, and in the Consistory of 18 May 1970 the Holy Father announced the forthcoming canonisation of forty new saints, the Blessed Martyrs of England and Wales.[16] Following the unanimous vote in favour of the Resolution by all members of the Consistory, it was stated that 'the Church intends to stress and hold up for the admiration not only of Catholics, but of all men, the example of persons unconditionally loyal to Christ and to their conscience to the extent of being ready to shed their blood for that reason'. Three months after Fr Caraman left St Edmund's, the Cause reached its long-awaited climax on 25 October 1970. Pope Paul VI went out of his way to mollify Anglican sensitivity of the saintly status being conferred on English Roman Catholics who had died for the Faith. The ceremony in Rome was cut from the customary five hours to just over two, but – as reported next day on the front page of *The Times* under the headline 'The Pope's Hopes for Unity with Anglicans' – it was distinguished by 'colourful aspects such as the presentation of traditional gifts – bread, wine, candles, flowers, and a pair of doves – to the Pope by the Postulator, or Advocate of the Martyrs' Cause,

Jesuit Fr Paoli Molinari'. In his address, Paul VI concentrated on reconciliation between Rome and the Anglican Church, and he prayed that the blood of the martyrs would heal the four-hundred year old wound between the two churches.[17]

Although Fr Caraman was not mentioned in the *Times* report, his role in the successful outcome of the Cause was acknowledged: he was asked to take part in the offertory procession and the ceremony of the presentation of gifts to the Pope in the middle of Mass. Before he left England, Fr Caraman confessed that he was 'very nervous about Rome, though I am sure there will be some very happy interludes', and added, 'I want to give him [the Pope] the doves in a cage, but I think there would be difficulty in retrieving them after-wards and bringing them back'.[18] Katie, a daughter of his close friends, the McEwens of Marchmont, collected birds, and Philip felt the doves would make a wonderful present for her. When he returned to his hotel on the evening of the great day, he wrote an ecstatic letter:

> *Haec dies quam fecit Dominus.* I gave my doves to Paul VI. When I asked the keeper of the papal aviary whether I could keep them he replied that they belonged to the Pope. I am pursu-ing the matter and I *hope* to bring them ultimately to Marchmont. It was grand to hear my heroes declared saints.[19]

This rare excursion into the limelight was not the only inter-ruption to work on his book. Following the winding up of his appointment at St Edmund's, he was called upon to give eight-een spiritual conferences to the monks of the Downside community in Somerset, an undertaking which not only prevented him from returning to Norway in the summer, but also called for considerable preparation.

Once Fr Caraman had given up the safe haven of his congenial rooms at Ware, the question of where he should be based also recurred. This time the problem was resolved by the generosity of Robin and Brigid McEwen, who offered him the hospitality of their stately home in Scotland. A Catholic family of considerable creative achievement, John McEwen, the first baronet, was a politician, poet and author, and a regular contributor to *The*

Month when Fr Caraman was editor of the magazine: his son, Robert, who inherited the title, was an eminent lawyer, and illustrated the wildlife story *Ring of Bright Water*. Philip had been a frequent and regular visitor to their family seat at Marchmont in the Scottish Borders since 1953, staying for a few days, sometimes for longer, and on one occasion spending Christmas with them. The house itself is thought to have been designed by William Adam, father of Robert Adam, and was built in the mid-eighteenth century on the site of a castle once owned by the Earls of Marchmont. The fact that the house had a private chapel was, for Fr Caraman, a special attraction. When the McEwens heard that he needed a tranquil base where he could write, and from which he could travel for his research, they offered him a home. The Jesuit was able to console himself with the thought that in accepting the McEwen's invitation his motives were not entirely selfish. He would, he told Lita Anker, 'look after the Catholics in the area, about forty of them'. who were nearly all members of the extended McEwen family. Fr Caraman said Mass each day in the chapel, and every Sunday when he was there he took a Parish Mass in the nearby town of Eyemouth. Lady Brigid McEwen recalls that Princess Margaret was present when Philip said Mass in the chapel in October 1971, and that HRH commented afterwards on its similarity to the Anglican service; she had never before attended a Mass.

The McEwens' offer of hospitality was accepted with relief and delight by Caraman. After paying Brigid and Robin a visit in the summer, he told them that after two days back in London he was 'convinced that Marchmont is the place for me in my advancing years ... I miss the trout for breakfast and so many other kind attentions from the children and you'. The light duties, and comfortable surroundings suited Fr Caraman admirably. 'If I took any other job I would not be free to travel as I want', he told Lita Anker shortly before he moved up to Marchmont. His travel plans were extensive. 'I shall be out of England for at least six months next year, mostly in South America. I start at Buenos Aires and work my way up through Paraguay and Eastern Bolivia and parts of Brazil to Peru.' He had booked a passage on a cargo boat leaving England in late

January or February, in order to reach South America in time for the autumn there, which he had been told was the loveliest time of the year. In the meanwhile, he hoped to fit in a trip to Spain. As things turned out, he spent Christmas back in Oslo at the behest of Bishop Gran, and returned to Marchmont for a fortnight in January before setting off on his adventure to the southern hemisphere. 'In a few years' time I shall be too old for long journeys', Philip told Lita in his sixtieth year, 'I want to do my travelling before I go blind or lame'. Fortunately, he never suffered from either disability, and his thirst for travel and determination of spirit propelled him onwards until the age of eighty-six.

☙

Had Fr Caraman not chosen to devote his life to the priesthood, to the Society of Jesus and to Jesuit history, he might have earned his living as a travel writer. With its vivid personal observations, the journal Philip kept of his visit to South America in 1971 is even more readable than the perceptive travelogue he had made of his East African experiences four years earlier.[20]

The agenda for the 1971 journey was very clear. Fr Caraman intended firstly to garner vital material for his book from archives in Buenos Aires, and then visit the actual sites of as many of the original Jesuit mission settlements as he possibly could. His talent for getting to know, and for getting on with, people in all walks of life smoothed his path, and his warm personality quickly won him an entrée to the means of achieving his goals. After short stops at Rio de Janeiro and Santos, the cargo ship arrived on schedule in Buenos Aires on 25 February. Wasting no time, Fr Caraman immediately established contact with Fr Furlong, 'a spry eighty-two-year-old Jesuit', who had devoted his life to the subject of the Jesuit Reductions, and had 'written more than anyone else on it'. He immediately promised Philip 'every kind of help'. Fr Furlong also told him of 'all the sources no one had yet used', and introduced the younger Jesuit to the National Archives, where he was 'given VIP treatment'.

Later the old priest familiarised him with other academic institutions in the city, and Fr Caraman complained that 'Fr Furlong
is packing weeks of work for me into every day'.

Fr Caraman was delighted to discover that Fr O'Farrell, the
Provincial, who lived only fifteen minutes' walk away from the
Jesuit house where he was quartered, had been educated at
Beaumont: the two men immediately got on well together, and
shortly after Philip's arrival O'Farrell laid on a special meal in
his honour, despite the fact that it was Lent. 'Best of all',
commented the visitor, the Provincial 'asked whether I would
like to drive with him to Cordoba ... which he has to visit ...
Once there I would have his car for [an] excursion I want to
make.' This greatly simplified Fr Caraman's plans: it saved him
the expense of an air ticket and solved the problem of how he
would get up-country without doubling back on his tracks later
on.

Within ten days of Caraman's arrival in Buenos Aires, he met
the Raynals, a family of prosperous cattle-dealers to whom he
had an introduction from London. When he was lunching with
them on barbecued beef in the garden of their mansion, the
youngest son – aged about twenty-six – became excited when he
heard about Philip's proposed trip to the remote Jesuit sites in
Paraguay and Brazil. Named Abbott Lorenzo, the young man
'looked a real gaucho', and was the manager of a company
running four large ranches in the Provinces of Santa Fé and
Cordoba. 'The gaucho', as Philip called him, and two of his
brothers had started a private airline, and said he would put the
company plane and a truck at the priest's disposal: he would
take his photographic equipment and a gun, and see that Philip
was housed in the *estancias* of his friends during their travels.
Raynal senior promised to equip him with an 'authentic gaucho
hat' for his safari.

The crucial contact with Lorenzo Raynal provided Philip with
an unrivalled way of reaching the most inaccessible sites on his
extensive wish list. In April they visited some of the Reductions
on the east bank of the Uruguay river, and others located in
Argentina and across the river in Paraguay. On one memorable
flight, flying at low altitude for 120 miles, they followed in

reverse the route down the upper Parana taken by Padre Ruiz de Montoya in his attempt to lead a group of Indians to safety in 1631. The chapter in *The Lost Paradise* entitled 'The Great Exodus' describes how Montoya tried to save the lives of some 12,000 Guarani people threatened by massacre or enslavement by marauding Mamelucos. The expedition's journey downriver, and its encounter with the terrifying Guaira falls, which at extreme flood have over eight times the volume of Niagara, is one of the most vivid and dramatic episodes in Caraman's book.

In May on another excursion in the Reynal plane, this time to the Chiquitos area in Bolivia, the party was joined by Bridget Astor who turned out to be a competent photographer. This trip was one of several on which Philip landed on a primitive airstrip. Then, travelling on jungle tracks in 'a very ancient and battered jeep with no spare tyre', whose speedometer and fuel gauge had ceased to work, the party eventually reached San Miguel, where they found a 'superb timber and adobe church (almost cathedral size), with huge pillars of hard forest wood now like iron; almost whole church in same condition as when built in 1720 by Martin Schmit, an Austrian Jesuit'. On the evening of the same day at the mission of San Rafael, Fr Caraman made an astonishing discovery:

It was dark when we were taken into the loft [of the church] to see the old organ built by the Indians at [the] same time as [the]church: people had come here from Chile and Peru to hear the music and see how instruments were made. I had read that nothing was known of the music of the missions ... and all scores had been lost. The Father flashed his torch onto a cardboard box lying in dust near the organ – it was full of music written out by Indians in the eighteenth century. The simple nun grabbed a bunch of scores roughly in her hand, and I screamed – the paper was near perishing. What might be there God knows! The priest realised the fantastic (possible) importance of the find, and offered me the whole box, but there was danger of losing it in the dark, particularly if we had to sleep in the jungle ...

Noting this incident in his book, Fr Caraman substituted 'a wooden box' for one of cardboard, which seems more likely to be accurate.

Another jungle expedition was particularly fruitful. On his arrival in Asuncion, he was welcomed by the British Ambassador to Paraguay, Brian MacDermott, who was described by Philip as 'a very fine R. C. and a friend of my best English friends in Oslo'. MacDermott not only undertook to look after Fr Caraman's post but to give him protection 'in the event of a revolution'.[21] He also took a great interest in Philip's research, and drove him to see six of the more remote Paraguay Reductions. Then during his stay in the country Caraman met Fr Melia, 'a learned man' who had devoted much of his life to studying the culture of the Guarani people, one of the principal tribes featured in the story of the Jesuit Reductions. After an initial show of reluctance, Fr Melia agreed to take Caraman with him on one of his visits to visit a tribe living in an isolated area; the journey by bus and on foot was arduous, but Melia 'knew exactly what bush to stop [the bus] at along the road through the jungle'. The two priests reached a group of Indians 'gathered round an adobe hut and an open shelter with a thatched roof in which a fire was burning. Apart from their clothes ... they resembled in every other way the primitive Guarani as they were in the days of the Conquistadores.' Fr Melia told Philip that unless he had been on terms of trust with the Indians, they would have resented the intrusion of outsiders.

On his return to civilisation, Caraman immediately had his pictures of the Guarani developed, and was overjoyed with the results of his 'hit or miss photography'. Throughout his travels he was concerned about getting illustrations for his book, and on this visit to the jungle believed he had 'certainly got at least half a dozen possible illustrations – I think even more'. As things turned out, only one of his pictures – a delightful shot of a young Guarani girl – was used in the book, although several of Bridget Astor's photographs were included. Philip's anxiety over illustrations would have been compounded had he known at the time that they would appear in the book printed on matt rather than glossy paper, losing in the production process much of their impact.

Fr Caraman was constantly aware of the unsavoury nature of the ruling regimes in the countries he visited. At times his movements were hampered by political events. On his drive to Cordoba with Fr O'Farrell he was annoyed when, owing to riots and unrest in the city, they were 'stopped by the military' and a 'rather menacing situation [developed] as four soldiers with guns covered the car front and behind'. Movements in and around Cordoba were restricted, which he found an 'abominable nuisance as there are places I must see in the neighbouring countryside'. In line with what he had been told by Graham Greene, he heard 'hair-raising stories from the Provincial about the Jesuits in Paraguay', and was told 'it was safe to stay with the Jesuits in Asuncion, but [he] should be ready to escape to the MacDermotts at the Embassy'. The Jesuit house had been raided and the priests there beaten up by Stroessner's men less than a year earlier.

Whilst Fr Caraman was able to take the unpleasant political situation in his stride, he was less detached when it came to the poverty he encountered everywhere he went. Sightseeing in Buenos Aires shortly after his arrival, he discovered that:

> Next to the cathedral, on a site that is best in town and must be worth millions, a huge Curial administration building [is] going up. Aghast, for presumably the diocese of Buenos Aires could be run from 2 or 3 flats, [I] understand now what the third world priests were campaigning against. Unbelievable *folie de grandeur* in country where a vast percentage of people have meat to eat and nothing else ... The Cardinal Archbishop, to whom I have an introduction and will not take up, [is] an old man of eighty-two whose thinking processes are medieval.

Arriving at the Jesuit house in Asuncion, he immediately appreciated the hardships endured by his brother priests. He was 'shown into the poorest room I have ever slept in – whether in Africa or Europe', and realised that 'the priests here live on the smell of an oil rag'. Despite their poverty the priests all seemed very happy, he noted. He was still staying with them on 1 May, and commented that it was:

> a day I used to like, before St. Philip was pushed out to make room for the workers – and the fact of it here where the peasants

... form ninety per cent of the people and have no say at all in the government ... the wealth is very largely in the hands of two per cent ... and the country is run in the interests of a party.[22]

Fr Caraman's concern reached out to the people he encountered along his way. During his journey with Ambassador MacDermott, the weather turned wet and – unseasonably – bitterly cold. It was almost impossible to keep warm: Philip was shivering despite having put on several pullovers, and borrowed 'a very heavy long overcoat' from his host, an officer in the Paraguayan army with whom they were staying. During a sleepless night, Philip was aware that 'the house was guarded all night by a poor Paraguayan conscript who patrolled the garden wearing only a poncho for warmth under his raincoat'. This momentarily soured his sense of satisfaction in reaching the sites of several of the more isolated Reductions during the journey.

After this excursion, Fr Caraman developed a heavy cold, one of only a few minor ailments he experienced during a hectic and physically demanding schedule. He suffered from a mild bout of sunstroke after a 'very pleasant picnic lunch', lost a filling from one of his teeth after eating beef at an *asado* meal on a cattle ranch, and suffered a 'frightful headache' after a lengthy, bone-shaking journey in an overcrowded bus with a drunken driver, during which the man sitting behind him attempted to pick his hip pockets, and Philip had to remove his spectacles for fear that they might be broken.

Considering his frail physique, and a record of serious illness, Fr Caraman displayed remarkable resilience during the months he spent in South America. Buoyed up by the nature of his enterprise, and the excitement of travel and discovery, there was no time for depression or stress-related illness. By the time he wrote an exultant 'End' to his journal, Philip had acquired a remarkable personal insight into the historical setting of the Jesuit missions in Paraguay, and achieved almost everything – and in some respects far more – than he had hoped for when he originally planned his journey. All that remained was for him to get down to the lonely work of actually writing his book.

Fr Caraman returned to Marchmont with good intentions, and
spent most of the remaining months of 1971 staying with the
McEwens, working more or less without interruption until
March of the following year. His method of writing *The Lost
Paradise* followed much the same pattern as that used in his
previous book, *Norway*: he wrote principally in manuscript on
the right-hand side of a double sheet of A4 paper, the left hand
page being used for sentence and paragraph corrections. His
work was heavily self-edited, with numerous 'cut-and-paste'
deletions and insertions, which probably caused his typist more
than a few headaches: an aide-memoire of points to be included,
with bibliographical references, preceded each chapter.[23]

Fr Caraman's writing formula was self-critical and, to some
extent, laborious, and sustained effort over a protracted period
was more than his chronically restless nature could endure. In the
spring of 1972 he accepted an invitation to the United States,
where he worked as an assistant priest at St Aloysius Rectory in
Great Neck, in New York state. The temporary appointment
caused him some amusement, as he described to his sister,
Claire:

> Apart from locking a man in church all night – he was found
> curled up under a statue of St Joseph in the morning – I have
> made no major gaffe. One day a week I take off to lunch or dine
> with a friend in New York, otherwise I work quietly here in the
> hope of being given some remuneration for my services at the
> end ... The food is made to taste all the same, whether it is
> lobster, chicken or steak. I don't know how it is done ... Pretty
> well every other object in my room is some sort of telephone,
> bell or communication device. All very INefficient [*sic*].[24]

Two weeks later he made another comment on his stay in Great
Neck:

> Fortunately the parish priest here is not Irish. The Irish clergy
> are all IRA sympathisers – some of the younger ones are very
> violent. I dread meeting them for they are ill-mannered and bring
> up the question of Ulster every time.[25]

The summer and autumn brought another diversion. After only a couple of months back at Marchmont, Philip succumbed once more to the lure of Norway. Amidst the exhilaration of his tour of South America the country had never been far from his mind: on a visit to a primitive area in Argentina, he had noted that a sanitation system devised by the Jesuits was 'far more hygienic than any equivalent arrangement I had met in the Norwegian countryside'. Later, when he was told by a bishop in Paraguay that he had only 'twenty priests in his diocese which took in 218,000 Christians', Philip commented, 'what a contrast with Oslo where there are twenty-four priests for 1,800 Catholics'. Having been responsible for establishing a Jesuit presence in Norway, he was overjoyed when two parishes in the country were taken over by the Society: the invitation to stand in for fellow Jesuits during their holidays appealed both to his sense of duty and to his yearning for Norway.

The tasteless fare Philip had eaten in New York, together with his long experience of Norwegian food, and the knowledge that he would have to cook for himself during the summer and autumn, inspired him to take a Cordon Bleu cookery course, before once more crossing the North Sea. 'I have never really been taught [to cook]', he told his sister. Packing his books into his Simca, he said that his three months as locum parish priest would be spent in writing quietly. That was his intention. All went well for a time: in a letter from the presbytery at Lillehammer he told Lita that only about 'one person calls every three days', and having been alone for two and a half weeks he had 'finished the first chapter of my book'. Fr Caraman explained that he had left 'the first and last (the most difficult chapters) to the end'. Every morning he went out to do his shopping and 'clowned with the attendants in the store'. But with a house of his own, albeit on a temporary basis, he could not resist the temptation to return some of the hospitality he had received from his friends over the years. Excitedly, he looked forward to entertaining a house party made up of Robin McEwen, his host at Marchmont, Lady Taylor, an elderly lady he had met on the cargo boat to South America, and Wenche Koren. Their visit was to be the 'great test' of his newly acquired culinary skill. He regarded the various recipes he had for soups as his greatest challenge. 'I have some lovely fresh deep frozen raspberries (about which even I cannot go wrong), and some excellent *torsk* (cod)', he wrote, but 'the soup – that will be the test'. He also discovered that self-catering, combined with the work of sacristy and church, was more time-consuming than he had foreseen. The book remained unfinished.

The pleasure Fr Caraman experienced in having a house of his own was some compensation for the responsibilities of running a parish, but it was only a temporary arrangement: a permanent and satisfactory solution to the problem of where he should live still eluded him. Marchmont provided ideal conditions for writing: he was happy there, and enjoyed the company of the McEwens and of their children and friends, 'so many nice people seem to gather round you', he told Brigid on one occasion. But Philip probably felt that he had imposed long enough on their hospitality, and once again consulted Fr Martin D'Arcy about where he should go. D'Arcy, who was based at Mount Street, tried to persuade him to return there. 'You might be happy here, as there are some very good people', he wrote.[26] But his protégé's almost pathological dislike of the Mayfair community persisted, as did his distrust of 'the handful of men who move in the corridors of power' in the English Province.

Philip Caraman found a more congenial home in a Jesuit parish in Wiltshire, and on his return from Norway he moved into the presbytery of Fr John Tranmar, a priest with whom he had always got on well. 'It is very pleasant here and ideal for my work – a sleepy old village with a fine 13th century church on which I look out as I sit typing here at my table. And I have friends too not far away', he explained to Lita from Tisbury. The small town had another, strong, attraction for him. The parish serves the magnificent chapel of New Wardour Castle, a jewel of Catholic recusant history set in parkland once owned by the Arundell family, who still live nearby. Celebrating Mass in this beautiful setting was a duty close to Fr Caraman's heart, and one he undertook gladly, bringing out the chapel's medieval vestments to show his visiting friends.

Work on the book seemed to make good progress, and in

April 1973 he wrote the Introduction, in which he described the background to a number of the previous studies on the subject of the Jesuit Reductions, and explained that in *The Lost Paradise* he had merely tried to tell the story of 'the whole Republic, its foundation, early failures and eventual success', leaving readers to draw their own conclusions about the value of the Jesuit colonial experiment.[27] But Fr Caraman's problems did not end there. Between absences from Tisbury, and parish duties in support of Fr 'Jack', work on the detailed footnotes, references, appendices, bibliography and complicated maps rumbled on into the summer: by then he was thoroughly fed up with the whole business. 'I am still working on my wretched book ... when I have handed it in to the publishers then I shall be able to think of going away', he wrote, complaining of endless interruptions at Tisbury.

The fact that he was working with a new publisher may have added to his difficulties. Fr Caraman's long association with Longmans, and with John Guest who had been a respected friend of many Catholic authors, came to an end when the firm was taken over by Pearson Education shortly after the publication of *Norway*. Philip's agent, Deborah Rogers, introduced him to Sidgwick & Jackson, who brought out his next two books. Once *The Lost Paradise* was in their hands, Fr Caraman was free to indulge in the leisurely travel he revelled in. In the spring of the following year, having assisted Fr Tranmar with the Easter services, he set off on an extended tour of Spain, landing at Bilbao, and progressing via Burgos and Jerez to stay with Lita in Estepona, returning to England by way of Madrid. It was a welcome interlude. Publication of the book was still a long way off, and in September 1974 Fr Caraman expressed his frustration, saying, 'If I live to 1976 probably five books will come out under my name, but at the moment there are all kinds of hold-ups'. The work on which he had embarked with such enthusiasm, and to which he had devoted so much scholarly research, was testing the bounds of his patience.

This was one of the periods of uncertainty which Fr Caraman experienced during the middle years of his life. Although he was comfortably based at Tisbury, and played a useful part in the pastoral life of the country parish, it was a time of comparative aimlessness: awaiting the publication of one book, he had no plans for another, and lacking either royalties or a project to attract funding from the Jesuits he was short of money. Distant travel was not an option: a wet week spent in Ireland with friends, and the odd visit to Scandinavia were the most he could manage. In the new year of 1975, Fr Philip's thoughts turned to old age. He advised Lita Anker to reconcile herself to the passage of time, telling her that he had just read the following: 'all you that are desolate at the approach of age, be merry: it is not what it looks like from in front and from outside. There is a glory in all completion, and all good endings are but shining transitions.'

These not altogether gloomy thoughts may have been prompted in part by unaccustomed idleness, but probably owed something to the recent death of Auberon Herbert at the age of only fifty-two, and the severe deterioration in the health of Fr D'Arcy. Herbert's mother, Mary, had died in 1971, and Auberon's death marked the end of a long era during which Fr Caraman had enjoyed their hospitality at Pixton on innumerable occasions. Bridget Grant, Auberon Herbert's sister, recalls that Philip 'preached most beautifully' at his memorial service.[28] He also contributed an essay to a tribute to Herbert, which was published privately by a number of friends, including Isaiah Berlin and Malcolm Muggeridge. Caraman commented that Auberon 'set particular store on his friendships, which were diverse and world wide. There were few places ... where he did not have friends; all had a deep affection for him, admired his integrity, smiled at his foibles, ...'[29] Fr Caraman would not have appreciated that in the eyes of *his* friends these words applied to himself.

In 1975, Fr Caraman attended a Golden Jubilee Mass, celebrated by Bishop Butler, at St Teresa's in Hertfordshire, the parish his father had founded in the chapel of the family home in Elstree when Philip was fourteen. René was always a distant father-figure, in the manner of a Levantine paterfamilias: Fr Martin D'Arcy on the other hand had assumed the role of surrogate father in Philip's life, in matters both spiritual and temporal, and now he too was nearing his end. In 1975 he suffered three brain spasms, and was more or less confined to the house in Mayfair. D'Arcy's increasing frailty was another signpost to impending old age.

The autumn at last brought the publication of *The Lost Paradise*. Fr Caraman's spirits were to some extent restored by the good reviews which appeared in all the leading papers, including *The Observer* and the *Spectator*. Writing in *The Sunday Times*, Hugh Trevor-Roper commented that the book was 'a fascinating study of the Jesuit Reductions and of a model Indian settlement in colonial Paraguay ... Father Caraman has recreated it with learning, objectivity, personal investigation in South America, and a happy style.' The *Sunday Telegraph* reviewer, the Earl of Birkenhead, said it was a beautifully written book 'of great scholarship which leaves one with affection as well as respect for the Jesuits'.

The review in *The Tablet* was written by Fr Caraman's old friend, and erstwhile theatre critic for *The Month*, actor-writer Robert Speaight. His piece was perceptive and complimentary: praising the author's 'exacting scholarship, clear narration and diligent research', he continues:

> He [Caraman] has visited Paraguay, and seen for himself what remains of the Reductions. He gives a vivid description of the country, and what he has to say of the Indian tribes ... is of great anthropological interest ... [The Jesuit fathers] were of many nationalities ... [and] the impression remains of incredible courage and hardihood, and of an intelligence that was always ready to learn ... The government of the Reductions in Paraguay ... was infinitely more constructive and humane than the *encomiendas* under Spanish colonists ... that the Indians learnt the rudiments of the Christian faith and the technique of a co-operative economy is among the miracles of missionary enterprise ...

The review praises Fr Caraman for not wasting 'his rhetoric over the iniquitous suppression' of the Jesuit regime in 1767 and the expulsion of its priests from the Reductions in the following year. Speaight added the comment that 'today when the social problem in Latin America cries to Heaven for vengeance ... the Jesuit Reductions may well have something to teach the predatory capitalism of the *estancias*'. The article concluded that the Jesuits had taught the Indian tribes to be 'happy, and enlivened the practice of their religion with the arts of visual, musical and even theatrical display', and that Fr Caraman had 'condensed his story into a narrative which is consistently readable'.[30]

Taking justified pride in his work, Philip sent copies of *The Lost Paradise* to a number of friends, including Muriel Spark in Rome, and Graham Greene's ex-mistress Catherine Walston, who thanked him warmly for his present. The only acknowledgement Fr Caraman received from Greene himself was a note, typed and signed by Elizabeth Denys, his sister and acting secretary, saying, 'Mr Greene, who is in France, has asked me to thank you very much for sending him a copy of your book *The Lost Paradise* which he much looks forward to reading'.[31] This was followed by a brief letter, again signed by Denys, in which Greene said: 'How kind of you to send me your book about the Paraguayan *missiones*. Alas! I shall never be able to return to Paraguay until General Stroessner has gone to his disagreeable account. I am glad you managed to evade being expelled from Paraguay or kidnapped in Argentina.'[32] Later, Philip told a friend that Greene's impersonal reaction destroyed any lingering affection he still had for the writer, and there is no evidence to suggest a resumption of their relationship after this time.

A more bitter pill was the news that Fr Caraman's story of the Reductions had been hijacked by Hollywood, and that the award-winning scriptwriter Robert Bolt was working on a screenplay about a Jesuit mission in eighteenth-century Paraguay. Philip admired Bolt's work on *A Man For All Seasons*: still having strong ties with the theatrical world, he had allowed the playwright to see a copy of *The Lost Paradise* before it went on sale to the public. Caraman and his agent felt that the research and groundwork provided by the book should receive some acknowledgement: Bolt and a phalanx of Californian-based corporate lawyers disagreed. The dispute rumbled on for months. In April, 1976 Bolt addressed a letter from Beverley Hills to Philip at the 'Jesuit House' in Mount

Street, saying he had been 'taken aback' by the request for an acknowledgement. He added that the film was going well, although he feared that 'as a piece of re-created history' Philip would find it 'rather more re-creative than historical'.

The situation deteriorated when the American lawyers stepped in, and Caraman's literary agent advised him to take legal advice before pursuing the matter further, commenting that the Americans 'did not intend to budge an inch'. The Hollywood legal guns submitted that Bolt had been working on the subject of his screenplay for 'quite sometime' before he read *The Lost Paradise,* and that the film company in question had engaged an anthropologist as a full-time research assistant who had 'located and reviewed a substantial amount of original source material dating back several hundreds of years'. They contended that this research had been passed on to Robert Bolt as background material for his screenplay well before Caraman had sent him the book. The Jesuit was persuaded that his case was not strong enough to pursue satisfactorily, and the matter was eventually dropped.[33] *The Lost Paradise* quickly went into a reprint, but the wrangle soured Philip's enjoyment in his success: thanking Lita for her 'flattering remarks' about the book, he added: 'Robert Bolt is writing a film script based on the last chapters: it is for Paramount, but as there is no copyright in historical material, I don't even get an acknowledgement'. Ten years later, when Bolt's film *The Mission,* starring Jeremy Irons and Robert de Niro, reached the big screen, Philip heartily wished to disown any connection with it, and regarded the whole affair with a certain degree of bitter humour. In the meantime his life moved into a sphere remote from both the literary world of London and the squabbles and glitz of the Hollywood scene.

Notes

1 The word 'Reduction' (from the Spanish *reducir,* to reduce – into townships) is first found in an instruction of the Spanish Crown dated Saragossa 29 March 1503: it charges officials in Espanola

to bring all Indians into Reductions, with church, priest and school, and there, after giving them clothing, to introduce them into civilized life. Philip Caraman, *The Lost Paradise* (Sidgwick & Jackson, 1975), footnote p. 36.

2 Ibid. pp. 11–15.

3 Ibid,

4 Exchange of letters, Greene–Caraman, 13 Jan 1969 and undated, John J. Burns Library, Boston College (hereafter BC).

5 *The Month*, July 1956, vol. 16.

6 Letter, Graham Greene to Philip Caraman, 16 July 1969 (BC) © Francis Greene 2004.

7 Passages in this chapter based on Fr Caraman's letters to Lita Anker are not dated or noted individually.

8 Philip Caraman, Preface to *Norway*.

9 Ibid. pp. 19–20.

10 Letter, Graham Greene to Philip Caraman, 24 November 1969 (BC) © Francis Greene 2004.

11 Letter, Fr Martin D'Arcy to Philip Caraman, 25 November 1969 (BC).

12 Letter, Fr Martin D'Arcy to Philip Caraman, 3 April 1968 (BC).

13 Letter, Fr Martin D'Arcy to Philip Caraman, 21 November 1969 (BC).

14 Letter, Fr Martin D'Arcy to Philip Caraman, 10 December 1969 (BC).

15 Tom Burns, *The Use of Memory*, p. 140.

16 The Forty Canonised Martyrs included: thirteen secular priests, three Benedictines, three Carthusians, one Brigittine, two Franciscans, one Augustinian, ten Jesuits, and seven lay persons including three mothers of families.

17 *The Times*, Monday 26 October 1970, issue no. 58,006.

18 Letter, Philip Caraman to Brigid McEwen, 16 October 1970.

19 Ibid. 25 October 1970.

20 Fr Caraman's experiences in the Argentine, Paraguay, Uruguay, Brazil, Bolivia and Peru are described in seventy pages of carefully-written notes, which he sent back to Marchmont at various stages during his trip, possibly for safety and/or typing. Pages 29–40 are missing and have not been traced (Private Papers).

21 Letter, Philip Caraman to Brigid and Robin McEwen, Asuncion, 7 April 1971.

22 In the revised liturgical calendar, 1 May is dedicated to St Joseph the Worker.

23 The original MSS of *Norway* and *The Lost Paradise* are preserved

in the John J. Burns Library in Boston College.
24 Letter, Philip Caraman to Claire Cradock-Henry, 3 March 1972.
Philip Caraman Private Papers (hereafter PCPP).
25 Ibid. 18 March 1972.
26 Letter, Fr Martin D'Arcy to Philip Caraman June 1972 (BC).
27 Philip Caraman, *The Lost Paradise* (Sidgwick & Jackson, 1975),
pp. 11–15.
28 Letter to author, 22 May 2001
29 Philip Caraman, *Auberon Herbert – a Composite Portrait*, edited
by John Joliffe.
30 *The Tablet*, 22 November 1975.
31 Note dated 24 October 1975 (BC).
32 Letter dated 5 November 1975 (BC).
33 The foregoing is based on correspondence found in Philip
Caraman's Private Papers.

Chapter Ten

World's End

'Norway can become a disease', Fr Caraman warned an English friend who consulted him about a posting to Oslo. He spoke from experience. After leaving the country in 1968 to take up his appointment at St Edmund's, Ware, Caraman had returned on countless occasions, either to visit friends or to look after a parish whilst the regular incumbent was away on holiday. He always found some excuse to go back to the country which both fascinated and frustrated him in equal measure. After the publication of *The Lost Paradise*, with nothing to keep him in England, he accepted a deeper commitment to the Catholic mission in Norway, and agreed to Bishop John Gran's proposal that he should become parish priest of St Olav's, Tønsberg, for a period of three years from February 1976.

Before starting his new job, Caraman spent the winter in Norway, staying first in Oslo, and later moving up to Trondheim. His changing opinion of Trondheim reflected his attitude to Norway as a whole. 'Give me Trondheim any day to Oslo: it is a charming place, marvellous when the winter sun shines brightly down Prinsensgate', he told Lita, shortly after his arrival there at the end of 1975. But by New Year's Eve his enchantment with the ancient cathedral city had evaporated. 'They say it is the worst winter Trondheim has had within memory. I have seen the sun twice since 19 November; for the rest it has been blowing, snowing, raining', he wrote despondently. The months before taking up his parish appointment were spent in brushing up his linguistic skills. Despite the time he had devoted to learning the language when he first went to

Oslo ten years earlier, he lacked confidence in his own ability. 'I can still spend an evening, when necessary, holding my own in conversation in my atrocious Norwegian', he told Brigid McEwen, during one of his visits to Oslo from Marchmont.[1] But running a parish where many of the people understood no other language required greater fluency and hard work on his part. 'No-one ever told me that Norwegian was such a difficult language. I have done nothing ... except read, hear, speak, think, dream Norwegian. By mid-February I hope to be more than a beginner', he declared.[2]

At the age of sixty-four, this was Fr Caraman's first experience of being in sole charge of a parish, and he quickly discovered that language was only a minor consideration compared to some of the challenges posed by his other responsibilities. Within a few months he was complaining that 'there is far too much official work for the poor *sogneprest* in Norway. I am no good at it.' Parish accounts, form-filling, official returns and red tape was not work he found congenial. But the compensations for bureaucracy were considerable: he had a pleasant modern house, and a state stipend on which to support himself. He also had a free hand to organise his parish work and his private life in any way he wished. He was accountable to no one other than his friend Bishop John Gran, whom he went to see in Oslo several times a year, or who paid him a pastoral visit from time to time.

Fr Caraman was a conscientious parish priest. His sense of responsibility to his parishioners transcended any temptation he might have had to put his own interests first, nor was it in his nature to be idle. But for a man of his age the ministry was often daunting. Many of Caraman's problems were geographical: the pastoral area for which he was responsible approximated in size to Surrey and Sussex combined, and the problems of getting around some of the more rugged terrain, particularly in winter, were often insuperable. In summer the former whaling station of Tønsberg is a pleasant enough south coast town, attracting its share of holiday visitors: in winter it is sometimes cut off from all but the most determined travellers, its inhabitants isolated within their own community. In these circumstances it was hardly surprising that St Olav's had a floating congregation, with wide variations in numbers between winter and summer: it was unusual for him to see the same people in church regularly from one Sunday to the next. He got on well with his scattered parishioners, and within a few months of taking over admitted that 'I really like the people of Vestfold and would rather be with them than with any others'.[3] But he discovered that in winter 'the usual depression descends on my parishioners', triggering a cycle of 'divorces, separation and an urge for instant cremation'.

In many respects it was an unrewarding ministry. An article in the *Catholic Gazette,* written shortly after Fr Caraman returned to England, explains:

> The [low Mass-attendance] is mainly because of the long travelling distances involved but owes something to the ambivalent attitude of the people themselves to their religion. Confirmation ceremonies always draw their full quota of teenaged candidates, but [this] is traditionally one of the social highlights of family life. In some centres it is the *presence* of a Catholic priest that is important. In his role of witness a parish priest may be invited to talk about the Faith in a local school or give an interview to a newspaper explaining a Catholic point of view, without any thought of conversions resulting.

The article related that Norway's oil wealth, and the country's recent and sudden rise in prosperity had created a preoccupation with possessions rather than ideas, which inevitably mitigated against the practice of religion.[4]

In addition to the normal round of parish duties – baptisms, marriages and funerals – Fr Caraman held regular Saturday sessions for anyone wanting private instruction in the Catholic faith. He always prepared his sermons carefully, occasionally lamenting to friends that he thought they were wasted on his congregation. 'I have been very busy preaching good sermons in bad Norwegian', he wrote shortly after his first Christmas in Tønsberg. He was also responsible for the spiritual welfare of a community of Sisters of St Elizabeth, living close to his spacious church; the nuns, of mixed German and Polish nationality, ran a small school independently from the parish. The upkeep of the relatively new church and parish property caused more than a few problems. Explaining that he could not settle down to any creative work, Fr Caraman grumbled that 'I came here as a priest, but I have become a plumber, electrical engineer, builder, plasterer and decorator'. But before his first winter set in he reported that he had 'started Mass in Larvik and in Sandefjord once a month and I have a faithful little congregation in both places, about twenty in each. We have coffee and *smorbrod* afterwards. It is all very jolly.'

When Fr Caraman looked back on the years he spent in Tønsberg, he recalled a number of incidents connected with his ministry there with gentle amusement. Two of the stories related to 'the confessional'.

> There is always a curiosity among non-Catholics about the confessional. I mean what used to be called 'the box.' In Norway this curiosity is almost morbid. At times in Tønsberg a whole class from the local school would come to my church for a talk on Catholicism as part of their study of Comparative Religion. At the end when I told the teenage children they could look round the church there would be a rush to the back to see what lay behind the curtain on the penitent's side of the confessional. Those at the end of the line found it difficult to accept that there was nothing more than a kneeler and a crucifix there, and a chair on the priest's side.

Regretting the loss of 'the box' from some modern churches in England and elsewhere, Fr Caraman remarked that 'the old grille served at least as a protection at an attempt at assault', and related that on one occasion in a remote town in Norway, he had been asked to hear confessions in a dental surgery by another parish priest who had 'mischievously pumped up the chair above floor level'. One of his women penitents went through the ten commandments one by one, but was unable to recall what the seventh was about. 'I can't think of it myself', Philip answered spontaneously. The woman thought this so funny that she 'gave vent to her mirth by prodding me so painfully in the ribs, that I was alerted to the hazards of hearing penitents without protection from such assaults'.[5]

Whilst observation of human nature provided Philip with a constant source of interest and amusement, his comment that he was unable to settle down to creative work betrays the frustration he felt at being unable to exercise his artistic talents. For the first time in many years he was an author with neither a book in prospect, nor a job compatible with writing one. Instead, he started to paint. He took up painting as a hobby tentatively and almost as a joke at first, but with increasing confidence as time went on. His new-found talent was another source of fun between himself and his artist friends, John and Lita Anker and Wenche Koren. After illustrating *Norway*, Lita had moved on to portrait-painting, and had persuaded Fr Caraman to sit for her, much to his amusement. This portrait had become an ongoing joke between them: enjoying his new-found skill, he told her 'we can paint each other next summer'. Portraiture was not his forte, but his miniature landscapes are competent and atmospheric, and working on them provided him with many snatches of relaxed enjoyment.

Even had he wished to do so, it would have been impossible for Fr Caraman to embark on another historical study such as *Henry Garnet* or *The Lost Paradise* while he was in Tønsberg. He could not have carried out the exhaustive research necessary for such an undertaking from so remote a place without frequently abandoning his parishioners. There is no suggestion that he wanted to start such a work, at least for the time being. Although both these books had been successful and well-received, each in its time and in its own way was generated painfully, and had been the source of considerable grief. His reaction to *Garnet* was to write the more relaxed and idiosyncratic *Norway*. A follow-up to *The Lost Paradise* had not been proposed. But since his early years in Mayfair Philip Caraman had never been without an idea for some book or other buzzing round in his head; writing was embedded in the core of his being, and remained an unquenchable urge for self-expression. For the first and last time in his life he wrote a novel. It came relatively easily to him in the warmth of his lonely house during the long Norwegian winters. In February 1978 he told a friend, 'I have sent a scurrilous novel to Penguins and await their reaction. I fear it will be posted back to me.' It was – very quickly. Within a few weeks he reported: 'Penguins say they can't publish my novel "with assurance of sufficient success": I shall try another publisher that has asked to see it, then forget about it. I shall have to find something else to keep me sane next winter.' There is no indication that he used his agent as an inter-mediary, nor of the novel's story-line, or that it was submitted to the Jesuit censors. If the 'scurrilous' book followed up an idea he had considered some ten years earlier, then it was intended to shock. Just after he first moved to Oslo, he had written to Lita Anker saying:

> When I have finished my book on Norway ... I *may* start a novel. What I would like to do is a futuristic novel about the Church – with a black Pope in Rome (perhaps the year 1999), married priests and (!) Catholic Norwegians: also a new religious order of priests: neo-Jesuits, founded by Fr Anker (!) ... How do I introduce the love interest? I must ask Graham Greene whom I hope to track down [in Paris].

By the time his novel was finished over ten years later he was no longer corresponding with Greene, the book would never have passed the Society's censors, and, in the wrong hands, would have reinforced the suspicion in which he was held by his Jesuit brethren. It is a matter of speculation whether or not the book would have appeared under a *nom de plume* had it been accepted: we shall never know. The 'scurrilous' novel sank without trace – presumably destroyed by its author.

Fr Caraman's reputation would have suffered badly had the critical eyes of Mount Street, and the censure of his Provincial, penetrated as far as Tønsberg. Some of the people he entertained in his home would not have met with their approval. During his second year as parish priest he encountered a group of actors known as *Thesbiteateret* who were based in Tønsberg: their leading-light was a charismatic young Italian from Trieste named Gianni Lepre. Chronically short of money, and with nowhere to rehearse, Lepre and his friends were befriended by Fr Caraman, who permitted them the freedom of his house, which they exploited to the full. In October 1977, Philip reported that one night he had 'three actors dossing down on the ground floor', and the following evening he was 'asked to entertain eight of them along with an English clown: fourteen in fact, turned up and filled the house with smoke'; he added that he could not 'enquire too closely into their extra-matrimonial liaisons'.

Despite their chaotic lives the actors were a far from amateur group, featuring on national television, putting on *Peer Gynt* in the Amfiscenen of the National Theatre in Oslo, and making overseas tours. Philip warned a friend, who was contemplating sponsorship of a visit to an arts festival in England by *Thesbiteateret,* that Gianni Lepre 'has talent, unlimited charm and few scruples. What he has to offer to any festival will certainly be a more than worthy and worthwhile contribution. But I have warned you that he can be an appalling nuisance.' Fr Caraman, who in the past had worked with some of the leading directors and actors of stage and screen, was well qualified to judge their abilities. But his patience with the Italian and his friends was wearing thin:

> Last Saturday when he had nowhere to practise he begged me to let him have the use of my dining room: he used it, also my bedroom, bathroom, kitchen and spare room, as well as my sitting room where he had his players shouting out their parts. The Saturday before that he asked me whether I would entertain 8 [sic] of his group who were having a visit from an English actor – the boys brought their girl friends and vice-versa – so I found myself searching for food for fifteen. They leave every place utterly filthy, but I like them all the same – they are interesting, enthusiastic, frank and *un*reliable.

The actors continued to enliven Philip's life, despite the hassle and expense they caused him: the following spring he related a further chapter in their exploits, and issued another warning:

> Should you get involved with them remember that anything you have that they haven't is liable to become theirs for as long as they require it. Hence they have a claim to food, bed and bath

... particularly the bath. The other day, just before the Bishop
came here for the night, I saw a packet of hairpins lying around
in my bathroom and was able to remove it just in time.

Fr Caraman tolerated the lax morals and misdeeds of his
actors because the group worked with the handicapped, and he
said 'they showed great understanding and compassion which
endeared them to me'. Furthermore he believed in fostering
talent in those younger than himself: he encouraged Lita Anker
to draw, Muriel Spark and lesser known authors to write, and
actors to perform. His friendship for Gianni Lepre and his group
may also have been inspired by his belief in his mission to be
'a fisher of men', and in the hope that one day his generosity
and tolerance would be remembered by them as an example of
Catholicism.

Most of Philip's visitors were more conventional. His
brother, John, stayed with him when he was on leave from
Africa; a favourite nephew arrived very late one night from
England; Father Tranmar from Tisbury, accompanied by his
sister, came over for a holiday; the socialite artist Peter Coate
gave his host a colourful landscape as a memento of his stay.
All were made welcome by Fr Caraman who looked forward
ever more eagerly to visitors as his sense of isolation increased
with the passage of time. The young Irish priest Rory Mulligan,
who had arrived in Oslo in 1969 and assumed responsibility for
Catholic youth work in Norway, and Fr Olaf Waring went down
to Tønsberg as often as they could. And Caraman and Waring
sometimes made an excursion over to Sweden by ferry to buy
goodies, mostly food such as chickens for the deep freeze,
which Philip had discovered were cheaper there.

The times Philip looked forward to most eagerly were those
when he could visit Lita Anker and her family, or when they in
turn came to stay with him. After spending his sixty-fifth birthday with the Ankers, he wrote an effusive letter in gratitude for
'a marvellous party which I shall be able to talk about for a long
time – marvellous paté, parsley soup (recipe please), salmon and
masses of drink. A banquet fit for a king. And thank you for all
the loving toil that went into it.' He told her that when the

Ankers stayed with him they would not 'get such lovely food, but there will be plenty to drink'. Philip's affection for her was unchanged, and his feelings of fatherly interest are epitomised in a letter he wrote to her on another occasion when she had cooked a meal for him, and had lost her temper in the kitchen: 'Drive carefully, send me a postcard, say your prayers, forget your falcon, don't curse your oven, be good, enjoy your own company (as I do), read St Thomas, bless your children, give my greetings to John, sleep tight, watch your weight and pray for me.'

Unfortunately for Philip, the Ankers spent much of their time in Spain, and he was unable to see them as often as he would have liked. Preparing food, and cooking for his visitors was never a chore. Finding the ingredients to practise his culinary skills was another matter: most of his menus required items not available in a small Norwegian town, nor affordably in Oslo. Shopping lists made out either for potential visitors or ahead of his own snatched trips to England included: 6 bottles of Burgess Sauce Tartare, Harris Pork Shoulder, Bovril, Gentleman's Relish, Harrod's Paté and Fortnum & Mason's Pork Pie. He had expensive tastes and was always precise about the particular brand he wanted of any item: it was never just 'mayonnaise', it had to be Hellman's – no other would do.

On one occasion the provision and presentation of a meal for guests proved a regrettable source of distraction from his priestly ministry. An English couple, whom he had invited to have lunch with him after attending his Mass one Sunday, found him deeply upset. On returning to the presbytery, trembling with remorse, Fr Caraman asked if they had realised he had omitted to say the second part of the Act of Consecration during the Holy Sacrifice, and had forgotten to consecrate the wine. He was deeply mortified by this lapse in concentration, which may well have been caused by thoughts of the meal he was preparing for his visitors.

Despite any distraction it may have occasioned, Philip constantly urged people to call on him. 'This is a desperately lonely life and you would be doing me an immense kindness if you could call in here ... do come, I want only warning for a meal the day before', he told English friends living in Oslo. In winter, when visiting was often hazardous or impossible, the dark days passed slowly, and he was sometimes cut off from the outside world. Norwegians cope efficiently with their winter conditions, clearing snow almost as quickly as it falls. But in urban areas snow ploughed from roads is banked on to verges and piled, willy-nilly, across the entrance to private driveways and garages: moving a car from house to highway usually requires lengthy digging, and is a trial of strength particularly for anyone as elderly as Philip. Travelling in winter was an ordeal for him. 'I am not looking forward to driving around Vestfold in the winter', he decided before the first snow had set in or he had realised just how bad it would turn out to be.

His first winter at St Olav's was one of Norway's worst. In Oslo, the snow arrived in October, and was still falling steadily six months later: on the south coast it was worse. 'There was a bad patch of snow and ice [the other day]; the trains had to stop and all my meetings were called off'. Fr Caraman complained as the first flakes fell. Six months later, in April 1977, he wrote: 'An old lady in the parish here says that it has been the worst winter she can remember in her forty years in Tønsberg. I hope I shall not have to endure another such.' His hopes were in vain: the following March he reported that although the next winter had started later it had been even harder. The third winter in his appointment was no better: preparing to pack up and leave in March, 1979, he said he couldn't see himself 'getting off by car on summer tyres on 4th April if this weather continues. We are still in a wilderness of ice and snow here.'

Unlike the parish priests for whom he had acted as *locum*, Fr Caraman chose to take his holidays during the winter, rather than the summer months. 'I forfeited my summer holiday last year to be able to cut a slice off this Norwegian winter', he said after his first year in Tønsberg. But his prime concern was for his ministry: before arranging any breaks he made certain that another priest would replace him during his absences from St Olav's. A number of men helped him in this way: Father Dahl, a Norwegian Dominican from Oslo, looked after the church while Philip made a retreat in Denmark, and Fr Vranken, to whom he eventually handed over the parish, acted as supply priest when he had a holiday in Cyprus. When he could not find another priest to take the Sunday services, Fr Caraman dashed away on a Monday returning before the following weekend. Many of his business visits to England were hastily-snatched interludes into which he crammed as many events and appointments as possible. During a hectic few days in 1978 he flew to London on a Wednesday, went up to Stonyhurst 'to attend a Jesuit jamboree' the following day, was present at a two-day Provincial Meeting, returned to London to meet friends, including Alec Guinness, with whom he had lunch, and was back in Oslo within a week. He explained 'I can't stay longer [in England] though I should like to: anyhow it will cheer me up'.

Restricted by time, the few real holidays he had during his years in Tønsberg were never odysseys on the scale of some of his previous travels. He longed for the sun, and told Lita that he fancied going to North Africa: 'I have always wanted to see the Roman ruins at Carthage', he said. Later he changed his mind, and told her he was thinking 'of taking a package tour to see the Pyramids'. The Ankers were planning a visit to Morocco of which he was clearly envious: 'how wonderful to discover Moroccan mountains in your old age. I hope John will be inspired to do some striking paintings,' he told Lita. He would have been delighted had he known then that in very old age he too would discover the beauty of the Moroccan mountains.

When Fr Caraman returned from holiday there was always 'a mountain of correspondence to get through', to which he replied with his customary care and thoughtfulness. On one occasion, when he was living in Ware, he complained to his sister Claire: 'I sometimes wish I did not know so many people'. Although letter-writing added to his burden of paperwork, correspondence was his principal lifeline to friends and acquaintances during the years he was at St Olav's. His sense of isolation was often acute, the more so following the death of Fr Martin D'Arcy at the age of eighty-eight during the first year of Caraman's ministry in Tønsberg. D'Arcy's letters had been a supportive link with the Society of Jesus during Philip's years of self-imposed exile from London, particularly when he was living abroad.

D'Arcy's death, and the loss of the gentle, and sometimes corrective, guidance on which Philip knew he could rely, left a gap in the younger priest's life which would never be replaced. Theirs was a remarkable relationship. They had met initially as master and pupil, then as mentor and protégé, and finally had become the closest of friends, their association based on mutual affection and respect within their priestly vocation. The understanding between them had in due season been tempered by light-hearted fun and shared jokes. One of these was the joke about Fr O'Higgins, another related to Fr D'Arcy's physique. Fr Caraman related that 'in his youth D'Arcy was interested in boxing: he made a joke of his chest measurements whenever there was a question of my carrying his bags'.[6] On one occasion, after Fr D'Arcy had spent an evening with Philip in London, he sent a note from Mount Street saying, 'Keep the fare for the taxi, it will save to buy [you] a map of London, and also one of the bus routes. I got a bus within three minutes from the Edgware Road.'[7] – a reproof tempered with humour. D'Arcy's letters had kept Philip abreast of news of the Mount Street community, another link which was now severed. Evidence of the trust that had grown between them was the confidence Martin D'Arcy placed in Caraman as the older man experienced increasing depression and the ravages of old age. Almost ten years before his death, he wrote to Philip: 'If I die or go senile, I want you to take charge of my notes, mss, etc., If it be too much of a burden, do see to it that someone who is one with me in spirit does this job'.[8]

It was difficult for Fr Caraman to carry out D'Arcy's wishes to the full. He was not in England when the eminent Jesuit died, and the disposal of D'Arcy's papers fell within the jurisdiction of the Jesuit Provincial and was not, officially, a private matter. But after he returned to England Caraman was able to arrange for some of D'Arcy's prized vestments to be disposed of according to his wishes. In 1970, when Philip had been staying with the McEwens, Martin D'Arcy, who knew the family well, had sent the vestments to the chapel at Marchmont, saying he was 'so glad these vestments are being used as they should be and in such a Catholic home. So many lovely Church things, vestments

... chalices, statues etc are being thrown on the scrap heap or lying amid dust.'[9] In 1981 Caraman obtained the permission of the Jesuit Provincial for the vestments to be given outright to the chapel as a memorial to Robin McEwen who had recently died.[10]

Fr Caraman's relationship with Martin D'Arcy had matured over a period of almost forty years, and was a fundamental influence on the formation of Philip's character and outlook, and ultimately on the course of his life and career. Both men had experienced rejection and envy from a coterie of peers within the Society of Jesus, and much of Caraman's ambivalent attitude towards authority stemmed from his sense of loyalty to D'Arcy. The two men were linked inseparably in the minds of some of the older priests in the English Province: one told D'Arcy's biographer that he 'couldn't help regarding him [Caraman] as something of a snob and one of Fr D'Arcy's "long-haired" arty disciples'.[11] This was the type of criticism which Fr Caraman had learnt to expect, but he brushed it aside because it linked him with a priest and father figure for whom he had a deep regard. Following D'Arcy's death, however, this attitude served to increase Philip's sense of isolation and his sensitivity to criticism.

Outside the Society of Jesus, Fr Caraman had other confidants. Following the deaths of Evelyn Waugh and Martin D'Arcy, both of whom had been a source of strength and support in his life, Philip turned increasingly to another long-standing friend. Following the Jesuit's first encounter with Alec Guinness on the day Edith Sitwell was received into the Church at Farm Street in 1955, the relationship between the two men had burgeoned as time progressed. Closer to Philip in age than either Waugh or D'Arcy – there was less than three years between them – Caraman's friendship with Guinness was a more relaxed affair than his association with either of the older men. The unspoken deference with which he had treated both Fr D'Arcy and Waugh was replaced in Guinness's case with a brotherly regard, based on a shared sense of humour and purpose.

In his autobiography, Guinness describes in hilarious style an episode which took place a few years after his first meeting with Fr Caraman, when the Jesuit was still editor of *The Month*. Philip arranged for the actor, his wife Merula, and two others to attend the Pontifical High Mass celebrated by Pope John XXIII in St Peter's on the morning of Christmas. Their tickets were not for a particularly good position, and the party went along 'in grubby raincoats over old clothes'. Unexpectedly they were ushered into places of honour normally reserved for royalty on the High Altar, to the horror of Fr Caraman 'who was incorrectly dressed, looking rather like some crumpled curate from an impoverished English vicarage'. After Mass, the party were made to walk the full length of the Basilica behind the Pope's chair, and then rushed up to the roof where 'Fr Caraman insisted we should kneel in a lead gutter of trickling water to witness the Papal Blessing'.[12]

Their circle of mutual Catholic friends embraced, among others, Margaret and Giles FitzHerbert, and Brigid and Robin McEwen and their children. Lady McEwen recounts an anecdote relating to the time Fr Caraman was staying at Marchmont and writing *The Lost Paradise*:

> Fr Philip staying with us all that time, I couldn't bring myself to go to confession to him (since it might involve instances of my annoyance at him!), so when Robin and I were in London we thought we would go to confession in Westminster Cathedral ...
> As we emerged a figure detached itself from a dark pillar and said 'Biddy.' It was Alec ... I explained hurriedly in a whisper what we were doing there, because of not wanting to go to Philip, which he quite understood. He was on his way to the theatre ... and he too was going to confession.

The following Christmas the McEwens received a card from Alec Guinness in which he had written 'perhaps you would like me to hear your confession?'[13] It is unlikely that Fr Caraman was told this story, but he would probably have enjoyed the joke.

Humour, with a serious twist, was the basis of many of the letters Guinness wrote to Philip in Norway. At the time he was involved in playing Ben (Obi-Wan) Kenobi he wrote to Philip, saying:

Do you think that the ridiculous *Star Wars* is giving rise to a new heresy and I shall be called before the Inquisition? Actually I think that the 'Force be with you' line, which is in nearly all of the letters I receive nowadays – *could* be a goodish thing and slightly oppose the soccer hooliganism attitude to life.[14]

In this manner Guinness sometimes revealed his feelings about his roles and audiences to Philip, on another occasion reporting that he was 'up in London for the day from Bath – where I am playing to old stale Bath buns'.[15] But much of their correspondence was of a more serious nature, and revealed genuine concern for each other's welfare. When he heard that Guinness was in hospital for an operation, an anxious Caraman telephoned Merula to enquire after his friend's progress: in return Alec thanked Philip for his call 'across the North Sea and its rigs, oil pollution etc.' and hoped that all was well with the priest and that the 'nights [in Norway] are shortening properly and that you are not too lonely'.[16]

Guinness was concerned for 'Dear Blessed Philip', as he sometimes addressed him, in his Nordic ministry, and the warmth of his friendship may well have been a factor in Fr Caraman's decision to leave Tønsberg. By the spring of 1978, he had decided to leave the following year, and told a friend that 'the Bishop groaned a kind of blackmail groan when I told him I did not think I could continue here beyond my contracted three years. It was a fatal error to have learnt the language, even imperfectly.' By the high standards he expected of himself, Fr Caraman felt he was achieving very little. 'I am such an incompetent parish priest that it takes me three times as long to get anything done as it takes a normal parish priest', he confessed. Balancing his commitment to missionary service against what he could endure physically and mentally, he was defeated by a combination of a belief in his own inadequacy, the Norwegian winters, and his sense of isolation from those he loved. Inconsistent in his likes and dislikes of places and situations, he was constant in friendship. He may not have made converts, but the appointment in Tønsberg was not altogether bleak: apart from the odd bout of flu, and a bad fall on his way to the church one Sunday, his health had generally remained good: he enjoyed the freedom of having his own comfortable home: he had acquired a new hobby with his painting, and lived in a pleasant town in a scenic setting, where his brushes never lacked a worthy subject. Close to Tønsberg there is a wild and rugged stretch of coast jutting out into the Oslo Fiord known as *Verdens Ende*, and during the bitter winters, when he felt most alone, and feared for his life on the dangerous roads, Fr Caraman must have wondered if he really was living at the end of the world. Alec Guinness certainly thought he was, and did his utmost to persuade Philip to return to England. 'Why live in Norway? It must be just as cold here. And surely we in England can muster a far greater number of nasty people with souls for saving than you can in healthy Arctic climes,' he wrote.[17]

Once Fr Caraman had made a firm decision to leave Norway when his contract expired, Alec and Merula Guinness offered more than just sympathy. They offered him a home. Their house, Kettlebrook Meadows, near Petersfield in Hampshire, had a self-contained flat which they offered to let Philip live in rent free: he would only have to pay for heating and lighting. Outlining the proposal, the actor said he had discussed the idea with his parish priest and the Bishop of Portsmouth, both of whom agreed in principal. It was a generous invitation. Fr Caraman did not take up Alec's offer, although the bond between them remained as strong as ever: instead he accepted a commission which would take him to Rome, and to London, and give him another book on which to exercise his literary talents.

❧

In a career characterised by contrast, none could have been greater than Fr Caraman's life in Tønsberg and his move to the cosmopolitan buzz of the Eternal City. In the period following his ministry in Vestfold, Philip spent several lengthy spells working in Rome: these alternated with months spent either in London or in Tisbury, and were punctuated by visits to the United States and to Australia. An invitation to write the history of the Gregorian University of Rome provided the reason for his first session in Italy: it was a project he took up eagerly.

His book traces the story of the great Pontifical scholastic institution from the foundation of the Roman College by Ignatius Loyola in 1551, through the many ups and downs of its fortunes over the four hundred years to the eve of Vatican II. With archival material readily available, Caraman wrote quickly and with enjoyment. By highlighting the more dramatic episodes and colourful characters in his story, he succeeds in turning what could have been a recital of dry historical facts into an interesting and easy read. The controversial nature of Galileo Galilei's involvement with the College, an episode featuring Queen Christina of Sweden, events connected with the suppression of the Society of Jesus in 1773, and political upheavals following the French Revolution, all lend colour and verve to the history of a university which numbers some of Catholicism's brightest stars among its alumni. Canonised saints and *beatae* on its roll of honour cross the centuries, from Englishmen like Robert Southwell and Ralph Sherwin martyred under Queen Elizabeth I, to the Conventual Franciscan Maximilian Kolbe, who died at Auschwitz. Caraman comments that when Pope Gregory XIII was thanked in twenty-five languages for the lavish munificence which underpinned Ignatius Loyola's initial foundation, 'even he could scarcely have foreseen that four hundred years later his university of the nations would be attended by students from eighty-five or more countries and have professors from a continent then unknown'.[18] *University of the Nations* was an apt, if obvious, title for the book which was slanted towards the North American market and brought out by a leading American Catholic publisher, Paulist Press, without any of the delays which had plagued *The Lost Paradise*.

In his Introduction to *University of the Nations,* Fr Caraman revealed the ethos which guided his concept of writing history:

> It was my good fortune many years ago to belong to a small group of students who met every week in the rooms of Sir Maurice Powicke, the Regius Professor of History at Oxford, who would talk about long-forgotten bishops, kings and statesmen as though he had just come from entertaining them in the hall of his college. All that I learned then about the thirteenth century I have now forgotten, but one lesson I took away with

me, namely, that there need never be an excuse for making history dull.[19]

Caraman never lost sight of the principle he learned as a student at Oxford, and always sought to make his histories interesting for the non-academic reader. With his early books he achieved spectacular success, but some of his later publications were criticised for a lack of scholarship. Referring to this aspect of his work, Fr Fergus O'Donoghue, archivist of the Irish Province of the Society of Jesus, commented that

> his [Caraman's] writing was intended to make the Society better known, and to make both Jesuit and English Catholic history accessible to the average reader. Philip did not regard himself as a scholar of the first rank, but he knew that he wrote both easily and well. His books ... reflect his gifts, though his study of Henry Garnet reveals a capacity for deeper research when required.[20]

Fr O'Donoghue's accolade contrasts with comments levelled at Fr Caraman's writing elsewhere in the Society. When he was invited to write other Jesuit histories, in addition to that of the Gregorian University, he was labelled a 'hack' by some of his confrères. The criticism seems somewhat harsh: if every established writer who has been commissioned to produce work was labelled a 'hack', then the literary stables would be occupied by some very famous men and woman who are generally considered to be thoroughbreds, including William Shakespeare.

Caveats concerning his work lay in the future. Meanwhile Philip experienced a period of *rapprochement* with the Society of Jesus, during which the sorrows and problems of the past fell into perspective and he was able to enjoy an harmonious interlude in his Jesuit life. In September 1979 Fr Caraman became a Professed Father in the Society of Jesus, and was admitted to the fourth vow over and above the three vows of religion – poverty, chastity and obedience – made at the time of his ordination over thirty years earlier.

The fourth vow is a solemn *profession* of special obedience to

the Pope with respect to the Missions; that one would go wherever the Pope wished to send one, [explains Fr Richard
Randolph]. Those who can be professed of the four vows are
more usually those who have attained some degree of academic
or other excellence, or have been appointed to a position of
government or special responsibility in the Society ... it more
closely binds the Society and the professed member of the
Society together in a position of trust.[21]

Fr Caraman had waited until the age of sixty-eight for the
mark of approbation which had been accorded to Martin D'Arcy
when still a young man.

The grounds on which Fr Caraman qualified for profession
are explained in a letter he received the following year from the
Jesuit General, Fr Pedro Arrupe, to mark Philip's Golden
Jubilee in the Society. Fr Arrupe has been described as 'a
Basque with the lineaments of Ignatius Loyola', and as 'a man
of courtesy and charm with a hint of holiness', a polyglot who
had travelled throughout the world.[22] Although the letter
undoubtedly followed a standard format sent to all priests reaching the fiftieth anniversary of their entry to the Jesuit novitiate,
it is sufficiently personal to reveal both Arrupe's courtesy, and
his concern for one of his priests. From his office in Rome, the
Father General wrote:

You seem almost too active to me, Father Philip, to be a
Jubilarian! As you were here recently and will soon, I hope, be
here again, I will be able to thank you personally for all your
good work, past and present. Enough here to recall that your
service of the Lord has been very much an apostolate of the pen
– you were involved very soon after ordination both as editor and
author and I am told that you gave new life to *The Month* after
the war ... and your historical work has of course been highly
praised. I would like to pay tribute again to your great labours
as Vice-Postulator for the Cause of the English and Welsh
Martyrs. Those who are in a position to know judged your
contribution to be outstanding. And I must not forget your
unusual pastoral interlude in Norway. Thank you very much,
Father, in the name of the Society for all the good work that you
have done – and are continuing to do.[23]

Highlighting Fr Caraman's achievements, which he himself
sometimes doubted, the letter surely brought the Jubilarian
comfort and encouragement. The Jesuit General's letter noted
the fact that Philip had recently visited Australia: the work 'he
was continuing to do' was a commission to write a history of
the Society of Jesus and its Mission there. With the completion
of *University of the Nations,* this was another absorbing project,
and planning his journey to the far side of the world reflected
the *frisson* he still experienced at the prospect of travel to a
distant, and – for him – unknown continent. Long before the era
of low-budget airlines, Philip became an expert in travel
economy. He hunted down the best deals with dogged determination, passing on the fruits of his research to friends whom he
urged to take up the cheap offers of air, ferry and train fares
which he had discovered. He announced smugly that his ticket
to Australia allowed him to drop off at various points along his
route, including Hong Kong and other equally exciting places .
Thus the slightly-built, elderly, priest with a misleading air of
vulnerability and only light luggage travelled inconspicuously,
and contentedly, on yet another long-haul journey. After his
return, he said, 'I enjoyed all my time in Australia and had a
marvelous [sic] journey from Adelaide to Perth by train.' The
book which provided the excuse and the finance for Fr
Caraman's happy odyssey was less of a success. Publication was
subjected to endless delays, and six years later he reported that,
'Collins (Australia) are now making the excuse that they are
unlikely to sell enough copies to make ends meet. But I suspect
there have been anti-pommy machinations behind scenes.' His
suspicions were confirmed when the work was cast aside by the
Australian Jesuits. The history of the Province was produced by
Fr Peter Steele SJ, although Philip wrote a series of articles
under the title 'Early Days in the Australian Mission' for the
British Jesuit in-house publication *Letters and Notices* some
years later.

One of the problems posed by Caraman's peripatetic existence
at this time was the difficulty he had in finding somewhere to
write without interruptions. He frequently visited Tisbury,
helping Father Tranmar with parish duties as a quid pro quo for

a haven in which he could work, but his principal base in England was a presbytery in a quiet cul-de-sac in Wapping. At first he was delighted with his home at St Patrick's, with its address in London's East End docklands a far cry from Mayfair. Later the enchantment wore thin, and he moved from Wapping, explaining that he had little time for writing there because he 'served most of the day as doorman, telephonist and cook'. His new base was Southwell House, a Jesuit house of studies in Swiss Cottage with an active ministry run by a number of priests. It was a busy place, but convenient enough for the short periods Caraman spent in the capital.

Was it a desire to find a place where he could write without interruption, or another bout of the Nordic disease, which persuaded Philip to return to Norway? He surprised his friends, and possibly himself, by spending the harshest months of the winter following his visit to Australia at the Mariakirken in Lillehammer, a parish even more isolated than his former home on the south coast. The Jesuit General described Fr Caraman's years in Norway as an 'unusual pastoral interlude'. They were more than that: for Philip this was a missionary field for which he still retained a lingering sense of responsibility. It is likely that he succumbed to an urgent plea for help from Bishop John Gran, and in January 1981 he related that:

[The parish priest] moved off to a Monastery of Christ in the Desert in New Mexico leaving no one prepared to live here alone and care for 60 Catholics between here and Sognefjell. It suited me for three months for the purpose of writing without inter-ruption. I have had one caller since I came. Nearly every time the telephone rings it is the wrong number. I am not technically parish priest, so I pass on all the accounts, statistics, etc. to Oslo. The [new] parish priest is a Danish monk living as a hermit up in Lom. I have not seen him and would not know him if I met him. He spoke to me once on the telephone. He will have to come down from his fastness if anyone wishes to get married, a very improbable event today in Norway ...

Fr Caraman described the utter isolation of his existence, saying he had received only one visit from outsiders, two priests from Oslo, in two months: on their way back to the capital the priests' car had skidded forty yards into a snowbank, and ended up facing Lillehammer again. 'Otherwise I have neither seen, nor heard nor spoken to anyone here from one Sunday morning to the following Sunday.' The large, modern, church was, he said, 'built by a mad priest for a congregation that existed purely in his imagination and endowed with money from Essen. The largest number I have had, excluding 30 at Xmas, is 21.' On the first Sunday in January he had a congregation of eight.

Fr Caraman's loneliness was relieved by the solicitude of some of his friends: Colonel Kristen Kristensen, an army officer who had helped Philip with contacts when he was writing *Norway,* and his wife, Frances, supported him as they had throughout his years in Norway. An Englishwoman who had met her husband during the war, Frances was Cardinal Hume's sister, and a good friend of whom Philip was particularly fond: Fr Olaf Waring, unlike the parish priest of Lillehammer, persevered in his ministry and was only a phone-call away. He recalled a time when the snow had been especially heavy: 'It was one of those non-stop snows which we get occasionally – a fortnight of continuous falling snow. One was happy when it all finally stopped. But then, when after a few more days the snow began to fall again, Philip rang me in Oslo and exclaimed that if it did not stop he would surely go mad.'[24]

Other friends wrote with news from England. A letter reporting a public spat between Tom Burns, who was nearing the end of his time as editor of *The Tablet*, and another prominent English Catholic, Norman St John Stevas, aroused his curiosity. 'I would love to see the correspondence between Stevas and Burns, for I know them both and could not imagine two better seeded antagonists,' he confided, in a rare admission to acquaintanceship with celebrities. Consistently self-effacing, normally he never alluded in conversation to any of the famous writers, churchmen, politicians, and actors with whom he was on first-name terms. He never dripped names. Father Fergus O'Donoghue, who shared an office in Rome with Philip for six months, and was in contact with him for several years, put it well: 'Philip was ... a very discreet friend who knew many important literary figures, who moved in some socially exalted circles but never boasted of his 'connections', and made light of his friendships with some very famous people'.[25] It was hardly surprising that few people with whom he was in contact in his later life were aware of Fr Caraman's 'connections'.

The loneliness of Lillehammer did not deter Philip from returning to spend a further two months there at the end of the following winter, albeit this time for more selfish motives. After a brief visit to the United States in the summer of 1981, *University of the Nations* was successfully launched, and he was free to choose another subject to work on. The seeds of his next book had been sown over a decade earlier during his East African journey, and other pointers had aroused his interest during his work in the Jesuit archives in Rome. 'I am now engaged on a book on Abyssinia', he said, adding that he had 'a fair idea of the land and its people'. Caraman explained his choice of subject: 'In the early seventeenth century the Jesuits brought about a union of the Abyssinia Coptic church with Rome. It did not last long, but it is an interesting chapter in the history of the Jesuits which no one has attempted yet to write.' Inspiration for the new book was primarily rooted in Philip's passion for travel. In the course of his research work over the years he had taken notes for a book – which in fact was never written – intended as a study of three Jesuit journeys of exploration. One of these was the attempt made by Jesuits in Paraguay to find a passage through the marshes of the upper Paraguay river to their missions in the Bolivian province of Chiquitos: this formed part of the story of the Reductions told in *The Lost Paradise*. Another of these adventures – the journey of Bento de Goes from Lahore though Afghanistan in search of an overland route to China – eventually formed the basis of the last of Fr Caraman's Jesuit histories, and was published shortly before his death. The third study followed the late sixteenth-century travels of Pedro Paez in Yemen, which led to the exploits of the Spanish Jesuit and his companions in Ethiopia. The discovery in the Jesuit archives in Rome of four unpublished letters written by Paez added impetus to Caraman's wish to tell his story and that of the Jesuits in Ethiopia from 1555-

1634. His principal regret was that when he came to write the book the political situation made it impossible for him to follow 'the route from Massawa on the Red Sea to Fremona and on to Lake Tana, along which the Jesuits so frequently travelled'.[26]

On his second sojourn in Lillehammer, life was considerably brighter than on the first. His stint in the parish covered the weeks of Lent and Holy Week: although his congregations was still notable for its absence, the weather was far less depressing than during his stay the previous year:

> Yesterday [Ash Wednesday] I made, blessed and unliturgically distributed ashes to myself: not even a cat in the congregation in this splendid church built (and endowed) by a mad German without the bishop's leave ... This is the best part of the winter here. Cold, yes, but blue skies, sunshine, longer hours than in England, and no rail strikes to make visits to friends impossible.

Catering for himself in his isolated presbytery, thoughts of his larder preoccupied Philip. He had some Norwegian *flatbiff* which he was unsure how to deal with: 'all my attempts to make a decent meal with Norwegian meat have ended in totally taste-less brown linoleum', he complained. Although the fish from the nearby lake were excellent, the French Brie he had bought 'was hard and made rather tasteless from a long sojourn in a deep freeze'. Ten days before he returned to England there was heavy snow, and with everything in the country about to shut down for the Easter holiday he laid in provisions, and reported that he felt as though he was under siege.

His return to England in the spring of 1982 marked the end of the final chapter in Fr Caraman's ministry in Norway, during the course of which he had spent four Christmas days entirely on his own. At the age of seventy, he could no longer endure winter months spent in isolation, nor would he experience again the delights of the country's brief, idyllic, summers. He had contributed more than his share of pastoral zeal to this difficult mission, and his thoughts concerning Catholicism in Norway were tinged with disillusion. 'Few novices or church students go very far, and ninety per cent of my parish lose contact with the church after confirmation', he wrote shortly before he left

Tønsberg. He was dismayed at the morals of some of his parish-ioners, and, when questioned about the Church in Norway, replied, 'I dare not write about it'. Experience had taught him that the Norwegian missionary field was 'very stony ground' indeed. Some months after Philip left Lillehammer, John Gran, who was almost nine years younger, retired from his post in Oslo, and bought a house in Corsica. The Bishop's departure marked the end of Philip Caraman's love-hate relationship with Norway, although he still remained in contact with friends there, especially Fr Waring, and he retained an interest in the country's news and gossip for the rest of his life. To his amuse-ment, he learned sometime later that his years of labour as a parochial minister had earned him a small pension from the Norwegian government.

Notes

1 Letter, Philip Caraman to Lady Brigid McEwen, Oslo, 5 January 1971.
2 Unless noted separately, quotations in the first part of this chapter are taken from Fr Caraman's letters to Lita Anker and to the author. Those in the second part are from his letters to the author.
3 The area on the western side of the Oslofiord, lying roughly between Oslo and Tønsberg, is the district known as Vestfold.
4 June Rockett. Essay entitled 'Mission North' in the *Catholic Gazette*, vol. 71, issue no. 2, February 1980, p. 18.
5 Notes in Philip Caraman's Private Papers (heareafter PCPP).
6 Based on note left by Fr Caraman among papers now in Boston College.
7 Letter, Fr Martin D'Arcy to Fr Caraman, 6 June 1970, John J. Burns Library, Boston College (hereafter BC).
8 Ibid. 5 February 1967 (BC).
9 Letter, Fr Martin D'Arcy to Lady Brigid McEwen, 8 October 1970.
10 Letter, Philip Caraman to Lady Brigid McEwen, 30 June 1981.
11 Letter, H. J. A. Sire to author, 25 May 2002.
12 Alec Guinness *Blessings in Disguise* (Hamish Hamilton Ltd, 1985, & Fontana Paperbacks, 1986), pp. 77–8.

13 Letter, Lady Brigid McEwen to author, 30 April 2003.
14 Letter, Alec Guinness to Philip Caraman, 31 January 1978 (PCPP).
15 Ibid. 26 September 1976.
16 Ibid. 13 May 1977.
17 Ibid. 2 January 1977.
18 Philip Caraman, *University of the Nations* (Paulist Press, New York/Ramsey, 1981), p. 145.
19 Ibid. p. 2.
20 *Letters & Notices*, vol. 94, Spring 1999, no. 415, p. 939.
21 Letter to author, 23 May 2002.
22 Tom Burns, *The Use of Memory*, p. 173.
23 Letter, Fr Pedro Arrupe SJ to Philip Caraman, 8 September 1980 (PCPP).
24 Fr Olaf I. Waring, letter to author, based on Obituary Notice, September 1998.
25 *Letters & Notices*, vol. 94. Spring 1999, no. 415, p. 939.
26 Philip Caraman, Introduction to *The Lost Empire. The Story of the Jesuits in Ethiopia. 1555–1634* (Sidgwick & Jackson, 1985).

Part Four
A Place of Rest
1982–1998

Chapter Eleven

The Herb Garden

Few men who are committed to the religious life, and remain faithful to their vow of obedience, can be certain where their work and vocation will take them. Except in retirement the majority of priests have no guarantee of a permanent home. In this respect, Fr Caraman was considerably less fortunate than many of his Jesuit brethren, who had a family haven to which they could return from time to time. Never 'settled' in any one place for more than a few months or weeks, the parish in Tønsberg, and the house at 31 Farm Street where he had lived for fourteen years during his years as editor of *The Month*, were the closest he had ever come to an undisturbed existence. Accustomed to moving from one base to another, he betrayed no sign of tiring of his peripatetic life: writing was the spur which goaded him on.

Even as a septuagenarian, Fr Caraman often had two or more projects on the go at the same time. The history of the Jesuits in Ethiopia was still unfinished when he returned to Rome to work on another Jesuit enterprise in which a number of his confrères of different nationalities were also engaged. This was the ambitious *Diccionario Historico de la Compania de Jesus*, to which he contributed some twenty essays. His articles were written in English and later translated. Some idea of the magnitude of the task is given in a letter Caraman wrote four years later:

I wrote [an article] on Jesuit chaplains for a Dictionary of Jesuit History still in the process of production. [My essay] started with the first Jesuit chaplain who around 1540 crossed the Elbe in a local skirmish, got biffed on the head with a cannon ball but nevertheless preached a fiery sermon at Passau three days later and lived to a ripe old age without ever taking any medicine in his long life. The article – about 10,000 words – is unlikely to be published in my lifetime. It covered the chaplains in the Spanish Armada and went down to the Vietnam War.[1]

Although Fr Caraman wrote quickly, work on the Dictionary kept him in Rome for the greater part of 1982. Describing the six months during which he shared an office in the Jesuit Historical Institute with Philip, Fr O'Donoghue said that he 'found him to be loyal, pleasant, humorous and hard-working. Philip was . . . a good companion.'[2] But beneath the surface the Institute was a factious place: Jesuits are by nature individual-ists, and – it is said – do not adapt readily to teamwork. Another member of the Jesuit writing team with whom Philip got on well was Fr Francisco de Borja de Medina: this friendship, and the turf wars endemic to the Institute at the time, had repercussions when Caraman embarked on a life of St Ignatius Loyola a few years later.

Fr Caraman had other friends in Rome, as he had almost everywhere else he went. When she was at home during one of his prolonged visits, he went to see Muriel Spark, with whom he had remained in touch since his days as editor of *The Month*. These social calls provided an enjoyable break from the austere, and sometimes acrimonious, atmosphere of the Institute and the Jesuit's *Casa degli Scrittori* in the Via dei Penitenzieri, where he was quartered whilst working on the Jesuit dictionary. Philip also kept his ties with Norway alive through contacts with the Norwegian community in Rome, for whom he said a Christmas Mass in the church of San Carlo, where a chapel used by the group has what Philip termed a 'very militaristic picture' of St Olav.

Although he spent some of the winter months there, Philip never felt particularly well in Rome. More than twenty years earlier, when he started work on the Cause for the Forty Martyrs, he had suffered ill health during his visit, and his expe-rience of the Roman climate had not improved with the years. Whilst researching *The Lost Paradise* in the city, he had burnt himself badly and said he had 'a ghastly time in hospital there'. Later, when he complained to Muriel Spark of how ill he felt during another visit, she told him:

> The air of Rome is now officially declared to be polluted over the danger mark. I seldom go there – only to collect mail and pay bills. When I finish my current novel I hope to find another house somewhere else. I am sure the air and water of Rome contributed as much to your poor health there as the wine.[3]

Fr Caraman did not find London any more agreeable than Rome, and escaped from Southwell House whenever he could. He made frequent visits to rural Wiltshire to help Fr Tranmar, and expressed the gratitude he felt for the haven provided by the parish by writing and publishing a pamphlet on the history of the chapel at Wardour. 'Give me Paris, Rome or Vienna', Philip had declared when he was based in Oslo: now city life no longer suited his health or temperament. Within a few weeks of returning from Rome, he set out for Zimbabwe: on this occasion the long-haul journey was not undertaken for pleasure, but to see his 'ancient brother'. 'I am taking *his* leave, so to speak, in reverse', Philip said.[4] The brothers did not meet again. Fr John Caraman died on 27 July 1983, within a few months of Philip's return to England, but the visit had been providentially timed and given John 'great happiness', according to the Jesuit who wrote his obituary.

The void experienced by the loss of his brother was eased for Philip by a friendship which developed between himself and Fr Richard Randolph, who had spent over twenty years in Africa as one of John Caraman's fellow missionaries. Randolph retired from Zimbabwe and joined the Jesuit community in Farm Street as Minister and domestic bursar in the year John died. Later he said that he was fortunate to have had both Caraman brothers 'as a good friend in Christ'. When Philip asked him why he had taken so readily to his company, Fr Randolph replied that it was because he had so much liked his brother.[5]

Philip Caraman, living in Swiss Cottage, and Fr Richard in Farm Street, discovered they had much in common, including a shared sense of humour and a love of travel. Initially their joint excursions were day trips to Boulogne. Fr Randolph described a typical day out:

> Often we met at Charing Cross by the earliest tube trains, and travelled by rail to Folkestone to breakfast on the channel ferry to Boulogne. There we arrived in time to stroll to a brasserie, called Chez Alfred, for an inexpensive but delicious lunch. We then climbed up to the upper town, explored about, and made sundry small purchases of continental culinary goodies to take home, as well as material for a supper on the return journey to Charing Cross. We would arrive back at our respective destinations by 10 p.m. This we repeated several times as an exhilarating and often hilarious way of going out for the day.[6]

Fr Randolph came to know Philip well during these and subsequent travels in his company: he remarked that Fr Caraman had inherited his father's business acumen and had a grasp of finance which was unusual in a Jesuit, many of whom, he said, have no idea at all of the use and value of money. On their trips, Philip always offered to pay for things, then decided he had no money, and finally, at the end of the day, suddenly found that he had and duly paid up. 'His appetite for business and a bargain always induced him to think that anything (a can of sardines for example) bought abroad was better value than one purchased in England, and had a certain *cachet* on account of its continental origin.'[7] Philip certainly made much of the Brie and other cheeses he found in the specialist shop in Boulogne, and on a visit to friends in Folkestone demanded a trip to the local fishmonger whose catch, he was certain, would be superior to anything he could buy elsewhere. Later, the Jesuits' expeditions flourished into longer holidays abroad, and towards the end of Fr Caraman's life, Richard Randolph became one of his closest confidants and friends.

There were other diversions. When he was staying at Southwell House, Fr Caraman was once again in demand as a religious adviser to film and TV companies. To his cynical amusement, he was invited to contribute to the filming of *The Mission*, and was also involved with a play for the BBC entitled *The Holy Experiment*. Alec Guinness too was anxious to enlist his help: 'Will you be in London on the second or third [of next month]? If so would you like to make yourself useful on one of those afternoons helping me rehearse the [Tridentine] Mass which is at the end of Graham's *Monsignor Quixote* ... I *hope* the TV company will suggest a fee, but if they don't I will.'

Two weeks later Guinness sent Philip another note, saying that should Fr Caraman be unable to get to the rehearsal of the adaptation of Greene's novel, 'then please don't worry, as I'm sure we could find someone else but it would be nice for me if it was you'.[8]

The artistic content of Guinness's work was frequently a topic of discussion between them. A couple of months previously, Alec had sent the priest a note about the recently completed film *A Passage to India*, in which he played the part of Professor Godbole for David Lean. He told Philip that 'the film is good (except for the last ten minutes, which are banal) but I am afraid I am quite awful in it. But really embarrassing. I am afraid judgement becomes feeble with age'.[9]

With continual requests to conduct weddings and funerals, Fr Caraman was once again prominent in London Catholic circles in a manner reminiscent of his years in Mayfair. But the role of popular priest was no longer acceptable, especially as it interfered with his writing. In a letter from Rome early in 1986, he said that he was planning to 'bury' himself 'deep in the West Country' in order to write his next book. 'In London I find myself caught up in social-pastoral-personal problems', he revealed. He also expressed a fear that 'apart from a business visit to the US in June, I think my travelling days are over'. He had however enjoyed a painting holiday in Ithaca the previous October, although the weather had let him down. His travelling days were far from over: he merely feared they might be.

The move to the West Country was delayed by further visits to Rome. *The Lost Empire* came out in the summer of 1985. Three years earlier, Fr Caraman's agent had arranged for all rights in this, and his other books, to be assigned to the Jesuits: this may have been a ploy to forestall another dispute similar to that which had arisen following publication of *The Lost Paradise* in 1975. There was no need for worry. The story of the Jesuits in Ethiopia never attracted the same attention, nor the acclaim, accorded to the earlier book, although the African story was a considerably less complicated narrative than Caraman's history of the Jesuit Reductions in Paraguay.

In Pedro Paez, *The Lost Empire* has a bold and charismatic hero, whose exploits dominate the book. The author's best writing describes the Spanish Jesuit's abortive attempt to reach Ethiopia from Goa. In this seven-year ordeal, Paez and another Jesuit were shipwrecked, captured by pirates, imprisoned, and forced to work as galley slaves. During their captivity the Jesuit piests were force-marched through the deserts of the Hadhramaut, and Paez was the first traveller from the West to leave a description of that inhospitable land. Eventually, after finally reaching Ethiopia, he made many journeys of exploration, and wrote a long and comprehensive book on the country, in which 'his description of the source of the Blue Nile occupies only four out of 1,128 printed pages'. More than a century and a half later, James Bruce of Kinnaird, 'the first Briton to travel in Ethiopia after the Jesuits had left ... [came] with the declared purpose of discovering the source of the Nile ... [and was] compelled to claim what Paez had never claimed, that he was the first European to have found the springs of the great river'.[10]

The final act of the story of the Jesuits in Ethiopia is no less tragic than their expulsion from South America at the time of the suppression of the Society, which Fr Caraman had related in *The Lost Paradise*. Following Paez's death from fever in 1622, the Emperor wrote extolling his virtues to the Jesuit Provincial in Goa, describing him as 'our spiritual father, bright sun of the faith that cleared Ethiopia of the darkness of Eutyches'. And in 1936 the historian, Sir Wallis Budge, commented that Paez was 'a deeply religious and learned man, whose body and brains were working at all times to spread the faith which he professed'.[11] His success as a missionary and explorer was spectacular, but within twenty years of his death his achievement, in winning the allegiance of the Emperor and of many of his subjects to the Church of Rome, was thrown away by the blundering and insensitive arrogance of Paez's successor Alfonso

Mendes. A few pockets of loyalty to the Pope lingered on, but with the departure of the Jesuits, and the exclusion of foreigners from the country, Ethiopia once again became isolated from the rest of the world.

Such are the vagaries of publishing and reviewing that Fr Caraman's well-written and dramatic story made few ripples on the literary scene, although Sidgwick & Jackson's production of the book, with an intriguing cover design and high-quality illustrations, was superior to the work they had done ten years earlier on *The Lost Paradise*. Perhaps in the meantime the public had lost interest in tales of Jesuit derring-do. The genre was no longer fashionable.

Fr Caraman considered a biography of Edmund Campion for his next writing project, but was dissuaded. A study of the Jesuit martyr had been made by Evelyn Waugh, and possibly Philip was wary of treading in his master's footsteps. It is not immediately clear why he settled instead on St Ignatius Loyola, whose life and works had already been studied and written up by numerous other writers and scholars, including Caraman's old history master, Christopher Hollis. Possibly he felt that new material concerning Ignatius's life, which Philip had learnt about from conversations in Rome with the Spanish historian Francisco de Borja de Medina, would add a new dimension to his narrative: ostensibly the biography was written to commemorate the fifth centenary of the birth of the saint. If some of his fellow Jesuits were less than enthusiastic about Fr Caraman's project, at least he received encouragement from another writer whose opinion he valued. Muriel Spark told him that 'a life of St Ignatius sounds just your thing but I imagine very arduous to do thoroughly. Anyway he was a good soldier like you – an affinity between the biographer and the subject always makes for good results'.[12]

Fr Caraman was working in Rome when he received distressing news: Margaret FitzHerbert had been run over and killed by a car as she was crossing a road in north London on her way to an art gallery with some friends on 28 January 1986. Meg, whom he had known since she was a young child and who died in her early forties, had brightened his days with her warmth

and her wit, and her loss left a void in his life. The priest and
Waugh's favourite daughter had remained in close contact,
however far apart their respective travels had taken them, and
their fondness for each other was unchanged despite the trau-
matic events surrounding Caraman's dismissal from Farm Street
over twenty years earlier. She often sent him news of her children, and in a letter to Norway, when she and Giles FitzHerbert
were about to take up a post abroad, Meg wrote: 'I think it
would be nice if you retired soon from your arduous missionary
work and joined us *en poste* as tutor for the children and chaplain to the diplomatic community wherever it might be'.[13]

Fittingly, as she had worked with him on the Cause, Margaret
and Giles were in Rome at the time of the Canonisation of the
Forty Martyrs; over the years she had come to know a number
of Fr Caraman's other friends, including Muriel Spark and Alec
Guinness, both of whom expressed their sadness at her death in
letters to Philip. Two days after Meg was killed, Alec told the
priest that he was 'deeply *distressed* and *shocked*' at the news.
Three years earlier, the daughter whose ability to complete a
full-length book Evelyn Waugh had doubted, was shortlisted for
the Whitbread prize for Biography.[14] Margaret FitzHerbert's
story of the life of her grandfather, Aubrey Herbert, depicts an
extraordinary man of action, a traveller and politician, who was
twice offered the throne of Albania, and was the figure on
whom, it was said, John Buchan had modelled the romantic hero
of *Greenmantle*. Philip Caraman had always encouraged Meg to
write since her days as his secretary in Farm Street, and took
paternal pride in her success long after her untimely death.

Margaret was buried beside the graves of her parents, Laura
and Evelyn Waugh, on the hill beneath their former home at
Combe Florey. Thanking Fr Caraman for his panegyric, Meg's
brother, Auberon Waugh, told the priest that he was grateful for
his 'calm and benign presence on that sad occasion'. The house,
overlooking the burial plot outside the village churchyard at
Combe Florey, was now the home of Auberon and his wife
Teresa; a tribe of other Waughs, Herberts and FitzHerberts, was
dotted about the countryside on the fringes of Exmoor. In 1971,
Giles and Margaret had bought a rambling property at Cove,

north of Tiverton, where a gaggle of their own children, and a host of cousins, could enjoy the freedom of a vast garden: some years later Septimus, another of Evelyn Waugh's sons, moved to Cove House with his family. A few miles further up the picturesque Exe valley was Herbert territory, presided over now by Laura Waugh's sister, Bridget Grant, from a farm on the outskirts of Dulverton. The Herbert family mansion at Pixton had been sold and converted into apartments, but the little church established by Mary Herbert in the town remained as a memorial to her concern for the welfare of local Catholics. At the entrance to the courtyard leading to the church of St Stanislaus, Bridget Grant's son-in-law, Ian Fraser, owned a property standing directly on the narrow pavement of Dulverton High Street named Bridge House. Given rent free, this was where Fr Caraman came in the summer of 1986 to work undisturbed by the pressures of London, and to live quietly, close to friends whom he had known for over forty years, and among whom he was peaceably at home.

Despite its imposing name, Bridge House was little more than a labourer's cottage near the disused stable which had provided the site for Mary Herbert's church. The front door on Dulverton High Street opened into the sitting room, whence a narrow staircase wound to the upper floor with two bedrooms and a bathroom. A second room downstairs served as dining-room and study. Through the reasonably well-equipped kitchen, the back door led to a few feet of patio-garden, and a gate into the yard of the church. A larger house adjacent to the church had served as a presbytery for Canon Ronald MacDonald, who retired after more than thirty years as parish priest of St Stanislaus shortly before Fr Caraman's arrival; this rather gloomy diocesan property was not offered to Fr Caraman, who was not regarded as Canon MacDonald's replacement. The Dulverton parish has one of the smallest congregations in the Catholic Diocese of Clifton, although it covers a large area. The Bishop was unable to find another priest for this isolated parish, and when Philip moved to

Dulverton he himself was long past retirement age. It was not foreseen that he would undertake a permanent pastoral role.

The cottage was by no means ideal for an old man living alone. Although Fr Caraman recognised its drawbacks, he was content with Bridge House: it was the first place he could call his own since leaving Tønsberg seven years earlier. In an interview with a Catholic journalist a few years after he went to Dulverton, Caraman explained that he had acted as a holiday supply priest there for many years, starting in 1946, and added that he liked it. 'It's quiet, and I can get on with my writing', he said.[15] At last he felt 'settled'. Now that he had the freedom to cook for friends, he planted herbs in the tiny, south-facing patio beyond his back door. The fun of trying out new menus and entertaining guests had been denied him when he was living in the impersonal atmosphere of a large Jesuit house. For a while he also grew a few vegetables in the garden alongside the empty presbytery, but the work soon proved too arduous, and the vegetable plot was abandoned. Knowing his enjoyment of food and wine, Fr Caraman's larder was rapidly showered with goodies. Alec Guinness was slow off the mark, but characteristically generous with his contribution. Three months after Philip moved into Bridge House, Guinness wrote to say:

> I have asked Berry Bros & Rudd of St. James's St. to send you half a dozen bottles of wine as a house-warming gift. I imagine they will take a week or ten days to reach you. Nothing at all grand but drinkable I think. Certainly not of the quality for you to put before Bron Waugh when you entertain him. You would be advised to ask him to bring his own. It was good seeing you looking so well and happy. Obviously Dulverton suits you.[16]

The quiet Exmoor town did agree with Philip: his work went well and the biography of St Ignatius made good progress. He considered Collins as a publisher, but following his work on *University of the Nations*, Fr Caraman looked increasingly towards the United States for interest in his books. Before moving to Dulverton, he had arranged for his 'papers', as he referred to them, to go to the John J. Burns Library in Boston College. This valuable archive contained many of the letters and cards he had received from well-known literary figures, including Edith Sitwell, Evelyn Waugh and Graham Greene, when he was editor of *The Month*. There were also personal letters he had received from them in a private capacity after his dismissal from Farm Street. During the 1990s, towards the end of his life, other letters written to Fr Caraman during the years he spent in Dulverton were added to the archive. It is probable that his decision to send his valuable papers to the Jesuit college was influenced by the American, Fr Francis Sweeney, a friend of Thomas Merton's, whom Philip had known for many years. Although the archive found a suitable home in a Jesuit institution, Caraman's unilateral action did not go down well with some of his confrères in the British Province of the Society when in due time it was discovered what he had done. This was another bone of contention between Fr Caraman and the hierarchy in Mayfair. The Archive of the British Province is housed in Mount Street, and there is little doubt that memories of the unpleasant saga played out there in 1963 influenced Caraman's decision to favour Boston College.

Shortly after his move to Dulverton, Caraman contacted the Loyola University Press in Chicago, in an attempt to resurrect some of his early books in the United States and generate additional royalties. The reaction from the Loyola publishers was disappointing. The Jesuit director, Fr Daniel L. Flaherty, replied to Fr Caraman's inquiry about printing a new edition of *The Hunted Priest*, the title under which his life of John Gerard had been published in America, by saying, 'we don't feel there is enough general interest in Father Gerard at the moment to make a reprint "marketable" here in the States'. The Elizabethan anthology, *The Other Face*, which had been so well received in England, fared no better. Fr Flaherty started by admitting he was not 'familiar' with the book and would have to look at a copy in the University library before replying. He then decided *The Other Face* was 'a very interesting book, but not for our audience I'm afraid. More than likely ... a new reprint would find a market in Britain.' He then turned to another of Fr Caraman's books, *The Lost Paradise*, probably unaware that his remarks would cause Philip more pain than pleasure.

With the impending release here of *The Mission*, starring DiNiro and Irons in a script by Robert Bolt, we are hoping for some renewed interest in Fr. McNaspy's *Lost Cities of Paraguay* which we published in 1983. That prompts me to ask about the status of your *Lost Paradise*. Is it still in print? If not, who holds the rights?

A couple of weeks later, Fr Flaherty followed up this query, inadvertently rubbing more salt into Fr Caraman's wounds:

I see that a 1985 edition of *The Lost Paradise* was put out for $16.95 by Notre Dame University press and is being distributed by Harper & Row. Hope the movie helps sales. I haven't seen the film, but I have seen articles by Dan Berrigan (who worked with the film company) and C.J. McNaspy (who read the Bolt script) on the 'historicity' – or lack thereof – of the movie.[17]

Fr Caraman also had worked with the film company, but his brush with Robert Bolt and Hollywood still rankled. 'I can claim to have stirred up interest in Colonial Paraguay but do not father the film on me,' he wrote after *The Mission* had been released in England. To anyone who had read *The Lost Paradise*, it was obvious that the film was a travesty of Philip Caraman's painstakingly researched facts. Bolt's story starts in 1758, reaching its climax twenty years later against the dramatic background of the Iguazu Falls and the eviction of the Jesuits from their missions in Paraguay. Linking Montoya's attempted rescue of Guarani Indians from predatory slave-traders with the expulsion of the Society from South America in 1768, the playwright conveniently managed to lose over one hundred years of Jesuit history along the way. One or two scenes in the film succeed in capturing the utopian ideal of the established Missions, and the screenplay conveys the disaster inherent in their dispersal. The entrancing tune played on the pan pipes by Jeremy Irons, which contributed greatly to the film's success, was accurately based on the musical ethos of the Missions. But the Cardinal–narrator's statement that the survival of the Jesuits in Europe depended on their obedience to his order to leave South America is an over-simplificaton of a complicated political situation. It is remarkable how many scenes in *The Mission* are set against the roaring beauty of the Falls which Fr Caraman had described so vividly in *The Lost Paradise*.

Philip gave vent to his feelings in a conversation with Fr Richard Randolph, who wrote: 'The film *The Mission*, which was based on the book, but with all sorts of inept alterations, inexactitudes and much histrionic licence, was an embarrassment to him. When I asked him what he thought of it, he replied "Splendid rubbish! The plain facts of the true story would have been much better theatre".'[18]

Fr Caraman's advisory role was given the barest acknowledgement. As the long list of credit rolls interminably through the final reels of the film, his name appears among a galaxy of others whom 'we should also like to thank', somewhere after those of the wig-makers, kitchen assistants and make-up artists who had worked on the set.

There is no cinema in Dulverton, and had he received a more obvious acknowledgement it is still unlikely many of its residents would have known about Fr Caraman's connection with the highly acclaimed film. No celebrity status was attached to the old priest encountered buying a winter coat in the charity shop, or seen shopping for groceries in the High Street. He became a familiar and much-loved figure in the town, exchanging pleasantries with almost everyone he met: before long he was also the official parish priest of St Stanislaus. To begin with, Fr Caraman had said Sunday Mass for Catholics who otherwise would have faced a long journey to attend church. He also said a weekday Mass in Latin for Bridget Grant and a handful of others: when more and more worshippers turned up in the week, Latin was replaced by Mass in the vernacular, although he never introduced the exchange of the Sign of Peace into his liturgy, and chose to distribute the Sacred Host to communicants kneeling at the altar rail in the old manner rather than into the hands of those standing before him. He never invited his congregation to communicate from the chalice, although the Bishop of Clifton made it known he wished the Eucharist to be administered under both kinds throughout his diocese. The congregation at St Stanislaus had been dwindling for a number of years because, it was said,

Canon MacDonald in old age had upset and alienated many of his parishioners. With Philip's arrival numbers increased dramatically, and local Catholics, who officially came under St George's parish in Taunton, were soon requesting baptisms, marriages and funerals, which he was not permitted to conduct. Philip took pity on his unofficial flock, and two years after moving to Bridge House he was officially authorised to act as parish priest.

As he recalled the burden he had carried in his only other appointment as a parish priest, it was not a role Fr Caraman took on lightly in his late seventies. Inevitably his mind went back to the years he had spent in Tønsberg, and he admitted that he didn't know how he had managed to survive his time there. Now living in a very different environment, Philip recalled an occasion in Tønsberg when a lady had presented a child for baptism:

> 'What's the child's name', I asked.
> 'Odin', she said.
> 'Any other name?'
> 'Yes, Thor.'

In the end he had added the name of (St) Olaf out of despair.

Both Fr Caraman's parishes were set in beautiful surroundings, attracting crowds of summer visitors: each place, in its own way, was isolated in winter. But similarities end there. Whereas in Tønsberg Philip had struggled to keep up with accounts, official returns and other paperwork, in Somerset a group of willing parishioners shouldered these and other administrative burdens. Pagan names were not requested when he baptised the Catholic babes of Dulverton, and at Bridge House Fr Caraman never experienced the loneliness he had known in Norway. He entertained, and was entertained by friends old and new, revived links with his past, and quickly forged a warm relationship with members of his congregation. Philip's luncheon parties became a regular feature of Dulverton life, his adventurous cooking garnished with herbs from his little garden. In John Smith the Jesuit found a brilliant administrator who soon sorted out the parish finances in his role as Treasurer. John recalls that when he gave Philip some good claret for Christmas, the priest said, 'That is the best thing you could have given me'. But later, when John was invited to dinner with the Bishop of Clifton at Bridge House, and offered to bring the wine, Philip told him not 'to waste good wine on the Bishop'. The Jesuit's sense of mischief had not been quenched by age. He criticised Bishop Mervyn Alexander's literary style, and refused to read verbatim the Lenten and Advent Pastoral Letters sent to every parish in the diocese. Instead Fr Caraman paraphrased the text for his congregation, commenting in private that Mervyn Alexander 'cannot write English', which seems a little unfair to a good pastoral Bishop.

Once he was officially appointed parish priest, Fr Caraman started to make a number of aesthetic improvements to his little church, several of which were designed to highlight the important part the Herbert family had played in the history of St Stanislaus. Over a period of years, with financial backing from generous patrons and parishioners, a fumed chestnut statue of St George was commissioned from Septimus Waugh, sculptor and artist son of Evelyn and Laura, and a window commemorating Margaret FitzHerbert was installed. The centre panel of the window was the work of Irish stained-glass artist Evie Hone, based on a mediaeval statue of St Mary dug from the bogs of Connemara: emblems associated with the Forty Martyrs of England and Wales were also incorporated into the design of this window – a reminder of Meg's work for the Martyrs' Cause. The last work of art Fr Caraman commissioned for the church was a set of four windows by Silas Wood of Birmingham, representing the four evangelists as depicted in the Apocalypse.

Apart from Bridget Grant, and Herbert and Waugh family members who kept a watchful eye over Fr Caraman's welfare, other helpers who gathered round were mostly people unknown to him before he settled in Bridge House. Before long, however, news of his arrival reached other Catholics in the area, and friends from the past appeared to swell his congregation. From the far side of Exmoor, Philip was contacted by politician and writer Sir John Biggs-Davison, who was a Conservative Minister for Northern Ireland, and had been a contributor to *The Month* when Philip was editor.[19] Caraman describes how the

Minister 'came out of church with a kind of quizzical smile and a humorous twinkle in his eye, often expressing a singular point of view on a topic of the day.'[20] When Biggs-Davison became seriously ill, Philip visited him, and was with him on the afternoon before he died. Invited to preach the homily at the politician's funeral, Philip remarked the day before that he hoped he would not be blown up by the IRA.

Another figure from the past appeared from Tiverton. This was John Skinner, who as a young Jesuit scholastic had accompanied Fr Caraman on merry excursions in search of Henry Garnet and other recusant heroes, and who later turned to journalism and writing when he left the Society of Jesus. When they met again in Dulverton, John had long been married, and he and his wife were warmly welcomed by Philip for whom the younger man still retained a great deal of respect and affection. They had known each other for nearly thirty years, and Skinner remembers that Fr Caraman once asked him if his decision to leave the Society had been influenced by the Farm Street débâcle. The reply was an emphatic 'No'. John Skinner was responsible for writing the obituary published in *The Times* on Fr Caraman's death, and observed him closely during the last decade of his life. He noted that Philip 'wouldn't hear any criticism whatsoever' of Pope John Paul II, and when John murmured against the Pontiff, Caraman retorted that he thought 'history would judge him a very great Pope'.[21] Skinner remarked that this was a very happy time for Philip: other old friends also found him more contented and at peace than ever before.

The leisurely pace of his ministry suited the old Jesuit, and his sense of fun was much in evidence. He wrote a series of cameos of Dulverton life under the title *Journal of a Country Priest*; he considered, and later rejected, the idea of publishing these sketches, but the idiosyncratic style of the Journal reflects Fr Caraman's warmth and humour in a way none of his other writing ever does. In the *Journal*, as in his letters, his compassion, tempered with occasional flashes of annoyance and frustration, speaks to the reader directly, undisguised by the narration of historical facts.

Before Philip Caraman moved to Dulverton, relations between Anglicans and Catholics in the town had not been particularly good. But within a few months of his arrival he accepted an invitation to talk to a small group which gathered once a month at the farmhouse of Beth and Robert Eden, an Anglican lay reader with responsibility for some of the more isolated churches on Exmoor. This meeting, undreamt of in the days of Canon Macdonald, went well. And the warmth of Fr Caraman's relations with clergy of other denominations is reflected in two entries in his journal:

> If you happen to be short sighted as I am there are hazards in greeting people in the High Street. Yesterday I hailed warmly, as I thought, the Reverend Mr Flatt, a retired stand-in vicar living in nearby Brushford: he was once very kind to me over a burial in his churchyard. We would always have a jolly talk when we ran into each other in town. I broached several ecumenical topics and wondered why I got no response. Soon after we parted I realised I had been talking with the man who runs the Dry Cleaning plant round the corner from here: he had the same round smiling, highly coloured, face and the same flaxen hair as Mr Flatt.[22]

A subsequent entry in the Journal records that one afternoon Fr Caraman met 'the real Mr Flatt . . . such a nice man'. In mid-winter the clergyman was looking 'very *sportif* in a light suit that would be more suitable wear in Dominica than in Dulverton'. Philip wished he came more into his life, and wondered if there was a Mrs Flatt. 'I know so little about him, he is warm-hearted, natural and really concerned about his friends', he added.[23]

As a parish priest of the old school, Fr Caraman liked to take the catachetic classes for children preparing for their First Confession and Holy Communion himself. He felt it was his duty to do so: in his opinion this was something which should not be delegated to the laity as it was in most other parishes by the end of the twentieth century. In a hangover from the days of his youth, Philip held his classes on a Saturday morning, a most inconvenient time for some of the families concerned. But the priest was devoted to the children in his little flock, and recorded, with amusement, that 'after I had prepared two bright boys, brothers, for their first confession the younger one asked me, "Father, can we go to confession together? We commit the same sins."'[24]

Old-fashioned in his ways perhaps, but Fr Caraman continually laboured to keep his scattered congregation up to the mark. By way of exhorting his listeners to attend an occasional weekday mass during Lent, he drew yet again on his experience of Norway. He told his parishioners the story he had heard when he first went to the country in 1965: the tale of the old priest who said his weekday Mass in an empty church, reciting the liturgy 'in two tones, his natural bass for the priest's part, a treble for the server's response,' and waggled 'his right leg to which a small bell was attached by an elastic band around the ankle' at the Sanctus, the Elevation of the Host and the Agnus Dei. The story had the desired effect on the congregation of St Stanislaus, and Fr Caraman was 'never without two, three and sometimes six at weekday Mass during the rest of Lent'.[25]

Ash Wednesday brought its own hazards. One year, Fr Caraman related that:

> There was a sizeable group this morning to hear the prophecy of Joel setting the tone for Lent. The ashes were sent to me from Taunton by a church student, a very traditional, impeccably orthodox young man, who believing that the sign of penitence should be carried on the forehead throughout the day, mingled the ashes with glue. Some twenty of my small flock went out into the High Street like sheep branded for the slaughter. In the evening there were no takers.[26]

Philip Caraman frequently mused on the changes and alterations to Catholic liturgy and practice which had been introduced since Vatican II. Another entry in the *Journal of a Country Priest* was inspired by he disappearance of the biretta from the wardrobe of Catholic priests. The day after conducting a burial in a rainstorm he wrote:

> Much ancient wisdom gathered from the Church's experience

over the years has been jettisoned in unseemly haste since the second Vatican Council ... Without a biretta my hair was tousled and dripping before I was half way through the committal. Where was my biretta, the only covering I could have worn without disrespect for the dead: I must have cast it away or left it behind in one of my moves.

He remembered how 'a group of wandering players, the Thesbit Theatre', had asked him for the loan of a biretta for one of their productions when he was in Tønsberg. He no longer had one even then. As he returned to Bridge House after the funeral, and dried his hair, he 'wondered why all the graveyards in West Somerset – King's Brompton, Skilgate, Brushford, Dulverton itself – are all on hilltops exposed to cold driving rain'.

Fr Caraman's patience was sometimes stretched to the limit. He tells the story of the woman living 'behind Crispin's restaurant in the High Street', who asked him 'to do something about strange phenomena in and around her house'. She reported doors opening mysteriously, strange knocking and noises. He duly went round the house with Holy Water and 'a sprig of box', and when he was about to leave the woman 'opened the door into her garden and pointed to a dead branch of an apple tree lying just outside'. This she associated with the devil. 'There had been a high wind the previous night', Philip concluded caustically.

Far more distressing for Fr Caraman was the same woman's reaction when she heard that he was about to go into hospital in Taunton to undergo an operation for cancer. On the Sunday morning when he was preparing to leave home 'for a *major plus* abdominal operation', she called on him 'convinced that she had been endowed with healing powers which could be effective only by means of close bodily contact'. She advanced on Philip across his sitting-room, with arms outstretched, forcing him to retreat into the kitchen. Having fought off her physical embrace he then had to counter her 'request, almost a demand, to join her at Stonehenge for the celebration of the autumn solstice'. She told him that his presence there with her Druid companions would render his operation unnecessary. 'What concern she had for me!' was Philip's only comment.[27]

The news that Fr Caraman had been diagnosed with cancer in the summer of 1989 was received with sadness and concern by the many friends to whom he wrote asking for prayers. 'Light a candle for me in the church,' he requested. Tidings of his operation reached Norway, and Lita Anker passed the news on to John Gran, who was full of advice and opinions. Early in his illness Philip was visited by Fr Michael Campbell-Johnston, the Jesuit Provincial, whose leather-clad figure arrived one Saturday on a motor-bike, startling Philip's congregation with his unconventional appearance. He arrived just as Fr Caraman was experiencing a particularly trying weekend, with a group of noisy teenagers quartered in the Activity Centre adjacent to the church.[28] The Provincial helped the old priest sort out some of the young people's problems, and one wonders if he might not, at the same time, have suggested that Fr Caraman might enjoy a less stressful life in a Jesuit house without the responsibility of running a parish. But the two men got on well enough: Philip admired Fr Campbell-Johnston's work in South America, and retained an abiding interest in the plight of the poor in that continent – a legacy from his travels there nearly twenty years earlier.

News of Fr Caraman's cancer brought reassurance from Alec Guinness, who wrote at the end of August, thanking the priest for letting him know the date of the operation: 'I have carefully marked [the date] in my diary. Please try to rid your mind of anxiety. Difficult I'm sure, but I am sure all will be well. You won't have the energy for writing for a week or so, but, if possible do get someone to telephone me and give me news of you'.[29]

Fr Caraman accepted his illness with remarkable equanimity. The evening following his doctor's diagnosis, he wrote in his Journal:

My doctor said that he would pass me on for examination to a surgeon in Minehead. I am rather too old to be cut up once again. This morning, however, as I was having my early cup of tea in my pyjamas thinking of what might lie ahead, I felt a deep peace almost sensibly spreading through me. It was something I had never experienced before. I reflected how marvellous it would be to die now. The feeling was so comforting that I began to fear that it might be just selfishness, or possibly cowardice, in wanting to be quit of further work and worry. I leave it like that.[30]

In this time of crisis, Fr Caraman was fortified by the well-spring of inner strength and certainty which so often he had drawn upon to give comfort and advice to others. In the past, that spring had seemed to run dry at times, or been choked by worldly cares, when he himself needed solace. His quiet acceptance, and the prayers and good wishes of his friends and family carried him through to a successful recovery. He survived to experience both worry and enjoyment, and to work for several more years as a country priest in the service of his little flock.

Notes

1 Philip Caraman, letter to author, Dulverton, 18 December 1986.
2 *Letters & Notices*, vol. 94, Spring 1999, no. 415. p. 939.
3 Unpublished letter, Dame Muriel Spark to Philip Caraman, 30 December 1986, Philip Caraman Private Papers (hereafter PCPP) © Muriel Spark 2004.
4 From a letter to the author dated 2 March 1983. Quotations in this chapter which are not noted separately are from Philip Caraman's letters and cards to the author.
5 Fr Richard Randolph SJ, *The Month*, June 1998, p. 250.
6 Ibid.
7 Author interview with Fr Richard Randolph.
8 Alec Guinness to Philip Caraman, letter, 28 February 1985, and card, 16 March 1985 (PCPP).
9 Card, Alec Guinness to Philip Caraman, 28 December 1984 (PCPP).
10 Philip Caraman, *The Lost Empire. The Story of the Jesuits in Ethiopia 1555–1634* (Sidgwick & Jackson, London, 1985), pp. 105 and 106.
11 Ibid. p. 132.
12 Letter, Muriel Spark to Philip Caraman, 30 December 1986 (PCPP) © Muriel Spark 2004.
13 Letter, Margaret FitzHerbert to Philip Caraman, 3 November (?) 1966.

14 Margaret FitzHerbert, *The Man Who Was Greenmantle* (John Murray, 1983).
15 *The Catholic*, published by the Catholic Truth Society, Summer 1992. p. 3.
16 Letter, Alec Guinness to Philip Caraman, 29 October 1986 (PCPP).
17 Letters, Daniel L. Flaherty SJ to Philip Caraman, 7 and 22 October 1986, John J. Burns Library, Boston College.
18 Fr Richard Randolph in *The Month*, June 1998, Second New Series, vol. 31. p. 250.
19 Essays contributed by John Biggs-Davison to *The Month* during Fr Caraman's editorship include 'The Meaning of Commonwealth', February 1959, vol. 22, p. 69.
20 From the Homily given by Fr Caraman at the Requiem Mass for Sir John Biggs-Davison at St Petrock's Church, Somerset, 23 September 1988.
21 During one of his visits to Rome Fr Caraman was presented to John Paul II, and a personal Christmas card from the Pope is preserved among his papers.
22 Philip Caraman, 'Journal of a Country Priest', undated and unpublished (PCPP).
23 Ibid.
24 Ibid.
25 Ibid.
26 Ibid.
27 Ibid.
28 Fr Caraman continued to live in Bridge House after he was confirmed in the appointment of parish priest of St Stanislaus, while the former presbytery was converted into an activity/youth centre by the Diocese of Clifton.
29 Letter, Alec Guinness to Philip Caraman, Kettlebrook, 22 August 1989.
30 'Journal of a Country Priest'.

Chapter Twelve

A Country Priest

Few members of Fr Caraman's congregation realised that their priest led a double life. During his first ten years in Dulverton, Philip disappeared from time to time without explanation; now and then strangers to the town might be glimpsed calling at Bridge House. The Jesuit may have hoped to escape the social pressures of city life by burying himself in the West Country, but London – and his past – followed him to Somerset.

Fr Caraman was still in demand as a speaker and adviser on a number of topics, and he remained in touch with prominent figures in the Catholic Establishment, including Cardinal Basil Hume and Archbishop Luigi Barbarito, the Apostolic Pro-Nuncio. Caraman's prestige in the field of Elizabethan Catholic history was undiminished by time, and he received numerous requests for assistance from other writers interested in the period. In the notes which Philip prepared for a BBC talk by the historian A. L. Rowse in 1988, he laid great emphasis on the loyalty to crown and country of English Catholics during penal times, pointing out that any sympathy they had for King Philip of Spain at the time of the Armada was no more than a desire for freedom to practise their religion. The views of Rowse and Caraman on religious history were diametrically opposite, and it is a credit to the Jesuit's reputation that Rowse took the trouble to consult him.[1]

The part Philip had played in the Cause for the Forty Martyrs continued to bring requests for guidance, including one from Mgr Ralph Brown of the Westminster Archdiocese in connection with the proposed canonisation of Blessed Adrian

Fortescue: the relaunch of the sometime defunct *Catholic Times* was marked by a major article written by Fr Caraman on the subject of the English and Welsh martyrs. Rarely did he turn down a request for an article or for advice, replying at great length to his correspondents, and often following up their pleas for information by undertaking troublesome research on their behalf. But in February 1991, when he was approached by the Board of Governors of Campion Hall to write a history of his old Alma Mater, the invitation was declined.[2] The reasons for this are not known: possibly Philip felt it was too big an under-taking, and one which would have entailed abandoning his niche as parish priest in Dulverton. Later, this invitation and its non-acceptance had an unfortunate sequel.

For some years before Fr Caraman fled to Somerset, he had been targeted by authors engaged in writing biographies, or editing the letters, of the notable Catholic writers with whom he had been closely involved. The rich seam of his correspondence with Edith Sitwell had provided material for a book of her *Selected Letters* edited jointly by Derek Parker and John Lehmann – Rosamond's brother – in 1970, and a decade later his reminiscences had given Sitwell's biographer, Victoria Glendinning, valuable material. Some of his memories of Edith Sitwell he kept to himself. He never lost his affection for her, and thought of her sometimes in Dulverton; an entry in his Journal reveals:

> This Sunday morning was my bad day. I forgot to turn over the page of the altar missal and read the introductory verse from the previous Sunday of Lent. Then I started the Gloria. When there was no response from the congregation I held up my hands in apology. This was nothing like as bad as the occasion when I was acting as assistant to an archbishop at a private confirmation. When I held up the book for the ritual of the sacrament he looked at me in bewilderment: it was open at the page for the service of blessing a cemetery. The confirmed was Dame Edith Sitwell.
>
>   In the course of preparing her for reception into the Church, I visited Renishaw. Sitting there one morning facing each other across the fireplace in the large drawing room I happened to speak of the now forgotten Ember days. 'Ember, O, ember!' she

said. The word had struck a cord [sic]; an idea for a poem had germinated in her poetic soul.[3]

Other friends from the past were recalled less readily, and the West Country did not always provide the hideaway Philip had hoped for. Authors anxious to raid his store of memories soon caught up with him, and a sense of weariness creeps into his dealings with some of the writers who approached him. Within a year of his arrival in Dulverton he received a letter from Michael De-la-Noy saying he had 'been commissioned by Bodley Head to write a biography of Edward Sackville-West', and would the Reverend P. Caraman help him? 'I understand it was you who received Eddy Sackville, and that you were staying with him when he died. You may imagine that his conversion, and his death, are matters of great interest to me,' pleaded the writer.[4] Philip answered by return of post:

> I did not know him [Sackville-West] all that well, though I did stay with him twice at Clogheen ... It was not I, but a Fr Hubert McEvoy, who received him into the church, either at Boscombe or Bournemouth where he was the Superior of the Jesuit parish ... Nor was it I who was with him when he died, but his old friend from broadcasting days, Fr Pemberton, who died a few years ago.

Fr Caraman added some anecdotes and observations about his visits to Clogheen, and signed off by saying, 'I seldom come to London. And when I do my visits are very short.' Politely, he offered to rack his memory for further recollections, and offered to meet De-la-Noy either in London, or in Dulverton should the author care to visit him.[5] The detached tone of Philip's letter is in marked contrast to the warmth and concern expressed in the letters he had written to 'My Dear Eddy' when he was editor of *The Month*; his friendship with Sackville-West had been, in its time, far closer than he admitted to the biographer.

Philip was wary of reviving the past, and was prudent to be so. He was a jealous guardian of Evelyn Waugh's reputation, and sensitive to any derogatory remarks made about the author. In private Caraman brooked no criticism of his friend: in public his championship of Waugh involved him in lengthy sessions with would-be biographers and commentators. Interviewed by Nicholas Shakespeare for a BBC documentary, Fr Caraman sat somewhat stiffly before the cameras, and emphasised the aura of serenity that had surrounded Waugh on the morning of his death.

This programme was judged a success, but a lengthy interview with one of Evelyn Waugh's biographers, Martin Stannard, had an unfortunate outcome for Philip. He discovered, when the last volume of the professor's major work came out in 1992, that the author had dwelt at length on the events in Farm Street leading to Philip's dismissal from *The Month* in 1963, on the part played by Margaret FitzHerbert in the drama, and on Waugh's reaction to the débâcle. The book leaves the reader with the impression that the cause of Caraman's depression at the time, and his subsequent nervous breakdown, was his relationship with Meg. Philip is described by the author as a 'young priest' in May 1960 (he was then forty-eight years old), and it is alleged that although his love for Waugh's daughter was entirely pure, it was nevertheless passionate, and that her marriage introduced an awkward husband on to the scene. In writing his biography, Stannard seems to have been unaware both of Caraman's impossible workload, and of the friction and personality clashes within the Jesuit community in Mayfair, which were responsible for Philip's erratic behaviour during and after the crisis. It is improbable that Fr Caraman would have mentioned such deeply personal matters to the biographer; if these factors were discussed during their interview then Stannard chose to overlook them. The book also repeats the misleading rumour that Fr Caraman was 'sent' to Norway, an error apparently made in ignorance of the Jesuit's long-standing friendship with John Gran and the Bishop's invitation to Oslo. Stannard contends that the events in Farm Street in 1963 were a 'terrible disappointment' to Evelyn Waugh, who until that time had always 'maintained a special admiration for the Jesuits'. But in the letter already quoted in Chapter Six of this book, Waugh told Caraman that the priest's 'behaviour in this whole business . . . has done more to fortify my belief . . . in the divine institution of the Society of Jesus in particular, than any event in my life as a Catholic'.[6]

Fr Caraman's dislike of Professor Stannard's book goaded him into writing several pages of notes in which he listed points which the author had got wrong. He sent these notes to another biographer, Selina Hastings, who was researching her own book on Waugh when Stannard's came out. She had introduced herself to Philip by letter in September, 1987, and quickly forged a warm relationship with him, very different from his encounter with Martin Stannard, whom the Jesuit had disliked even before publication of his book.

Selina Hastings says that Philip was 'immensely kind to me when I was working on my life of Waugh'.[7] He in turn enjoyed her company. Sympathetic and a gifted writer, Hastings was someone with whom he found it easy to work, and to talk to when work was done. She made the long journey from London to Bridge House on more than one occasion, and treated him to a good lunch at the Carnarvon Arms Hotel, which in those days was Dulverton's best restaurant. When Philip was ill in 1989, Hastings was one of the many friends who wrote to him expressing concern; she also confided to him some of her feelings about her work as a biographer. Describing an interview with Giles FitzHerbert, she told Philip that:

> He was extremely civil, and his memory was marvellous especially about staying at Pixton, but of course my nerve failed me, and I couldn't bring myself to ask what I really wanted to know about Margaret. This is the part I hate about biography – having to ask perfect strangers the kind of impertinent question one would hardly care to put to one's best friend of ten years standing ... You are so lucky dealing with people who have been dead hundreds of years who are in their way saints.[8]

Philip Caraman's friendship with Selina Hastings took him back into the world of the authors he had known, and their writing, in a way few other contacts managed to do in the last decade of his life. After his recovery from cancer, it was to her, and probably to no one else, that he read an extract from the Journal he was keeping of his life in Dulverton. On her return to London after one of her visits, Hastings wrote to him, saying, 'I do hope you will write that autobiographical diary. The small extract you read me was quite irresistible.'[9] Two months later, knowing of Caraman's meetings with Rosamond Lehmann many years before, she wrote telling him about the writer's death, reporting that 'it was very quick and painless'.

Apart from Waugh, the only writer Fr Caraman discussed with Selina Hastings at any length was Graham Greene, 'whom he admired but was wary of,' she says.[10] Following an introduction from Hastings, Philip was approached by Michael Shelden who was working on a biography of Greene. His book came out in 1994, after Graham's death: it is a sceptical and challenging appraisal of the novelist, particularly of his sexual morality, and the writer concludes that the value of Greene's life lies in his best writing rather than in his moral excellence. Discussing *The End of the Affair*, the biographer says that Greene 'has shown much ingenuity in abusing the God of Christianity', and that one passage in the novel 'must certainly stand as one of the gems in the history of blasphemy'. Shelden then relates that in the 1950s, when questioned about his commitment to Catholicism, Greene claimed that he always submitted his manuscripts 'to Father Philip Caraman, one of the leading Jesuit intellectuals, for guidance'.[11] There is no evidence among Philip Caraman's papers to support Greene's claim that he monitored the novelist's work. In fact the Jesuit's comment to Waugh that he thought *The End of the Affair* to be 'beautifully written and a great technical achievement, but I read it with sadness', seems to indicate that the Jesuit had no veto over the work.[12] Shelden remarks that 'Greene was delighted to hide behind his friendship with the priest whenever it seemed convenient.' Little wonder that Fr Caraman had learnt by experience to be 'wary' of Greene.

At about the time that Philip met Professor Michael Shelden, he was contacted from San Antonio in Texas by Graham Greene's official biographer, Norman Sherry. The priest felt that he had been somewhat abrupt when Sherry first telephoned him, and apologised for his discourtesy. To begin with the biographer appears to have been unaware that Caraman had deposited the archive of letters he had received from Greene in the Burns Library in Boston College; later, after he had spent two days at the College going through the letters, he wrote to Philip wondering if others, which he had not seen 'could be opened to Graham's authorised biographer'.[13] At the time he was in contact with Caraman, Sherry's main area of research seems to have centred on Greene's affair with Catherine, and he questioned Philip about what he knew and thought of her. 'When did you first meet Catherine Walston, and did you live at their home, and in what capacity?' he wanted to know. Fr Caraman had stayed with the Walstons on more than one occasion, and visited their home in Ireland, but it is unlikely that he told Sherry anything significant about either his relationship with the family, or about his involvement with Greene and his mistress at the time of their affair. Such sensitive matters he kept to himself.

It was probably with mixed feelings and vexed memories that Philip attended Greene's grand Memorial Mass in Westminster Cathedral two months after the writer's death in 1991. Cardinal Basil Hume was present at the Mass, and – in addition to the principal celebrant – four other priests concelebrated at the high altar. Fr Caraman was not one of them. If the Jesuit did not readily express his sentiments about Greene, the reverse was not true. 'I hope [Philip] never knew how deeply Graham hated him,' says Selina Hastings, who had known the novelist well.[14] Whether or not he realised the depth of Greene's dislike, Fr Caraman went to the Mass in the company of Muriel Spark and Alec Guinness, and attempted to hide behind the actor when they were caught on camera emerging from the Cathedral. That evening, Fr Caraman's furtive figure appeared on nationwide TV news programmes, and the secret of the prominent part he had played in the lives of Catholic celebrities was out at last. The news caused quite a stir in the quiet town of Dulverton, and came as a surprise to most of his parishioners.

෴

Once settled in Somerset, Fr Caraman saw much more of members of the Herbert and Waugh families than he had for some years. His friendship with them now extended over four generations, and included not only Evelyn and Laura Waugh's children, but their grandchildren. The relationship between Auberon Waugh – now living in his father's old home at Combe Florey – and the Jesuit was never the same as that enjoyed by Philip and Evelyn, nevertheless the two men were on good terms. Bron was running the *Literary Review* at the time, and asked Fr Caraman to review Peter Levi's *The Frontiers of Paradise: A Study of Monks and Monasteries*. In his piece, entitled 'Being a Monk is Fun', Philip described the book as 'very original', and writing with a light touch commented that he had the 'impression that hermits are making a come-back. I have met several in remote places abroad', no doubt remembering the disappearing act of the parish priest of Lillehammer.[15] The literary relationship between Bron Waugh and Philip continued with a review by the Jesuit of Waugh's autobiography *Will This Do?* when the book came out in 1991. Bron thanked him for an 'excellently charitable review', and added:

> I'm sorry the libel bits [in the book] bored you, but then I rather enjoy the occasional dead theological controversy too. Perhaps you were overfed with dead theological controversies while training for the priesthood. I like the way you have chosen to illustrate your piece with a great grinning photograph of Archbishop Worlock [of Liverpool]. I have cut it out to make it look as if it is the Archbishop who is testifying to the niceness of Bron Waugh. I hope I shall see you before Christmas to thank you in person for your generosity.[16]

While Bron Waugh's literary reputation flourished, Fr Caraman's was on the wane. He was still invited to write articles and give talks, but his books no longer attracted the attention they had ten years earlier. The first to appear after he became parish priest of Dulverton was his life of Ignatius Loyola.[17] Publication of the biography was plagued by a number of unforeseen problems and eventually became the source of considerable bitterness and disappointment to its author. One of the reasons Fr Caraman had been attracted to the subject of the Jesuit founder was a rumour about new material concerning the life of the Saint which he had picked up when he was working in Rome on the Jesuit Dictionary. A fellow writer at the Jesuit Historical Institute, Fr Francisco de Borja de Medina, had told Philip that another Spanish Jesuit, Fr Fernàndez, had written an eighty-page essay on the subject of a certain Maria de Loyola who may have been the natural child of Ignatius. Shortly before he was diagnosed with cancer, Caraman wrote to Fr Fernàndez, seeking his permission to use this sensational revelation in his biography and citing the passage he intended to include in the book. The quotation refers to some money which Ignatius [Inigo] had collected from the Duke of Najera and had then divided among certain individuals to whom 'he felt some obligation'. The passage read:

> He [Ignatius] does not specify either the obligation or the individuals, but it is now thought that he may have been making provision for a child he had fathered. Recently it has been discovered that the Duchess of Najera in her last will left money to a Maria de Loyola who had been brought up in her household. As all the bastard Loyola children, apart from Maria, are known, it is conjectured that she may have been Inigo's daughter.

In his letter to Fr Fernàndez, Caraman emphasised that he did not 'want to steal the result of your long researches', and asked the Spanish Jesuit to allow 'this passage to stand *with full acknowledgement to yourself* in the way you would wish'.[18]

The illegitimate daughter did not survive the scrutiny of the Jesuit censor: the passage quoted by Philip in his letter to Fr Fernàndez was excised. In its place, Ignatius is described as having written 'somewhat enigmatically' of arranging for the money due to him to be divided 'among certain individuals to whom he felt some obligation'.[19] Fr Caraman was seriously ill when he was working on the final phases of the book, and had passed it over to the Jesuit scholar appointed by the Provincial to act as censor. Enquiries, directed through the Historical Institute, concerning reliable documentation to support the existence of the bastard child proved unsatisfactory, and following discussion with Collins, the book's publishers, she was removed from the text. It is emphasised that this was done not because of the nature of the revelation, but because of the lack of sound evidence to back it up. When Philip recovered from his illness and realised what had happened to his 'scoop', he was greatly put out. Although the incident embittered a previously warm relationship between Caraman and the historian responsible for altering the text, the priest concerned probably acted in Philip's best interests. Recent research proves that the documentation purporting to prove that Maria de Loyola was the natural child of Ignatius was unreliable: a confusion over names, and a complicated genealogical tree appear to have been responsible for the error. The root of Fr Caraman's grievance was, probably, the sense that the friendship he had forged with Fr Francisco de Borja de Medina in the partisan atmosphere of the *Casa degli Scrittori* had been betrayed. Friendship always meant more to him than the exigencies of scholastic minutiae, although in this case the academic details were hardly trivial.

The trials brought about by *Ignatius Loyola* did not end there. A review in the *Catholic Historical Review*, the influential journal of the American Catholic Historical Association, which has a wide circulation in the United States, was critical of the book, and upset Fr Caraman because it was written by yet another Jesuit whom he had regarded as a personal friend.[20] A generation younger than Philip, the American historian Fr Thomas M. McCoog had got to know Caraman well when he was based at Southwell House: with a shared interest in literature and Elizabethan history, the two priests had gone to the theatre together, and enjoyed each other's company when their visits to London coincided.

Whilst Fr Caraman's *The Lost Empire* was largely ignored by the critics when it appeared in 1985, Fr McCoog gave it a glowing review:

Philip Caraman ... began his celebrated career with important studies of the early Jesuit mission to England. Largely through his translations the exciting stories of John Gerard and William Weston reached a wider public. The stories that he has pursued in recent years have been no less exciting or important. His learned study of the Jesuit *reductions* in Colonial Paraguay, *The Lost Paradise*, analysed an important episode in Jesuit history.

Now in *The Lost Empire,* written with the same objectivity and in the same flowing style, Caraman has produced the first study in any language of the Jesuit enterprise in Ethiopia.[21]

Following the effusive praise for Philip's previous book, McCoog's review of *Ignatius Loyola* was an unwelcome surprise. In his essay the historian drew attention to inaccuracies in the book, and criticised the author for accepting and relating facts concerning St Ignatius which were no longer in line with current thinking and research. In summary, McCoog deemed the book to be devotional rather than an accurate, up-to-date, historical work. These unfavourable comments wounded Philip's ego where it was most vulnerable. His Achilles' heel had always been the pride he took in his work as a Jesuit historian; it was a small vanity pinpointed by his mentor Fr Martin D'Arcy when he teased him about Fr O'Higgins. Clearly, this joke had irritated Philip. With his biography of the saint he had wandered into the minefield of Ignatian studies, into territory hotly contested by historians, particularly those who are members of the Society of Jesus. He was castigated for his temerity, and reacted resentfully rather than as the good soldier Muriel Spark had praised him for being.

The relationship between Fr McCoog and Philip Caraman deteriorated further when the American invited Philip to join a team of writers preparing a collection of essays to mark the centenary of Campion Hall. The scope of the publication was clearly defined in advance: it was agreed by the Master and Thomas McCoog, who had been appointed as editor, that the proposed book should be academic in nature rather than a 'coffee-table' presentation. Despite their previous spat, McCoog, who was probably unaware of the invitation to write a history of the Hall sent to Philip previously, asked him to contribute an essay on Campion. He agreed, but when the article was submitted it contained what Fr McCoog describes as 'sloppy' mistakes: in one instance Philip had referred to Robert Dudley as 'John'. Simple errors were easily corrected, but in the editor's view the essay was uninformed by current historical thinking, and the older priest appeared to be unaware of recently published studies by some of the other contributors to the symposium, a number of whom were eminent historians. McCoog then offered to send Philip the relevant papers, which he thought would not be obtainable easily in 'the back of beyond' – in distant Somerset. Whilst Caraman agreed to correct the obvious errors, he refused to change anything in his essay, whereupon the American declined to publish it. Acknowledging that Fr Caraman was 'the best stylist' of all the writers involved in the project, McCoog asked him if he would write a short biography of Campion as an Introduction to the collection, weaving in the work of the other contributors. Philip did not accept. Fr McCoog admits that their relationship was 'soured'; the priests met again on one or two occasions, but their friendship, in the words of the younger Jesuit, 'was not what it had been'.[22]

These setbacks did not quench Fr Caraman's zeal for work. As he reached his eightieth birthday in the summer of 1991, with his energy restored following his recovery from cancer, he was still looking for subjects for his pen. The birthday was marked by good wishes from many of his friends, and gifts included the portrait painted by Lita Anker. One letter Philip received to mark the occasion brought him news and gossip from Norway, although he regarded the writer with some scepticism. In the long epistle John Gran wrote from Oslo, the Bishop said he hoped that God would bless Philip's 'eighty years and also those to come, and may they be many'. Gran said that he was keeping well, with his 'scant seventy-one [years]', and that he was 'just back from Corsica after six weeks of a mixture of holiday and hard work with guests'. He told Philip that he was 'finally trying to write his memoirs', and that he was 'bored to death thereby. There won't be many readers indeed, and no publisher if they're in their right mind, but then few are nowadays.' The Bishop said he no longer had cause to visit Great Britain 'my chosen country', and added, 'Corsica of course is not France ... in any real sense, but it is where I like to be the most'.[23] Encouraged by John Gran, Fr Caraman had devoted many years of his life to the Norwegian mission: now the Bishop had deserted Norway to spend much of his time in the house he had bought in Corsica. The Jesuit was disillusioned. Furthermore, while he may have agreed with Gran's opinion of publishers, Philip took a dim view of the concept of memoir-writing.

In the days before they parted company, Fr Caraman had discussed possible subjects for books with Thomas McCoog, who suggested that he might write a memoir based on his relationship with the Catholic authors with whom he had been involved. Philip dismissed the idea: the fact that it was mooted suggests a certain lack of empathy between the two priests. Modest and self-effacing, Fr Caraman would never submit for publication a memoir in which, by its nature, he himself would play a prominent part. When eventually John Gran sent him a copy of his memoirs, Philip remarked caustically, 'Why did he bother [to write this]?', and on hearing that an acquaintance had self-published his life-story he raised his eyes mockingly to heaven. Later, a book he read as background material on the last of his Jesuit histories attracted the disapproving remark, 'It [the book] is quite helpful, but why does the author keep on bringing himself into the story?'[24]

There is no doubt that a memoir of Fr Caraman's involvement with the literary figures and prominent Catholics whom he had known and worked with would have attracted considerable interest. He would never write it. In addition to his respect for the privacy of his friends, and his desire for anonymity, there is another possible reason for his reluctance to air his reminiscences. The key lies in two of his early books, *John Gerard* and *Henry Garnet and the Gunpowder Plot*. In both Fr Caraman lays great emphasis on Garnet's refusal to divulge the secrets of the confessional despite the threat of martyrdom. In an Appendix to the autobiography of John Gerard, (my italics: JR) Philip wrote: 'In practice no priest, *either then or now,* with knowledge of a thing in two distinct ways, viz. under the most inviolable secrecy and from his own observation, would venture to use his "simple knowledge" at the risk of seeming to violate the sacramental seal [of Confession]'.[25]

Fr Caraman had been confessor to many of the celebrities he was invited to write about: how could he remember which of his recollections was, or was not, a matter of 'simple knowledge', or something he had learned under the sacred seal of the sacrament of Confession? With the passage of time it was impossible for him to be certain.

Fr Caraman's interest in the English martyrs was undiminished. He was disappointed to learn from a journalist, sent by the Catholic Truth Society in 1992 to interview him about his life and work, that only three of the pamphlets he had written for the CTS were still in print. The interviewer described him as 'the distinguished Jesuit writer' and commented that Dulverton was 'the last place I expected to find so cosmopolitan a priest'.[26]

Fr Caraman's next book marked a return to safe territory after the criticism he had received over *Ignatius Loyola:* it was set in penal times in the West Country, in an era and in an area he knew well. Contrary to the opinion expressed at one time by Protestant historians, it is now accepted that the Reformation in England was not welcomed with general enthusiasm for change on the part of ordinary folk as once was thought. Nowhere was loyalty to the Old Faith stronger than in Devon and Cornwall, where a large section of the population rose in rebellion in support of retaining the Latin Mass against the substitution of Archbishop Cranmer's First Prayer Book. This episode in English history, known as the Prayer Book Rebellion, reached its brutal climax in the West Country with the defeat of the rebels in 1549 in Exeter, only a short drive from Philip's parish in Dulverton. Four of the recusant leaders were sentenced to be hanged, drawn and quartered at Tyburn: less prominent rebels suffered a martyr's death in the West Country: others who had taken part in the uprising had their lands confiscated or were penalised with heavy fines.

The story of the Rebellion was not an original subject, but it was a drama after Fr Caraman's heart, and one to which, with his knowledge of the period, he could add his own insights and comments. He enjoyed the research – much of which was based on local records – and had great fun driving round in his car tracking down material. His problem lay in finding a publisher for what was, in effect, recycled history. He sent the typescript to Sidgwick & Jackson, who had published *The Lost Paradise* and *The Lost Empire,* and was put out when they failed to send him even an acknowledgement. The publishing world was changing rapidly, and the days were gone when his name and his Fellowship of the Royal Society of Literature carried weight. He fared no better with other mainstream publishers, consoling himself with the excuse that the book was 'an awkward length', too short for a major historical work, too long for a monograph. In the end Fr Caraman got in touch with an independent firm in nearby Tiverton, and was delighted when they agreed to publish his *Western Rising*.[27] He quickly forged a rapport with one of the firm's directors, Steven Pugsley, echoing his association with John Guest of Longmans many years earlier.

Meeting Fr Caraman for the first time in the priest's old age, Steven Pugsley commented on his 'quiet sense of humour' and his dry wit. Both attributes were in evidence as Philip set about the business of finding illustrations for *The Western Rising*. One excursion a week before his eighty-first birthday in the summer of 1992, found him at his most mischievous and un-ecumenical. Here I must break Fr Caraman's cardinal rule for writers and tell the story in the first person. When he was on one of his periodic visits to Tisbury, I arranged for him to go round Wilton House, seat of the Earls of Pembroke, which he had not visited although the house had been open to the public for many years. The search was on for a portrait of Sir William Herbert, who was created first Earl of Pembroke in 1551 following his part in defeating the Catholic rebels and suppressing the Western Rising. At the time of our visit to Wilton House, the controversy concerning the ordination of women in the Anglican church was hot news. As we sat in the reception office, waiting for a VIP guide and free entrance to the house, Philip suddenly pronounced in a loud voice, 'in a hundred years time the Anglican Church will have ceased to exist'. Our tour of the house coincided with the filming for TV of one of Sister Wendy Beckett's art appreciation programmes; when we reached the Old Masters in the famous Inigo Jones Double Cube Room, the Carmelite nun was ensconced in a corner of the room apparently lost in quiet contemplation in preparation for her act before the

cameras. 'Do you suppose she is in ecstasy?' whispered Philip
with a grin. Some months later he told me that he hoped 'the
Carmelite will bring in vocations to the Order'.

In the end Fr Caraman decided not to use the portrait of the
Earl we found in the house. In November 1992 he wrote from
Dulverton saying, 'there is no hurry because I have lost the first
five chapters of my book in my computer'. A month later, when
I told him the price the Wilton House Estate would charge for
use of a colour transparency of the portrait, he wrote again:

> Sixty Pounds plus VAT seems a pretty steep fee ... The 1st Earl
> was such a nasty man that I don't feel like spending all that
> money on a reproduction of his ugly visage ... I particularly
> resent paying such a sum to the descendants of the rogue who
> destroyed the [Wilton] Priory in order to build himself a palace.

The picture of the Earl did not appear in the book.

Another story, told in Dulverton, again reveals Philip in
mischievous mood. The writer and Reader in Church History at
Cambridge University, Eamon Duffy, called on Fr Caraman at
Bridge House; accompanied by one of Philip's parishioners,
they processed to the medieval church in the hamlet of
Morebath, scene of Duffy's book *The Voices of Morebath*,
which was published after Fr Caraman's death.[28] At the church
they were met by a startled patrician woman arranging flowers,
who questioned why three strange men were visiting so remote
a church. 'We've just come to claim what is our own,' Philip
retorted, remembering the religious turbulence that had overtaken the villagers of Morebath four hundred years earlier.

The Western Rising came out in the spring of 1994.
Publication of the book was underwritten by Fr Caraman,
presumably with the backing of the Jesuits, and he busied
himself advertising it among his many friends. 'Get your bookshop to order a number of copies – they should go like the
proverbial hot cakes,' he wrote. A couple of months later he
reported that the book was 'selling well in these parts'.[29] The
first print-run of a thousand copies soon sold out, and the book
went into a second edition. Sales were boosted by a puff from
Auberon Waugh in his 'Way of the World' column in *The Daily*

Telegraph: the writer tied in a description of the book to a comment on the recent ordination of thirty-two women priests in the Anglican cathedral in Bristol:

> A fascinating new book by the historian Philip Caraman describes the West Country rebellion of 1549, suppressed with great cruelty . . . and scarcely mentioned in any history books . . . yet an estimated 4,000 Cornishmen and Devonians were killed . . . and a further 1,000 executed before the uprising was put down.
>
> At the weekend a gathering was held to launch *The Western Rising,* published at the conspicuously low price of £9.95 by Westcountry Books of Tiverton. Talk at Rothwell and Dunworth's bookshop in Dulverton, where the meeting took place, was largely on the possibility of another West Country uprising, this time against the Careyites.[30]

The antiquarian bookshop of Rothwell & Dunworth, a few yards from Bridge House across the High Street, was a constant source of joy to Fr Caraman, for whom one of life's greatest pleasures was browsing among books. It was also his good fortune that the owners, Caryl and Richard Rothwell, were Catholics and faithful parishioners of St Stanislaus. Caryl's father had been a contributor to *The Month* when Philip was editor: Richard is an artist. Running the shop with their son Max, who had been educated at Ampleforth, the Rothwells were almost his closest neighbours during working hours; when Philip felt lonely, which was not often in Dulverton, he had only to cross the street to enjoy sympathetic company. This he did on many occasions, even minding the shop for brief periods when the person in charge went out on an errand. He was overjoyed if he made a sale. It was Max Rothwell who introduced Fr Caraman to the technicalities of a computer, when, at the age of eighty, he was presented with one by another of his parishioners. Before long Philip was extolling the advantages of the machine to some of his writer friends, including Selina Hastings. When things went wrong, and he 'lost' his work among the microchips, he sent an SOS across the road, and Max sorted out the problem for him. In return the young man was frequently entertained at one of the priest's little luncheons: he recalls that there was usually a bright 'young lady' among the other guests, one of the many whose company Philip still enjoyed in old age.[31]

The warmth and friendship surrounding Fr Caraman in Dulverton convinced him that there was nowhere else he would prefer to live. When some of his Jesuit brethren questioned why he had 'buried' himself in so remote a part of England, they failed to appreciate the affection in which he was held by his parishioners, and the love and devotion he dedicated to them in return.

❧

Shortly after Philip moved to Dulverton, Fr Richard Randolph also left London: he too went to live in the West Country, first as assistant, and then, following Fr John Tranmar's retirement, as parish priest of Tisbury. Both friends were now country priests: both still enjoyed travelling abroad, especially to France. Their one-day excursions had extended into longer journeys, which Fr Randolph recalled later with pleasure:

> We went to the Pyrénées and hired a car. It was notable that Philip preferred to sit outdoors at a café table, drinking a cordial and watching and quickly noticing the passers-by. When I had met him in Rome ... I had realised that he suffered from vertigo. He could not bear to stand on a flat roof within six feet of the edge. In the Pyrénées, on hairpin bends being driven up the side of minor mountains, he would clutch the gear-lever, 'to keep himself from falling out of the car'.

Whilst searching for a certain ruined abbey, the two priests 'met another baffled motorist who asked, "Où se trouvent-t-ils les ruines de l'abbaye?", to which he received the answer, "On ne peut pas les trouver. Mais nous voici, nous sommes deux abbés, mais pas encore tout à fait ruinés!" (or words to that effect).'

On another occasion, the Jesuits went to Strasbourg and toured the vineyards of Alsace by bus: later, when the Communist regime was toppled, they travelled to Prague. Fr

Randolph relates that 'On all these excursions [Philip] was a constant companion, always walking a few paces behind. When one turned round to say something . . . he had gone! Kidnapped? Run over? Fallen down a subway? Lost? But usually he could be run to earth, reading a pamphlet in a bookshop, or in a delicatessen pricing a salami'.[32]

These journeys always had a religious undertone. In Colmar the priests saw the famous crucifixion of Grunewald's altarpiece, which Fr Randolph thought was hateful: Fr Caraman remarked that crucifixion was not a pretty thing anyway. For their holiday in the Pyrénées, the priests were lent a house in le Boulou close to where there are several Romanesque churches. In the nearby village church of St André, one of the patron saints of his father, Philip sat for a long while lost in prayer and contemplation: when he heard that one of his friends was about to visit the same area he sent a postcard of the church saying, 'This is very close to where you intend to stay: it has a very special atmosphere: and there are others like it'. In the simple beauty of these ancient churches the old priest found the rest which so often had eluded him.

'Senior moments', albeit minor in nature, were increasing in number. Before leaving for Brittany, Philip mislaid his passport and only retrieved it at the last moment: about to depart for le Boulou in French Catalonia he told everyone, mistakenly, that he was going to stay in Andorra, and he sometimes repeated his favourite stories several times to the same listener. But his passion for travel burned as strongly as ever, and longevity did not deter him from making adventurous journeys. Iceland was the only country in Scandinavia he had never visited, and when the Bishop of Reykjavik invited him, Philip accepted with alacrity, returning to Dulverton full of praise for the natural wonders he had seen there, particularly the geysers. He never returned to Norway, although he remained in touch with Fr Olaf Waring by telephone, and his intelligence network kept him informed about what was going on there. When the country elected its first woman prime minister, he sent a gleeful note saying, 'my friend Oskar Garstein who taught [Prime Minister] Gro [Harlem Brundtland] at the cathedral school in Oslo told me

that she possessed everything except a heart'. After the Duchess
of Kent's conversion to Catholicism, he reported that:

> Two weeks ago the Duchess of Kent was staying with friends in
> the region of Lillehammer. She set out for Mass there but could
> not get through the snow drifts. Meanwhile the parish priest was
> waiting for her arrival before starting Mass. As Lillehammer has
> no airport it is doubtful whether anyone will get through for the
> Olympic games.[33]

Fr Caraman was always intrigued by the British Royal Family
and their Norwegian cousins. Another Jesuit, Fr Claudio Rossi,
commented on this: 'With so many friends among the great and
the good, and with my own love of gossip, I wish [Philip] had
name-dropped but he never did. The only titbit that I recall was
that he told me that Lord So and So described to him the Royal
family's spirituality as "Three Cheers for God."'[34] On another
occasion Philip remarked that 'Her Maj. [*sic*] is very Germanic
in her zeal for protocol – especially when it is a question of
medals'.[35]

   Fr Rossi spent eight years in the Diocese of Clifton, and after
Philip's death he commented on their friendship: 'not being a
fellow academic, maybe we did not threaten each other and so
we got on very well. Philip was warm, friendly, good fun, with
a solid uncomplicated faith.' He added that Fr Caraman 'was a
good solid, pastoral, parish priest'. But Philip was beginning to
feel his age. Reaching his eighty-third year he was in good
form: in a cheerful card, Alec Guinness remarked that it was
'good to hear you on the telephone sounding so chirpy, 38 I
think rather than 83'. In contrast there were days when he felt
tired and no longer able to cope with running a parish and some
of the problems it brought. He had to endure the unwanted
attention of vandals, who ripped the parish notice board on the
High Street off the wall, tore up hand-written notices at the
church entrance, and broke into the sacristy and the adjoining
youth hostel. 'Nothing stolen, just vandals out for destruction.
And there is a youth who rings my door bell often when I am
busy at my desk and disappears into thin air before I can come
down and catch him,' Philip related in his Journal.

Educated and ordained in the pre-Conciliar era, Fr Caraman was wearied by expectations that he should change the style and manner of his ministry. He noted sardonically in his Journal:

A circular arrived entitled *Improve Your Service*. It offered a pastoral summer school where I could bring up-to-date my priestly techniques to meet the challenge of the 'nineties': I would be taught to deal with difficult situations and to help people to discover a sense of vision and purpose in their lives. It was highly recommended by ... a former Minister of the Good News Crusade. I wonder what Newman would have said to such an offer?

Fr Caraman added that the proposed plan required that he should still be 'an active parish priest at the age of eighty-eight.'

In winter a chill wind funnelled down the Exe Valley into his inadequately heated cottage: it was a time of penance for Philip. After one 'desperately grey and wet winter in Dulverton', he jumped at an invitation to stay in Morocco: the visit was repeated in subsequent years, and he looked forward eagerly to these holidays as a time of warmth and rest.

Fr Caraman's host was the British Ambassador, a senior diplomat with a distinguished career who had served in Cairo, Kabul, Baghdad, the Lebanon and the Sudan. Sir Allan Ramsay's knowledge of the Arab world, and of Islam, was both extensive and erudite, and impressed Philip who was a novice in this branch of religious studies, although it was one that had always intrigued him. Sir Allan and his wife Pauline were Catholics who met the Jesuit during his ministry in Dulverton. As their guest, the old priest lived in a comfort and style reminiscent of some of the other grand houses in which he had been entertained earlier in his life: Pixton and Stonor, Clogheen, Renishaw, Montegufoni, Combe Florey and Marchmont, were all a far cry from his labourer's cottage. The Residence in Rabat was the last to be added to the list, and enjoyed one unexpected advantage shared by some of the others. On condition that the Ramsays attended Sunday Mass in the Cathedral, the Ambassador had been granted permission from the Catholic Archbishop to have a small chapel in the Residence, in which the Blessed Sacrament was reserved. The chapel was converted from a storeroom, and here Fr Caraman and other visiting priests could celebrate Mass if they wished to do so. To Philip this was a great blessing.

During one of his holidays in Rabat, Philip fulfilled a long-held wish to see the mountains of Morocco, which he had envied Lita Anker for visiting years earlier. He had great affection for Pauline Ramsay, and she twice acted as his guide and escort on journeys to the High Atlas in the embassy Discovery. Mountain roads, and narrow hairpin bends, induced a bad attack of vertigo in Fr Caraman who clung desperately to Pauline as they drove ever higher. But once they reached the top he was blissfully happy, and revelled in the view and the delights of the adventure. The highlight of one trip was Glaoui Kasbah in the Middle Atlas, near Marrakesh, and the excursion was the source of much fun and laughter, particularly when Philip and Pauline Ramsay tried to smuggle into hotel rooms the wine and other necessities for the priest's daily celebration of Mass.

One journey took place during the holy month of Ramadan, and both Fr Caraman and Pauline were conscious of the fact that their Moroccan driver could not eat during daylight hours. A bond of great sympathy developed between the priest and the driver – a simple soul – who said of Philip 'he is a good man'. This perception was echoed by the other servants in the Residence, all of whom were Muslims; they considered it a privilege to have Fr Caraman among them, and one of the maids, of her own volition, looked after and cleaned the chapel daily before his Mass.[36]

On his return to Dulverton after one holiday in Morocco, Philip recalled his experiences there to illustrate a Sunday sermon. It was a characteristic reaction to events that had fired his imagination. His sermons were greatly looked forward to by his congregation, not only for their brevity, but for their unfailingly thoughtful content and gentle delivery. Fr Caraman's homilies were deceptively simple, and – like his own religious faith – uncomplicated by theological niceties. The careful planning and writing that went into his sermons was never apparent to his listeners, one of whom was convinced they deserved a wider audience than the congregation of the little church of St Stanislaus.

The widow and family of John Biggs-Davison had, like the family of Evelyn Waugh years earlier, been grateful to Fr Caraman for the panegyric he had preached at the statesman's funeral. They invited Philip to prepare a selection of his sermons for a book which was published and printed privately by the family in 1995 under the title *Lord and Master*. The tribute to Biggs-Davison appeared at the end of the book under the title 'Quiet Crusader'. The thoughtfully arranged sermons capture the essence of Philip Caraman's preaching, and represent a series of short meditations which a reader may 'pick up, open anywhere, and read for five or ten minutes,' as he had remarked when recommending another book to Lita Anker.[37] Ever sensible of his own shortcomings, on the title page of one presentation copy of *Lord and Master* Philip wrote, 'Sermons, heard and unheard, certainly unheeded by me'.

In addition to the story of the Prayer Book Rebellion, *Lord and Master* was one of three books Philip was working on during the last years of his life. His appetite for writing was never satisfied. *A Study in Friendship – Saint Robert Southwell and Henry Garnet* was largely based on research he had done for the translation of the John Gerard and William Weston auto-biographies, and for his biography of Henry Garnet, with whom Southwell had effected a clandestine landing near Folkestone at the start of their mission to England in 1586. Of the two Jesuit martyrs, Robert Southwell plays the more prominent role in Caraman's study: his 'poems form a considerable part of [the] book [and] are set in the framework of Garnet's letters'.[38] Describing the close friendship that developed between the two hunted priests, Fr Caraman says there was 'nothing sentimental ... it was a deep rooted human affection balanced by a shared burning zeal for the kingdom of God on earth that brought them together'.[39] In relating the story of Southwell's martyrdom, Philip gives graphic details of the torture inflicted on the saint by Richard Topcliffe, who was described by John Gerard as 'a cruel creature [who] thirsted for the blood of Catholics ... old and hoary and a veteran in evil'.[40] Caraman's vilification of

Topcliffe amounts to a personal vendetta conducted retrospectively against the man who inflicted unimaginable sufferings on heroic Jesuits: to Philip the persecution experienced by English Catholics in penal times was living history. The love of friends, both given and received, played such an important part in his life that *A Study in Friendship* was a fitting book to appear in Philip's last years.

The most taxing of the books he was working on was a history of the Jesuit mission to Tibet, which highlighted the exploits of members of the Society who pioneered routes across the mountain ranges north of India. This book was the last of a trilogy based on Jesuit explorers and adventurers in unknown regions of the globe, of which *The Lost Paradise* and *The Lost Empire* were the first two. *Tibet – The Jesuit Century*[41] covered the only area of which Fr Caraman had not had personal experience. Research for the book meant that Philip had once again to work for several weeks at a time in the central Jesuit Archives and in the Jesuit Historical Institute in Rome. Research and writing a major history did not sit easily with pastoral responsibilities which had increased as the congregation of St Stanislaus grew in size. In September 1995 the parish and his friends celebrated the fiftieth anniversary of his ordination: as the infirmities of old age multiplied, he could no longer both write and attend to parish duties. He confessed that, 'I am playing [sic] seriously of retiring from here early next year: I am now in my tenth year in Dulverton: aches and arthritis won't go away. I have not any idea yet where I might be sent to. I am in Rome for a month from 25th October to finish off a book.' Some six weeks later he said that 'a priest is coming to take over in my absences [in Rome and Morocco]. If he finds the place suits him he will replace me around Easter [1996] when it looks as if I shall go to Farm St. That is the plan. But I don't know how well it will work out.'[42]

It didn't work out. In March 1996 Philip returned from Morocco to snow and ice on Exmoor, and no immediate hope of being replaced in Dulverton. He could, quite simply, have handed in his resignation to the Bishop of Clifton, but the idea of leaving his people without a priest was, to him, unthinkable.

The prospect of living in Mayfair[43] may have played some part in his decision to stay on in Somerset, but uncharacteristic behaviour betrayed his exhaustion. Philip grew cantankerous: he was agitated, complaining of the noise, when John Smith's wife hoovered the church: the presence of small children at Mass in St Stanislaus irritated him, and he asked one family with several boys to go elsewhere. They left the parish. Increasing infirmity brought the realisation that he could no longer drive round the country lanes to visit and take communion to the sick, so he agreed, somewhat reluctantly at first, to the commissioning of lay ministers of the Eucharist, including a woman. Belatedly he saw the advantages of some of the changes that had taken place in pastoral practice, and permitted women readers at Mass. This led John Smith to conclude that in his final years Fr Caraman was no longer so critical of the post-Conciliar Church as once he had been.[44] His weariness manifested itself in other ways. Preaching a homily on the Gospel story of the Samaritan woman whom Jesus met at the well-side, Philip told his congregation that – like Jesus – priests sometimes felt tired and thirsted for rest from their labours. But, following the example of his Jesuit forefathers in penal times, Fr Caraman soldiered on.

Following Sir Allan Ramsay's retirement, the delights of Morocco were no longer on offer for Philip's holiday in the winter of 1996. He looked elsewhere for warmth and sunshine, and spent February 1997 in Barbados, staying in a Jesuit house used by the Society as a haven for priests working in the Guyana mission. The holiday was not an unqualified success. Barbados wasn't his scene, and the accommodation was neither as comfortable nor as restful as the Residence in Rabat: the long-haul flight too must have been trying for a man in his mid-eighties, although this was something Philip would never admit. In the hope that Bishop Alexander might one day find a replacement for him, Philip promised himself a retirement present. His curiosity about the world and its people, their countries, customs and languages was undiminished by age: he told friends and parishioners that he was planning a voyage on the *St Helena*, the small cargo ship making the regular run from Barry in Glamorgan to deliver mail and supplies to the remote island in the South Atlantic: after spending a week on St Helena, he would travel on to Cape Town and return home by air. This was one journey he would never make.

In September 1997, Philip went on a painting holiday to Brittany, staying with Pauline and Allan Ramsay near the pretty port of Audierne. On a country road on Cap Sizun they found one of the ancient chapels he loved to visit. Near the holder for votive candles in the Chapel of Our Lady of the Seven Sorrows at Langroas, hung a prayer* which in various forms has recently made its appearance in a number of churches in other parts of France. The prayer was copied and taken home to Dulverton. The peaceful holiday came to an abrupt end when Philip suffered a severe heart attack, and was rushed into hospital in Douarnenez. It turned out that the head of the heart unit was one of the best known cardiologists in France, and after spending nine days there Philip was flown home. After his return, Philip extolled the benefits of travel insurance, which had covered his medical and repatriation expenses.

The heart trouble finally clinched the matter of Fr Caraman's retirement. Now there was no question of his living alone in Bridge House with its difficult staircase, nor of continuing as parish priest of St Stanislaus. The Bishop at last had a candidate lined up for the post – a former Anglican – but he had not yet been ordained as a priest: as a deacon he could not say Mass nor administer the sacrament of Confession. Philip moved into Three Acres, a small nursing home at Brushford, a couple of miles down the Exe Valley from Dulverton, and celebrated parish Mass when he was well enough to do so. St Stanislaus relied increasingly on visiting priests, who often came from Taunton. Officially, retirement was set for the New Year of 1998, and to mark the occasion Philip donated a votive stand to the church as a farewell gift, along with a framed copy of the

---

* Published in P. Caraman, *Meditations for Tomorrow*, Burns & Oates, 1998. The prayer appears at the end of this book.

prayer he had discovered in the chapel of Langroas to hang beside it. Incapacity did at least spare him from banishment to one of the houses where the Jesuits lodge their old and infirm priests: instead the Society footed the bill for the nursing home, where he could be visited by his numerous friends in the area, and keep his old telephone number, a line of communication on which he relied heavily.

Philip never reconciled himself to the loss of his independence. There was always one more book he wanted to research, write and publish, or one more country or continent he hoped to visit. As his heart condition deteriorated, and he fought for breath, he realised that travel was impossible: writing exhausted him, and he became increasingly unhappy and frustrated. Fortunately, work on *Tibet*, which mirrored in miniature some of the complications he had encountered in writing *The Lost Paradise*, was largely completed, and the book was in the hands of Steven Pugsley in nearby Tiverton. The publisher had agreed to take on the book although it fell outside his normal list, after the success of *The Western Rising* and because of his friendship and admiration for Fr Caraman.[45] With the completion of *Tibet*, Philip was preparing a new edition of his sermons, following popular request for a follow-up to *Lord and Master*. This posed no problem: his computer accompanied him to Three Acres, and no outside research was involved. He also started making notes for an autobiography. At one of their meetings, Steven Pugsley suggested the book, but realised that Philip's innate modesty might deter him from writing it. The biographical work which Philip had in mind was intended, he said, as a record for his family of its history and genealogy. With his computer, and through correspondence with cousins on the Continent and with friends living in Eastern Europe, he gradually gathered a considerable amount of background material. As he worked, Philip made hand-written notes recalling incidents in his early life, and laying down the guidelines he intended to follow. The autobiography he had in mind would, he said, be 'mainly my own S.J. life or rather connected to S.J.s: no gallery of notables but only close friends who are or were notable'. Before the phrase 'no gallery of notables', he originally wrote 'no name-dropping',

but then deleted it. The handwriting, which started clearly as Fr
Caraman chronicled family history, gradually became an almost
illegible scribble as his health deteriorated in the final weeks of
his life, and he realised time was running out.

In the New Year of 1998, Philip had one or two spells in
hospital, and eventually he had to be connected to an oxygen
cylinder to assist his breathing: this necessitated a move from
his upstairs room in Three Acres to a small room on the ground
floor with limited outlook. Visitors were aware of his distress,
although he was unfailingly courteous and welcoming, and still
enjoyed his food. When he knew a friend or former parishioner
was planning a visit, he telephoned a request for some tasty
addition to the nursing-home fare, which he complained about
although the food was really very good: smoked salmon was still
his favourite, but avocado pears, which he said were good for
him, and a particular variety of sardines from Sainsbury's were
also on his request list. When we visited him towards the end of
March, he told us despondently that he could no longer work for
more than half-an-hour a day on his autobiography: he earnestly
asked all his visitors to pray for him.

When Philip received an advance copy of *Tibet* from Steven
Pugsley, he was appalled to find that one of the illustrations had
been bound into the book upside down. Throughout the production work on the history, Fr Caraman had stressed that he
wanted the book to be well presented, and Pugsley remarked on
the courtesy he managed to muster despite his acute disappointment and the physical duress he was experiencing.

Claire Cradock-Henry, Philip's only surviving sibling and in
poor health herself, travelled over from Surrey to see him in
March. Jesuits came down from London: Fr Holt, who was a
contemporary, remarked that he found it rather a long journey.
Fr Richard Randolph had less distance to travel from Tisbury,
and paid the dying priest a long visit in April. To this close
friend Philip confided his wishes concerning his few possessions, although in law this testament probably carried little
legality. Fr Randolph later described what passed:

Philip asked me to help him summarise his dispositions, the

[Jesuit] Provincial willing, of the most treasured things he had about him: a retirement gift of two watercolours of Cader Idris: a treescape painting by Pavel Tchelitchew given him [by Sacheverell] in memory of Edith Sitwell; ... a silver ciborium and communion plate, made by William Phipps, silversmith to the Queen, and marked P C 1965, and given to him as a leaving present from the staff of *The Month* ... These dispositions and some others were, I understand, readily approved by a willing Provincial.[46]

The testament contained two further clauses. In the first, Philip requested that Fr Olaf Waring should be the principal concele-brant at the Funeral Mass he knew would be held for him at the church in Farm Street after his death, and that the Jesuits should pay Pastor Waring's fare from Norway. In the second Philip asked that 'a good stock' of his books should be held at the shop in Farm Street, because, he said, he still had 'many friends living in Mayfair'.[47] Philip followed this up with a phone call to Norway, during which he asked Fr Waring 'to say some words' at his Requiem Mass.[48] Fr Randolph's visit occurred shortly after the death of the former Provincial, Fr John Coventry. On being told of Coventry's death, Philip reflected that three out of the four leading players in the drama that had taken place at Farm Street in 1963 were now dead. 'I am the only one still alive', he added quietly. Remembrance of the traumatic episode still troubled him.[49]

Fr Caraman's end did not come easily, and the sense of peace he had experienced at the time of his cancer operation seemed to elude him. Visitors became fewer in number; he was often too exhausted to talk much, although his telephone was still a lifeline. Alec Guinness called regularly to enquire, anxiously, how he was. The actor's official biographer, Piers Paul Read, noted that many of Guinness's conversations with friends were conducted by telephone rather than by letter, and this is certainly true of the friendship between Philip and Alec. Read also remarks on the sadness felt by Alec and Merula Guinness as, one by one, their close friends predeceased them.[50] Philip's imminent death was, perhaps, particularly painful to Guinness who, after an operation some years earlier, had written – half in jest – to the Jesuit, saying, 'Five days ago I left hospital after my *fourth* hernia operation. Surely that will see me out. If you are good enough to speak of me at my funeral mass, you could say "he was a Martyr to the Hernia." '[51] A friendship which began on the day when Edith Sitwell was received into the Church over forty years earlier was drawing to its close, and Philip would not be there to speak at Alec's Funeral Mass.

Philip's last days were often confused, and difficult for the faithful friends who attended him. Some of his possessions were still at Bridge House, and he was particularly upset when a piece of fine embroidery work done by Claire when she was at the Royal School of Needlework could not be found. An old Norwegian fisherman's jersey made of oiled wool, rank with dirt, had also disappeared, much to his distress. It had been a present from Lita Anker nearly thirty years earlier: he wanted it near him, along with the memento of Claire, and the copy of Margaret FitzHerbert's book which he kept beside his bed in the nursing home.

Shortly before he died, Philip's mood changed: he telephoned Richard Randolph in as excited a voice as his failing breath would allow, to say he had found a perfect prayer: *Include me, Domine, in imis Cordis Tui visceribus*. Fr Randolph translated this as 'Fold me in the depths of Your Love, O Lord.'

Fr Philip Caraman died on 6 May 1998. His Funeral Mass, at which the preacher was Bishop Mervyn Alexander of Clifton, was held in Dulverton a week later. He was buried in the cemetery of the church in Brushford, overlooking the Exe valley, and in due time lines from the ancient prayer of the Church, the 'Dies Irae', which he had chosen before he died, were inscribed on his gravestone as he had requested:

> *Qui Mariam absolvisti,*
> *Et latronem exaudisti,*
> *Mihi quoque spem dedisti.*

A country priest, buried in a country churchyard, with the words of a humble penitent inscribed on his memorial. At the end this is how he wanted it to be.

Notes

1 Information concerning Fr Caraman's activities and contacts described in this and the following paragraphs is taken from his letters and papers in the John J. Burns Library in Boston College (hereafter BC).
2 Letter, 13 February 1991 (BC).
3 Philip Caraman, 'Journal of a Country Priest', undated, unpublished, Private Papers (hereafter PCPP).
4 Letter, Michael De la-Noy to Philip Caraman, 28 May 1987, British Library (hereafter BL).
5 Letter, Philip Caraman to Michael De-la-Noy, 29 May 1987 (BL).
6 Martin Stannard, *Evelyn Waugh – No Abiding City. 1939–1966*, pp. 428, 460–1, 468–9.
7 Selina Hastings, letter to author, 1 May 2003.
8 Letter, Lady Selina Hastings to Philip Caraman, 6 September 1989 (BC).
9 Letter, Selina Hastings to Philip Caraman, 16 January 1990 (BC).
10 Selina Hastings, letter to author, 1 May 2003.
11 Michael Shelden, *Graham Greene. The Man Within* (Heinemann, London, 1994), pp. 377–8.
12 Chapter Five of this book, note 11.
13 Letter, Norman Sherry to Philip Caraman, 22 April 1992 (BC).
14 Selina Hastings, letter to author, 1 May 2003.
15 *Literary Review*, June 1987, pp. 8 and 9. Peter Levi's book was published by Collins Harvill.
16 Letter, Auberon Waugh to Philip Caraman, Combe Florey, 22 November 1991 (BC).
17 Philip Caraman, *Ignatius Loyola. A Biography of the Founder of the Jesuits* (Harper & Row, San Francisco, 1990).
18 Letter, Philip Caraman to Fr Fernàndez SJ, 21 June 1989 (BC).
19 *Ignatius Loyola*, p. 33.
20 Fr Thomas M. McCoog SJ, *Catholic Historical Review* 77 (1991) pp. 513–14.
21 Thomas M. McCoog, *The Month*, December 1985, 2nd New Series, vol. 18, no 12, pp. 432–3.
22 Author interview with Fr Thomas M. McCoog SJ, 29 July 2003.
23 Letter, John Gran to Philip Caraman, 4 August 1991 (BC).
24 Philip Caraman read Patrick French's *Younghusband – The Last Great Imperial Adventurer* (HarperCollins, 1994) when writing *Tibet – The Jesuit Century*.

25 Appendix F, *John Gerard. The Autobiography of an Elizabethan,* lst Edition, p. 272.
26 Christopher Ralls, Article entitled 'Profile of Philip Caraman' in *The Catholic* (Catholic Truth Society), Summer 1992, p. 3.
27 Philip Caraman, *The Western Rising 1549. The Prayer Book Rebellion* (Westcountry Books, 1994).
28 Eamon Duffy. *The Voices of Morebath. Reformation and Rebellion in an English Village* (Yale University Press, 2001).
29 Philip Caraman, letters to author, 3 (?) March and 8 May 1994.
30 Auberon Waugh, 'Way of the World', *The Daily Telegraph*, 23 March 1994.
31 Author interviews with Caryl, Richard and Max Rothwell, March/ April 2003.
32 Richard Randolph, *The Month*, June 1998, 2nd New Series, vol. 31. no. 6. p. 251.
33 Philip Caraman to author, notelet, 23 June 1989 and letter, 3 June 1994.
34 Claudio Rossi SJ, *Letters & Notices*, Spring 1999, vol. 94, no. 415, p. 939.
35 Philip Caraman to author, card, 30 March 1991.
36 Author interview with Allan and Pauline Ramsay.
37 See Chapter 8. The book, entitled *What Law and Letter Kills*, has not been tracked down by this author.
38 Philip Caraman, *A Study in Friendship. Saint Robert Southwell and Henry Garnet*, Introduction to edition published by Society of Jesus in India, 1991. A second edition was published by the Institute of Jesuit Sources in the U.S.A.
39 Ibid.
40 Philip Caraman, *John Gerard*, lst Edition. p. 68.
41 Philip Caraman, *Tibet. The Jesuit Century* (Halsgrove, 1998).
42 Philip Caraman, Letters to author, 3 September 1995 and 19 October 1995.
43 Fr Caraman would have lived in the Jesuit house at 114 Mount Street, the presbytery for the Church of the Immaculate Conception in Farm Street.
44 Author interview with John Smith.
45 Author conversation with Steven Pugsley.
46 Fr Richard Randolph SJ in *The Month*, June 1998.
47 Author interview with Fr Richard Randolph.
48 Fr Olaf Waring, undated letter to author.

49 Fr John Coventry died on 9 April 1998: Fr James Walsh predeceased him in 1986. Margaret FitzHerbert's death on 28 January
1986 is described in Chapter Eleven of this book.
50 Piers Paul Read, *Alec Guinness. The Authorised Biography*
(Simon & Schuster, 2003), p. 570.
51 Alec Guinness, letter to Philip Caraman, 28 October 1982.

Epilogue

On the morning following Fr Caraman's death, *The Times* and *The Daily Telegraph* carried obituary notices paying tribute to his life as a writer and a priest. The piece in the *Telegraph* glossed over the story of Philip Caraman's dismissal from Farm Street in 1963, but accurately described other episodes in his eventful life. In *The Times*, John Skinner highlighted Fr Caraman's hidden ministry in Dulverton, the success of his Elizabethan historical works and his role as a spiritual adviser.

The Jesuits lost no time in reclaiming one of their own. A fortnight after the Funeral Mass in the little church in Dulverton, a solemn Memorial was celebrated in the splendour of the Church of the Immaculate Conception in Mayfair. The preacher quoted some of Fr Caraman's own words in an attempt to reach an understanding of his life: 'If the talents are taken to include not only God's gift of mind, heart, soul and body, but also temperament, inherited fears, opportunities of education and upbringing, and even psychological deviations, it is possible to form a tentative but necessarily inexact estimate of the response of the soul to grace.' When Fr Pedro Arrupe congratulated Fr Caraman on the occasion of his Golden Jubilee in the Society in 1980, the Jesuit General prayed that God's graces might continue to descend on him 'during many more years in the peace and happiness' of his Jesuit vocation. At times, Philip Caraman's vocation had been far from peaceful, but his loyalty to the Society of Jesus was never in question, at least in his own mind: some of those who attended the Memorial, and were acquainted with the vicissitudes of his life as a Jesuit, may well have disagreed.

In line with Philip's request, Fr Olaf Waring came over from Norway to take part in the Mass at Farm Street. But all did not go as the dying priest had wished. Whilst acknowledging the kindness of the Jesuit Superior, Pastor Waring says:

> Philip had in fact asked me personally to say some words ... I was prepared to do so when I went to London but it was clear that the Fathers at Farm Street did not know anything about the request, so I just concelebrated. It was a great privilege anyway; but truth to say I was a little bit disappointed because Philip had asked me personally. In the case [sic] I never mentioned Philip's request.[1]

Apart from his enduring friendship with Fr Waring, it is possible that Fr Caraman's request was motivated by a wish to draw the Society's attention to Norway: he knew that successive British Provincials had failed to appreciate the country's importance as a missionary field. Philip was never given the credit he deserved for his labours there.

The division of opinion within the Society concerning Fr Caraman was immediately apparent to an outsider. Fr Waring remarked that:

> My general impression has always been that Philip was the object of some envy and nastiness ... from his own brethren within the Society of Jesus in England. Of course the generation gap has to be taken into account. At Philip's funeral it became apparent to me that the younger Jesuits did not quite appreciate Philip's qualities. I found myself getting a little un-amused. *The Daily Telegraph* obituary had a little remark about 'his room at Farm Street [when he was editor of *The Month*] was beautifully furnished and decorated in contrast to the Spartan standards prevailing elsewhere in the establishment'. What nonsense that is. That Philip had a sense of the artistic is of course true. But the impression given is that there was some sort of luxuriousness with which he surrounded himself – not so![2]

Controversy concerning Fr Caraman continued for some time.

The issue of the Jesuit house magazine *Letters & Notices* which came out in the autumn of 1998 featured obituaries of Philip Caraman and of his former Provincial, Fr John Coventry. Philip's was remarkable for the derogatory tone of the principal contribution. This engendered such a storm of protest, from priests both in and beyond the British Province of the Society of Jesus, that six months later *Letters & Notices* published a sequel in which Philip's admirers were given an opportunity to have their say.

Opinion and counter-opinion sallied back and forth, and embraced not only Fr Caraman's personality but his books. As a result of the hold-up caused by the printers' error over the illustrations, *Tibet – The Jesuit Century* came out just before Philip died, and a notice of the book did not appear in *The Month* until the following year. Fr Francis Edwards, the Jesuit historian who reviewed the book, conceded that it was 'an absorbing story', but remarked that 'the accounts of the journeys [of the Jesuit explorers] seem at times confusing'.[3] Had Philip been alive, this criticism, like the earlier one of *St Ignatius*, would have upset him, as it questioned his reputation as a raconteur of Jesuit travel sagas.

Fr Caraman's last book was published posthumously, as he realised in the last few weeks of his life that it would be. Shortly before he died he told me: 'I am calling my new medit-book *Meditations for To-morrow*' [sic]. Philip particularly wanted a good-looking production in memory of his friendship with Stanley Morison, one of the distinguished men who had guided his triumphal revival of *The Month*. The book was underwritten by the Jesuits, and placed with Burns & Oates, a pale ghost of the once great Catholic publishing house then in the care of Paul Burns, a nephew of Tom Burns who had run the firm during its heyday when Philip was editor of *The Month*. When the book came out in November 1998 it was marred by a number of printing errors which would have annoyed and disappointed Fr Caraman, and been viewed with horror by Stanley Morison: this may have been the result of inadequate proof-reading due to Philip's ill-health when he was preparing the book. (It is unlikely that the author intended to create a new race known as

Hews, possibly derived from a fusion of Hebrews and Jews.)[4]

Many of the spiritual reflections in Caraman's earlier book of sermons *Lord and Master* are repeated in *Meditations for Tomorrow*. The arrangement of the two books is almost identical, but the second book includes a number of previously unpublished pieces, notably on the subjects of Marriage and the Eucharist. The reflections on Matrimony were derived from notes Fr Caraman had kept of sermons given at some of the many weddings at which he had been asked to officiate both in London and elsewhere. Both books are a welcome legacy to admirers of Philip Caraman's homilies, although much of his appeal as a preacher lay in the manner of his delivery. It was said of another great preacher, Mgr Ronald Knox, whose copious sermons Fr Caraman had edited, that he spoke his own words badly from the pulpit. Of Philip the reverse was true.

Meditations for Tomorrow carries a Foreword, written at Philip's request by Sir Allan Ramsay, which serves not only as a Prologue but as a glowing panegyric to the author of the sermons. Allan Ramsay points out the 'universality' of the meditations, and their appeal 'to everyone, of whatever religion, believer and unbeliever alike'. He remarks on the priest's devoted service to the parish of St Stanislaus during the last twelve years of his life, and extols Fr Caraman 'as one who gave his life to his faith, in the traditions of the great Society of which he was proud to be a member and for the cause of whose English and Welsh martyrs he laboured in his researches and his writings'. The book closes with a copy of the prayer Allan Ramsay and Philip had discovered during their stay in Brittany, and there is an unattributed drawing by Pauline Ramsay of the wayside chapel where it was found.

Comment concerning Fr Caraman has not been confined to Jesuit circles: since his death his name has cropped up in a number of publications in a variety of contexts. In *Catholics*, an overview of the progress of Britain's Catholic community during the twentieth century, the author Dennis Sewell presents a number of vignettes of prominent Catholics, including Fr Caraman.[5] The brief reference to the Jesuit concentrates on his role as editor of *The Month* and on his literary converts,

describing Rosamond Lehmann as 'the one that got away'.
Intended as little more than an introduction to a passage about
Catholic novelists and literary figures, no mention is made of
Philip Caraman's books, nor of his role as Vice-Postulator of
the Cause of the Forty Martyrs: this despite an historical sketch
of Catholic persecution in penal times at the beginning of the
book. In contrast several pages of *Catholics* is devoted to his
well-known contemporary Mgr Alfred Gilbey, whom the Jesuit,
in the last decades of his life, had neither the position, the financial means, nor the slightest wish to emulate as a popular priest.
Doubtless Gilbey provided better copy than Fr Caraman.

Sewell dismisses Fr Caraman in a few short paragraphs, but
the reference is anaemic in comparison to the bitterness directed
at Philip by Garry O'Connor in his unofficial biography of Alec
Guinness.[6] The writer drove down to Dulverton in January,
1988 hoping that Philip would provide him with an introduction
to Guinness, and in the expectation that the Jesuit might be
cajoled into making some intimate revelations concerning the
actor. O'Connor describes Caraman as 'a thin spare man with
glasses and wiry white hair who wore a fisherman's jersey ...
[he] was seventy-eight years old, though looked barely older
than sixty-five'. The physical description is perceptive, but there
are a number of inaccuracies in the book in addition to the
mistake over Philip's age; Dulverton is erroneously located in
North Devon, and O'Connor says that Caraman was Alec's
confessor and the priest who introduced him to the Catholic
Church. Guinness himself testified that he was received into the
Church by Fr Henry Clarke on 24 March 1956, and researches
for this book have not uncovered any evidence to suggest that
Fr Caraman was Guinness's confessor. The anecdote related by
Lady Brigid McEwen (describing her encounter with Guinness
in Westminster Cathedral) seems to hint that he was not. In his
autobiography Guinness described Philip as a loving friend, and
it was this friendship that O'Connor attempted to exploit for his
unofficial biography. He committed a grave blunder. Fr
Caraman's unshakeable loyalty to his friends was recognised by
all who knew him: he never indulged in gossip, nor willingly
discussed anyone, particularly a public figure like Guinness,

except perhaps with a bona fide mutual friend. Philip's obduracy in the face of O'Connor's probing drew a harsh response from the would-be biographer, who said he 'shuddered in his unfriendly presence', made sarcastic comments about the lunch provided for him after his journey, and described the old priest's hospitality as 'minimal'. 'By a little stretch one could imagine him as a priest in charge of the Inquisition,' O'Connor added.

The book would have infuriated Philip for its discussion of Alec Guinness's putative homosexuality, just as comments denigrating the memory of Evelyn Waugh upset him. On the other hand, O'Connor's remarks about himself probably raised a dry smile from beyond the grave.

In contrast, Guinness's official biographer, Piers Paul Read, clearly understood and acknowledged the bond of friendship between Philip and the actor. The biography came out in the autumn of 2003: it contains almost no correspondence between the two men, because – as Read points out – Alec's preferred line of communication was the telephone, nor does the author mention Philip as one of the Guinness's many guests at their home, Kettlebrook Meadows, although the priest certainly stayed there on more than one occasion. Read does not claim, as O'Connor had, that Fr Caraman was Alec's 'confessor': instead, towards the end of the book, he makes one perceptive observation about their relationship, which aptly embraces Evelyn Waugh:

> He [Alec] had no regular spiritual director except, possibly, Fr Philip Caraman who, one suspects, was no more likely to say anything harsh to Alec than to Evelyn Waugh, and may have accepted the view of both men that, while the Grace of God may not have made them much better, its absence would have made them much worse.[7]

This passage from a Catholic writer confirms the testimony of many others who benefited from Philip's gentle spiritual advice.

When Fr Caraman entrusted his last wishes to Richard Randolph, he said that he hoped copies of his books would be made available for friends in Mayfair to buy. Some of the later works did not sell well, and stocks of *Tibet* and *Meditations For*

Tomorrow remain unsold. But Philip Caraman's earlier books, particularly his stories of the Elizabethan martyrs and *Norway*, are long out of print, and change hands at many times their original sale price. A well-known second-hand bookshop in Oxford, specialising in Catholic books,[8] has a steady turnover in works by Fr Caraman; *The Lost Paradise*, which to some extent is regarded as a seminal work on the Jesuit Reductions in South America, is the book requested most frequently. As a readable historian, Philip is not forgotten.

Fr Caraman did not live to witness the demise of 'his magazine', *The Month*, nor the withdrawal of the last Jesuit parish priest from Tisbury and historic Wardour which terminated the Society's association with the parish after more than four hundred years. Both events would have saddened him. In contrast, it is only recently that the value of Fr Caraman's work in Norway has become apparent. The Church in this unpromising missionary field, which Philip nursed through lean times and often despaired of in private, has blossomed with a significant influx of Catholic immigrants from South-East Asia. In the twenty-first century Vietnamese priests run the churches in Tønsberg and Larvik, and are involved in work in several other areas. The West Country parish to which Philip devoted his last years is also vibrant with an active congregation: a new priest, Fr Robert Miller, has updated the liturgy but inherited his predecessor's love of the unusual church of St Stanislaus.

In a tribute in *The Catholic Herald* to the billionaire Sir Paul Getty, Dom Antony Sutch wrote, 'no one ever knows another fully; that is the realm of God'. A biographer is aware of the wisdom of this statement, but remembrance surely has some validity. Fr Caraman is remembered in Norway as 'a wonderful priest – and personality'.[9] and in Dulverton he is still spoken of with affection by Catholics and non-Catholics alike.

Notes

1 Fr Olaf Waring, undated letter (August 2001) to author.
2 Ibid.
3 Francis Edwards SJ, *The Month*, July 1999, vol. 32, no.7, 2nd New Series, pp. 285–6.
4 Philip Caraman, *Meditations For Tomorrow* (Burns & Oates, 1998), p. 67.
5 Dennis Sewell, *Catholics – Britain's Largest Minority* (Viking, 2001).
6 O'Connor, Garry, *Alec Guinness – the Unknown (A Life)* (Sidgwick & Jackson, 2002).
7 Piers Paul Read, *Alec Guinness – The Authorised Biography* (Simon & Schuster, 2003), pp. 568–9.
8 St Philip's Books.
9 Fr Rory Mulligan SM, card to author, 12 September 2003.

Evelyn Waugh

The Panegyric by Fr Philip Caraman, SJ

The full text of the panegyric preached by Fr Philip Caraman, SJ at the Requiem Mass, celebrated in Latin, in Westminster Cathedral on Thursday 21 April 1966.

This gathering is for prayer. It is also an expression of our regard for a man universally admired for his gifts and deeply loved by many friends.

Christ commanded us to trade with our talents. This Evelyn Waugh did. He sought perfection in his craft and came nearer to achieving it than perhaps any man of his time. But the way he cultivated his gifts was only one manifestation of his fidelity – the virtue marked the whole man.

It is a detail, perhaps, but a significant one, that throughout his career as a writer he remained faithful to the same publisher and to the same literary agent. At the end of his life his closest friends were among those he first met in his youth. It was this fidelity that made them put a special value on his friendship. While he playfully exaggerated their foibles, he was penetrating in his praise. Also he served his friends when they were dead. I mention only Alfred Duggan and Mgr. Knox.

It is not an accident that *A Handful of Dust* is generally reckoned the best of his earlier novels. It was written when he was still wounded by the failure of loyalty. Under the shock he sought a faith that would underpin morals. He found it, assisted by Fr. Martin D'Arcy, to whom he dedicated and gave his book, *Edmond Campion*.

'Conversion,' he wrote, speaking of himself in the third person, 'suggests an event more sudden and emotional than his calm acceptance of the propositions of his faith – in early manhood when many Englishmen of humane education were falling into Communism.' Unlike them, he remained steadfast.

Here, in the shrine of English Catholicism, I must speak of his fidelity to the Church in which he lived for thirty-six years until his death. Certainly he would charge me with absurd exaggeration if he heard me say what I believe to be true, that he did equal service to his Church by his example as by his books. It was to be expected of a man who fought with eminent bravery for his Sovereign in the late war that he should remain outstandingly loyal to his Church in the crisis caused by the Vatican Council. He was deeply disturbed by the revolution in the outward forms of worship but accepted it in a spirit of soldierly obedience.

There was no man in England more entitled to give his opinion on the new English liturgy. Yet, when on the first Sunday, Mass was said in English, he was asked about it, he answered instantly: 'The question does not arise.' Only when he was outraged beyond Christian endurance by manifest heresy, did he express himself in a letter to the press. The letter, I recall, touched on the Eucharist. He showed the anger Christ had when he cleansed the Temple.

It has been truthfully said by a Catholic friend that the tabernacle and the sanctuary lamp were for him the symbols of an unchanging Church in a crumbling society. There is a futuristic short story of his which describes how, after an atomic explosion on London, a man emerges and wanders about a dead and ruined city till he is drawn by the distant sound of a bell, and, making his way into a cave below Piccadilly Circus, sees a cluster of shawled women huddled round a priest as he offers Mass. When the priest turns round with a gesture and phrase the survivor recognises, he is seen to have a black face.

The Mass mattered for him most in his world. During the greater part of his lifetime it remained as it had done for centuries, the same, and everywhere recognisable, when all else was threatened with change. He was sad when he read of churches in which the old altar was taken down and a table substituted, or of side altars abolished as private Masses were held to be unliturgical or unnecessary. With all who know something of the pattern of history, he was perturbed.

It was a struggle to accept it all, but he did accept it, and with enviable fidelity. The calmness that was evident in the last weeks of his life was a sign that the struggle had been won. To those who were with him on his final day – his family and a priest (he surely prayed for this) – nothing was more manifest than the way God had arranged his end as a mark of gratitude to a faithful servant.

I should be doing him the greatest disservice if I did not beg you all here to pray for him now: not only his friends who owe him this, but all who would make some return for the pleasure they have derived from his pen.

This perfect craftsman must through your prayers be made the perfect man before he can join the company of Campion and Helena. Only the saints, as he wrote himself, have conformed completely in their lifetime to the will of God. He would expect everyone here, each in his own way and with integrity, to pray for his soul.

The intersection of time and eternity is a mystery. But we know this: that, while those who are nearest to him by natural ties must wait a little before they meet him again, for him the meeting will be as tomorrow.

He would want them to seek their comfort in the faith he so firmly held and be assured that his companionship continues though its character is altered. They can be certain also that God above all others cannot fail in faithfulness to those who have been loyal to him. *Requiescat in pace.*

Prayer

To be said on offering a candle

I do not know how to pray
I am here to light a candle
I realise that it is nothing much, this candle
It represents almost nothing of myself
Nothing of my work
Nor did I pay much for it
Indeed it cost me less than the price of a single meal
It is no more than a sign
the sign that I want to share a few moments
Alone with you in silence
   The sign that I have come here knowing
   That you are present
   That you can see me
   That you are no stranger to my life nor to
Its problems and present difficulties, my home,
My children, my work, my obligations,
My family and friends, my future, my health, and
     the particular problem
Which brings me here today.
   I am lighting this candle in the knowledge that
The bread which sustains me throughout
My daily life comes from you.
   I know this ever since Jesus, Your Son, taught
Me to ask you for it in my prayers,
Saying, before inviting me to ask it of you,
That you love me as a Father and
That I can always turn to you for help
   and speak to you as such.

Fr Caraman's Books

1951 *John Gerard. The Autobiography of an Elizabethan.* Translated from the Latin with an introduction by Graham Greene (Longmans, Green and Co.)

1955 *William Weston. The Autobiography of an Elizabethan.* Translated from the Latin with an introduction by Evelyn Waugh (Longmans, Green and Co.)

1957 *Henry Morse – Priest of the Plague* (Longmans, Green and Co.)

1960 *The Other Face. Catholic Life Under Elizabeth I* (Longmans, Green and Co.)

1963 *Saint Angela. The Life of Angela Merici, Foundress of the Ursulines (1474–1540)* (Longmans, Green and Co.)

1964 *Henry Garnet 1555–1606 and the Gunpowder Plot* (Longmans, Green and Co.)

1966 *The Years of Siege* (Longmans, Green and Co.)

1967 *C.C. Martindale. A Biography* (Longmans, Green and Co.)

1969 *Norway* (Longmans, Green and Co.)

1975 *The Lost Paradise* *an account of the Jesuits in Paraguay 1607–1768* (Sidgwick & Jackson).

1981 *University of the Nations* *The Story of the Gregorian University with Its Associated Institutes, the Biblical and Oriental 1551–1962* (Paulist Press, New York/Ramsey).

1985 *The Lost Empire.* *The Story of the Jesuits in Ethiopia 1555–1634* (Sidgwick & Jackson)

1990 *Ignatius Loyola* (Collins/Harper & Row) San Francisco

1991   *A Study in Friendship*
Saint Robert Southwell and Henry Garnet
(Institute of Jesuit Sources) St. Louis U.S.A.
1994   *The Western Rising 1549. The Prayer Book Rebellion*
(Westcountry Books)
1995   *Lord and Master*
(Privately Published)
1998   *Tibet. The Jesuit Century*
(Halsgrove)
1998   *Meditations For Tomorrow*
Posthumous   (Burns & Oates)

Pamphlets written by Fr Caraman for the Catholic Truth Society

1975   *Edmund Campion*
1977   *St Cuthbert Mayne*
1978   *Margaret Clitherow*
1980   *The Curé d'Ars* (illustrated)
1981   *St Nicholas Owen – Maker of Hiding Holes*
1985   *St Philip Howard*
1985   *Holiness*
1986   *Margaret Clitherow* (illustrated)
1986   *The Jesuit Republic of Paraguay*

As editor
1976   *Praying Together*

Note on Primary Sources

The archive deposited by Fr Philip Caraman in the John J. Burns Library in Boston College is the principal source of material published for the first time in this book. This archive includes letters written by Evelyn Waugh, Graham Greene, Dame Edith Sitwell and other members of the Sitwell family, Fr Martin D'Arcy SJ, and many of Fr Caraman's other correspondents.

The Archives of the British Province of the Society of Jesus in London are the source of other previously unpublished material including a number of Thomas Merton's letters. The Manuscript Department of the British Library has a small Caraman collection: this also has proved to be of significant importance.

Fr Caraman was a prolific correspondent, and his letters to friends, including myself, have been used liberally in this work.

I have also had access to papers Fr Caraman entrusted to a friend shortly before his death. These papers have been another invaluable source, and include the notes he made for an autobiography during the last months of his life: these notes gave me the information on his family background and early years which I have used in the first two chapters of the book. It is expected that this archive will be placed in the public domain in due course.

I must thank the British Province of the Society of Jesus for granting me permission to quote the writings and letters of Fr Caraman and the letters of Fr Martin D'Arcy and other priests of the Society of Jesus.

I would like to express my gratitude to Mrs Teresa D'Arms, Mrs Bridget Grant and Lady Teresa Waugh for generously allowing me to quote letters written by Evelyn and Laura Waugh, Mary Herbert and Auberon Waugh, and to Christopher Sinclair-Stevenson for passages from the letters of Sir Alec Guinness. I am also grateful to the Merton Legacy Trust for permission to use extracts from Thomas Merton's letters. I should also like to thank David Higham Associates for permission to quote Graham Greene and Dame Edith Sitwell and other members of the Sitwell family. My thanks are due also to Dame Muriel Spark and David Higham Associates for allowing me to cite a passage from *Curriculum Vitae* and one of her letters.

I also wish to thank Lady Selina Hastings, Piers Paul Read, and H. J. A. Sire for allowing me to quote from their letters and published work.

All those mentioned above have been most patient in replying to my letters and requests, and I would like to record my gratitude for their courtesy and acknowledge their help in writing this book.

Every effort has been made to contact all persons holding rights in extracts quoted in this book. I apologise if anyone has inadvertently been overlooked: the author and publishers will be pleased to rectify any omission as the opportunity arises.

June Rockett – 12 January 2004

Select Bibliography

BOOKS

Amory, Mark.   (Editor) *The Letters of Evelyn Waugh*
                    (Weidenfeld & Nicolson) London 1980

Burns, Tom.   *The Use of Memory. Publishing and
                    Further Pursuits*
                    (Sheed & Ward) London 1993

Cooper, Artemis.   (Editor) *Mr Wu and Mrs Stitch. The
                    Letters of Evelyn Waugh and Diana
                    Cooper.*
                    (Hodder & Stoughton) 1991

De-la-Noy, Michael. *Eddy. The Life of Edward Sackville-
                    West.*
                    (Bodley Head) London 1988

Donaldson, Frances. *Evelyn Waugh – Portrait of a Country
                    Neighbour*
                    (Weidenfeld & Nicolson) London 1967

Duffy, Eamon.   *The Voices of Morebath. Reformation
                    and Rebellion in an English Village*
                    (Yale University Press) New Haven
                    and London 2001

FitzHerbert, Margaret. *The Man Who Was Greenmantle*
                    (John Murray) 1983

French, Patrick.   *Younghusband
                    The Last Great Imperial Adventurer*
                    (HarperCollins) 1994

Glendinning, Victoria. *Edith Sitwell, A Unicorn Among Lions*
                    (Weidenfeld & Nicolson) London 1971

Greene, Graham.   *The End of the Affair*
                         (Heinemann) London 1951
Greene, Graham.   *A Burnt-Out Case*
                         (Heinemann) London 1961
Greene, Richard.   *Selected Letters of Edith Sitwell*
                         (Virago) 1997
Guinness, Alec.   *Blessings in Disguise*
                         (Hamish Hamilton) London 1985
Hastings, Selina.   *Evelyn Waugh. A Biography*
                         (Sinclair-Stevenson) London 1994
Hastings, Selina.   *Rosamond Lehmann*
                         (Chatto & Windus) 2002
Heath, Jeffrey.   *The Picturesque Prison – Evelyn
                         Waugh & His Writing*
                         (Weidenfeld & Nicolson) London 1982
Holroyd, Michael.   *Works On Paper*
                         (Little Brown) 2002
Lehmann, John.   Editor (with Derek Parker) *Edith
                         Sitwell – Selected Letters*
                         (Macmillan) 1970
Lehmann, Rosamond.   *Album*
                         (Chatto & Windus) 1985
Merton, Thomas.   *Entering the Silence – Volume 2 of the
                         Journals of Thomas Merton*
                         Edited by Jonathen Montaldo
                         (Harper) San Francisco 1997
Mockler, Anthony.   *Graham Greene – Three Lives*
                         (Hunter Mackay) Scotland 1994
O'Connor, Garry.   *Paul Scofield – The Biography*
                         (Sidgwick & Jackson) 2002
O'Connor, Garry.   *Alec Guiness. The Unknown*
                         (Sidgwick & Jackson) London 2002
Pearce, Joseph.   *Literary Converts: Spiritual Inspiration
                         in an Age of Unbelief*
                         (Harper Collins) London 1999
Read, Piers Paul.   *Alec Guinness, The Authorised Biography*
                         (Simon & Schuster) 2003

Salter, Elizabeth.   *A Memoir of Edith Sitwell*
                         (The Bodley Head) 1967

Shelden, Michael.   *Graham Greene. The Man Within*
                         (Heinemann) London 1994

Sherry, Norman.   *The Life of Graham Green Vol. 2*
                         1939–1955
                         (Jonathan Cape) London 1994

Sire, H. J. A.   *Father Martin D'Arcy. Philosopher of*
                         Christian Love
                         (Gracewing) 1997

Sitwell, Osbert.   *Laughter in the Next Room*
                         (Macmillan) 1949

Spark, Muriel.   *Curriculum Vitae*
                         (Constable) 1992

Spurling, Hilary.   *The Girl from the Fiction Department*
                         (Hamish Hamilton) 2002

Stannard, Martin.   *Evelyn Waugh – No Abiding City*
                         1939–1966
                         (J.M. Dent) 1992

Various   *Auberon Herbert. A Composite Portrait*
                         Edited by John Joliffe. Privately
                         Published. 1976

Waugh, Auberon.   *Will This Do? The First Fifty Years of*
                         Auberon Waugh: An Autobiography
                         (Century) 1991

Waugh, Evelyn.   *Edmund Campion.* (Longmans, Green
                         & Co.) 1935

West, W.J.   *The Quest for Graham Greene*
                         (Weidenfeld & Nicolson) London 1997

White, Antonia.   *The Hound and the Falcon. The story*
                         of a reconversion to the Catholic Faith
                         (Longmans, Green & Co.) 1965

NEWSPAPERS – PERIODICALS – MISCELLANEOUS

The Catholic (Catholic Truth Society) – Summer 1992
Catholic Directory – Various dates
Catholic Gazette – Vol. 71/2 1980

Horizon – Various dates
Letters & Notices (Jesuit in-house periodical) – Various dates.
Literary Review – June 1987
The Month – Various dates
Northern Catholic Calendar – 1934–1937
Stonyhurst Magazine – Various dates
The Tablet – Various dates
The Times – Various dates
The Times Literary Supplement – Various dates

Index

Note: Numbers in italics indicate plates. References to Philip Caraman use the abbreviation PC.

Agius, Dom Ambrose 84
Alexander, Mervyn, Bishop of
    Clifton 281, 313, 318
Allen Hall, Ware see St Edmund's
    College
Andria, Malvina d' 8
Andria, Maria and Peter d' 8
Andria, Monica de 8
Aniteb (family home) 8, 9
Anker, Elinor 193
Anker, Iver 193
Anker, John 166, 181, 191–2, 193,
    197, 201, 211, 243
Anker, Lita 146, 179, 181, 185,
    189–90, 194, 211, 286, 318,
    Pl. 16a, b
  as artist 243, 246, 300
  and Catholicism 163, 196–8
  and illustrations for *Norway* 192,
    211, 217, 243
  in Spain 165, 193, 196, 232,
    247
Aquaviva, Claudio SJ 148
Arden, John 92 n.2
Arrupe, Pedro SJ 257–8, 322
Astor, Bridget 225, 226
Auden, W. H. 52
Australia, PC's visit 258

Baddesley Clinton 116
Balladur, Edward 7
Barbarito, Luigi, Apostolic Nuncio
    289
Barry, Alterlius (godfather of PC) 9
Barry, Paddy 113, 150
Basset, Bernard SJ 23, 43, 124
Bates, H. E. 52

Beardsley, Aubrey 57
Beaton, Cecil 152
Beaumont School (St John's) 132,
    154, 224
Belloc, Hilaire 42, 102
Benedict XV, Pope 28
Benevolent Society for the Relief of
    the Aged and Infirm Poor 28
Berlin, Isaiah 39, 233
Berrigan, Daniel 55, 278
Betjeman, John 52
Biggs-Davison, Sir John 281–2,
    311
Bodkin, William SJ 32
Bolland, Joseph SJ 65–6, 100, 137
Bolt, Robert 212, 235–6, 278
Boothe-Luce, Clare 99
Borja de Medina, Francisco de SJ
    268, 273, 297–8
Boston College: and D'Arcy 131
  John J. Burns Library 152, 174,
    276–7, 294–5
Bourne, Cardinal Francis
    Alphonsus, Archbishop of
    Westminster 9–10, 28
Bowen, Elizabeth 62
Bowra, Maurice 40
Boyle, Desmond SJ 120
Bray, Gen. Sir Robert 162
Bridge House, Dulverton 275–81,
    285, 289, 293, 309, 314, 318,
    Pl. 23
Bristol University, Catholic
    chaplaincy 209
Brodrick, James 67, 72–3
Brook, Peter 75–6
Brown, Mgr Ralph 289

Brownell, Sonia (née Brownell)
61–2, 136
Bruce, James 272
Bruning, Heinrich 40
Brushford: PC's grave 318, *Pl. 24*
Three Acres nursing home
314–18
Budge, Sir Wallis 272
Bunn, Mary 137
Burns & Oates (publisher) 324
Burns, Paul 324
Burns, Tom 21 n.12, 49, 51, 57,
98–9, 136, 219–20, 260

Campbell, Roy 86, 88–9, 105
Campbell-Johnston, Michael 286
Campion, Edmund 273
Campion Hall, Oxford 39–44, 120,
131, 153, 195, *Pl. 4*
centenary history 290, 299–300
Campion House, London 129
Cannon, Denis 75
Caraman, Abraham 3–5
Caraman, André (grandfather of
PC) 5, 8, 9
Caraman, Artin (father of Abraham
Caraman) 3, 6
Caraman, Artin (later Pascal; son of
Abraham Caraman) 5
Caraman, Betina (née Pasqua;
mother of PC) 6–7, 15, 22, 30
Caraman, Claire Mary (sister of
PC) 8, 31, 195, 229, 316, 318
Caraman, John Andrew SJ (brother
of PC) 8, 123, *Pl. 21*
death 269
in novitiate 22, 29, 30
PC's relationship with 13, 30–1
PC's visits 201, 203–6, 269
visit to PC 246
Caraman, Margaret Mary (Mother
Mary of St John; sister of PC)
8, 10, 29
Caraman, Paul (great-grandfather of
PC) 5
Caraman, Pauline (great-aunt of
PC) 10

Caraman, Philip George SJ *Pl. 1,
6, 20*
appearance 3, 13, 326
character: discretion 260–1
generosity 188, 190
humour 14, 18, 35–6, 123,
151, 168, 176, 194, 269,
303
love of history 11, 16–17, 27,
33–4, 36, 70–1, 114–15,
162, 255–6
love of theatre 76–7
love of travel 38, 82, 115, *Pl.
17*, 172, 178, 184–6, 207,
212–13, 214, 222–3, 232,
261, 306–7
as public speaker 17–20, 289
restlessness 181, 184, 207, 229
death and Memorial 317–18,
322–4
education and training: academic
achievements 17, 43–4, 67,
132, 210
at Campion Hall 40–4, 120
at Heythrop College 30, 31–3,
44, 49
at Manresa House 20, 22–7
at St Beuno's 50–1
at Stonyhurst 12–19, 23
family: background 3–8
childhood 8–11
friendships 43, 52, 79–85, 122–4,
128, 138–40, 177, 233,
269–70, 298
with women 84, 146, 165,
194–6, 246–7, 273–4,
293, 306
see also Anker, Lita;
FitzHerbert, Margaret;
Greene, Graham;
Guinness, Alec; Sitwell,
Edith; Waugh, Evelyn
ill-health 23, 80–1, 113–14,
168–9, 228, 268–9, 314–16
cancer 285–7
depression 164–5, 168, 198–9,
292

fatigue 123-5, 168-9, 177-9,
    313
nervous breakdown 133,
    141-2, 292
and novitiate 22-44, 154
at Heythrop 31-3
at Manresa House 20, 22-7
as teacher 33-4, 35-6
in old age 123-4, 267-87,
    289-318
recreation: cooking 24, 230-1,
    247, 276, 280
painting 243, 254, 271, 314
relationships: with brother 13,
    30-1
with father 8, 29-30, 233
with fellow Jesuits 121-2, 231,
    244, 251, 256, 258, 277,
    298-300, 323
with office staff 114, 117-19,
    121, 123, 128-31, 133,
    139
with superiors 128-30, 131-44
religious life 25-6
Golden Jubilee as Jesuit 257-8,
    322
Golden Jubilee of ordination
    312
Memorial 322-3
ordination 44, 49
and other churches 283
solemn profession 49, 256-7
see also spiritual direction
travels: Africa 201-9
Australia 258
Barbados 313
France 185-6, 314
Germany 36-8
Iceland 307, *Pl. 17*
Morocco 249, 309-10, 312
Norway 152-4, 159-81,
    184-201, 209, 216-18,
    223, 230-1, 239, 259-63,
    Pl. 15
Rome 112, 113-14, 119, 212,
    218, 254-5, 267-9, 271,
    312

South America 222-8, 230,
    286
Spain 232
United States 229, 261
working life: as editor of *The
    Month* see *The Month*
as parish priest 239-49, 252-4,
    259-63, 267, 279-87,
    289-318
as Professor of Church History
    209, 211, 214-15, 218,
    221, 239
as Vice-Postulator for Forty
    Blessed Martyrs see Forty
    Martyrs
writings: *C. C. Martindale* 24-5,
    30, 144, 171-2, 177-8,
    186-90, 195-6
critique of 256
*Diccionario Historico de la
    Compania de Jesus* 267-8
Henry Garnet 142-3, 146-50,
    164, 170, 243, 256, 301
Henry Morse 105-6
Ignatius Loyola 273, 276,
    296-9
John Gerard 33, 70-1, 72,
    95-6, 147, 277, 301
Journal of a Country Priest
    282-5, 293
Lord and Master 311, 315, 325
*The Lost Empire: the Story of
    the Jesuits in Ethiopia*
    202, 261-2, 267, 271-3,
    298-9
The Lost Paradise 78, 214-16,
    224-6, 229, 232, 234-6,
    239, 243, 252, 261,
    277-9, 328
Meditations for Tomorrow
    324-5, 327-8
Norway 172, 179, 181, 185,
    186, 190-2, 200, 210-11,
    216-18, 243, *Pl. 16a*, 328
novel 24-4
The Other Face 34, 106-7,
    116, 169-70, 277

*Saint Angela: The Life of
    Angela Merici* 143–4
A Study in Friendship 311–12
Tibet – The Jesuit Century 312,
    315, 316, 324, 327–8
University of the Nations
    254–6, 258, 261, 276
The Western Rising 302–3,
    304–5, 315, *Pl. 23*
William Weston 81–2, 95–6,
    147
The Years of Siege 169–70, 186
Caraman, René André (father of
    PC): death 27–9
  in London 5–7, 9–10, 28
  marriage 6–7
  personality 203
  relationship with PC 8, 29–30,
    233
  and Smyrna 3, 4, 5, 11–12, 28
Caraman, Rosalie (née Roboly) 5,
    12
Caraman, Veronica Mary (sister of
    PC) 8
Cardinale, Hyginus Eugene,
    Archbishop of Nepte 175
Catesby, Robert 148
Catholic Evidence Guild 17, 19–20
Catholic Gazette 241
Catholic Huts Council 28
Catholic Times 290
Catholic Truth Society 302
Cecil, Sir Robert 147, 148
Chesterton, G. K. 98, 216
Christina of Sweden 255
Clark, Sir Kenneth 122
Clarke, Fr Henry 326
Clarke, Richard SJ 35
Claver House, Pimlico (Jesuit
    hostel) 138, 140, 151, 201
Clogheen *see* Cooleville
Clonsilla (cruise ship) 212, 214
Coate, Peter 246
Collins, Dorothy 98
Collins (publisher) 258, 276, 297
Combe Florey (Waugh home)
    100–1, 123–5, 129, 137–9,

141, 173–4, 274, 296
Compton-Burnett, Ivy 62
Connolly, Cyril 52–3, 61, 83, 122,
    136
Cooleville (Clogheen, Tipperary)
    84–5, 161, 291
Cooper, Lady Diana 109, 122
Copleston, Frederick SJ 33
Corbishley, Tom SJ 131–2
Corby, Blessed Ralph 34, 36
Corby Hall retreat house,
    Sunderland 34–5
Corby Hall School, Sunderland
    35–6, *Pl. 3*
Corrigan, Terence SJ 146, 163
Cove House, Tiverton 274–5
Coventry, John SJ: academic
    achievements 43
  death 317, 324
  and dismissal of PC 120, 128–34,
    137, 140–1, 189
  as English Provincial 120, 146,
    169
Cradock-Henry, Claire *see*
    Caraman, Claire Mary
Craman, Anais (née Issaverdens) 5
Crane, Paul SJ 138
Crusade of Rescue 10, 28

Dahl, Fr 248
Dahl, Roald 216–17
D'Arcy, Conyers SJ 44 n.1
D'Arcy, Martin C. SJ *Pl. 12*
  death 249–50
  as English Provincial 32, 44, 49,
    66–7, 70, 106
  and Farm Street 120, 186, 210,
    218, 231
  as father-figure 233, 250–1, 299
  and favouritism 43, 67–8
  and Forty Martyrs 219
  ill-health 233–4
  at Manresa House 23
  as Master of Campion Hall
    39–44, 153, 195, *Pl. 4*
  and *The Month* 49, 52, 53, 55,
    113, 136

The Nature of Belief 88
and PC in Norway 152-3, 164-5,
169, 177, 179
and PC as Professor of Church
History 209-10, 214, 218-19
and PC's difficulties with
superiors 131-4, 142, 210
and Sitwell 85, 86-7, 88, 90,
105, 152
solemn profession 257
as Stonyhurst master 15-16
and *The Tablet* 219-20
and Waugh 53, 166, 172, 175,
177, 331
De la Baume, Xavier Rénom 163,
180
De-la-Noy, Michael 291
Denys, Elizabeth 235
Dru, Alick 42
Dru, Gabriel (née Herbert) 42
Dudfield, Louisa (godmother of PC)
9
Duffy, Eamon 304
Dulverton: bookshop 304, *Pl. 23*
Bridge House 275-81, 285, 289,
293, 309, 314, 318, *Pl. 23*
St Stanislaus Church 102, 275,
279-84, 312-15, 325, 328,
Pl. 22
see also Pixton Park

Earle, Jock SJ 133
ecumenism, and Forty Martyrs 140,
219-21
Eden, Beth and Robert 283
Edwards, Francis SJ 324
Eliot, T. S. 55
Elizabeth I 33-4, 70-1, 81-2, 95-6,
106, 110, 146-7, 170
Ethiopia: Jesuits in 261-2, 267,
271-3
PC's visit 201-2

Farm Street, Mayfair: and D'Arcy
120, 186, 210, 213, 218
Church of the Immaculate
Conception 44, 88-91, 114,
151, 322, *Pl. 5*
and office staff 114, 117-19,
120-3, 128-31, 139
PC's removal from 129-30, 138,
140, 154, 170, 218, 322
'writers' house' 67-8, 82, 114,
117, 120-1, 124-5, 128-9,
267
see also Mount Street
Farquhar, Sister 150
Farwell, Victor OSB 44 n.1
Fernàndez, Fr 297
FitzHerbert, Giles 121, 128, 130,
142, 174, 212, 252, 274, 293
FitzHerbert, Margaret (née Waugh)
Pl. 22
death 273-4, 281, 320 n.49
and Evelyn Waugh 166, 172, 176
friendship with PC 185, 212,
252, 318
and *Henry Garnet* 143, 150
marriage and family 122-3, 142,
174, 292
working for PC 114, 117-19,
121, 123, 128-31, 133, 193,
292
Fitzmaurice, William SJ 35
Flaherty, Daniel L. SJ 277-8
Fleming, Ann 117, 122, 141
Fortescue, Blessed Adrian 289-90
Formosa, Fr 174
Forty Martyrs: beatification 111
canonisation 209, 220-1, 274,
289, *Pl. 18*
delays and problems 139-41,
146, 184, 219-20
and ecumenism 140, 219-21
illness and overwork of PC
113-14, 115
office staff 117-21, 129-30, 139
Fraser, Ian 275
Furlong, Fr 223-4

Galileo Galilei 255
Garnet, Henry SJ 115-16, 142-3,
146-50, 207-8, 256, 311
Garstein, Oskar 145, 161, 307-8

Gerard, John 70–1, 115, 147, 208, 277
Germany, PC's visit 36–8
Gielgud, John 76, 194
Gilbey, Mgr Alfred 326
Gill, Eric 39, 164
Glendinning, Victoria 290
Glover, Dorothy 77
Godfrey, Cardinal William 119, 164
Graham, Cunninghame 215
Gran, John Willem Nicolaysen 286
    as Bishop of Oslo 146, 197, 263, *Pl. 13, 14*
    memoirs 300–1
    ordination 144–5
    and PC in Norway 160, 163, 184, 189–90, 200, 209, 211, 216, 223, 239–40, 259, 292
    and Second Vatican Council 167
The Grange (family home) 9–11, 28
Grant, Bridget (née Herbert) 42–3, 173–4, 233, 275, 279, 281
Grant, Eddie 42
Great Neck, New York State 229
Greene, Graham *Pl. 7*
    and D'Arcy 39, 53
    biographies 76–8, 79, 294–5
    and Catholic Church 74, 79
    cooling of friendship with PC 134–5, 235, 294–5
    death 295
    early friendship with PC 71–9, 81, 99–100, 103–4, 166, 215–16, 218, 227
    and Martindale 75, 171–2, 186–7, 195
    and *The Month* 53, 55–6, 60, 63–5, 71–2, 78, 100, 137
    and Sitwell 105
    and Waugh 99–100, 134, 172–3, 177
    writings: *Brighton Rock* 74
    A Burnt-Out Case 135
    The Comedians 185
    The End of the Affair 65–6, 73, 77–8, 100, 294
    'The Hint of an Explanation' 56

Monsignor Quixote 271
    'Pius XII – The Paradox of the Pope' 64–5
    The Potting Shed 76
    The Power and the Glory 75–6, 83, 172
Greene, Vivien 100
Gregory XIII, Pope 255
Grene, Christopher, *Collecteana* 34
Guest, John 83, 141, 186–7, 211, 232
Guinness, Alec 212
    biographies 317, 326–7
    conversion to Catholicism 89, 326
    and death of PC 317–18
    friendship with PC 50, 90, 114, 249, 251–4, 274, 276, 286, 295, 308
    and homosexuality 327
    and Edith Sitwell 89–90, 251
    and theatre 270–1
    and Waugh 90
Guinness, Merula 252, 253, 254, 317
Gunpowder Plot, and Garnet 115, 147–9, 170
Gurrin, Basil SJ 41

Hanshell, Deryck SJ 54, 57, 59
Hartley, L. P. 122
Hastings, Selina 197, 293–5, 305
The Haven (summer house) 13
Heath, Edward 45 n.20
Hebblethwaite, Peter 136
Heenan, Cardinal John Carmel, Archbishop of Westminster 152, 153, 164, 166, 175, 209, 219
Henry VIII, and Forty Martyrs 110–11
Herbert, Auberon 42–3, 101–2, 107, 173, 233
Herbert, Aubrey 274
Herbert, Laura *see* Waugh, Laura
Herbert, Mary (Mrs Aubrey Herbert) 102, 173, 186, 233, 275

and D'Arcy 42
and Campion Hall 39
friendship with PC 43, 100,
    176–7
Heythrop College 27, 30, 31–3, 44,
    49
Hochwalder, Fritz 215
Hodder preparatory school 13
Hollis, Maurice Christopher 16, 273
Holroyd, Michael 176
Holt, Geoffrey SJ 13–14, 15, 23,
    24, 26–7, 316
The Holy Experiment (television
    play) 270
Homes for Destitute Catholic
    Children 28
Hone, Evie 281
Hopkins, Gerard Manley 51, 61
Horizon (periodical) 52–3, 56, 60,
    61–2, 83, 136
Horner, David 88, 107
Hume, Cardinal Basil, Archbishop
    of Westminster 289, 295

Iceland, PC's visit 307, *Pl. 17*
Issaverdens, Jacques (uncle of PC)
    10, 11
Issaverdens, Leontine 12

James I and VI 147–8, 170
Jarrett, Bede OP 75
Jesuit Historical Institute (Rome)
    218, 268, 297, 312
Jesuits: in Ethiopia 261–2, 267,
    271–3
as family 31
in northeast England 34–5
in Norway 145, 163–4, 230
PC in novitiate 20, 22–44, 154
PC's relationships with superiors
    128–30, 131–44, 277
Reductions in Paraguay 214–16,
    223–6, 228, 232, 234–5,
    278, 328
at Stonyhurst 15–16
suppression 70, 234, 255, 272
in Tibet 312, 315, 324

see also Campion Hall; Heythrop
    College; Manresa House;
    The Month
John XXIII, Pope 124, 252
John, Augustus 39, *Pl. 12*
John, Henry 21 n.12
John Paul II, Pope 38, 112, 282,
    Pl. 17, 119

Kay, Hugh 136
Keane, Henry SJ 50–1
Keatinge, William 44 n.1
Keen, Mary 130
Kennedy, Ludovic 109
Kenya, PC's visit 201
Kettlebrook Meadows, Hants.
    (home of Alec Guinness) 254,
    327
Knox, Ronald 60, 97–9, 325, 331
Kolbe, Maximilian 255
Korda, Alexander 76–7
Koren, Wenche 146, 164, 185, 192,
    194, 211, 230, 243
Kristensen, Kristen and Frances 260

Ledochowski, Fr 32
Lee, Laurie 53
Lehmann, John 122, 290
Lehmann, Rosamond 84–5, 86,
    108, 197–8, 294, 326, *Pl. 10*
Lepre, Gianni 244–6
Letters & Notices 33, 49–50, 258,
    324
Levi, Anthony 108
Lewis, C. S. 40, 61
Lillehammer, PC as parish priest
    259–63, *Pl. 15*
Longford, Frank Pakenham, Lord
    39, 154
Longmans (publisher) 61, 139, 143,
    186–7, 207, 217, 232, *see also*
    Guest, John
Loyola, Maria de 297–8
Loyola, St Ignatius 144, 255
biography by PC 273, 276, 296–9
Spiritual Exercises 25–6
Loyola University Press 277

Lygon, Hugh 180
Lygon, Lady Mary 108–9

MacDermott, Brian 226, 228
MacDonald, Canon Ronald 275,
 280
Malraux, André 6, 99
Manning, Henry Edward,
 Archbishop of Westminster 76
Manresa House, Roehampton 20,
 22–7, *Pl. 2*
 curriculum 27–8
 and domestic training 24
 Jesuit spirituality 25–6
 and recreation 24–5
Marchmont (home of McEwens)
 186, 221–3, 229, 230, 231,
 250, 252
Margaret, HRH Princess 222
Mariakirken, Lillehammer 259–63,
 Pl. 15
Marie de Saint Polycarp, Sr (cousin
 of PC) 10–11
Martindale, Cyril SJ 67, 123, 140
 and Greene 75, 171–2, 186–7,
 195
 Life of R. H. Benson 67
 as Master of the Juniorate 27
 PC's biography 24–5, 30, 144,
 171–2, 177–8, 186–90,
 195–6
 and St Beuno's 51
Mass: importance for PC 199–200,
 222, 310
 Latin 173–6, 279, 302
 vernacular 117, 124, 173, 279,
 332
Mathew, Gervase OP 75
May, Edwin 28–9
Mayer, Blessed Rupert 37–8
Mayfair *see* Farm Street, Mayfair;
 Mount Street
McCoog, Thomas M. SJ 298–301
McEwen, Brigid 186, 211, 221,
 229, 231, 240, 252, 326
McEwen, John 221–2
McEwen, Katie 221

McEwen, Robin 186, 211, 221,
 229, 230, 231, 251, 252
McNabb, Vincent OP 19
McNaspy, Fr C. J. 278
Melia, Fr 226
Mendes, Alfonso 272–3
Merici, St Angela 115, 143–4
Merton, Thomas 54–5, 57–60, 210
Miller, Fr Robert 328
The Mission (film) 235–6, 270–1,
 278–9
modernism, Catholic 187–8
Moffat, Fr 136, 218–19
Molinari, Paul SJ 111–12, 113,
 117, 140, 221
The Month 73–4
 and D'Arcy 49, 52, 53, 55, 113,
 136
 closure 136, 328
 dismissal of PC 136–9, 189, 292
 editorship of PC 49, 51–68, 72,
 75, 80–1, 91, 96–9, 112–13,
 135–6, 145, 267, 305
 and Greene 53, 55–6, 60, 63–5,
 71–2, 78, 100, 137
 and Norwegian Church 145–6,
 162
 'Saints' series 63–4, 83, 97
 and Sitwell 105
 and Waugh 53–4, 57–8, 61, 63,
 65–6, 96–7, 137–8, 292
Montoya, Ruiz de SJ 225, 278
Moore, Henry 52
Morison, Stanley 52, 324
Morocco, PC's visits 249, 309–10,
 312
Morse, Henry 105–6
Mortimer, John 109–10
Mortimer, Raymond 80, 135
Mount Street, Mayfair, Provincial
 House 50, 120, 121, 129, 131,
 169, 218, 231, 277
Muggeridge, Malcolm 43, 101, 233
Mulligan, Fr Rory 205, 246

Nabokov, Vladimir, *Lolita* 105
New Wardour Castle, Wilts. 67, 231

Newman, John Henry 61, 84, 99
'Nini' 190, 194
Norway: and Catholicism 144–6,
    162–3, 180–1, 185, 199–200,
    205, 239, 262–3, 323, 328
  food and drink 159, 161–2, 167,
    180, 230, 262
  language 160–2, 190, 200,
    239–40, 253
  PC in 152–4, 159–81, 184–201,
    209, 216–18, 223, 230–1,
    Pl. 15
  PC as parish priest 239–49,
    252–4, 259–63, 267, 280
  travel in 172, 178–81

O'Connor, Garry 326–7
O'Donoghue, Fergus SJ 256,
    260–1, 268
O'Farrell, Fr 224, 227
O'Higgins, Fr 210, 250, 299
Oldcorne, Fr 149
Orwell, Sonia 61–2, 126, *Pl. 9*

Paez, Pedro 261, 272
Pakenham, Frank (later Lord
    Longford) 39
Paraguay, Jesuit Reductions
    214–16, 223–6, 228, 232,
    234–5, 278, 328
Parker, Derek 290
Pasqua, Adelina 8
Pasqua, Betina *see* Caraman, Betina
Pasqua, Francesco 6
Paul VI, Pope 199, 220–1, *Pl. 18*
Paulist Press 255
Peters, W. 73–4
Petit, John Edward, Bishop of
    Menevia 117
Piers Court (Waugh home) 53, 80,
    100
Pius XII, Pope 64–5, 137
Pixton Park, Somerset 42–3, 53,
    100–2, 123, 173–4, 186, 211,
    233, 275
Plessington, Blessed John 121
Plunkett, Blessed Oliver 129

Powell, Anthony SJ 143
Power, John 44 n.1
Powicke, Sir Maurice 255
Prayer Book Rebellion 302–3,
    304–5
Priestley, J. B. 52
profession 49, 256–7
Pugsley, Steven 303, 315, 316, *Pl. 23*

Ramsay, Sir Allan and Lady
    Pauline 309–10, 313, 314, 325
Randolph, Richard SJ 257, 279,
    316–18, 327
  and John Caraman 203, 269
  and Jesuit training 26–7
  and The Other Face 106
  travels with PC 269–70, 306–7
Raynal family 224
Read, Piers Paul 317, 327
Renishaw Hall, Sheffield 87, 88,
    104, 290
Rhodesia (Zimbabwe), PC's visit
    201, 203–9
Rieber-Mohn, Hallvard OP 145,
    162, 211
Roberts, Archbishop 91
Rogers, Deborah 232
Roman Catholicism: and Armenian
    community 4–5
  and Caraman family 9–10
  under Elizabeth I 33–4, 70–1,
    81–2, 95–6, 106, 110,
    146–7, 170
  in England 6, 9, 16–17, 42, 99
  Irish 35
  and modernism 187–8
  in Norway 144–6, 162–3, 180–1,
    185, 199–200, 205, 239,
    262–3, 323, 328
  and religious vocations 22
  restoration of hierarchy 110, 111
  see also Forty Martyrs
Rome: Gregorian University 254–6,
    258, 261
  Jesuit archives 70, 215, 312
  PC in 112, 113–14, 119, 212,

218, 254–5, 267–9, 271, 312
Rose, Alban 140
Rossi, Caludio SJ 308
Rothenstein, Elizabeth 52, 61
Rothenstein, John 52, 57, 61
Rothwell, Caryl 305, *Pl. 23*
Rothwell, Max 305–6
Rothwell, Richard 305
Rowse, A. L. 289
Royal Family, British 308
Royal Society, PC's membership
    141
Rubbra, Edmund 57
Rudderham, Joseph, Bishop of
    Clifton 140
Rushton Hall 116

Sackville-West, Edward 86, 90,
    101, 108
  friendship with PC 79–81, 84–5,
    161, 191, 291
  and Greene 79, 80, 135
  and *The Month* 62–3, 79–80
  and Waugh 80
Sackville-West, Vita 62
Sacred Congregation of Rites 111,
    119
St Beuno's College, Wales 32, 50–1
St Edmund's College, Ware 209,
    211, 213–14, 218, 221, 239
St John Stevas, Norman 260
St Lawrence, Raleigh 125 n.10
St Olav, Tønsberg 239–49, 252–4
St Patrick's, Wapping 259
St Stanislaus Church, Dulverton
    102, 275, 279–84, 312–15,
    325, 328, *Pl. 22*
St Teresa of the Child Jesus, parish
    9–10
Salter, Elizabeth 150
Scofield, Paul 75–6
Scriptorum 67, 113
Second Vatican Council 117, 119,
    220, 284–5
  and Gran 167
  and Waugh 124, 173, 175, 332–3
Sewell, Dennis 325–6

Shakespeare, Nicholas 292
Shawe-Taylor, Desmond 80
Shearer, Moira 109
Sheed, Frank 19
Shelden, Michael 294
Sherry, Norman 76–8, 79, 294–5
Sherwin, Ralph 255
Sidgwick & Jackson (publisher)
    232, 273, 303
Sims, Fr 9–10
Sire, H. J. A. 14, 23, 32, 35,
    131–2
Sitwell, Edith 101, 121–2, 141,
    166, *Pl. 11*
  and D'Arcy 85, 86–7, 88, 90,
    105, 152
  conversion to Catholicism 85–91,
    196, 251
  correspondence with PC 87,
    104–5, 107, 113–14, 150,
    290
  death 151–2
  and *The Other Face* 34, 106–7
  PC as spiritual director 85, 87–8,
    91, 104, 107, 150–1
Sitwell, Francis 122, 151, 154
Sitwell, Georgia 107–8
Sitwell, Osbert 85, 88, 107, 152,
    178, 212, 215
Sitwell, Reresby 122
Sitwell, Sacheverell 85, 107–8, 141
Skinner, John SJ 115–17, 282, 322
Smith, Ian 201, 207
Smith, John 280–1, 313
Smith, William Peers SJ 26
Smyrna (Izmir)
  and Caraman family 3–6, 7, 13
  destruction 12–14, 28
Snow, Sir Charles 122
Society of Jesus *see* Jesuits
South America, PC's travels in
    222–8, 230, 286
Southwell, Robert 255, 311
Southwell House (Swiss Cottage)
    259, 269, 270, 298
Spark, Muriel 83–4, 166, 235, 246,
    268–9, 273–4, 295

Speaight, Robert 45 n.21, 57, 77, 234–5
Spender, Stephen 122, 166
spiritual direction 105, 108–9, 124, 169, 176
  and Lita Anker 196–8
  and Alec Guinness 327
  and Rosamond Lehmann 84–5, 197–8
  and Edward Sackville-West 80
  and Edith Sitwell 85, 87–8, 91, 104, 107, 150–1
  and Antonia White 82–3
Spiritual Exercises (Loyola) 25–6
Spitzbergen, PC visits 191–2
Stannard, Martin 117, 292–3
Steele, Peter SJ 258
Steuart, Roy SJ 137
Stevenson, Quentin 90, 105
Stone, Reynolds 52
Stonor Park, Oxfordshire 116, 173
Stonyhurst College: archives 17, 33–4, 70, 95
  and Catholic Evidence Guild 17, 19–20
  Debating Society 18–19, 36, 99–100
  discipline 14–15
  origins 16–17
  PC as pupil 12–20, 23
  PC as teacher 33–4
  religious ethos 15
  teachers 15–16
Strauss, E. B. 63, 103, 173
Stubbs Society (Oxford) 41
Sudan, PC's visit 208
Sutch, Dom Antony 328
Svejdar, Honor 212
Sweeney, Fr Francis 55, 210, 277

The Tablet 56–7, 96, 136, 219–20, 234, 260
Taylor, Lady 230
Teilhard de Chardin, Pierre 58
Tertianship 50
Tesimond, Fr 148
theatre: ban on attendance 75–6

  PC's assistance to Guinness 270–1
Thesbiteateret 244–6, 285
Thomas, Dylan 53
Thorman, Joseph, Bishop of Hexham and Newcastle 35
Thorn, Finn D. OP 145
Tibet, Jesuit mission 312, 315, 324
Tigar, Clement SJ 129, 152, 219
Tisbury, Wilts. 231–3, 254, 258–9, 269, 303, 306, 328
Tomlinson, Mgr George 175
Tønsberg (Norway), PC as parish priest 239–49, 252–4, 267, 280, 285
Topcliffe, Richard 311–12
Tranmar, John ('Jack') SJ 231–2, 246, 258–9, 269, 306
Tresham, Sir Thomas 116
Trevor-Roper, Hugh 97, 234
Trondheim 239
Turner, Vincent 43
Tyrrell, George SJ 187–8

Uganda, PC's visit 208
Undset, Sigrid 146
United States, PC's visits 229, 261
Urban VIII, Pope 111

Van Zeller, Dom Hubert 173
Vatican, Sacred Congregation of Rites 111, 119
Vignaux, Ernest SJ 50–1
Von Lintzgy, Audrey 130
Vranken, Fr 248–9

Walsh, James SJ 113, 117, 120, 128–31, 169, 320 n.49
Walston, Catherine 77–9, 100, 135, 171, 235, 295
Walston, Henry 77
Walton, Sir William 122
Waring, Olaf I. SJ 122
  and death of PC 317, 323
  friendship with PC 160–1, 164, 198–200, 246, 260, 263, 307
Watson, Peter 136

Waugh, Auberon 42, 153, 274,
  296, 304–5
Waugh, Evelyn 39, 141, 273, *Pl. 8*
  biographies 291–3
  correspondence with PC 97–8,
      112, 114, 118–19, 123–4,
      130, 134, 141, 153–4,
      167–8, 277
  death 174–8, 292
  depression 153, 164, 166–7,
      172–3
  friendship with PC 7, 96–103,
      107–9, 117–19, 122–5,
      129–31, 133–4, 137–8, 150,
      172–6
  and Greene 99–100, 134, 172–3,
      177
  and Knox biography 97–9, 331
  and Merton 54, 58–60
  and *The Month* 53–4, 57–8, 61,
      63, 65–6, 96–7, 137–8, 292
  panegyric by PC 175–7, 331–3
  'Pinfold episode' 102–3, 172
  and Pixton Park 42–3
  and Sackville-West 80
  and Sitwell 89–90
  and *William Weston* 95–6
  writings: *Basil Seal Rides Again*
      153
    Edmund Campion 331
    A Handful of Dust 331
    The Loved One 55–6, 58
    The Ordeal of Gilbert Pinfold
      103
    St Helena 96–7
    Tourist in Africa 204
Waugh, Hattie 117, 128, 130, 139,
    153, 174
Waugh, James 138, 174
Waugh, Laura (née Herbert): and
    Auberon Herbert 101
  and death of Evelyn 174, 176–8
  marriage to Evelyn 100, 102–3,
    141

  and Meg FitzHerbert 121
  and PC 123, 125, 138–9
  at Piers Court 80
  at Pixton Park 42, 53
Waugh, Margaret (Meg) 114,
    117–19, 121–3, *see also*
    FitzHerbert, Margaret
Waugh, Septimus 154, 174, 275,
    281
Waugh, Teresa (wife of Auberon)
    119, 176, 274
Welch, Denton 80
Weld, Thomas 17
West, W. J. 78
Westminster Cathedral Chronicle
    120–1
Westminster Catholic Federation 28
Westminster Eucharistic Congress
    (1908) 110
Weston Hall, Shropshire 107
Weston, William 81–2, 95–6, 115,
    147, 208
Whinney House, Gateshead 34
White, Antonia 82–3
Whittaker, Paul SJ 35
Wiel, Evelyn 90
Wilson, Angus 166
Wilson, Harold 201
Wilton House 303–4
Wingfield-Digby, Robert 43
Winsnes, A. H. 146
Wiseman, Cardinal Nicholas,
    Archbishop of Westminster 111
Wolfit, Donald 215
women, friendships with 146, 165,
    194–6, 246–7, 273–4, 293, 306
Wood, Silas 281
Woodruff, Douglas 56–7, 98,
    219–20

Zambia, PC's visit 208
Zimbabwe, PC's visit 269, *see also*
    Rhodesia